Kazuo Ishiguro: new critical visions of

Kazuo Ishiguro is one of the finest conte
that increasingly rare distinction of being a ...
with the general reading public and is also well-respecteu ...
academic community. *Kazuo Ishiguro: New Critical Visions of the Novels*
presents a good number of fresh perspectives on the author's work
that will appeal to those who read him for pleasure or for purposes of
study.

Established and rising critics reassess Ishiguro's works from the early
'Japanese' novels through to his short story cycle 'Nocturnes', paying
particular attention to *The Remains of the Day, The Unconsoled, When We
Were Orphans* and *Never Let Me Go*. They address universal themes such
as history, memory and mortality, but also provide groundbreaking
explorations of diverse areas ranging from the posthuman and 'minor
literature' to ethics, science fiction and Ishiguro's musical imagination.

Featuring an insightful interview with Ishiguro himself, this collection
of essays constitutes a significant contribution to the appreciation of
his novels, and forms a lively and nuanced constellation of critical
enquiry.

Preface by Brian W. Shaffer. Essays by Jeannette Baxter, Caroline Bennett,
Christine Berberich, Lydia R. Cooper, Sebastian Groes, Meghan Marie
Hammond, Tim Jarvis, Barry Lewis, Liani Lochner, Christopher Ringrose,
Victor Sage, Andy Sawyer, Motoyuki Shibata, Gerry Smyth, Krystyna
Stamirowska, Motoko Sugano, Patricia Waugh, Alyn Webley.

Sebastian Groes is Senior Lecturer in English Literature at Roehampton
University.

Barry Lewis is Senior Lecturer in English at the University of Sunderland.

other books by the editors

Also by Sebastian Groes

Ian McEwan: Contemporary Critical Perspectives
Kazuo Ishiguro: Contemporary Critical Perspectives (with Sean Matthews)
The Making of London
Julian Barnes: Contemporary Critical Perspectives (with Peter Childs)

Also by Barry Lewis

Kazuo Ishiguro
My Words Echo Thus: Possessing the Past in Peter Ackroyd

kazuo ishiguro
new critical visions of the novels

edited by
sebastian groes and barry lewis

First published 2011 by
PALGRAVE MACMILLAN

Palgrave Macmillan in the UK is an imprint of Macmillan Publishers Limited, registered in England, company number 785998, of Houndmills, Basingstoke, Hampshire RG21 6XS.

Palgrave Macmillan in the US is a division of St Martin's Press LLC, 175 Fifth Avenue, New York, NY 10010.

Palgrave Macmillan is the global academic imprint of the above companies and has companies and representatives throughout the world.

Palgrave® and Macmillan® are registered trademarks in the United States, the United Kingdom, Europe and other countries.

ISBN 978–0–230–23237–2   hardback
ISBN 978–0–230–23238–9   paperback

This book is printed on paper suitable for recycling and made from fully managed and sustained forest sources. Logging, pulping and manufacturing processes are expected to conform to the environmental regulations of the country of origin.

A catalogue record for this book is available from the British Library.

A catalog record for this book is available from the Library of Congress.

10 9 8 7 6 5 4 3 2 1
20 19 18 17 16 15 14 13 12 11

Printed and bound in China

contents

v

contents

contents   vii

part v *when we were orphans*

part vi *never let me go*

list of illustrations

All images are reproduced courtesy of The National Museum of Modern Art, Tokyo, and where specified, the copyright-holders. Every effort has been made to trace all copyright-holders, but if any have been inadvertently overlooked the publishers will be pleased to make the necessary arrangement at the first opportunity.

list of abbreviations

AFW   *An Artist of the Floating World*
N   *Nocturnes*
NLMG   *Never Let Me Go*
PVH   *A Pale View of Hills*
RD   *The Remains of the Day*
U   *The Unconsoled*
WWWO   *When We Were Orphans*

Parenthetical references to works by Kazuo Ishiguro in this volume are to first editions published in the United Kingdom, unless notes suggest otherwise.

preface

brian w. shaffer

Like most dedicated, enthusiastic, long-standing readers of Kazuo Ishiguro, I first made the acquaintance of his work not in the early and mid-1980s, with the appearance of the early short fiction and the two 'Japanese' novels – the subtle, sublime, psychologically inflected *A Pale View of Hills* (1982) and the historically and politically resonant *An Artist of the Floating World* (1986) – but in the waning moments of the 1980s, with the emergence of the Booker Prize-winning *The Remains of the Day* (1989), which catapulted the thirty-five-year-old author to fame on both sides of the Atlantic and beyond. My experience of Ishiguro's astounding, structurally and tonally 'perfect', third novel – his first novel to be set in Britain, I would soon learn – prompted me to circle back to these earlier Japanese novels, which only confirmed, in my eyes at least, in their masterful antic-ipations of *The Remains of the Day*, this author's importance to contempo-rary British (and indeed to world) fiction. That this important new voice in British fiction belonged to a person of Anglo-Japanese background only piqued my interest and curiosity all the more.

Since then, like so many thousands of other readers in English-speaking nations and in the three dozen or so non-English-speaking countries in which Ishiguro's work has appeared in translation, I have devoured with the hungriest of eyes, and with the utmost appreciation of the author's artistic vision, each new novel, story and screenplay that has emerged. *The Unconsoled* (1995), *When We Were Orphans* (2000) and *Never Let Me Go* (2005), each in its own way, grew out of and yet broke with the earlier Chekhovian and Jamesian novels, instead echoing, variously, the likes of Dostoevsky, Kafka, Conan Doyle and the science-fiction tradition in surprising and highly effective ways.

Having twice met and interviewed Ishiguro during these same twenty years only deepened my appreciation for the fiction, in particular its fascinatingly reticent protagonists. For while Ishiguro as an interview subject is as engaging, forthcoming and revealing as one could possibly wish, his fictional protagonists (and to a certain extent the novels themselves), by contrast, stubbornly resist tidy readings, fixed meanings or interpretive closure. Indeed, my favourite two sentences ever uttered about Ishiguro's art – Mark Kamine's quip that 'few writers dare to say so little of what they mean as Ishiguro'[1] and Salman Rushdie's observation that 'just below the understatement of [*The Remains of the Day*'s] surface is a turbulence as immense as it is slow'[2] – attest to this fundamental, characteristic quality of Ishiguro's fiction.

Having lived with and written about Ishiguro's art – the stories, novels and screenplays – for more than two decades, and having taught the majority of his works multiple times, there can be little doubt that it is the accomplished novels that constitute his profoundest contribution to contemporary literature. It is therefore high time that a critical volume specifically devoted to the novels – one that probes them from multiple perspectives and through various critical and contextual lenses – comes forward to assess, engage and further 'open' this enigmatic, interpretively reticent work. Although the past decade has seen into print a number of books and articles on Ishiguro's fiction, *Kazuo Ishiguro: New Critical Visions of the Novels* is the first multi-author volume to focus specifically on the six masterful novels. Groes and Lewis's volume, to my mind the most penetrating single-volume assessment of Ishiguro's fictional art yet ventured, features the work of eighteen scholars from five countries (in Europe, North America and Asia). These eighteen essays, while they can profitably be read individually, collectively forge a series of provocative dialogues and conversations – encompassing socio-psychological, scientific, philosophical, musical, biographical, political, colonial and postcolonial, national and transnational paradigms – that transcend any single one of the essays; the volume as a whole is worth even more than the sum of its valuable parts. This dialogic aspect of the volume should come as no surprise when one notes that many of the essays collected here emerged from the same academic gathering, 'Kazuo Ishiguro and the International Novel: A One-Day Conference,' that took place in Liverpool in June of 2007. Indeed, many of the contributors literally heard each other's essay drafts and took part in a conversation. The result of this conversation is the rich and heterogeneous volume you hold in your hands.

In this same spirit of critical dialogue and conversation, *Kazuo Ishiguro: New Critical Visions of the Novels* concludes with a provocative new interview with Ishiguro himself – an interview that rounds out well the collection in its engaging treatment of numerous subjects and texts discussed in the volume's critical essays, and in its opening up, like the volume as a whole, of new directions for Ishiguro criticism.

notes

1. Mark Kamine, 'A Servant of Self-Deceit', *New Leader*, 13 November 1989, 22.
2. Salman Rushdie, 'What the Butler Didn't See', *Observer*, 21 May 1989, 53.

acknowledgements

The editors and publisher wish to thank Kazuo Ishiguro for his generous support of this book. This collection is partly the result of the 'Kazuo Ishiguro and the International Novel' conference, staged at Liverpool Hope University, on 7 June 2007. Liverpool Hope University is thanked for its generous support of the conference and a profoundly inspiring author event. We would like to thank Amanda Hopkinson and Valerie Henitiuk of the British Centre for Literary Translation for granting us permission to reprint Motoyuki Shibata's essay 'Lost and Found: On the Japanese Translations of Kazuo Ishiguro', which was first published in *In Other Words*, 30, 32–9. We are grateful to the National Museum of Modern Art, Tokyo, for granting permission to publish the paintings by the Japanese war artists included in this volume; and we are grateful to the Japan Artists Association Inc. (JAA) for the arrangement of the copyright. Motoko Sugano's help was invaluable in this process. Thanks are also due to Brian W. Shaffer for his illuminating Preface to this volume. Vic Sage and Pat Waugh are thanked for their ongoing support of our academic lives and their brilliant contributions to this volume. We thank Sean Matthews for his advice in the various stages of the production of this book. Both editors would particularly like to thank Sonya Barker at Palgrave Macmillan for her valued support of this project. Sebastian Groes would like to thank his wife, José Lapré, for her support in often trying times. Barry Lewis would like to thank the Culture and Regional Studies Beacon at the University of Sunderland for funded teaching assistance during the latter stages of the editing of this volume.

SEBASTIAN GROES
BARRY LEWIS

contributors

Jeannette Baxter is Senior Lecturer in English Literature at Anglia Ruskin University. She specializes in twentieth- and twenty-first century writing, in critical and cultural theory, and is the author of *J. G. Ballard's Surrealist Imagination* (Ashgate, 2008) and editor of *J. G. Ballard* (Continuum, 2009).

Caroline Bennett is Senior Lecturer in English Literature at Liverpool Hope University. She has published work on Isabel Allende, Ian McEwan and sacred spaces, and is currently writing on spirituality in the poetry of Elizabeth Jennings.

Christine Berberich is Senior Lecturer in English Literature at the University of Portsmouth. Her research interest focuses on Englishness and national identity. She has published on writers including Evelyn Waugh, Anthony Powell, George Orwell, Julian Barnes and W. G. Sebald, and is the author of the monograph *The Image of the English Gentleman in 20th-Century Literature: Englishness and Nostalgia* (Ashgate, 2007).

Lydia R. Cooper is a Visiting Assistant Professor of American Literature at Monmouth College, where she teaches contemporary American literature. She is the author of a book on Cormac McCarthy (Louisiana State University Press, 2011). Her essays have appeared in journals such as *ISLE: Interdisciplinary Studies in Literature and Environment*; *Critique*; *The Canadian Review of American Studies* and *Papers on Language and Literature*.

Sebastian Groes is Senior Lecturer in English Literature at Roehampton University. He specializes in modern and contemporary culture and literature, and in representations of cities. He is the author of *The*

Making of London (Palgrave Macmillan, 2011), editor of *Ian McEwan* (Continuum, 2009) and co-editor of *Kazuo Ishiguro* (Continuum, 2009) and *Julian Barnes* (Continuum, 2011).

Meghan Marie Hammond is a doctoral candidate in English Literature at New York University, writing a dissertation on the role of empathy in first-person literature by Henry James, Ford Madox Ford, Virginia Woolf and Kazuo Ishiguro.

Tim Jarvis works at the Institute of Education. His research interests include radical and experimental fiction, and the Gothic and horror tradition. His fiction was published in *Prospect Magazine, Leviathan 4: Cities* (Night Shade, 2004), *New Writing 13* (Picador, 2005), and in *DWB* (Louvain, 2005). Criticism was published in *Material Worlds* (Cambridge Scholars, 2007).

Barry Lewis is Senior Lecturer at the University of Sunderland, and has held posts at the University of Newcastle, the University of Trondheim and Stavanger College in Norway. He is the author of *Kazuo Ishiguro* (Manchester University Press, 2000) and *My Words Echo Thus: Possessing the Past in Peter Ackroyd* (University of South Carolina Press, 2007).

Liani Lochner is a doctoral candidate in the Department of English and Related Literature at the University of York where she is completing a thesis on literature's challenge to totalizing discourses in the work of Kazuo Ishiguro, Salman Rushdie, J. M. Coetzee and Aravind Adiga.

Christopher Ringrose is Principal Lecturer in English and Head of Learning and Teaching in the Arts at the University of Northampton. His interests include contemporary writing and children's literature, and recent publications include essays on Ben Okri and on new historical fiction for children. He is an Associate Editor of *The Journal of Postcolonial Writing* and of Routledge's *Annotated Bibliography of English Studies*.

Victor Sage is Emeritus Professor of English Literature in the School of Literature and Creative Writing at the University of East Anglia. He has published extensively on the Gothic tradition, including *The Gothic Novel: A Casebook* (Macmillan, 1990), *Gothick Origins and Innovations* (Rodopi, 1994) and *Le Fanu's Gothic: The Rhetoric of Darkness* (Palgrave Macmillan, 2003). For Penguin Classics he has edited Charles Maturin's *Melmoth the Wanderer* (2000) and Sheridan Le Fanu's *Uncle Silas* (2001). Sage has also published a collection of short stories, *Dividing Lines* (Chatto and Windus, 1984), and two novels, *A Mirror for Larks* (Secker and Warburg, 1993) and *Black Shawl* (Secker and Warburg, 1995).

Andy Sawyer is librarian of the Science Fiction Foundation Collection, and Course Director of the MA in Science Fiction Studies at the University of Liverpool. He is Reviews Editor of *Foundation: The International Review of Science Fiction* and has published widely on science fiction and fantasy, including essays on Ursula K. Le Guin, Terry Pratchett and Ramsey Campbell. With David Ketterer he has co-edited an edition of John Wyndham's previously unpublished novel *Plan for Chaos* (Liverpool University Press, 2009). He is the 2008 recipient of the Clareson Award for services to science fiction.

Brian W. Shaffer is Professor of English and Dean of Academic Affairs for faculty development at Rhodes College, in Memphis, Tennessee. He is the author of several books, including *Reading the Novel in English, 1950–2000* (Wiley-Blackwell, 2006), *Understanding Kazuo Ishiguro* (University Press of Mississippi, 1998) and *The Blinding Torch: Modern British Fiction and the Discourse of Civilization* (University of Massachusetts Press, 1993). He has co-edited *Conversations with Kazuo Ishiguro* (University Press of Mississippi, 2008), *A Companion to The British and Irish Novel, 1945–2000* (Blackwell, 2005) and *Approaches to Teaching Conrad's* Heart of Darkness *and 'The Secret Sharer'* (Modern Language Association of America, 2002).

Motoyuki Shibata is Professor of American Literature at the University of Tokyo. He has written widely on contemporary literature in English, including essays on Paul Auster and Kazuo Ishiguro. He has translated many novels by contemporary American authors, including Paul Auster, Steve Erickson, Steven Millhauser, Richard Powers and Stuart Dybek. He was winner of the 27th Suntory Prize for Social Sciences and Humanities for *American Narushisu* (*American Narcissus*). He is a regular contributor to the Japanese magazines *Coyote* and *Monkey Business*.

Gerry Smyth is Reader in Cultural History at Liverpool John Moores University. He has published widely on music and the novel, and on Irish cultural history. His recent publications include *Music in Contemporary British Fiction: Listening to the Novel* (Palgrave Macmillan, 2008) and *Music in Irish Cultural History* (Irish Academic Press, 2009).

Krystyna Stamirowska is Professor of English Literature at the Institute of English, Jagiellonian University, Krakow, Poland. Her publications include *Representations of Reality in the Post-War English Novel 1957–1975* (Universitas, 1992) and *B. S. Johnson's Novels: A Paradigm of Truth* (Universitas, 2006). She has published numerous articles and chapters in books, including four essays on Ishiguro.

Motoko Sugano teaches at Takushoku University in Tokyo, Japan. Her research interests include the representation of imperialism in Kazuo Ishiguro's work and (post-)colonial literatures in English by writers from South-East Asian countries.

Patricia Waugh is Professor of English Literature at Durham University. She has taught widely in nineteenth- and twentieth-century literature and literary theory and criticism, and she specializes in twentieth- and twenty-first-century literature, relations between modernism and post-modernism, women's writing and feminist theory, utopianism, literary criticism and theory, and literature, philosophy and science. She has edited numerous books and her monographs include *Metafiction* (Routledge, 1984); *Feminine Fictions* (Routledge, 1989); *The Harvest of the Sixties* (Oxford University Press, 1995); *Revolutions of the Word* (Edward Arnold, 1997); and she is currently completing two books, *Thinking with Feeling: Literary Humanities and the Biologisation of Culture* and the *Blackwell History of the Novel 1945–present*.

Alyn Webley wrote his doctoral thesis, 'The Vocational Imperative: Kazuo Ishiguro's Fictions and the Discourse of Denial', at the University of Glamorgan. He has published a paper, 'Making and Breaking Hegemonies: Ishiguro and History', in *Postgraduate English*. He is currently working as a freelance reviewer and as a reader for the Welsh Books Council.

introduction: 'it's good manners, really' – kazuo ishiguro and the ethics of empathy

sebastian groes and barry lewis

Kazuo Ishiguro is one of the most accomplished and celebrated writers of our time. He has produced a body of best-selling work that receives consistent praise from both academic and broadsheet critics whilst appealing to a global readership. At the age of five Ishiguro arrived in the United Kingdom as a Japanese immigrant, and his work combines his unusual perspective and fine intellectual acuity to portray a wide variety of places, characters and concerns, particularly exploring the effects of class, ethnicity, nationhood, place and morality, as well as the issues surrounding artistic representation itself. He was marked out as an extraordinarily gifted graduate of the University of East Anglia's MA in Creative Writing, and his first two, 'Japanese' works pointed to the emergence of a major writing talent in the early 1980s. His work was included twice in *Granta* magazine's 'Best of Young British Novelists' list (in 1983 and 1993); his work has been translated into more than thirty languages; he has won many literary prizes; and all but one of his works has been nominated for the prestigious Booker Prize, which he won for *The Remains of the Day* (1989), a modern classic. This novel was adapted into an Oscar-winning blockbuster, and the adaptation of *Never Let Me Go* (2005) into an equally successful film further underlines the appeal of Ishiguro's work to extraordinarily wide audiences.

Although primarily a novelist in the mould of classic writers of the humanist tradition, Ishiguro has also written across genres and for other media. After declaring that he uses 'the short story form as a way to work out ideas for [his] novels', he surprised his readers with a cycle of interconnected stories, *Nocturnes* (2009).[1] Ishiguro has also writ-ten a number of teleplays and screenplays for films, including James

Ivory's *The White Countess* (2005), and song lyrics for jazz singer Stacey Kent's album *Breakfast on the Morning Tram* (2007), which continue to underscore that, in Barry Lewis's words, 'the concepts of dislocation and homelessness . . . are versatile tools for exploring the richness of Ishiguro's writings'.[2] This diversity and range of his writing was further demonstrated in the surreal masterpiece and homage to Kafka, *The Unconsoled* (1995). *Never Let Me Go* is a stunning affirmation of his ability to think about ethical dilemmas without compromising the art of storytelling.

The contributions to this volume of criticism suggest that the power of Ishiguro's fiction lies in its ability to make us care about the world, about other people, about ourselves. The carefully crafted narratives invite us to invest our time and emotions in his fictional worlds and characters. This ethical imperative is Ishiguro's signature. We do not just feel for the fictional characters, but we are also impelled to speak on behalf of them, however different from us they appear to be. Victor Sage stresses the role of the reader in this process: 'despite, or perhaps because of this absence, its cruelty and pathos stand out and the reader is obliged to supply the emotions'. Think of Ono, the disgraced Japanese painter of *An Artist of the Floating World* (1986), whose sly, self-important understanding of himself is quashed by his daughter Etsuko; or of the butler Stevens, in *The Remains of the Day*, whose barely acknowledged realization that he has wasted his life in the service of an undeserving lord comes too late; or of Kathy H. and her fellow clones in *Never Let Me Go*, whose terrible predicament forces us to reflect upon our own humanity and respond with an outcry of injustice. They are not necessarily likeable characters, but Ishiguro's craftsmanship transfigures our imaginative response to them and provokes a human, sympathetic response. As Motoyuki Shibata argues in his chapter, it is the protagonists' failure of empathy that makes Ishiguro's work engaging: 'yet in spite of all these distances, or possibly *because of* them, we are moved; Ishiguro's characters' very inability to connect emotionally with others or with themselves makes the . . . books emotionally powerful. That is the real Ishiguro magic'.

Authors write with what creative writing students would call an 'Internal Judge' or an 'Ideal Reader' looking over their shoulder; what characterizes Ishiguro is his sensitivity to the variety of his readers. As he put it in an interview: 'I should talk to people in a way that they understand. If you're talking to someone who just flew in from China or Rome you will talk to them in a slightly different way than to someone who has grown up alongside you because you know they're not going to get the same cultural references. It's good manners, really'.[3] Ishiguro's work reduces references specific to place and culture to make his narratives 'universal', yet his reference to 'good manners' does not simply refer to etiquette or decorum but to his work's profound engagement with moral questions. There is also the sense that Ishiguro's own awareness of his status as a famous writer generates a responsibility towards his audiences. In the interview featured in this volume, he states:

> I feel a certain kind of relationship with my readership. There is a readership out there that will follow you into all sorts of interesting places. Particularly today, there is this highly sophisticated mass-readership out there. . . . They're not intimidated by strange things: they just don't like boring, pretentious self-indulgence. There's a readership out there hungry for new adventures. (p. 261)

Ishiguro trusts his readers, and we can trust him. Echoing the feeling of many readers, Haruki Murakami notes: 'in all my years of reading Ishiguro, he had never disappointed me or left me doubting him'.[4] It is this reciprocal awareness that makes moral agents of him and us. As with other authors, Ishiguro is aware of the contradictions and ambiguities of modern life, but rather than subscribing to the uncertainty, partiality and relativity in our understanding of ourselves and the world, he imbues his characters with the sense that their acts and choices *do* matter. Victor Sage therefore notes that Ishiguro's writing has 'a moral and ideological force that gives the work of this novelist a special place in the post-war novel'.

Ishiguro exploits several narrative techniques that regulate our emotional and intellectual engagement with his characters towards the practice of an ethics of empathy. From classic Greek tragedy, he draws his own version of dramatic irony: we have more knowledge and insight than the often self-deluding narrators, which makes us frustratingly powerless. Ono, Stevens and Kathy H. never quite reach the point of *anagnorisis*, that moment of insight or self-recognition that would enable them to steer their lives in different directions. In the spirit of classical tragedy, Ishiguro's fictions evoke a purging mixture of fear and, above all, pity. One may recall the heartrending close of *Never Let Me Go*, where Kathy H. stands alone before an empty Norfolk field after losing all her friends to a horrific organ-harvesting programme that will soon demand her life as well. Then there is the narrator in 'Malvern Hills' (2009), who, blinded by the arrogance of youth, is unable to see that the disillusionment of the older Swiss couple, Tilo and Sonja, will become his as well. *When We Were Orphans* (2000) asks us to leave behind two displaced orphans which, as Christopher Ringrose notes in his chapter, is 'not a cheap irony – two ruined people clinging together and lying to each other – but a rich one touched by tenderness'.

Ishiguro is also adept at leaving blanks and gaps in the narrative that draw the reader in still further. The complex shifts in time and geographical dislocations in a novel such as *A Pale View of Hills* (1982) force us to make links between seemingly unconnected events, and by doing so we glimpse the protagonists' secrets and hidden traumas. In the controlled interaction between revelation and concealment, the explicit and the implicit, we become woven into the invisible web that is the process of reading.

This masterly control over the text also manifests itself in Ishiguro's linguistic scrupulousness. Most famously, the story told by Stevens's father in *The Remains of the Day* of the tiger that is killed and removed from the dining room ends with the exquisite line: 'dinner will be served at the usual time and I am pleased to say there will be no discernible traces left of the recent occurrence by that time' (*RD* 36). In *When We Were Orphans*, the contortions of phrasing produced by Christopher Banks in his biographical account are both attempts to cover up his past and curious markers that alert the reader to his misrepresentation: 'from behind the cheerful anecdotes, there was emerging a picture of myself on that voyage to which I took exception' (*WWWO* 27). This self-deceiving language, as Sage notes in his chapter, 'strikes a pang in the reader'. Ishiguro does not succumb to the powerful pull towards the colourful language of affliction pervasive in contemporary writing. His texts prefer stoicism, which encourages the reader's steadfast acceptance of a detrimental situation.

Ishiguro's strategies for arousing empathy are supplemented by slippages of address to the reader. The curious 'you' to whom his narrators refer assumes that we are of a similar nature to them. But we, the addressees, are not butlers or clones. The 'you' spoken by the protagonists is not universal, but our acts of mental translation turn it into what Andrew Gibson calls a 'complex, ambiguous split-space' where 'identities twist round into each other and the reading subject becomes a profoundly ambivalent construction'.[5] In the act of bridging this hiatus, we extend the tragically limited consciousness of the narrators until we carry the burden of their trauma and the guilt these characters feel at their complicity in sustaining undesirable social systems. Although the protagonists lack the power to change their ways, we sense that we ourselves can – and must – forge a renewed agency.

The recent (re)turn to the study of empathy within literary studies brings Ishiguro's work to the fore. Krystyna Stamirowska explores ethics in relationship to language and identity in Ishiguro's work, arguing for subtle differences in his representation of gender. Although she acknowledges that Ishiguro's starting point for writing characters are human emotions that we all share, she also argues, contentiously, that whilst Ishiguro's 'male narrators have a stilted discourse that indicates emotional and ethical immaturity, his female protagonists express a more supple and ethically responsive discourse'. Meghan Marie Hammond continues this debate about Ishiguro's ethics by focusing on the complex role of genre in *The Remains of the Day*, in which Stevens struggles to find the appropriate narrative mode that will allow him to tell his life story. The novel is a travel narrative and road novel; an oratorical autobiography and apologia for a life's work; a state-of-the-nation novel; a love story and a romance; and, at times, a confession. This profusion of genres and their different rules of representation prevent, rather than help, Stevens from achieving the social and personal history that would have allowed him to acknowledge and atone for his part in Lord Darlington's serious political and, above all, moral mistakes.

Despite his desire to write universal narratives, Ishiguro is also a contemporary writer whose work investigates the state of the world today. Over the past few decades, we have experienced a proliferation of new technologies and modes of commanication; an omnipresent mass media; ever-faster forms of transport; and forces of globalization that have shrunk our horizons and propelled us into an increasingly 'virtual' experience of the world. These forces challenge the subject's autonomy and diminish our capacity to take responsibility for ourselves and others, and also, crucially, our ability to feel and feel *for*. Fredric Jameson calls this the 'waning of affect', whilst J. G. Ballard refers to it more abruptly as the 'death of affect'.[6] Ishiguro's ethic of empathy criticizes this condition, as Patricia Waugh states in her essay: 'the emotional absence and ethical failure enacted as [the theme of Ishiguro's books] is ironically and disturbingly redeemed by our proper responses as readers, pathos worryingly elicited in our recognition of the cultural apathia of an increasingly posthuman age'. Ishiguro's work forces us to establish a profound and meaningful connection with others by emphasizing the importance of our mindful use of language, and in doing so makes a serious claim for the novel form as an important representational form that allows us to exercise our imagination.

Ishiguro's ethics of empathy are directly related to the post-war consciousness. Unlike Rushdie, say, whose literary energies and emphasis on 'newness' derive from a triumphant, post-imperial spirit, Ishiguro is what the Germans call a *Nachkriegskind*: a child born into a generation that lives, and writes, in the shadow of the Second World War. This generation had no active role in – or made no direct contribution to – the atrocities perpetrated during that conflict, but they struggle to live as the inheritors of those tragic events which shaped them through their parents' experience. In this sense, Ishiguro has contributed to the post-war ethos shared by writers such as Ian McEwan, Graham Swift, Julian Barnes and Martin Amis. But whereas the novels of McEwan, Amis and Rushdie often arouse controversial, divisive reactions, Ishiguro's work has continuously generated a uniting, consolatory response across the globe. Unlike the often spectacular and sensational panoramas presented by his peers, Ishiguro's narratives are quiet and shrewd, and closer to the ethical questions and dilemmas evoked by J. M. Coetzee's work – but without the self-reflexive, metafictional game-playing. Coetzee's interest in the writing of Jewish–Russian exile Joseph Brodsky (1940–96) is shared by Ishiguro, who gave his name to the composer and conductor in *The Unconsoled*. Brodsky never addresses politics directly, observes Coetzee, but looks to great literature rather than politics, philosophy or religion for redemption by setting classic literary form as 'an example of moral and ethical purity and firmness'.[7]

More indirectly, Ishiguro keeps company with an earlier generation of writers such as J. G. Ballard, Kurt Vonnegut, Joseph Heller, Saul Bellow, Primo Levi, Jorge Semprún, Günther Grass and Harry Mulisch. These writers lived through the extraordinary eruption of violence between 1939 and 1945, and witnessed the savage effect of dehumanizing forces. A steady, if understated, attention to the atrocities and disasters of the twentieth century is characteristic of Ishiguro's narratives. The first two major works, *A Pale View of Hills* and *An Artist of the Floating World*, are indirect meditations on the consequences of the destruction of Nagasaki and Hiroshima by the atomic bomb; Japan's role in the Second World War is viewed from another perspective in *When We Were Orphans* and *The White Countess*; *The Remains of the Day* engages with British fascism in the run-up to the War and the waning of post-imperial power in its aftermath. The inescapable importance of the Second World War for Ishiguro is placed in a historical context by Christine Berberich, who suggests that *The Remains of the Day* functions as a therapeutic process of working through collective trauma whilst warning against the dangerous social and moral regression of the Thatcherite celebration of Englishness and Victorian moral values. *The Unconsoled* (1995) is a working-through of the traumatized East European consciousness after the collapse of dictatorial Communist regimes; and *Never Let Me Go* can be read, as Sage suggests, as an analogy of American slave culture, whilst the novel also reworks the fascist logic that led to the advocacy of eugenics and, eventually, the obscenity of the concentration camps.

Ishiguro has voiced his concern at the erosion of the protections accorded to civilians in recent conflicts and genocides, which suggests that his work is more political than some accounts (including, at times, his own) would suggest.[8] The novels of Ishiguro focus on episodes in modern history that confront us with the limits of our humanity and the problem of making sense of a seemingly senseless world. The work makes us aware of this irony, yet it is an unpostmodern, non-nihilist form of irony, as Christopher Ringrose explains in his reading of *When We Were Orphans*. Ringrose notes that it is the (religious) spirit of Kierkegaard that can be found in the complex forms of irony that Ishiguro's text evokes, and which prevent closure. He has, instead, made it his task to contribute towards the recovering of the human element. Mr Stevens's desperate quest to locate 'a little of that crucial quality of "dignity"' (*RD* 70) in his life story is telling. Ishiguro's project is similarly an attempt to recover human dignity and to restore the possibility of giving meaning and value to human life. Lydia R. Cooper frames *The Remains of the Day* and *Never Let Me Go* in the post-Holocaust ethical philosophy of Hannah Arendt and Jorge Semprún. Cooper shows that within 'autonomy-denying systems' such as Darlington Hall and Hailsham the narrators' willing postponement of an awareness of their situations, and their acceptance of a lack of autonomy, renders them complicit in the atrocities committed by their respective societies. Ishiguro's novels are, according to Cooper, 'haunted by glimpses of a radical empathy that could undermine' these systems. Liani Lochner continues this debate by showing how *Never Let Me Go* can be interpreted as a criticism of scientific discourse, which has a tendency to normalize the clinical, rationalizing values upon which it is built. For Lochner, 'Ishiguro posits the novel itself as a form of culture that can recuperate the "human" from science's purely mechanistic and materialistic definitions'.

Ishiguro's fiction often explores innovatively more popular forms or genre fictions, such as the detective novel in *When We Were Orphans* (2000) and science fiction in *Never Let Me Go*. Alyn Webley shows that Ishiguro stretches the conventions of the detective genre by making Christopher Banks, the protagonist of *When We Were Orphans*, forge an identity as a detective in order to hide the true nature of the problems he is trying to solve. Andy Sawyer traces how *Never Let Me Go* fits in a recent genre of 'outsider science fiction' by operating within a sci-fi register and exploiting the techniques of defamiliarization associated with that genre, but without conforming to its rules. These texts, like the others, unfold a dense and complex layering of meanings and a deeply resonant intertextuality that only the flexibility of the novel form allows. Ishiguro's work reminds us of Milan Kundera's claim that the strength of the novel lies not only in its 'spirit of complexity' but also in 'the spirit of continuity: each work is an answer to preceding ones, each work contains all the previous experience of the novel'.[9] And Murakami notes that Ishiguro's novels present a 'sort of composite universe' which is in dialogue with many previous writers, from Sophocles and Shakespeare to George Eliot and T. S. Eliot.[10]

What is also distinctive about reading Ishiguro's work is that it creates the sense that we are absorbed into a wider community that crosses geographical and linguistic barriers to stretch across the globe and through time. Victor Sage's essay therefore views Ishiguro's work through an anthropological framework in order to show how his novels persistently rework traditional rituals and rites of passage that operate across all cultures. Sage demonstrates that all of Ishiguro's novels subject such rites to an aesthetic and narrative interference that causes them to fail in their original function of progressing an individual to a new social stage and status within a particular culture. It is significant that Sage's exploration of universal reference in Ishiguro's work takes Shakespeare as its point of reference.

Ishiguro can be construed as a classic writer with affinities to the humanist tradition, which conflicts with the critical tendency to pigeonhole him as a postmodernist or, even more problematically, a postcolonial writer. Waugh notes that Ishiguro is often (mis)represented as an International Novelist in the mould of Rushdie whilst his work, in fact, 'does not easily "fit" the model of the international literary novel associated with post-modernizing experimentalism and flamboyant hybridity'. Waugh moves on to situate Ishiguro amongst two different strands of modernism. The first is that associated with the 'high modernism' of Eliot, Woolf and Conrad. These 'English' writers explored the depth of interior consciousness and its modes of representation, and they were concerned to find means of overcoming the 'dissociation of sensibility', or split between thought and feeling, that Eliot had identified as fracturing English literature since the metaphysical poets. The second strand of modernism is more continental and engages with the strange and surreal. Writers such as Kafka, Beckett and Albert Camus often exaggerated the split between thought and feeling by collapsing the boundaries between the internal and external or generating absurd, expressionist landscapes. Ishiguro's *oeuvre* straddles both these modernist camps: *An Artist of the Floating World* has affinities with the former, whilst *The Unconsoled* echoes the latter.

Ishiguro's labyrinthine and surreal fourth novel, *The Unconsoled*, lends itself particularly well to this critical reframing of Ishiguro as a late modernist. Jeannette Baxter explores the ways in which the legacy of the surrealists can be used to understand *The Unconsoled*'s complex narrative strategies of defamiliarization. Baxter cites Ishiguro's use of the labyrinth and other uncanny spaces as devices that disorientate the reader, turning *The Unconsoled* into a counter-historical, surrealist event. Tim Jarvis explores Deleuze and Guattari's concept of 'minor literature' to understand *The Unconsoled*'s engagement with Kafka: rather than focusing on the subject matter, Jarvis shows that Ishiguro's amplified evocation of Kafka's aesthetic and formal qualities is reflecting, and grappling with, an estrangement caused by the post-national and transcultural consciousness of the age of globalization. In Gerry Smyth's analysis of Ishiguro's engagement with music in *The Unconsoled* and in *Nocturnes* we find a tension between classic, Romantic and modernist conceptions of the arts. Smyth ponders upon Ishiguro's long-standing interest in music, noting that 'one of the principal recurring strategies of the "music-novel" is the introduction of music as a palliative effect in a range of crisis situations', another characteristic that Ishiguro's work offers us: the possibility of art as consolation.

Sebastian Groes also pays attention to the disruptive interventions of modernity into tradition by exploring Ishiguro's representation of East Anglia in *Never Let Me Go*. Ishiguro has often claimed that he uses England as a mythical place, but Groes points out that Ishiguro's fifth novel fits into a highly specific literary tradition of writing about East Anglia as a peripheral, melancholic space where symbolically the nation's collective memory is stored. Groes also suggests that Ishiguro punctuates this novel with bleak, haunting images drawn from a distinctly modernist legacy. The analysis of *Never Let Me Go*'s intricate temporality undertaken by Barry Lewis demonstrates how the compression of the lifespan of the clones throws up questions about time, consciousness and memory that are familiar to any reader of James Joyce or Virginia Woolf. Caroline Bennett also points out Ishiguro's elaborate use of temporality by focusing on the representation of children in Ishiguro's early work. She notes that they often function as vehicles for the displaced traumas of the adults: 'rather than showing a radical epistemological divide between the child and the adult, these novels suggest that the two roles are bound by degrees of unselfconsciousness and knowledge'. The blurring of the child and adult suggests that, particularly in the traumatized subject, there is no such thing as a clear division between the younger and older self.

Another form of exchange is traced by Motoyuki Shibata, who adds to the study of Ishiguro's work a short but illuminating account of the problems that occur when his novels are translated 'back' into

10 introduction

Japanese. What seems exotic to a Western audience loses its otherness for a Japanese readership, whilst Ishiguro's constrained, formal language is not perceived as unusual. Motoko Sugano provides us with a new insight into the reception of Ishiguro's *An Artist of the Floating World* in Japan. She continues Shibata's technical analysis of translation, but suggests that the Japanese audience had difficulties with this novel because of its representation of Japan's responsibility for its role in the Second World War, a topic that is still considered taboo in Japan. Her chapter is significant also for our understanding of Ishiguro due to its inclusion of actual Japanese war paintings by four of the many real-life 'artists of the floating world': Takeshiro Kanokogi, Ryushi Kawabata, Kakuzo Seno and Saburo Miyamoto.

Ishiguro's success with audiences around the world is driven by his unconditional commitment to understanding the world and its people, but also by his ability to provide consolation and a sense of community often seemingly lost in the contemporary, globalized world. And, as this volume of essays demonstrates, his work continues to stimulate lively and far-reaching debates amongst his critics.

notes

1. Kazuo Ishiguro in conversation with Sean Matthews, 'I'm Sorry I Can't Say More: An Interview with Kazuo Ishiguro', in Sean Matthews and Sebastian Groes (eds.), *Kazuo Ishiguro: Contemporary Critical Perspectives* (London and New York: Continuum, 2009), p. 122.
2. Barry Lewis, *Kazuo Ishiguro* (Manchester: Manchester University Press, 2000), p. 2.
3. Ishiguro in conversation with Claire Hamilton for 'Hamilton on Sunday', BBC Radio Merseyside; first broadcast 3 June 2007.
4. Haruki Murakami, 'On Having a Contemporary Like Kazuo Ishiguro', in Sean Matthews and Sebastian Groes (eds.), *Kazuo Ishiguro*, p. vii.
5. Andrew Gibson, *Postmodernity, Ethics and the Novel: From Leavis to Levinas* (London and New York: Routledge, 1999), pp. 199–200.
6. See Fredric Jameson, *Postmodernism* (London and New York: Verso, 1991), p. 10; J. G. Ballard, *The Atrocity Exhibition* (London: HarperPerennial, 2006), pp. 84–5, 108–9; originally published by Jonathan Cape in 1970.
7. J. M. Coetzee, 'The Essays of Joseph Brodsky', in *Stranger Shores* (London: Secker & Warburg, 2001), p. 158.
8. Kazuo Ishiguro in conversation with Martha Kearney in the Queen Elizabeth Hall, South Bank Centre, London, 13 May 2009.
9. Milan Kundera, 'The Depreciated Legacy of Cervantes', in *The Art of the Novel* (London: Faber, 1999), p. 18; first published in French as *L'Art du roman* in 1986 by Éditions Gallimard.
10. Murakami, 'Ishiguro', p. vii.

part i
critical overviews

1
kazuo ishiguro's not-too-late modernism

patricia waugh

summary

In this chapter Kazuo Ishiguro's credentials as an 'International Novelist' are examined and it is proposed that he is ambivalent towards the globalized, diasporic forces of postmodernism. Ishiguro's novels can be more fruitfully aligned with the first wave of internationalism associated with the modernists. His work has affinities with the 'High Modernism' of Eliot, Forster and Woolf in his concern for 'depth' and the exploration of interior consciousness; and also with the more Continental strain of modernism that produced expressionist landscapes and skewed plots. The case is supported by close readings of The Unconsoled *and* Never Let Me Go *in relation to concepts such as cosmopolitanism, stoicism and the objective correlative.*

kazuo ishiguro, postmodernism and the international novel

'The International Novel', a concept born in the early 1980s, was long overdue for many writers living in Britain. In 1957, Doris Lessing, who had lived there for nearly a decade, had bemoaned the insularity and parochialism of British writers and intellectuals. She commented wryly that the proclaimed New Left commitment to 'thinking internationally means choosing a particular shade of half-envious, half-patronizing emotion to feel about the United States; or collecting money for Hungary, or taking little holidays in Europe, or liking French and Italian films'.[1] There was little substantial change until 1980. In an editorial to the second *Granta Best of Young British Novelists* (1993), Bill Buford recalled the period leading up to the first volume of 1983. Before

13

1980, he claimed, there would have been no new young novelists to promote; the older generation (Iris Murdoch, Kingsley Amis, Angus Wilson, Muriel Spark and William Golding) were still going strong and, of younger novelists, the scene was entirely dominated by Martin Amis and Ian McEwan. But he goes on to describe how, in January 1980, it all began to change: he read a short story that seemed to offer something tantalizingly new, and eventually tracked its author, Kazuo Ishiguro, to a bedsit in Cardiff.[2] In 1981, Ishiguro's first novel, *A Pale View of Hills*, appeared, as well as Rushdie's *Midnight's Children*, Alasdair Gray's *Lanark* and Timothy Mo's first novel, *Sour Sweet*, about the experiences of a first-generation Chinese immigrant family in London.

However, though the 1980s saw the appearance of the 'International Novel' as a marketing phenomenon tied to economic and cultural globalization, literary internationalization was not a new phenomenon. The birth of internationalism as a defining feature of literary culture happened around 1910 and was tied to the rise of High Modernism. When Virginia Woolf famously wrote (in 1924) that in 1910 'human character' had changed, she was also responding to a sense of a new order, ushered in by European imperialism, the rise of consumer capitalism and the new technological inventions already compressing and accelerating time and space, such as the telephone and gramophone, the X-ray and the motor car.[3] E. M. Forster's *Howards End*, published in 1910, perfectly reflected the tensions of this earlier moment of 'internationalization' with its sense of an England dissolving into a global sea of capital rippling out from British imperial expansion. For Forster's London seems often to float on tropes of fluidity, as though its foundations were already shifting and heaving. When Margaret is driven to Howards End in Henry's motor car, even the earth feels like the sea: 'She looked at the scenery. It heaved and merged like porridge. Presently it congealed. They had arrived'.[4] Only when they reach Howards End, pastoral symbol of England, standing on firm land outside the imperial seas of Britain, solid in its ancient beauty, does she recapture 'the sense of space which the motor had tried to rob from her'.[5]

If the motor car and the dissolving island were defining metaphors for the sense of internationalism of early British modernist fiction, however, it is Rushdie's postmodern tropes of migrancy, nomadism and hybridity that have dominated descriptions of the second wave of fictional internationalization since the 1980s. The migrant and the nomad have provided powerful images for the postmodern sense of the incomprehensible global networks of capital and also of the new international novelist: a figure no longer tied to any one national tradition but rejoicing in the fluid, the disseminated and the rootless. Now, the novel, like the nation, must accept and welcome the *dissemination* and loss of identity feared by Forster as only ever the negative expression of imperialism. Embracing an ever-open sea of stories, Rushdie insists, referring to his contemporaries, 'we are inescapably international writers at a time when the novel has never been a more international form'.[6]

Ishiguro is sometimes presented as a novelist who has slipped comfortably, Rushdie-style, into this new role of International Novelist, working through its recognized modes of mimicry, ventriloquism and double perspective, taking on themes of global significance in virtuoso fictional performances that resist simple or particularized allegorical reduction. He has also expressed a sense of being born into a generation that felt stifled by the provincialism of the British novel at the end of the 1970s, but also by Britain's increasing marginalization within world politics: the 'Big Events' happened elsewhere. However, Ishiguro has also intimated more complex reservations about the effects of internationalization on fiction, aware that the new globalized fiction market and the celebration of the 'hybrid' are always open to orientalist pressures, the exoticization and appropriation of migrant and post-colonial experience. In an interview with the Japanese writer, Kenzaburō Ōe, he expressed concern that one of the effects of the internationalization and mass marketing of fiction might be the homogenization and erasure of cultural difference. This concern was first voiced by modernist writers and critics such as Forster, Eliot, Lawrence and F. R. Leavis (to whom Ishiguro refers in his interview with Sebastian Groes). In the Kenzaburō Ōe interview, he arrives at the following conclusion:

> Perhaps whether a writer is international or not is something that the writer cannot control. It's almost accidental. But often, I think, the deeper the work, and the deeper the truth of the work, the more likely it is to be international, whether the author is consciously addressing a small group of people or a large number of people.[7]

'Depth' is a key word here, a concept normally associated with literary modernism, for what is perhaps most evident about Ishiguro's writing – and evident to Ishiguro himself – is that his work does not easily 'fit' the model of the international literary novel associated with postmodernizing experimentalism and flamboyant hybridity. 'Depth', along with feeling, and the concern to overcome modes of 'dissociation of sensibility', was the preoccupation of English High Modernism. It was evident in Eliot's sense of poetry tapping into the 'deeper unnamed feelings which form the substratum of our being';[8] or in Woolf's sense of the modern novel pitched in the dark places of psychology; or in Conrad's preoccupation with the 'secret sharer', the hidden double or secret agent in the self, source of profound deception and self-deception; or Forster's concern with the undeveloped heart and the role of art in the refinement of feeling as essential to moral development. But there was another kind of modernism too, more European, and more strange and surreal, that functioned through exaggeration of dissociation, of the splitting of thought and feeling, of a kind of hyper-reflexive introspection producing expressionist landscapes divorced from bodily and material situations, collapsing the boundaries between internal and external. This alternative modernism begins with Dostoevsky and proceeds through Kafka, Beckett, Camus and Robbe-Grillet.

Ishiguro draws on both these trajectories of modernism, perhaps more on the first in his earlier writing and the second in his later works. Throughout his work, though, he explores loss, nostalgia and disorientation, the kinds of mental dislocation produced by traumatic histories and producing, in turn, a sense of blockage, suspension, the inability to move on. As much Beckettian as Forsterian in its effects, this impetus arises similarly out of the need to make meaningful narratives out of broken histories. The novels abound with traumas – personal, national, international; creativity is seen to arise out of the need to heal wounds, to find a consolation which, if it comes at all, comes almost always too late. Ishiguro might be thought of as an almost *too late, late* modernist. Like Ryder, reliving the moment when, as a small child, he realized that life's wounds (the tear in the rug) could be incorporated into imaginary play (the game with his toy soldiers), and that 'the blemish that had always threatened to undermine my imaginary world could in fact be incorporated into it' (*U* 16), Ishiguro's novels explore how the imaginary worlds produced out of nostalgic longing may be the necessary lies that we tell ourselves in order simply to survive psychically. Like Hailsham, they are imaginary utopian spaces, built out of nostalgia and providing emotional sustenance and consolation; but, equally like Hailsham, they may be not-so-noble lies covering over social injustice and exploitation, human outrages perpetrated on other humans in the name of utilitarian notions of the good. They may even fuel dangerous kinds of nostalgic mythologization of the 'greatness' of Britain, of its butlers and pastoral beauties.

The desire to reinvent old maps through insistent forms of self-deception is a constant theme, for it is the expression of a basic human need for attachment, belonging and care. Fictionality goes deep in Ishiguro, even when it is expressed through the seemingly superficial and the stereotypical. Iconic images from popular culture abound in his work: images already translated across geographies and discursive traditions. His butlers, detectives, clones and fantasies of superheroes and redeemers are all part of this economy. For the stereotype is always already the meaning of many copies. Ambivalent artifices of belonging, stereotypes are shortcuts, opening spaces for affective exploration. In reading his work, we constantly bump up against the familiar – the stereotypes of the ghost story, the detective story, the schoolgirl story, the tale of homecoming – but in uncanny and disturbing ways. This feeling of the uncanny, of encountering something familiar and yet displaced, is most obviously represented in *Never Let Me Go* through the figures of the children who are clones – human, and yet inciting a response of disgust at what is not quite human, as if they were *spiders* (*NLMG* 32), as Kathy H. recognizes. In *The Remains of the Day* (1989), Stevens's fulfilment of his butlering role is the performance of what is already a performance, a history of the 'great' butlers of England. The uncanny feeling is connected with the opening up of what Larkin called the 'long perspectives' that 'open out at each instant of our lives', linking us to our losses, as we constantly relive the past in present experience, in compulsive repetitions.[9]

affective cosmopolitanism and *the unconsoled*

In *The Unconsoled* (1995), Ishiguro brilliantly fictionalized his ambivalence towards the 'International Novel' for its potential sacrifice of the kind of 'depth' associated with the great modernist novels. Set almost entirely in a hotel in an unidentified middle-European town, the novel reads like the inner space equivalent of Fredric Jameson's hyperspace Bonaventure Hotel. Just as Jameson reads the Las Vegas hotel as an icon of international postmodernism, so Ishiguro's fictional hotel is a kind of map of the inside of the contemporary writer's mind and of the consequences for his or her creativity and self-identity of this 'internationalization'. In his account of the Westin Bonaventure Hotel in Las Vegas, Jameson provided one of the most resonant cultural images of postmodernity as a dizzying experience of loss of anchorage, of belonging and of spatial and temporal attachment. To walk through the building, a simulacrum of and substitute for the city itself, according to Jameson, is to become acutely self-conscious of the disjunctive relations between body, space and time in the contemporary world, and of our inability to orient ourselves in the time-space compressions and dislocations of capitalist globalization.[10]

Ishiguro's hotel appears to be another internationalized postmodern space, yet it also calls up, just as resonantly, earlier labyrinthine images from High European Romantic and modernist culture: Ariadne (on Naxos), Kafka's castle, Escher's drawings, Eliot's palimpsestic *The Waste Land* with its maimed Fisher King. These provide the infrastructure for a newly professionalized space of schedules, hurry, international business and endless busyness, the constant rehearsal for an opportunity that may never arrive, but for which one must always be prepared. From its comically kitsch beginning, with its atmosphere of Bergman meets Coen brothers meets Kafka with Austro-Hungarian décor *circa* 1930, a dash of German High Romanticism, and some French Decadence (with the sinister puppet-master Hoffmann presiding over the entire *mise en scène*), there ensues a surreal psychodrama. Time is projected onto the dimension of space. In an uncanny echo of ordinary residential experience in any international hotel, the experience of a place of professional reserve where strangers stumble into the intimacies of each other's lives, Ryder walks through walls and encounters dissociated or split-off versions of himself. He is granted a kind of uncanny omniscience as he telepathically enters the minds of others (who might also be projections of himself). The goal of his visit, the promised concert, never takes place; Ryder moves on, abandoning a woman who claims to be his wife and a possible son, Boris, who is more or less a stranger to his largely absent father. For over 500 pages, Ryder endeavours to find a space and time to rehearse and perform his art. But he has lost his 'schedule' and is forever hurried and harried by the numerous and varied demands made on him as redeemer of the lost triumphs of *Kultur* and community. The novel ends as he moves on to yet another European city, another peripatetic rehearsal.

When the novel was published, most reviewers and readers were entirely baffled. Few realized that Ishiguro began the novel after an exhausting world-promotional tour for *The Remains of the Day*, part of the process where the contemporary writer, like the book, has now become a packaged commodity, the possession of publisher, marketing agents, booksellers and international audiences, critics and reviewers. Viewed from this perspective, *The Unconsoled* is a meditation on the tension between historical ideas about the creative arts and their place in a culture, and the varieties of new external pressures on the contemporary writer in an internationalized culture market. What is celebrated as hybridity might also be experienced as the conflicting demands of political representation, ethical obligation and the commercial implications of producing creative work within a global economy. Competing historical images of authorship are carefully embodied in the varied cast of characters: Freudian neurotics, Romantic geniuses, traditional bards. Brodsky, like a maimed rock star returned from rehab, babbles continuously about his damaged genius and hysterically flaunts the wound that he believes places him beyond everyday moral obligation.

But Ryder, the lauded and serious contemporary international artist, is also expected to be part of a new cosmopolitan world of 'caring professionals', an international ethicist, compelled to respond to insistent and plural local demands, in a kind of parody of telescopic philanthropy.

Ryder's experience, of being unsituated and nowhere, is also the experience of any professionalized denizen of the new globalized world of cosmopolitan business and tourism. Yet Ishiguro's examination of cosmopolitanism goes deeper than this. The *cosmopolitans* in the original Stoic accounts were the children of Zeus who were also world citizens by virtue of their exercise of reason and their capacity to employ a universalizing and detached model of social justice. Pity, empathy and affect must be repudiated because to give way to the passions, even as compassion, would indicate a lower status, a loss of self-control and therefore a loss of *dignity* (a word much used in Ishiguro's work). For the Stoics recognized the cognitive power of feeling for evaluating and performing judgements, but they also saw feeling as producing the kinds of attachments that rendered the self vulnerable to forces from without and therefore beyond rational control. Stoic cosmopolitanism therefore aimed at a condition of *apatheia* that divests itself of attachment and aims at a cool universality. It was later reflected in the austere rationalism of mainstream traditions of ethical philosophy from Plato to Kant and in neo-Kantian ethicists such as John Rawls: to act ethically requires the denial of any affective attachment to the world.

Ishiguro ironizes the myopic limitations of this tradition through his many 'professionals', like Stevens, Ono and Ryder, who are each caught up in the most pervasive contemporary version of this Stoical conception of self-denial and self-control: the ideology of professionalism as a committed and efficient but 'cool' concept of service and duty. In its name, they perpetrate daily, on those who look to them for more intimate or loving *care and compassion*, numerous small acts of cruelty and neglect, sadism and torture. Etsuko's husband is only the first of Ishiguro's many characters whose professionalized refrain, 'I'm rather busy now', constantly evades the ethical demand of his family. Yet, for those who temporarily abandon their plans and schedules, small spaces open up for deeper self-recognition. In a Forsterian echo, Stevens motors off into the 'wilderness' in his borrowed car, at a stately speed, and although he fails to complete his perfect house 'plan', he does acquire some insight into his undeveloped heart and the recognition that domestic administration has been a poor substitute for a truly fulfilled life. As Ryder boards the tram at breakfast, moving on to yet another European city, conversing with the early morning worker, abandoning and rejected by Sophie and Boris, there is still a sense, at the very end, of stepping out into a more convivial civic world, the cosmopolitan fraternity offered by the great European cities that was first given expression in Gogol, Haussman and in Baudelaire's *flâneur*.

art and empathy: from care to social justice in *never let me go* and *the unconsoled*

In the current revival of the idea of cosmopolitanism as a new world citizenship, the novel, in Ishiguro's hands, becomes crucially important as a vehicle for the amplification and development of modes of feeling. In this sense, one can see the partial rootedness of his work in the earlier moment of European High Modernism with its equivalent preoccupations with globalization, internationalization and the importance of shared feeling. The novels are a literary meditation on *what it is to be human* as well as what it is to be British, or Japanese or American. At the centre of his fiction is the question of feeling: of whether art, in general, and the novel, in particular, can still provide a moral and political 'sentimental education', an education of the heart that is deeper and more ethically resonant than mere consolation. It is in this constant preoccupation with 'depth' as the aesthetic exploration and expression of feeling as a vehicle for ethical understanding that Ishiguro's work seems closer to modernism than postmodernism, constituting a *late* international modernism. Through his influence as a poet and a critic and as editor of *The Criterion*, the great shaper of international modernism was T. S. Eliot. In numerous ways, Ishiguro's aesthetic reflects the Eliotic and *modernist* concepts of 'impersonality' – formulated in his famous essay 'Tradition and the Individual Talent' (1919) – and the 'objective correlative' – formulated in the early 'Hamlet' essay (1919). Famously, Eliot argued that the poet's original emotion is transmuted – impersonalized into an 'objective correlative', a set of associations, images and verbal equivalents of a state of mind that is available for all. Because Ishiguro has made statements at odds with the purity of this early formulation, the close relation of his work to High Modernism has been overlooked. However, the concept of impersonality in Eliot's critical writing became much more nuanced than in this early formulation. The modified versions of the impersonality thesis, and his subsequent more open emphasis on the role of art as axiomatically the expression and refinement of depth of feeling, come close to Ishiguro's own understanding of the place of feeling and affect in art. Ishiguro has argued that writers write out of something that is unresolved deep down and, in fact, it's probably too late ever to resolve it. . . . The wound has come, and it hasn't healed, but it's not going to get any worse; yet the wound is there. It's a kind of consolation that the world isn't quite the way you wanted it but you can somehow reorder it or try to come to terms with it by actually creating your own world and your own version of it.[11]

Ishiguro is haunted by lateness, the sense that art can never provide complete reparation, but can provide relief through its capacity to remould old forms and to nuance understanding through a capacity to find verbal equivalents for complex states of feeling. At the end of *The Use of Poetry and the Use of Criticism* (1933), Eliot similarly describes the creative process as a long incubation where, as the shell cracks, there is a 'sudden lifting of the burden of anxiety and fear which presses upon our daily life so steadily that we are unaware of it'; but it is described as 'something *negative*: that is to say, not "inspiration" as we commonly think of it, but the breaking down of strong habitual barriers . . . relief from an intolerable burden'.[12] For Eliot, the concept of the 'objective correlative' described the capacity of the artist to arrive at modes of formal reparation or restoration which might provide a transitional space outside of purely subjective emotional states, transitional spaces that were available and open for shared or collective negotiation. For a contemporary international writer, that collective now refers not simply to a national or European readership but to a global audience, so the sense of how one might formulate and share the burden – without falling into allegory or parable – seems almost impossibly challenging. Moreover, for a novelist, as opposed to a poet, an 'objective correlative' must provide a recipe for the collaborative building of a world that is felt and processed as an experience, a world understood as construed through another mind, the imaginative basis for empathy. But one of Ishiguro's major themes is both the necessity for the cultivation of empathy and the necessity for knowing its limits. Imaginary projections onto the other may simply represent an extension of the individual's own self-regard and fear. Self-deceptions, lies and mimicry are perpetrated daily as camouflage and defence, fences against threats to the fences already interiorized in our psychic worlds.

In novels, existential and ontological threats of world-shattering significance are often conveyed through the ordinary and the quotidian: profound human isolation and loss through abandoned caps and shoes on a beach (in Daniel Defoe's *Robinson Crusoe*); or the fierce and dangerous yearning to belong and to be different in the various tilts of the Brodie set school hats in Muriel Spark's 1961 novel, *The Prime of Miss Jean Brodie*. Fences are crucial in both these novels: Crusoe establishes his human fiefdom with the building of his fence and Spark's novel begins with the image of the fence between the boys and girls as the basic instrument of segregation and belonging. *Never Let Me Go* and *The Unconsoled* are similarly novels preoccupied with clothing and with the making and breaking down of fences as a means of exploring the relations between art, emotion and justice: the human fears that drive us to belong and those which drive us to yearn for freedom and autonomy. In the opening chapter of *Never Let Me Go*, Kathy H.'s memories of Hailsham begin with a scene, of hidden schoolgirls gathered to spy on the boys' football game, which might have been extracted from any schoolgirl story (though there are strong resonances with Spark's). Kathy notices that Tommy is proudly – but foolishly in her eyes – distinguishing himself from the group by wearing a new polo shirt: she simply allows herself the thought, 'playing football in that. It'll get ruined' (*NLMG* 7). Something will get ruined: the reader senses something of greater import in Kathy's domestic concern with the shirt. Focalized through the perspective of the girls, the reader then witnesses Tommy's humiliation as, brimming with enthusiasm for play and pride in his new shirt, he is subjected to what is evidently a predetermined ritual of humiliation. Fascinated, the girls' (and the reader's) attention is arrested by the display of raw feeling as Tommy explodes into ballistic rage, 'raving, flinging his limbs about, at the sky, at the wind, at the nearest fence post' (*NLMG* 9). Laura, the mimic of his earlier performance, attempts to continue her comic turn by observing that Tommy is perhaps 'rehearsing his Shakespeare' (*NLMG* 10). Even Kathy, who later breaks away from the group to express genuine care and concern for Tommy, reflects: 'It was like he was doing Shakespeare and I'd come up onto the stage in the middle of his performance' (*NLMG* 10). The chapter concludes with Ruth's comment of 'Mad animal' (*NMLG* 11). If Tommy is not 'rehearsing his Shakespeare', then he is – what they all fear might be thought about themselves – merely a 'mad animal': something not quite human, not treated as quite human. Tommy is, appropriately, mad about it. The soiling of his shirt and the flinging of himself against the fence are Ishiguro's 'objective correlatives' for an emotional complex that encompasses, but extends far beyond, Tommy's own raw protest.

The world on which the mirage of Hailsham rests, a world of childhood dressed in nostalgia for Kathy H., is one of profound social injustice, built on utilitarian premises but contradictorily underpinned by a meritocratic infrastructure that allows the rich and the talented to prevail and triumph at the expense of the poor and the needy. In its materialism, even in its gestural welfare capitalism, it is a world whose liberal platitudes and shibboleths about the sanctity and quality of individual life rest on a 'slippery slope' philosophy of utilitarianism that ultimately leads to the perception of humans as expendable waste, meat – mad animals – if they are not functioning (deferential) cogs in the well-oiled machine. They are commodities in a culture of exchange, the fetishization of things and possessions, sales and tokens. They are zipped-up bags of organs that might be unzipped and dismantled, part by part. No wonder the children identify themselves with lost objects – precious rubbish that might be found again, in a field in unmapped rural Norfolk.

Childhood protects to some extent: Hailsham's 'guardians', as in Plato's *Republic*, disguise from them their true condition through a euphemistic vocabulary of 'donations', suggestive of free will and the encouragement of a creativity or expressivity that is implicit in the belief in a unique soul.[13] But Hailsham is actually an organ farm. The novel stages a debate about the place of art in a materialistic culture that views the body in entirely utilitarian terms. The children's treatment rests on the perpetuation of a (noble) lie that excellence in art might confer upon them the possession of an expressive identity akin to the possession of a soul. The guardians cultivate the lie in the belief that art might continue, in a culture of commodification and dehumanization, to confer selfhood through a Romantic-expressive notion of embodiment and emotional and subjective integrity and dignity. The novel appears to endorse this Romantic-expressivist aesthetic but additionally suggests – self-reflexively – that art should also function to articulate a sense of the actual erosion of the humanist notion of the self in a culture where materialism has paradoxically become the dominant metaphysics. Art must dislocate as well as console if we are to recognize ourselves through other lenses and see what we have or might become. The expression of *disgust* in Madame's face, the fear of contamination by spiders, is what makes Kathy aware that, for others, they are simply insects. Tommy must be 'rehearsing his Shakespeare' because the aesthetic act might be the only mode of redemption, the only available protection against identification with the abject, with contaminated matter: being a mad cow.

The etymology of the word *feeling* is from the Old Icelandic, *falmer*, meaning 'to grope towards'. Inhabiting the perspective of Kathy H. throughout the novel, the reader gropes for meaning through her struggle to convey complex feelings and an evolving conscience: her sense of complicity and guilt, compassion, protectiveness, self-justification and divided loyalty are present from the very first episode. For what is dramatized as the novel begins is the conflict over remaining part of the group – and therefore being complicit in its voyeuristic savagery – or acting on compassionate impulses that rebel against Tommy's treatment. What makes Kathy an ethical human being is that she leaves the group and risks her own subsequent exclusion, despite her awareness of her deep need for its protection, simply so that she can offer compassionate support to Tommy. Even as a professional carer, doing a 'pretty good' job, she is still pleased they could 'choose' their donors after six years. Why not, she says: 'Carers aren't machines . . . So when you get a chance to choose, of course you choose your own kind. That's natural. There's no way I could have gone on for as long as I have if I'd stopped feeling for my donors every step of the way' (*NLMG* 4).

Of all Ishiguro's novels, *Never Let Me Go* is perhaps the most dedicated to the complex ethics of care to the vulnerable condition of being a 'poor creature'. The image of Kathy H. holding the pillow and dancing to Judy Bridgewater's song, 'Never Let Me Go', conveys the fragility of the human self, but it is also a reminder of the capacity of art as a 'transitional object' – the song, the novel we are reading – to serve as an 'objective correlative' for its audience's complex projections. In the final visit to Madame and Miss Emily, Kathy H. discovers that for Madame the image was not of someone who will have a baby to care for (Kathy's understanding) but of 'a new world coming rapidly. More scientific, efficient, yes. More cures for the old sicknesses. Very good. But a harsh cruel world' (*NLMG* 248). Art as a 'transitional object' or Eliot's 'objective correlative' reunites rational thought and feeling and holds a mirror up to the complex social operations of these processes. Understanding might always arrive, in some sense, too late: like Ruth's resolve, after the beautiful vision of the blue boat, to tell Kathy the truth. Ethical understanding begins with the recognition that, though you and I may be looking at the same object or image, the world that you find in it may be a very different world from the one that I find there.

The ending of this novel is particularly poignant. A kind of horror is instilled at the human uses of the human and a kind of pity (Aristotelian *pathos*) for the fragility and vulnerability of a human identity so dependent on the suffering body. The emotional absence and ethical failure enacted as its theme are ironically and disturbingly redeemed by our proper responses as readers, a pathos worryingly elicited in our recognition of the cultural *apathia* of an increasingly post-human age. Yet, that we respond emotionally to a fiction, an artefact, just as the human clones who are its characters respond to each other, suggests that our humanness indeed rests upon our biological nature, but, also, and just as importantly, on how we represent to ourselves, symbolically, what we take that nature to be. The final image of Kathy staring at the rubbish and plastic caught and tangled along lines of barbed wire, flapping against the flat horizon, places in the foreground the fence with which the novel began and leaves the reader with a final image of the struggle of the clones to think of themselves as 'precious objects' and not simply rubbish for disposal.

The passage gathers together all the motifs of lost objects, rubbish, the body as expendable waste, throwaway consumer culture, the struggle to find meaning beyond fences, in its depiction of the bleak landscape, of barbed wire and loss. It offers an image of the body as waste unless redeemed through the power of the human imagination to project itself beyond the body and to enter empathetically into that sense of 'me' that exists for all others too. The phrase 'never let me go' has been considerably deepened and amplified by the end of the novel. For that same capacity to imagine and to anticipate and to emote that makes us human also functions to enhance many of the territorial fears and the dread of mortal ending that make us peculiarly complex poor creatures. Fences go up to protect against that most primitive of affects: the ravings of a mad animal against an unjust universe.

life's a rehearsal: shakespeare and the stoicism of seneca

The idea of 'rehearsing his Shakespeare' has other resonances in Ishiguro's work. There seems to be something disingenuous about Tommy's otherwise entirely genuine rage: an implication that he is performing, or rehearsing for a performance. And why are there so many instances in Ishiguro's novels when emotions are, indeed, self-consciously performed and staged, illuminated, or rehearsed for an imaginary audience, as *if they were already aesthetic*, or perceived that way, often by hidden and voyeuristic onlookers, as at the start of *Never Let Me Go*? In the early novels, moments of emotional recognition or emotional deception are consciously framed, significantly illuminated and the characters involved silhouetted, looming iconically, given a kind of visual depth and solidity as they appear from behind a screen in a shaft of light. Examples include: Ono summoned to his father's study almost paralysed with shame and fear as he stands under the halo of light, like a victim facing his torturer (*AFW* 42); or the way both he and Matsuda stare between the screen and out from the dark towards the light of the veranda, avoiding each other's gaze as they negotiate their way around their now unspeakable past (*AWF* 200); or where

Stevens, recalling the incident after he has requested that his father no longer wait at table because of his growing infirmity, sees William through a top floor window of the house, the daylight transforming Miss Kenton's figure into a silhouette (*RD* 66). Voyeuristically, they look out together onto the lawn, lit by sunlight and with the shadows of the poplars falling across; so the eye is taken to the figure of his father, pacing, mysteriously and very deliberately, compulsively and with a fierce intent, backwards and forwards from the steps to the lawn; this is physical testimony to the obsessional rumination that has clearly taken over his mind since the accident that has led to the reduction of his services. Grotesque or exaggerated gestures often accompany these illuminated moments: Ichiro slumping to the floor in mimicry of the Lone Ranger (*AWF* 30); the strange and disturbing glimpses of Hoffman thumping his brow and muttering 'An ox, an ox, an ox', as he rehearses the perversely willed encounter with his wife that (the hidden driver of the plot) will bring their marriage to its conclusion (*U* 383); Miss Emily, alone, pacing the floor and talking under her breath, assumed by Kathy to be 'rehearsing a lesson' (*NLMG* 41); or Miss Lucy, again caught voyeuristically, through the slit of a half-closed door in a room darkened by shut blinds, manically scrubbing out pages of close hand-writing so that the scratching noise is heard in the next room, 'like gas or steam escaping in sharp bursts' (*NLMG* 83).

Another of Eliot's essays, 'Shakespeare and the Stoicism of Seneca' (1927), throws some interesting light on these moments that are characteristic of Ishiguro's writing. The point of the essay was to show how the Elizabethans, lacking the moral underpinning provided by the Greek ideal of a *cosmopolis*, invented a weakened version of Stoicism as *consolation*: an exercise of emotional containment undertaken as the practice of cheering oneself up. This aesthetic performance, a private staging of the self to oneself, is most evident, Eliot writes, in 'the attitude of self-dramatisation assumed by some of Shakespeare's heroes at moments of tragic intensity'.[14] Othello is one such 'Senecan' tragic protagonist who, in his final speech, is '*cheering himself up*', trying to think well of himself, 'by adopting an *aesthetic* rather than a moral attitude . . . He takes in the spectator, but the human motive is to take in himself'.[15]

The fear of losing one's clothes in public, of slipping out of one's schedule or plot, or falling off the stage and into nakedness runs through all of Ishiguro's work: from the more conventional realist denial of the unreliable narrators of the early novels, seeking to cover over complex feelings of loss of status and power, bereavement, guilt and self-aggrandizement, to the emotionally projected and expressionist and strangely hyper-reflexive landscapes of the later novels. It is reflected in a continuous preoccupation with 'clothing': in Stevens's worries about what to wear as he embarks on his unanticipated journey and his disquisitions on butlering as more than the donning of a costume (*RD* 169). The fear of walking naked is the fear of emotional exposure, of being seen to be a mad animal; social encounter is presented almost always as a kind of ritualized performance which, if breaking with custom, may need careful rehearsal. However, in Ishiguro's work the performance provided for oneself, in private – the consolatory cheering oneself up as if on stage, in public view – is not quite the 'rehearsing Shakespeare' that it is in Eliot's account. Although it may often involve pride and self-aggrandizement, reassurance and self-deception, it is also often a fending off or a capitulation to a desperate sense of accountability to the invisible and haunting presences of the superegoic internalized parents, the social conscience and the law, or the deep internalization of an ethos of professionalized duty. When Stevens and Ono console themselves that they have done the state some service, the performance is not unlike Eliot's Othello; but when Tommy 'rehearses his Shakespeare' he is the poor, bare animal of *King Lear*, screaming at the universe, at the law, at the injustice of it all, at the invisible ties that bind humans to poverty or suffering, at the mortal body and the universal condition of inequality. If Eliot laments the substitution of an aesthetic attitude for a properly ethical judgement, Ishiguro shows again and again how the aesthetic is not simply a mode of self-deception, a staging of the self in ideal public dress (though sometimes it may be that). He also shows that, at the heart of what makes us ethical in the first place, is our imaginative and aesthetic ability to conjure counterfactuals or to empathize with other minds through imaginative projection. We must still learn, though, as Eliot so well understood, to recognize the moment when projection as self-dramatization begins to obscure clarity of vision.

The novel where Ishiguro walks most naked – a novel that is mostly about the fear of the embarrassment of walking naked, of being shamed and failing to perform – is *The Unconsoled*. Curiously, it is also a novel that reworks Eliot's *The Waste Land* – echoing its motif of 'HURRY UP PLEASE IT'S TIME', its quest for redemption amongst broken fragments of tradition, its hallucinatory voices, its central character who, like Tiresias, has already foreseen all.[16] Set alongside its analysis of the mundane travails of the contemporary internationalized artist is a more flamboyant and expressivist late Romantic myth of the artist as redeemer: the Wagnerian hereditary genius recapitulating a tradition of the *Volk*, the myth that was central to the revival of militaristic nationalisms across Europe. Images of the *Volk* and *Gemeinschaft* rub up against those of the world of schedules, professional conferencing and arts management, often in a single economical conceit, like the porters' dance, a *Volkish* performance of professional prowess that leads to the death of Gustav. This is an entirely staged world, where art is the *only* consolation and therefore the entire arbiter of value. Goodness is measured as taste. Merit rests on aesthetic accomplishment and performance: marriages are made and broken over the possession or otherwise of good taste. Children who fail to achieve stern performance standards are abandoned or punished. Conflicts about modernization and civic pride rest on controversies about aesthetic form or performance style. Everyone cheers themselves up constantly in the mode of Eliot's reading of a degenerate Stoicism.

Ryder seems not to know whether he belongs to this space of nowhere that is somewhere, or whether he is the stranger come to redeem it. The reader does not know either; nor if the entire novel is simply the projection of a performer who, caught between conflicting demands, traditions and professional pressures, has thrown away his schedule to retreat into the chaotic labyrinth of an internal world which might somehow nourish the next creative burst. He tries to engage, but the burdens are excessive; to resolve them would require an intimacy with local conditions that he has neither the time nor the desire to acquire. Ryder is a Parsifal returned to the contemporary Waste Land to see if, this time, he might ask the right questions and lift the curse from the land, healing by inspiration its wounded king, the aged, broken and alcoholic alter ego Brodsky. Yet Brodsky is also the Nietzschean Dionysus from *The Birth of Tragedy* and *Twilight of the Idols*, a reworking of the legacy of German Romantic thinkers such as Herder and Schelling (for whom Dionysus stood as a symbol of the poetic imagination) into a symbol of psychic renewal through a self-dissolution involving an ecstatic release of the instincts in primordial and communal ritual ecstasy. In the nursing and caressing of his wound he is also reminiscent of another powerful figure of the artist, the Philoctetes of Edmund Wilson's Freudian essay 'Philoctetes: The Wound and the Bow' (1941). This essay is a powerful account of artistic creativity as an outgrowth of individual psychopathology, of the idea that creative vision is inseparable from disability and sickness, and that art is the consolation for the pains of being human.[17]

Ryder too has found childhood consolation for his wounds in art and, like Philoctetes, is also the artist as outcast. But, like Brodsky, he is so narcissistically preoccupied with his wound that he cannot attend to his interlocutors. Miss Collins tells Brodsky that his obsession with his 'wound' has rendered him blind to the needs of his community, so that his art can never redeem the city or offer solace and direction, and that the nursing of the wound has become an end in itself:

> You'll never be able to serve the people of this city, even if you wanted to. Because you care nothing for their lives. That's the truth of it. Your music will only ever be about that silly little wound, it will never be anything more than that, it'll never be anything profound, anything of value to anyone else. (*U* 499)

Brodskyian dissolution is Ryder's future if he cannot learn to care and if he persists in his complicity with either an unreflective or narcissistic myth of the artist as redeemer in its commercialized guise of postmodern nomadism. Something more than consolation might still be achieved through art if subjective feeling is transmuted through an Eliotic and professional separation of the man who suffers and the man who writes – into a carefully honed and crafted aesthetic performance that might express shared forms of human belonging and difference – a new version of Eliot's tradition. Theodor Adorno's late modernist belief, expressed in his *Minima Moralia*, was that 'it is now virtually in art alone that suffering can still find its own voice, consolation, without immediately being betrayed by it'.[18] For that to happen, art must still create an adequate 'objective correlative': not an easy task when one is an International Novelist and when one's audience is spread across the entire globe. But that is why Ishiguro is a late, but hopefully not too late, modernist.

notes

1. Doris Lessing, 'The Small Personal Voice', in Tom Maschler (ed.), *Declaration* (London: Macgibbon and Kee, 1957), p. 24.
2. See Bill Buford's Introduction to *Granta 43: Best of Young British Novelists* (Harmondsworth: Penguin, 1993), p. 11.
3. Virginia Woolf, 'Mr Bennett and Mrs Brown', in Leonard Woolf (ed.), *The Captains's Death Bed and Other Essays* (New York: Harcourt Brace Jovanovich, 1950), p. 96.
4. E. M. Forster, *Howards End* (Harmondsworth: Penguin, 1941), p. 185.
5. Ibid., p. 188.
6. Salman Rushdie, *Imaginary Homelands* (London: Granta, 1992), p. 20.
7. Kenzaburō Ōe, 'The Novelist in Today's World: A Conversation', *boundary 2*, Fall 1991, 117.
8. T. S. Eliot, *The Use of Poetry and the Use of Criticism* (London: Faber and Faber, 1933), p. 155.
9. Philip Larkin, 'Reference Back', *New York Review of Books*, 2 (9), 11 June 1964.

10. Fredric Jameson, *Postmodernism, or The Cultural Logic of Late Capitalism* (London: Verso, 1991), p. 41.
11. Allan Vorda and Kim Herzinger, 'Stuck on the Margins: An Interview with Kazuo Ishiguro', in Allan Vorda (ed.), *Face to Face: Interviews with Contemporary Novelists* (Houston, TX: Rice University Press, 1993), pp. 30–1.
12. Eliot, *Use of Poetry*, pp. 144–5.
13. For further details of the education and duties of Plato's Guardians, see Plato, *Republic*, trans. F. M. Cornford (New York: Oxford University Press, 1970), pp. 63–7, 111–18.
14. T. S. Eliot, 'Shakespeare and the Stoicism of Seneca', *Selected Essays*, (London: Faber and Faber, 1932), p. 129.
15. Ibid., p. 131.
16. T. S. Eliot, 'The Waste Land', in *The Complete Poems and Plays of T. S. Eliot* (London: Faber and Faber, 1969), p. 66.
17. Edmund Wilson, *The Wound and the Bow* (Oxford: Oxford University Press, 1941).
18. Theodor Adorno, *Minima Moralia* (London: Verso, 1982), p. 312.

2

the pedagogics of liminality: rites of passage in the work of kazuo ishiguro

victor sage

summary

Kazuo Ishiguro's fiction is consistently interested in the complex nature of ritual structures, which, originally, in primitive societies, were meant to replace phases of inertia in the relations between individuals and the group. In Ishiguro's work, however, rites of passage are often interrupted, or they fail completely, due to a method of often ironical narration that reveals moral and political crises. Ishiguro's narrators are left searching their own memories for a key to the value of their own lives, which potentially fills the inertia and assuages the guilt of their existence. Although there are hints sometimes of a consolation for the emerging loss, it is the reader who is asked to assume responsibility for perceiving the disturbing void of liminality that lies beneath their often apparently confident identity and close relation to social groups.

rites of passage: a very brief introduction

One way of approaching the fictional narratives of Kazuo Ishiguro is via an anthropological model that critically frames their persistent exploration of the complex nature of ritual structures. Arnold Van Gennep's *The Rites of Passage* (1909) breaks down the process of negotiation between individuals and the group – known as rites of passage – into rites of separation, transition and incorporation. His account of these rites opposes physical and biological versions of energy:

> It is necessary that two movements in opposite directions be separated by a point of inertia, which in mechanics is reduced to a

31

minimum by an eccentric and exists only potentially in circular motion. But, although a body can move through space in a circle at a constant speed, the same is not true of biological or social activities. Their energy becomes exhausted and they have to be regenerated at more or less close intervals. The rites of passage ultimately correspond to this fundamental necessity, sometimes so closely that they take the form of death and rebirth.[1]

Victor Turner's reflections on the relation between the liminality of ritual and the logic of literary genre are also apposite to the representation of rites of passage in Ishiguro's work:

If the liminality of life-crisis rites may be, perhaps audaciously, compared to tragedy – for both imply humbling, stripping, and pain – the liminality of status reversal may be compared to comedy, for both involve mockery and inversion, but not destruction, of structural rules and overzealous adherents to them.[2]

One may be reminded instantly of, say, *King Lear* in the first case and of *Henry IV* in the second. Critics have made these points over the years from Northrop Frye onwards, which Ishiguro, as a student of literature, would no doubt have noticed. Shakespeare's dramatic work evidently manages both structures. Ishiguro's own work, though often bleak, is never tragic in mood; but it has much in common with the second case, namely the relation between rites of status reversal and separation, and the comic. Humiliation and isolation that has a ritualized aspect to it is a key theme; but its structure is, broadly speaking, comic, and there are moments of what Van Gennep refers to as 'incorporation' – the return of the individual to the group – too. This is not to say, however, that such patterns of narrative are not painful or touching, or even relieving, sometimes uniquely so. But they also have a moral and ideological force that gives to the work of this novelist a special place in the post-war novel.

'precautionary steps': an artist of the floating world

Let me begin by pin-pointing an incident in Ishiguro's second novel, *An Artist of the Floating World* (1986). This novel is narrated by Masuji Ono, a painter who finds himself discredited after the Second World War for doing what at the time he thought was right. The 'present' action of this book – that is, Ono's most recent layer of memory – takes place in 1948 and 1949, triggered by a visit of Ono's eldest daughter, Setsuko, who arrives with her little boy, Ichiro, Ono's grandson. Setsuko wants to discuss with her father the new marriage plans of her sister, Noriko, whose earlier attempt at marriage has failed. Now a new evening of introductions, a *miai* (a mutual inspection of the bride and groom by the two sets of relations), is planned over a meal in a hired hotel room with the Saito family, whose son, Taro, is most eligible. Setsuko is particularly concerned to alert Ono to his role in this event and to the investigation of the Saito family into his past. The implication, very indirectly put by Setsuko, is that, unless he takes 'precautionary steps' (*AFW* 42) this time, there is a risk that the new negotiations may be adversely affected (as, she alleges, happened last time) by Ono's past. His post-war reputation has changed drastically. Japan's cultural mood has shifted away from aggressive nationalism and imperialist expansionism to Western, American-style, democracy and post-war corporate industrial development. There is a vivid picture in this novel of the conflict between generations, which we gradually piece together through Ono's meandering, layered, and not always perfectly reliable, acts of memory.

Ono's vocation as an artist has certainly been tested: he tells us how his father, who has done his best to initiate him into the mysteries of accountancy, summons him into the reception room one day. This room, normally reserved for visitors, is one from which Ono has been banned from entering until the age of twelve. His father is sitting 'at the centre of the light' (*AFW* 43) with a heavy earthenware pot in front of him. This puzzles the young boy because the pot is normally only produced for guests:

> I sat in silence while my father looked through my work. He would regard each painting for a moment, then lay it to one side. When he was almost half-way through my collection, he said without looking up:
> 'Masuji, are you sure all your work is here? Aren't there one or two paintings you haven't brought me?'
> I did not answer immediately. He looked up and asked: 'Well?'
> 'It's possible there may be one or two I have not brought.'
> 'Indeed. And no doubt, Masuji, the missing paintings are the very ones you're most proud of. Isn't that so?' (*AFW* 43)

His father is careful to point out the skill of some of these works, before his son is sent away and the smell of burning permeates the house. The formality and cruelty of this scene makes a strange, hidden ceremony of the action; moreover, his mother opposes it, and it seems to take place on the authority of a wandering village priest who has made an 'assessment' of the weaknesses of the infant Ono (*AFW* 46). Ono gives up the precious paintings, but begins at this moment to defy his father, who wants him to go into business, and who apparently performs this action to deter him from seeking a career as an artist. Instead, it makes him more determined. This is a rite of separation. Ono leaves home and starts at the bottom; he joins a firm of commercial artists in the big city, who work in large groups. We see one of the important themes of Ishiguro's later fiction emerging here – that of loyalty to the social group and the ritual exclusion of dissent. Ono is such a dissenter: he leaves the graphics factory that produces geishas and cherry trees, making a leap in the dark, and manages to join the studio of a fine-art painter. Moriyama is committed to representing the ephemeral scenes of the 'floating world', the erotic beauty of the courtesans of the pleasure districts of the pre-war city which, from the perspective of the textual present, has been all but destroyed by the Second World War. Much of Ono's most remote layer of reminiscence about his pre-war youth takes place at Mrs Kawakami's, the last bar of the old neighbourhood to survive, hanging on amidst the bulldozers of the immediate post-war reconstruction.

In that set of pre-war narratives of memory, the young Ono changes the style and subject matter of his painting and becomes a 'traitor' to his master, Moriyama, who seeks, just like Ono's father, to confiscate and to burn his paintings. This event, however, is focused by another earlier intermediate scene, in which Sasaki, the leading pupil of Moriyama, is excluded by the group of apprentices, including tacitly Ono himself, for having 'betrayed' the master by questioning his methods. The scene is overheard by Ono, who is lying awake in his room. He hears Sasaki's footsteps as he goes from room to room, begging for a response, and he listens to the silence that comes back each time. In the end, Sasaki reaches the room next door, where his closest friend lives:

> 'You and I have been good friends for many years,' I heard him say. 'Won't you at least speak to me?'
> There was no response from the person he had addressed. Then Sasaki said:
> 'Won't you just tell me where the paintings are?'
> There was still no response. But as I lay there in the darkness, I could hear the sound of rats scuttling under the floorboards of that decaying room, and it seemed to me this noise was some sort of reply. (*AFW* 142–3)

This final part of the rejection scene is painfully drawn out. Sasaki begins by asking his anonymous friend for his paintings – he has nothing else to take with him. Then he asks for the friend to turn to him, to acknowledge his existence and to offer him, at least, his good wishes for the future, but he is not given 'even one word of comfort' (*AFW* 143). Eventually, Ono hears the slide of the screen door and the sound of Sasaki's steps moving away across the yard.

The ritual structure of this scene is uncluttered by description of individual motivation. Despite, or perhaps because of this absence, its cruelty and pathos stand out and the reader is obliged to supply the emotions of the listener, Ono (will he be next in line to reject him?) and those of the rejected Sasaki. And these effects come home to the reader all the more because Ono has already suggested to us the unreasonableness of the master's reaction by pointing out that the leading pupil matures precisely by seeing beyond his master's work; but, as he 'helpfully' (i.e. tactically) explains, the master's emotions make it sometimes impossible for him to regard the situation in any other way than as 'treachery' (*AFW* 142).

But what happens here to Sasaki is a forerunner of what will come to Ono himself, hence the rhetorical tactic. In a provocative gesture, he shows his latest painting to one of his old friends, the 'Tortoise', who predictably calls him a 'traitor' and immediately spreads the news. Ono is still living in the decaying, rat-infested villa when he learns that the master has taken some of his paintings while he is out. There is a deceptively mild-sounding conversation between the master and Ono in a storeroom, and then again at twilight, in a pavilion in one of the city's parks, as Ono is asked to light some lanterns. This is the beginning of the end. Silence falls now when he enters a room. It is clear that his fellow apprentices have been fully mobilized to reject, humiliate and drive him out: not crudely instructed by the master, but by merely breathing the atmosphere of fanatical loyalty at the villa. Like his father, the master is politely anxious to recover the rest of Ono's paintings, declaring himself 'interested' in seeing them. But Ono refuses the request because he knows that they will be burnt. The master immediately proceeds to the consequences, asking if he 'has made arrangements' (*AFW* 180), and Ono's reply is that he has made no arrangements whatsoever. Moriyama then predicts that his pupil's subsequent career will be a failure. The cruel, but restrained, ritual of rejection is conducted by the master in profile, not looking at his pupil. But at this moment of 'vindictiveness', he steps out of role, symbolized by his profile becoming full-face. A moral conflict – in which Ono assumes he is behaving as a free individual, not simply an institutional figure – becomes visible.

Ono's memory of this scene is permeated by a smell of burning that lingers, drifting into his recollection of later periods of his life, and compromising what appears to be this emergent moral perspective that protrudes from the purely ritual aspect of the scene. Instead of what the master savagely predicts for him here, Ono becomes the leader of a new art movement that forsakes aestheticism for, first, social realism and then imperialist propaganda. He renames his painting 'Complacency' – an image of three, ragged, poverty-stricken urchins whom he has actually observed and painted from life – with the title 'Eyes to the Horizon' (*AFW* 168–9). Through the acrid, smoke-filled mist of memory, we see that Ono himself, at the height of his influence, foolishly, but almost, as he struggles to see it, inadvertently, betrays his most talented pupil, Kuroda, by naively drawing the attention of the 'Cultural Committee of Unpatriotic Activities' to the content of his paintings (*AFW* 183). Kuroda is jailed, his work destroyed and his future as an artist, it seems, is completely ruined. The ritual structure of separation and expulsion from the group, the rite of passage, is overlayed by not only a moral, but a political question here, which was latent in the earlier scene with the master. Now Ono has become the master and triggers the ritual of separation from the other side. That is perhaps why he is willing to extenuate Moriyama's behaviour in the earlier scene, because he himself understands the ironic way the moral energy of his own position has been swallowed up by the inertia that the rite of passage is originally designed to replace. The familiar political question in Ishiguro's writing about how moral passivity leads to fascism is also mediated, paradoxically, by the ritual content of this repeated scene.

In fact, after the war, by the irony of history, when the whole political climate has reversed, Kuroda gains the reputation of a political martyr and is reinstated, obtaining a post at a college, while Ono himself is vilified and loses his reputation and status. It is this loss of status and reputation, in relation to another set of rites of passage, the marriage of his younger daughter, which provokes a dark suspicion. Underlying the unreliability of his memory and the puzzlement and stridency of his denials, there lurks the possibility that, instead of living a life of solid achievement (albeit with questionable periods of power and influence), there has been no substance at all to what Ono been doing as an artist. All has melted away now without a trace, and he has effectively wasted his whole life. He has been plunged again into a state of liminality from which, this time, there will be no rebirth, except as 'Father', a Lear-type figure ruled by his daughters without authority within his own family. This figure of 'Father' recurs in Ishiguro's novels and, Van Gennep notes, this transition is a ritual identity for some societies, rather than something that simply comes with a certain age.[3]

All this is triggered by the visit of Setsuko, who counsels her father about his part in Noriko's *miai*. To begin with, Ono can see that the occasion for Noriko is very tense, and she is wholly unsuccessful in presenting herself. Mindful of Setsuko's nervously euphemistic advice, Ono takes the initiative and denounces his former political past to the assembled relations of the groom. As he sees it, this creates the turning point for Noriko, who relaxes in her surprise at his outburst and reveals her forthright and likeable character to the groom. But later, Setsuko denies that she asked him to take 'precautionary steps' and claims instead that his unexpected outburst had simply bewildered them all, including the groom's family, the Saitos. Ono is quite proud of his decision, but what the reader realizes, through these otherwise bafflingly polite misunderstandings with his daughter, is that there are ritual manoeuvrings going on here too. Even his questionable periods of collusion with imperial power in the past have all evaporated away and mean nothing to the new generation. That is why his action of self-denunciation 'puzzled' (*AFW* 191) Noriko, because it assumed 'Father's' importance. But, as Setsuko explains to 'Father', all he was, after all, was only a painter, and that makes him, from a wider political point of view, inherently unimportant. Beneath her tetchily impeccable politeness to 'Father', all Setsuko is worried about now is that he should not commit suicide like the composer, Yukio Naguchi, and bring shame on them. The fact that he suspects Setsuko of parroting the opinions of her husband, Suicho, does not make the underlying bleakness and falsity in Ono's eyes of what she asserts to him any less bleak and untrue, as we can see from the stridency of his denials to the reader (*AFW* 194).

The underlying shape of rites of passage, of ritual humiliation and separation, and of the price of 'incorporation', of acceptance or reabsorption into a group or institution, is repeatedly present throughout this text. This is true even at the level of memory closest to the frame-narration itself, and thus closest to the reader.

'as indeed i am myself': *the remains of the day*

Ishiguro's third novel, *The Remains of the Day* (1989), is equally a series of embedded and interrupted rites of passage. This novel focuses on the master and servant relationship, rather than the master and pupil, but its preoccupations are quite similar to *An Artist of the Floating World*: the unreliability of memory, the agency of self-deceit, the way that language hides meaning, and the possibility, which needs to be evaded at all costs, that one has wasted one's whole life. His narrators are searching for something hidden in their own memories, a key to the value of their lives, something that promises to fill the inertia and assuage the guilt of their existence. Although there are occasional hints of a consolation for this loss that can emerge for the characters, the reader is presented with the disturbing void of liminality that undermines the often apparently confident identity of the narrators and their close relation to certain social groups.

The narrator, Stevens, is a man who must inhabit totally his role as servant, thus leaving no space for living, for a private life, for the life of his emotions. Stevens is a man almost without identity apart from his function. Yet there are tiny signs that constantly escape round the edges of this cardboard cut-out of a man, this comic Jeeves-like stereotype of 'professionalism' and utter loyalty to his master, Lord Darlington, providing us with fleeting glimpses of his suppressed being.

The person who both sees and manages to provoke many of these escapes of 'personality', emotion, and even anger in Stevens is Miss Kenton, the housekeeper. On this level, the text is a romantic love story that never happened: Stevens and Miss Kenton spend much of their time fencing, in irritable politeness, as Stevens resists her attempts to make him humanly aware of certain facts that he wants to avoid. In the comic dialogue about the Chinaman (*RD* 57) there is a perfect displacement of a life-crisis into the small change of their quotidian roles. The servants use a restricted code of politeness and 'correctness', a copy at fault only in its perfection, which contrasts with the ease of their masters' articulation. Stevens seeks in this dialogue to resist Miss Kenton's efforts to tell him that his father, who is employed in the house as an under-butler, is becoming confused and losing his grip on the job. Stevens seeks to make Kenton look stupidly fussy and even a little mad. Inevitably, Stevens's father has a fall, in front of some guests, while carrying a tray. It is agreed that he be relieved of some of his duties. Stevens climbs to his father's attic bedroom:

'I have come here to relate something to you, Father.'
   'Then relate it briefly and concisely. I haven't all morning to listen to you chatter.'
   'In that case, Father, I will come straight to the point.'
   'Come to the point then and be done with it. Some of us have work to be getting on with.'
   'Very well. Since you wish me to be brief, I will do my best to comply. The fact is, Father has become increasingly infirm. So much so that even the duties of an under-butler are now beyond his capabilities. His lordship is of the view, as indeed I am myself, that while Father is allowed to continue with his present round of duties,

he represents an ever-present threat to the smooth running of this household, and in particular to next week's important gathering.' (*RD* 65)

The slip into the third-person 'Father' exposes the ritual formality of the separation and is reminiscent of Setsuko's address to Ono above. But it is hopelessly mixed up with feelings that even Stevens the narrator (as opposed to Stevens the protagonist) cannot express, locked as he is into his role. The clumsy self-importance and slavishness of the phrase 'as indeed I am myself' strikes a pang in the reader, and points up the contrast of 'Father's' brusque dismissal of the child, Stevens – we never learn his Christian name – whose rank is above him. Two systems, family and employment, collide here in this confused and failed moment of ritual separation.

The dissolution of Stevens's father is inevitable, but in a rare moment of explicitness the text draws attention to its ritual aspect. It defamiliarizes the embarrassment of the moment, deflecting it into a comically solemn strangeness:

At the far end of the corridor, almost in front of the large window, at that moment filled with grey light and rain, my father's figure could be seen frozen in a posture that suggested he was taking part in some ceremonial ritual. He had dropped down on to one knee and with head bowed seemed to be pushing at the trolley before him, which for some reason had taken on an obstinate immobility. (*RD* 93)

Ritual is ironically invoked here because it is, in fact, absent: 'Father' has simply carried on as usual like a robot and paid no attention. This is a picture of the inertia of death-in-service, an emblem of Stevens's own condition, which he cannot afford to acknowledge. When 'Father' actually dies, Stevens is unable to be present, due to his 'important' role downstairs at Lord Darlington's international conference.

It is this inertia in the relations between individuals and social groups that, Van Gennep argues, it is the function of rites of passage to renew. The whole of *The Remains of the Day* is, from this point of view, an interrupted or failed rite of passage, in which Stevens fails to encounter that which will separate, transform and reincorporate him into the world as a citizen of it. The personal, moral and political crisis created by his inertia is at its most serious in the episode of the dismissal of the two Jewish housemaids. Even though he makes out retrospectively that his instinct opposed the idea, he colludes with his employer's anti-Semitism, brings Miss Kenton to the brink of resignation and triggers her disillusion and disappointment in him as a possible partner and love-object. His apparent coldness on the day makes his choice even worse for the reader, and indeed for Miss Kenton, than if he had spoken openly about those 'instincts' – but for Stevens there is no relation between the act of speaking and the existence of instincts. In the theatre of service, language is robbed of almost all spontaneity, all passion, desire, curiosity – Hermione Lee calls it 'this cauterised narrative voice', and Stevens's inertia is prolonged until the end of the text from this point on.[4]

This inertia, however, threatens to be subverted in two striking scenes of ordeal which allude, temptingly, in their structure to ritual humiliation. The first is a comic misunderstanding, reported in the frame-narration, in which he is mistaken for a gentleman by a company of Devon villagers. It is a mistake that Stevens passively allows to take place by not declaring himself, and then encourages by a series of completely misleading declarations, which give the impression that he 'consorted' with Winston Churchill, Anthony Eden and Lord Halifax and 'had their ear' (*RD* 188) in matters of foreign policy. The doctor, Carlisle, sees immediately what is going on, and the reader cringes throughout, because the threat of Stevens's exposure and humiliation as a charlatan is ever present. Carlisle decides not to humiliate Stevens in front of them but insists on having a chat with him in the morning, whilst alerting him that he is aware of the deception. This is one of the few times we glimpse Stevens on the point of being initiated into society, the world outside Darlington Hall. However, he manages to deflect his own position of subservience, and thus defer his initiation into the social world, by carnivalizing it, a motif that in some ways anticipates the fictional method of *The Unconsoled* (1995).

The second ordeal, linked with this by Stevens the narrator, ostensibly because of the theme of 'dignity', is a painful ritual humiliation. It is an incident that occurs during the 'international conference', when one of the guests, a Mr Spencer, calls for Stevens and savagely makes a spectacle of his lack of education in front of his employer, Lord Darlington, and several other giggling guests, in order to score a fascist point. Spencer wishes to prove to them that parliamentary democracy is a ridiculous error. Again, the scene is drawn out in repeated waves, climaxing in the threat (the actuality, to all but himself) of Stevens's public humiliation, which even Lord Darlington seems to recognize, as he tries, kindly but ineffectually, to dismiss him from the room. Having asked Stevens a dense and complex question about Laval's economic policy, Stevens has recourse to the butler's answer to all things he cannot deal with: that he is unable to be of assistance (*RD* 195). This provokes bursts of suppressed laughter from the audience in the library which, at the climax of the repeated phases of the scene, turns from suppressed giggles to open and hearty laughing. Spencer's opportunistic political point is developed perfectly from the image of the humiliated individual before them. Spencer states that the nation continues to believe in the notion that decisions are left in the hands of 'our good man here and to the few million others like him'. Spencer notes that it is no wonder that England is unable to find a solution to the nation's difficulties and mockingly states that 'you may as well ask a commit-tee of the mother's union to organize a war campaign' (RD 196). The remark is followed by open, glib laughter, after which Lord Darlington excuses Stevens.

Ostensibly, the rhetorical reason why Stevens narrates this incident is that it justifies him to his anonymous interlocutor ('you'), who is also apparently a member of the butlering 'profession'. It is an incident in which he managed to keep his dignity, through his quick-witted profes-sionalism, and he presents this ordeal as a rite of passage into becoming a mature and (he almost dares to think) a 'great' butler. The irony of the exchange from the reader's point of view is that the rite of passage ought to be a rite of separation, but the moral and political structure of this ritual humiliation is tied to the butler's position of passivity. This fact is underlined by his inclusion of Lord Darlington's attempt to shield him and protect him, almost like a child, which, for Stevens, triumphantly reasserts the theatre of service as a benign conspiracy between master and servant. The irony emerges at the point at which the rite of passage becomes visible, is arrested and cannot be fulfilled. Thus, the liminality of the narrator is terminally prolonged.

'a faint disturbing phantom of a ritual action': never let me go

There is evidence of continuity, in the presence of the embedded and interrupted ritual structures outlined earlier, in Ishiguro's later work. *Never Let Me Go* (2005), for instance, passes from the master–servant relationship, seen from the point of view of the loyal servant, to the narrative of a member of a slave class told in another restricted code. The significantly narrowed and politely stilted version of the institu-tionalized language of teenage adolescent pupils is haunting precisely because it is evidently not a transcription: there is little demotic, no obscenity, no real slang and no serious swearing, for example. This 'cauterizes' the surface of the text itself, giving it the pathos of a slightly ceremonial effect, a restricted code which bears comparison with that of Stevens. The text again uses the device of an anonymous interlocutor, 'you', who is another slave at another 'institution', to whom Kathy H., the narrator, addresses her narrative like a letter. Ishiguro inevitably selects a register of politeness for his narrative voices, and such euphemism irritates and mesmerizes in equal measures, extending far beyond literary elegance. In the case of *Never Let Me Go*, the 'H' of Kathy H. is not a surname, but merely an alphabetical indication of her place in a series.

Set in the late 1990s, the subject matter of this novel is sensational, futuristic (although set in an 'alternative' 1990s) and nightmarish: the systematic breeding of generations of cloned humans purely for the purpose of donating their organs for spare-part surgery. Conventionally, the topic belongs to science fiction, fantasy and horror: one thinks of Mary Shelley's *Frankenstein* (1818) and *Blade Runner* (1982, director: Ridley Scott), both of which feature scenes of Faustian confrontation between creature and creator. Indeed, this novel drives towards that scene of revelation as its climax. And as she abandons them, and turns back to her own ending, Madame – the friend of head 'guardian', Miss Emily – calls the clones 'you poor creatures' (*NLMG* 249), which gestures towards the creator/creature opposition.

The originality of Ishiguro's text is that it never treats its Orwellian subject matter melodramatically. Instead, it proceeds by the moderate, sensitive, minutely observed reportage of the central narrator and witness, Kathy H., who looks back over the course of her young life, and the familiar rites of passage of the young lives of her fellow students at 'Hailsham'. Everything is mediated through the life of the institution, the comforting house jargon of the boarding school and the group of friends, who are remarkably (and peculiarly, from the point of view of a transcription of 'normality') loyal to that institution, despite their differences with each other. We listen in to their intimate exchanges. Of course, the 'ordinariness' of all this is a fiction; pure theatre. The language of Hailsham is a tissue of euphemisms: the term 'student', for example, means 'clone'; the teachers are 'guardians' (with a nod to Plato); dying is 'completing'. The whole school environment is a fiction. But the reader can almost forget this, because the students themselves do not fully understand their situation. They are, as Kathy puts it crucially, 'told and not told' (*NLMG* 79).

This situation – the fact that there is no future for these slaves, that they are *already liminal* – gives an oddity to the standard institutional humiliation scenes that are reported to us, an oddity which is not at all apparent to begin with. The opening scene finds a company of girls gathered in the Sports Pavilion, standing on stools and benches, looking out through the high windows across the North Playing Field, at some boys who are about to choose a scratch team to play football (*NLMG* 7). The scene acts as a good character-sketch of the three main protagonists: Ruth, mercurial and Machiavellian, is a leader of groups; Tommy, autistic, stubborn, but athletic, is the vulnerable outsider and born victim; and Kathy, the empathetic narrator, is the go-between, who is already able to put herself in his emotional place, and who has spotted that the favourite polo-shirt he is wearing is going to get filthy. The team-picking is pure pretence: everybody knows Tommy is a better player than any in Senior 3, the year above him, but they are determined to exclude him. Naively, eagerly, he waits to be 'first pick' (*NLMG* 8). His actions are reported by Laura, the clown of the group:

> Laura kept up her performance all through the team picking, doing all the different expressions that went across Tommy's face: the bright eager one at the start; the puzzled concern when four picks had gone by and he still hadn't been chosen; the hurt and panic as it began to dawn on him what was really going on. . . . I was watching Tommy; I only knew what she was doing because the others kept laughing and egging her on. Then when Tommy was left standing alone, and all the boys began sniggering, I heard Ruth say:
>   'It's coming. Hold it. Seven seconds. Seven, six, five . . .'
> She never got there. Tommy burst into thunderous bellowing, and the boys, now laughing openly, started to run off towards the South Playing Field. (*NLMG* 8–9)

Tommy is left behind 'glaring after them, his face scarlet' (*NLMG* 9). Kathy approaches him, as he screams and shouts like an infantile Lear 'a nonsensical jumble of swear words and insults' (*NLMG* 9). When she offers him some briskly disguised sympathy, he strikes her. But he realizes later she was at least acknowledging him, and slowly a bond is formed. There are even rites of passage for slaves without a future and without a society to join, we might think, rather as Primo Levi finds underworld strata of trade in Auschwitz in *If This Is a Man* (1956). Yet this moment of liminality is simultaneously a vital howl of raw political and moral protest, an existential scream, on quite another level from the embedded but irresolvable institutional ritual in which it is apparently framed. The need for truth that runs throughout the novel drives the plot to its climax in the Plato's cave of Miss Emily's darkened front room in Littlehampton. For this is the small group of unstable individuals, Kathy and Tommy, and (posthumously) Ruth, which will finally push each other to get at the truth about Hailsham. It is Tommy's very awkwardness and stubbornness as an unregenerate, and later thoughtfully questioning, outsider-figure, which helps them puncture the inertial envelope of group consensualism. They are policed from generation to generation by their ritualized peer-group distractions, their vision of the past fuzzed at the edges by nostalgia and snobbery, a loyalty which has been fostered by the guardians at the School and which has prevented 'students' before them from breaking ranks. This mask of collectivity gives the reader part of the meaning (the bleak part) of the novel's title. The fulfilment of this quest to unmask the truth is no consolation, however; it can help them neither to live nor 'complete'; all they can do is literally hold blindly on to each other, hanging together in a parody of 'incorporation'. Afterwards, on the journey home from Littlehampton, Tommy asks to get out of the car, and Kathy eventually finds him in a field under an (almost) full moon 'raging, shouting, flinging his fists and kicking out' (*NLMG* 269) in the old way:

> He tried to shake me off, but I kept holding on, until he stopped shouting and I felt the fight go out of him. Then I realised he too had his arms around me. And so we stood together like that, at the top of that field, for what seemed like ages, not saying anything, just holding each other, while the wind kept blowing and blowing at us, tugging our clothes, and for a moment, it seemed like we were holding on to each other because that was the only way to stop us being swept away into the night. (*NLMG* 269)

This moment of sublime pathos is soon to be frittered away for these two survivors, in the comedy of stoical jokes about cows and mud as Kathy joshes Tommy back into life, such as it is, and they go on their temporary way. Now they will be able to part physically from each other for 'completion'. But this haunted, fragile moment of the clinging together of slaves in the face of 'the night' is reminiscent of the grotesque parody in black American slave culture of 'incorporation', which they turned to their own account in the musical form of the spiritual and then the blues. Victor Turner, with his Christian emphasis, would think of this moment as (achieved) 'communitas' and oppose it in a binary form to ritual. But here there is a faint disturbing phantom of a ritual action in the inertially repeated gesture that stands for a whole class of such gestures and gives the novel its title. Van Gennep seems closer to the effect here:

> Like children who have not been baptized, named, or initiated, persons for whom funeral rites are not performed are condemned to a pitiable existence, since they are never able to enter the world of the dead or to become incorporated in the society established there.[5]

notes

1. Arnold Van Gennep, *The Rites of Passage*, trans. and eds. Monika B. Vizedom and Gabrielle L. Caffee (Chicago: University of Chicago Press, 1960; originally published in 1909), p. 182.
2. Victor W. Turner, *The Ritual Process: Structure and Anti-Structure* (London: Routledge and Kegan Paul, 1969), p. 201.
3. Cf. van Gennep, *The Rites of Passage*, p. 85: 'Among the Masai of Kenya a boy cannot undergo circumcision, or a girl clitoral excision, unless the father has performed a ceremony called "passing over the fence", which signifies his acceptance of the status of an "old man", to be called from then on "Father-of-(his child).'
4. Hermione Lee, 'Quiet Desolation', in *New Republic*, 22 January 1990, 36–9; repr. in *Contemporary Literary Criticism*, 110 (1990), 233.
5. Cf. Van Gennep, *The Rites of Passage*, p. 160.

3
lost and found: on the japanese translations of kazuo ishiguro

motoyuki shibata

summary

Japanese translators of the novels of Kazuo Ishiguro are faced with a number of problems, especially with those texts that are based in Japan. A Pale View of Hills, *for instance, resembles not so much the Nagasaki of the late 1940s/ early 1950s as the Japanese films by Ozu depicting those times, so the 'translation' of the setting is not straightforward. Even the non-Japanese novels present difficulties. The narrators of* The Remains of the Day *and* Never Let Me Go *are given a special form of 'polite' speech in the Japanese translations to denote their humble and distanced personas.*

the unfaithful translation of *a pale view of hills*

You would think that an American translator of Haruki Murakami would have it easy: the immensely popular Japanese novelist is known for his love of American culture, high and low, his works are full of references to things American, and he himself has done excellent translations of writers such as F. Scott Fitzgerald, Raymond Carver and Grace Paley. Not necessarily easy, says Jay Rubin, the principal Murakami translator. Using as example a passage with a visual image involving combination salads and their ingredients, Rubin argues:

> Even in something so apparently straightforward as our example, much of which consists of a list of salad ingredients, there is no question of doing anything that could remotely be called a 'literal' translation. Written in a special syllabary used for foreign words, some of

the ingredients have a tantalizingly foreign sound and *look* in the Japanese text,[1] but they inevitably lose this quality when they are translated 'back' into English and are surrounded by other English words. . . . Paradoxically, then, the *closeness* of Murakami's style to English can itself pose problems for a translator trying to translate it 'back' into English: the single most important quality that makes his style fresh and enjoyable in Japanese is what is lost in translation.[2]

Moreover, a banal English cliché like 'bed of roses', Rubin notes elsewhere, though refreshing when literally translated and embedded into Murakami's original Japanese text, becomes nothing but a worn-out cliché again if it is translated 'back' into English. Obviously, the Murakami translator's lot is not really the bed of roses it seems to be.

Regarding this problem of translational 're-import', works by Kazuo Ishiguro, who left Japan for Britain when he was five and has apparently lost much of his Japanese speech, naturally invites comparison. This is true especially of his first two novels – *A Pale View of Hills* (1982) and *An Artist of the Floating World* (1986) – which are set in Japan and directly concern the 're-import' question. Does anything similar to what Rubin identifies occur when Ishiguro's 'Japanese' novels are translated 'back' into Japanese? Consider, for example, the following passage from *A Pale View of Hills*:

In those days, returning to the Nakagawa district still provoked in me mixed emotions of sadness and pleasure. It is a hilly area, and climbing again those steep narrow streets between the clusters of houses never failed to fill me with a deep sense of loss. Though not a place I visited on casual impulse, I was unable to stay away for long.

Calling on Mrs Fujiwara aroused in me much the same mixture of feelings; for she had been amongst my mother's closest friends, a kindly woman with hair that was by then turning grey. Her noodle shop was situated in a busy sidestreet; it had a concrete forecourt under the cover of an extended roof and it was there her customers ate, at the wooden tables and benches. She did a lot of trade with office workers during their lunch breaks and on their way home, but at other times of the day the clientele became sparse. (*PVH* 23)[3]

I assume that the 'steep narrow streets between the clusters of houses' and the 'noodle shop . . . situated in a busy sidestreet' would feel slightly exotic to English-speaking readers, if not overly unfamiliar. Naturally, this is not how the passage will strike Japanese readers. The small eatery with its wooden tables and benches, where 'salarymen' drop in for a quick bowl of *udon*, traditional Japanese fast food, will be entirely familiar to them. There is nothing exotic about it.

Yet perhaps that is not all. Even though the city of Nagasaki is as hilly today as it was just after the war, most tiny houses had probably been replaced by concrete apartment buildings by the time *A Pale View of Hills* first appeared. The *udon* diners are still as numerous in Nagasaki and other Japanese cities, but most of them have been taken over by chains instead of being independently run by a once prosperous middle-aged woman. In short, the passage will evoke a slight feeling of nostalgia in the Japanese reader's mind.

Subtly but definitely something is lost and something else is gained. Mild nostalgia in exchange for slight exoticism: not a bad transaction when so much more could have been lost in translation. At least it will not clash with the reading of the work as a whole. In this aspect, the translator of Ishiguro's Japanese novels is perhaps in a more fortunate position than the Murakami translator.

Ishiguro himself did not require a 'faithful' translation of *A Pale View of Hills*: according to the translator's Afterword, he specifically asked the translator to avoid using a certain *kanji* for a certain character, thereby assuming that the translator should select *kanji* for each character instead of using *katakana*, the usual option for names in novels written in English. This implies that Ishiguro took it for granted that the Japanese translation would contain information not included in the original – since *kanji* are ideograms, they can have highly symbolic resonances: there are a number of possibilities for *Sachiko*, for example.

Responses will vary among Japanese readers, depending especially on their age, whether they knew post-war Japan first-hand or not, and their familiarity with Nagasaki. What was interesting, however, when the Japanese translation of *A Pale View of Hills* appeared was that, at least judging by the reviews, readers did not really compare the novel with the actual Japan in the late 1940s so much as with the Japanese films depicting those times: especially films by Yasujiro Ozu. Taking their cue from Ishiguro's own admiration of that master chronicler of traditional (and transitional) Japanese families and marriages, more than one reviewer evoked Ozu's name for a shorthand description of the novel's atmosphere. As has been often pointed out, Ishiguro did not recover the Japan he once knew; he reinvented the Japan he (almost) never knew, using Japanese films and novels as his chief raw materials.

Yet there is often a distinct Ishiguro touch. Ishiguro claims, for example, that he had in mind Shu Ryuchi, a regular actor in Ozu movies, when he created the character of Masuji Ono, the artist in *An Artist of the*

Floating World, but there is a significant difference between Ryuchi (and the characters he plays) and Ono. In none of the Ozu movies in which Ryuchi appears does he ever play a sinister person – he simply seems *incapable* of any moral wrong – whereas the biggest question about Ono's past is whether what he did during the war was morally wrong or not.

This is not to say that reviewers and readers criticized Ishiguro's fictional world as derivative; rather, they perceived in his book a creative dialogue with the films. We still cling to the notion that novels should evoke a distinct sense of place. Yet the somewhat placeless quality in major contemporary writers such as Ishiguro, Haruki Murakami and Paul Auster, which seems partly caused by the fact that much of their fictional world is based on films and fiction rather than historical fact, compels us to revise that notion. In any case, we can say that something was inevitably lost, but something else was creatively gained in the Japanese translation of *A Pale View of Hills*.

the remains of the day is 'too good a novel'

A stranger case of loss, however, occurred in the translation of *The Remains of the Day*. Consider this passage:

> My father opened his eyes, turned his head a little on the pillow, and looked at me.
> 'I hope Father is feeling better now,' I said.
> He went on gazing at me for a moment, then asked: 'Everything in hand downstairs?'
> 'The situation is rather volatile. It is just after six o'clock, so Father can well imagine the atmosphere in the kitchen at this moment.'
> An impatient look crossed my father's face. 'But is everything in hand?' he said again.
> 'Yes, I dare say you can rest assured on that. I'm very glad Father is feeling better.'
> With some deliberation, he withdrew his arms from under the bedclothes and gazed tiredly at the backs of his hands. He continued to do this for some time.
> 'I'm glad Father is feeling so much better,' I said again eventually. 'Now really, I'd best be getting back. As I say, the situation is rather volatile.'
> He went on looking at his hands for a moment. Then he said slowly: 'I hope I've been a good father to you.'
> I laughed a little and said: 'I'm so glad you're feeling better now.'
> (*RD* 101)[4]

The unusual way he repeatedly addresses his father as 'Father' when he is right in front of him expresses well Stevens's emotional distance – or, more precisely, the repressive sense of propriety that forces him to place emotional distance between himself and his father (or anyone else, for that matter). The 'you' he uses in the last line above shows the limit of intimacy he feels he can afford.

So what? Can't the Japanese translator simply translate 'Father' as *Father*, and 'you' as *you*? He can, but something awkward happens. The Japanese are often accused of thinking that their culture is unique when it is not, but in the case of the use of the second person I think we can safely say that the Japanese language *is* rather unusual. We do not use the word(s) equivalent to 'you' anywhere near as often as English-speaking persons use 'you'. We avoid the second-person pronoun almost the way people in the Bible refrain from saying aloud Jehovah's name. Quite often, we grope in conversation for a way to address the person we are talking to without directly using 'you' (this can be maddening when someone's name is unknown). Therefore, it would be completely normal to address our father as 'Father' face to face: it would not sound as if we thought he was not there at all.

Perhaps unavoidably, Masao Tsuchiya, the Japanese translator of *The Remains of the Day*, translated 'Father' simply as *Father*, thus rendering Stevens's unusual way of talking to his father much less unusual. The son's clumsiness with emotional closeness is mostly lost in translation. On closely reading Tsuchiya's translation, one feels that he repeats the word *Father* too often, even when he can help it, and it might be that this was his compensatory attempt to indicate, rather ironically, Stevens's inability to connect emotionally with his father. But even if this were so, the intention is likely to be lost on readers who do not know the original: they would simply feel that *Father* appears excessively. In the end, there is no solution that would have preserved Stevens's odd address to his father. Fortunately, however, *The Remains of the Day* is too good a novel, and Tsuchiya too good a translator, to let this slight loss mar the work as a whole.

Did Ishiguro have in mind the Japanese avoidance of the second person when he had Stevens talk that way? It is a tempting thought, and those who would like to identify the English butler as a Japanese in disguise might claim that this supports their view. I am not, however, inclined to go too far in that direction. Even if Stevens does sound suspiciously Japanese in the conversation with his father, Ishiguro makes sure that the way he speaks is in perfect accordance with his personality.

'all these distances': *never let me go*

Tsuchiya also translated *Never Let Me Go*, and the consensus in Japan is that we are fortunate to have his excellent renditions of what are arguably Ishiguro's two best novels so far, although I also admire the sheer audacity of *The Unconsoled*.

These two books embody most clearly one of Ishiguro's basic views of life: most of us are in a position where we offer our service to someone higher, some cause or institution, and we can only hope someone up there will make good use of it. In short, 'we are all butlers'. All the important things have always already been decided by others. To generalize, this sense of predetermination is shared by other important contemporary writers, such as Murakami, Sebald and Raymond Carver. But whereas Murakami, for example, offers fantasies (in no pejorative sense) in which one small individual may have the chance to do battle with some big evil, at least through or in his or her imagination, Ishiguro's characters tend to be more stoic. They accept the fact of predetermination and try to make the best of it. The way they face the world is, for better or worse, quite humble.

To deal with this characteristic in *The Remains of the Day* and *Never Let Me Go*, Tsuchiya has employed a very distinct strategy, a special form of speech, which I do not think he has used when translating Michael Ondaatje or Frank McCourt, for example. Nor have other Ishiguro translators employed this strategy. Roughly speaking, when telling a story in Japanese, you have two options: what may be called the regular form and the polite form. For instance, 'he went to Liverpool' in the former would be *kare wa ribapu-ru e itta*, and in the latter *kare wa ribapu-ru e ikimashita*. The difference is generally marked by the verb at the end. The polite form is almost always longer and sounds more . . . polite.

In practice, almost all novels and stories are written or translated in the regular form. The polite form is rarely used, except when the narrator is politely addressing a specific person or persons, as in epistolary novels.[5] But it is this form that Tsuchiya employed in these two books. Although rather unusual for the translation of a novel, it is clearly a logical choice, especially for *The Remains of the Day*: there are a number of phrases that imply that Stevens is telling his story to a group of butler colleagues, and he is the type of person who would speak politely even to his peers. But I think that the form highlights other important characteristics of these two novels.

First of all, a narrator using the polite form naturally sounds *humble*. You feel that the listeners, readers, are more important than the speaker and that his or her story is offered *up* to you. Tsuchiya's translation of both books marvellously sustains this tone throughout. This is an artistic achievement in its own right, but also a faithful reflection of the humbleness that Ishiguro characters often adopt towards the world. In fact, in *Never Let Me Go*, Kathy H.'s use of the polite form is a little awkward, since she is also speaking to her peers, but would probably not talk so politely as Stevens. The sense of her humility, which is clearly underscored by the polite form, more than compensates for this awkwardness.

Second, and I think more importantly, politeness generally creates not intimacy but *distance*. By speaking politely, you distance yourself from your audience, creating the sense of holding back at the same time as you are opening yourself up. There are other kinds of distance involved as well. For one thing, both Stevens and Kathy H. maintain a certain distance from other characters, and from what they are talking about in general, especially the past events they are relating. They never immerse themselves in their pasts, and often try to analyse clinically, if not always entirely honestly, what happened in the past. In this respect, *Never Let Me Go* is much more subtle than *The Remains of the Day*: Stevens is a typical unreliable narrator, but he is unreliable in a very reliable way – once you get to know him you can usually see through him. It is not so easy with Kathy H., yet the fact remains that in both books the civil, courteous way the narrators talk emphasizes their emotional distance from others, and from the past.

Moreover, the two narrators distance themselves *from themselves*, especially in the case of Stevens. He does not really know what he feels – about Lord Darlington, about Miss Kenton, about his whole life – till the very end, at least on the articulate level. He does not know how to relate emotionally to himself, any more than to others. The translator of Ishiguro, therefore, will often have to try not to make his or her translation too lively or immediate.

These polite-speaking narrators, therefore, are doomed to distance themselves from readers, from other characters, from the past, and from themselves. And all these distances are wonderfully reproduced in the Japanese translations through Tsuchiya's use of the polite form. I think that this multiple sense of distance is even more conspicuously rendered – for the better, I would argue – in the Japanese translations.

Yet in spite of all these distances, or possibly because of them, we are moved: the very inability of Ishiguro's characters to connect emotionally with others or with themselves makes the two books emotionally powerful. That is the real Ishiguro magic. And I can assure English-speaking readers that that is just as beautifully conveyed through the polite language spoken by the Japanese-speaking Stevens and Kathy H.

notes

1. The Japanese language uses three sets of letters: *kanji* (Chinese characters, used for all sorts of concepts and things), *hiragana* (one type of syllabary, used for verbal hinges such as particles and conjunctions) and *katakana* (the other type of syllabary used for foreign words, to which Rubin refers here).
2. Jay Rubin, *Haruki Murakami and the Music of Words* (London: Harvill Press, 2002), pp. 288–9.
3. The Japanese translation, by Takeshi Onodera, was first published in 1984.
4. The Japanese translation, by Masao Tsuchiya, first appeared in 1990.
5. The polite form is also used often in children's stories, probably to help children feel that someone is talking directly to them (and perhaps to reinforce the impression that they are living in a polite world).

4

'one word from you could alter the course of everything': discourse and identity in kazuo ishiguro's fiction

krystyna stamirowska

summary

Discourse and identity have long been recognized as being intimately intertwined because language both expresses and constitutes our sense of self. At the same time, our idiolect and modes of speech contribute to how we see ourselves and shape and confirm our identity. In Ishiguro's writing, unadorned language is correlated with honesty, whilst elaborate language is correlated with moral confusion. This chapter examines the inflexible language of Ishiguro's insecure male narrators and contrasts it with the more supple and ethically responsive discourse of his female narrators.

'i have never had a keen awareness of my own standing': ishiguro's male narrators

The connection between discourse and identity has preoccupied twentieth-century linguists, anthropologists and social scientists as well as modernist writers. Both structural linguists (de Saussure, Jakobson, Benveniste) and anthropologists (Lévi-Strauss, Malinowski) tried to explain the nature of this link through the analyses of the uses of language in specific contexts.[1] Many of their conclusions were developed by the French psychoanalyst Jacques Lacan, who defined the unconscious as a structure analogous to language.[2]

The results of structural analyses of language, social behaviour and the human mind turned out to be highly relevant for the field of literary studies. Investigations of the connections between language and identity are particularly fruitful with respect to critical interpretation of the discourse used by the protagonists in the novels of Kazuo Ishiguro. Apart from establishing a firm connection between language and ethics, which encourages our 'reading' of characters through their speech, Ishiguro seems interested – as the interview with Sebastian Groes suggests – in examining a possible tie between discourse and gender. Whereas the male narrators use a stilted discourse that indicates emotional and ethical immaturity, his female protagonists' language is ethically both responsive and responsible.

The language used by Ishiguro's male protagonists is fraught with unease. It ranges from Ono's mixture of self-assurance and concealed anxiety in *An Artist of the Floating World* (1986); Stevens's over-correct, 'servant-emulating-his-betters' speech in *The Remains of the Day* (1989); the stilted inauthenticity of Ryder's monologues in *The Unconsoled* (1995); and the artificial efforts of Christopher Banks in *When We Were Orphans* (2000), whose discourse echoes that of many other (fictional) voices he has heard and tried to appropriate throughout his life.

Some of the characters' speeches illustrate an uneasiness and a perplexity reflected in a consistent preference for indirectness and elaborate understatement. Etsuko goes back compulsively to her traumatic experiences. She qualifies her reminiscences with comments on the general unreliability of memory in order to diminish the horror of past events by carefully undermining the accuracy of recollections: 'It is possible that my memory of these events will have grown hazy with time, that things did not happen in quite the way they came back to me today' (*PVH* 41). And again, later on: 'Memory, I realize, can be an unreliable thing; often it is heavily coloured by the circumstances in which one remembers, and no doubt this applies to certain recollections I have gathered here' (*PVH* 156).

Yet, unlike the male characters, Etsuko admits her complicity in a straightforward way. She acknowledges a 'selfish desire not to be reminded of the past' (*PVH* 9), and makes it clear that her first husband (whom she eventually left) was 'for the seven years he knew his daughter . . . a good father to her. Whatever else I convinced myself of during those final days, I never pretended Keiko would not miss him' (*PVH* 90). And later on, referring to her decision to leave for England, she adds: 'I knew all along that she [Keiko] wouldn't be happy over there' (*PVH* 176).

Etsuko's honesty prevails over her desire to delete or repress her past and is expressed through the factual tone of her language. It anticipates the directness and moral uprightness of another female protagonist-narrator, Kathy H., in *Never Let Me Go* (2005). When considered with reference to discourse and ethics, both of these female characters stand in sharp contrast to the male protagonists.

Ishiguro's male speakers, presented between *A Pale View of Hills* and *Never Let Me Go*, can be understood via the paradigm defining the relations between identity and discourse. The novels clearly foreground the connection between the way one *is* and the way one *speaks*.[3] Despite radical differences in terms of status, personality, age, background and occupation of Ishiguro's male protagonists, their awareness of the role of the linguistic dimension of identity and self-presentation is strikingly similar. They are concerned about their image, yet unsure how they are perceived by others. They all reveal false humility, wavering between self-esteem and self-deprecation. While the women are more realistic and capable of both confronting the truth about their lives and verbalizing this truth, the men never get beyond self-centredness and status-anxiety, which is reflected in their speech. In *An Artist of the Floating World*, Ono starts as a commercial painter and turns to art for art's sake, but ends up serving a political cause and promoting Japanese imperialism in the years preceding the war. Although after the war he carefully modifies his position, he still maintains that he acted in good faith and, more importantly, that his political errors did not damage his artistic reputation. At the same time, in a characteristic way, he maintains that 'I have never had a keen awareness of my own standing' (*AFW* 21), or 'I was never able to concern myself with matters of esteem' (*AFW* 64). This false humility, combined with a refusal to examine honestly one's past and one's choices, is revealed by and reinforced through the discourse of Ishiguro's male narrators. This is also characteristic of Stevens, Ryder and Banks. The circularity of this mechanism seems to be reflected in their respective itineraries, both on the physical and symbolic level: they end up more or less where they began, prevented from achieving their goals through either the sheer impossibility of their aims or by an innate selfishness.

In *When We Were Orphans* Christopher Banks sees himself mainly as the world reflects him, and tries to give more polish to this reflection. The formal style in which he converses with his associates reveals his anxiety about creating the right impression, and often brings to mind his predecessors, Ono, Stevens and Ryder. This is how Banks dismisses Sarah Hemmings, when she wishes to accompany him to a prestigious social event: 'Well, Miss Hemmings, it was very good to see you again. But now I must leave you and go up to this function' (*WWWO* 38). Although she is a woman whom he secretly admires, Banks fears that she will be perceived as a victim of her social ambitions. So when she repeats her request, she meets with another rebuff: 'I wish you a pleasant evening, Miss Hemmings' (*WWWO* 38). His manner of speech creates a false impression and conceals his very real interest in Sarah. His curiously formal and unsuitable style echoes the response Stevens makes to Miss Kenton following a similar personal approach: 'Miss Kenton, I do not understand you. Now if you would kindly allow me to pass' (*RD* 59). Pleading lack of understanding is an excuse and a camouflage for a profound, if unconscious, resistance against showing or acknowledging emotions. This refusal to acknowledge one's own feelings or those of others is a cause, and also a result, of one's inability to meet other people as fully autonomous, irreducible beings. It mars Stevens's life, just as it vitiates the lives of other Ishiguro protagonists.

Like Ono's identity, Banks's and Stevens's sense of self is largely constructed through language. Stevens not only carefully notes and imitates the modes of speech he hears from his betters, but, by his own admission, he reads simple romantic novels in order to improve his own English. Since he has little or no sense of self, his instinct is to emulate those whom he considers infinitely superior – not in order to become like them, but to be worthy of the privilege of acting in their service.

Stevens is not merely an isolated figure with an inflated ego, but also he has no authentic identity. His father's life has been very similar, and he too takes pride in being a superior butler. Stevens occasionally tells stories about his father's achievements as a form of thinly veiled self-advertisement. His equivalent in *The Unconsoled* is the hotel porter, Gustav, who also thinks in inflated terms of his modest job as something that is worthwhile and dignified. He demonstrates his professional standards by ignoring physical exhaustion and needlessly carrying suitcases in the lift. The absurdity of this incident is reminiscent of a very similar dissimulation performed by Stevens's father.

The Hayes Society of butlers has its counterpart in the Club of hotel porters in *The Unconsoled*. Their meetings seem to imitate gatherings of a professional association where members can discuss their common code and the rules they have agreed to observe. Like Stevens, Gustav takes pride in what he does and has no doubts about the respect due to the porters in his town. He talks to Ryder about his dignity and about the Club of hotel porters, in a manner similar to that of Stevens addressing other butlers during their meetings. Yet in Gustav's case, the absurdity is even more evident. Among the more grotesque elements of these porters are their self-adopted rules to impose unfeasible standards of duty; or the Porters' Dance which is performed, to general applause, on the tables of the Hungarian cafe in which they meet regularly. Reversing their respective positions, and unconscious of the irony produced by such a reversal, Gustav says to Ryder: 'We're not nearly as formal as we once were and it's been understood for some time that in special circumstances, guests could be introduced to our table. You'd be very welcome to join us, sir' (U 7). At the same time, he pleads with Ryder to mention the porters in his speech: it is through this borrowed voice, more prestigious than his own, that he hopes to consolidate himself in the eyes of others: 'one word from you could alter the course of every-thing' (U 295). Through Ryder's voice, a new identity could be created for Gustav and for the other porters of the city.

While Gustav's usual discourse differs from the one he hopes to borrow, Stevens speaks through the voices of others – mostly through Lord Darlington's. He never seems to acquire a voice of his own, as Meghan Marie Hammond argues in Chapter 7. On several occasions, Banks borrows self-consciously the registers of others in order to create a certain impression. Ryder moves in what seems to be a hall of mirrors and echoes. Other characters reflect and send back their image according to their own fantasies. Ryder's identity fluctuates and is remade on each occasion he meets somebody, either for the first time or after an interval, and especially when he is greeted familiarly by people whom he fails to recognize. However, those contingent meetings never turn into authentic encounters, in the ethical sense. They are not based on recognition of the autonomy and otherness of the people he meets.

Ryder's attempts to attune himself to his interlocutors result in increasing bewilderment and a near loss of his sense of self and purpose. The once-clear motive for his visit to the city, which is to give a concert, becomes obfuscated and almost forgotten, as he tries to adjust to stran-gers who compete for his attention. Motivated by politeness or a desire to please, he tries to listen to their urgent pleas, without really opening to the Other, or uttering anything other than empty promises. The long monologues, requests and appeals merge into a cacophony of voices devoid of meaning. Paradoxically, the urge by the numerous inhabit-ants of the city to articulate their hopes, and Ryder's acceptance of their requests, results only in a progressive confusion for all parties. Swamped by the demands of strangers, Ryder no longer knows what he is expected to do. The deluge of voices starts to affect him. Stephan Hoffman's pleading and his confidences about his parents' lack of approval evoke in Ryder memories of the troubled relations with his own parents. Stephan's confessions of anxiety and emotional dependence trigger a shift in Ryder's self-perception. The confident self-image of a successful artist is replaced by an anxious figure, reverting to an immature self awaiting a reunion with his mother and father. Incidentally, when his attention is focused on the fantasy of his parents' arrival and he asks about the arrangements made for their reception, his questions mirror exactly those which, in a comparable context, will be asked by Banks in *When We Were Orphans* (*WWWO* 281).

The frustration and guilt expressed by Hoffman's father and his fear of disappointing Mrs Hoffman generates unease in Ryder about his comparable neglect of Sophie. Ryder increasingly perceives himself through the discourse of others. Both Ryder and the reader seem finally lost in the resounding echoes, which affect the whole landscape or cityscape, drowning external reality in an unintelligible chorus. The surreal argument about a suitable location for Brodsky's deceased dog, which replaces what was to be a celebration of Ryder's visit to the city, is a perfect example of the growing destabilization. Speech, rather than defining and reaffirming identities, conveys a pervading sense of absurdity and contaminates both human relations and the inanimate space which the human figures inhabit. Common sense ideas, rules of conduct and assumed identities are undermined, reducing the occasion to chaos.

Despite their attitudes of humility and respect, expressed through repeated apologies and excuses, the requests of the citizens to Ryder are uttered in an impeccably polite manner that, nevertheless, carries overtones of insistence bordering on menace. The implied meaning concealed by the polite words contradicts the smooth surface, and Ryder gradually becomes aware that he is frequently confronted with threats tantamount to blackmail. Both sides play that game: while the inhabitants try to conceal their insistence and impatience, Ryder conceals his growing irritation. Their discourse becomes a game of deception in which the words, properly decoded, have a meaning that is the contrary of what they denote. When the hotel manager urges the half-asleep Ryder to take his time and not hurry to come down to meet him, his actual meaning is exactly the opposite. Ryder feels such pressure from the manager that he forgets his exhaustion and immediately gets up and prepares to go downstairs. People say what they believe they ought to say, yet, at the same time, attempt to convey what is essential to them. Contrary to their assurances, they do not see the musician as an autonomous person, but merely as a means through which to achieve an end.

The failure to present one's self and to enter into a relation with other selves leads to alienation and to destruction of human bonds. Despite endless encounters, the distance separating Ryder from others is ever greater, and even superficial understanding is barred. The hotel manager cannot reach out to his wife and their son cannot win the approval of the parents he loves; Miss Collins and Brodsky are divorced and estranged, and are unable to be reunited. Brodsky states: 'Please. We're old now. We don't have to argue like we used to. I just came by to give you the flowers. And to make a simple proposal.' But his appeal meets with instant rejection: 'it's much too late, there is nothing for us to discuss' (*U* 315). In a similar manner, Sophie, whom at first Ryder takes to be a stranger and does not even recognize as his former wife, appeals in vain for her husband to return to her and Boris. Ryder, for whom the only real existence is his own, is unable to transcend the horizon of his selfishness. Ultimately, speech gives way to permanent silence. Sophie refuses to listen to Ryder's vague promises; Gustav has not talked to his daughter Sophie for eighteen years now, even though he continues to see her regularly and helps take care of her son, Boris. As he explains to Ryder, they stopped talking for a relatively minor reason and it has simply remained that way.

When attending a dinner given in his honour, Ryder begins his address to the city's prominent citizens with a sequence of incongruous exclamations: 'Collapsing curtain rails! Poisoned rodents! Misprinted score sheets!' (*U* 145). These were selected beforehand as 'a really captivating opening statement' (*U* 136). His speech, meant to be encouragingly informal, disintegrates and the whole occasion collapses into chaos. Another significant occasion when Ryder is reduced to speechlessness is an encounter devised by his long-forgotten childhood playmate, Fiona. She is hoping to impress her false friends by showing her close relations with the much-coveted Ryder. At the crucial moment, when Fiona is being mocked yet again by her acquaintances, she urges Ryder to save her by introducing himself. Yet Ryder, already confused by his sudden failure to speak – he has just emitted a few pig-like grunts – is further paralysed by a glimpse of his reflection in the mirror hanging on the opposite wall of the room: 'I saw that my face had become bright red and squashed into pig-like features, while my fists, clenched at the chest level, were quivering along with the whole of my torso' (*U* 240). This shift in his self-perception, reflected in emotional and linguistic confusion, makes it literally impossible for him to declare his identity and reduces him to silence.

This deficiency of language precludes real dialogue and perversely enforces, rather than repairs, alienation. It is not surprising, therefore, that a non-verbal medium, music, acquires a magical role in the novel and comes to be seen as a panacea that could help transform chaos into order. Traditionally, music stands for harmony and coherence. The city dramatically lacks these qualities, and so music becomes a symbol through which its inhabitants express their hopes. Musicians are seen as particularly important, and the city's material and spiritual well-being is, in some mysterious way, dependent on their achievement. Ryder obtains a detailed view of the status attached to music, and is made doubly aware of the high hopes connected with his own performance and with the speech he is to give. The future of the whole town hinges on the success of the concert on Thursday evening.

Predictably, nothing goes according to plan. Ryder never manages to give either his recital or his address; Stephan's performance falls short of the parents' expectations; Brodsky arrives inebriated at the concert, leaning on an ironing board for support; and, as soon as he starts conducting, he loses balance and falls down. However, Ryder's essential selfishness, although consigning him to an inauthentic life in a self-created world of fantasy, stands him in good stead. He leaves the town behind, shakes the dust off his feet, and finds quick comfort in another casual encounter. He looks forward to his next engagement, this time in Copenhagen. This ending is a more ruthless version of the mild complacency shown by Ono, Stevens or Banks, after their own respective short-lived epiphanies.

kathy h.'s ethically responsive discourse in *never let me go*

In *Never Let Me Go*, Ishiguro radically changes the idiolect and voice through which his former, mostly male, protagonists narrate their stories. Their solemn and self-conscious language, bordering in some cases on self-parody, is now abandoned in favour of Kathy's speech which, though often clichéd and colloquial, epitomizes the immediate ethical response to the Other. Her speech is so offhand that Frank Kermode described it as a 'dear-diary' style.[4] As an adolescent, Kathy and her friends repeatedly used phrases such as 'that's rubbish' (*NLMG* 22); 'It's funny to think we got so worked up' (*NLMG* 38); and 'don't mess it up' (*NLMG* 100). Such casual expressions are in striking contrast to the formal mode of address of Stevens or Ryder.

One change that determines the ethical shift is the emphasis away from self-centredness to a clear focus on the Other. Kathy's identity is defined by her awareness of the reality of other people, which is to her the primary *donnée*. Consequently, her discourse constitutes itself as an act of reaching outside to the Other, rather than of expressing her own ego. In contrast to the typically self-centred figures in Ishiguro's former narratives, Kathy is the first narrator (with the possible exception of Etsuko) to change her mode of discourse from an overt or concealed monologue to a dialogue. Through her empathy, she enters a new ontological dimension occupied by others, whom she meets in a common space. Their existence is, to her, as real as her own. Her identity is re-established through a series of seemingly mundane encounters. However, when considered in their natural sequence, these encounters are easily seen as ethical, rooted in the act of meeting and accepting responsibility for the other person.[5]

The highly significant opening episode, as remembered by Kathy many years later, shows her sharing the general amusement at the expense of Tommy, who is acting awkwardly and unable to control his anger. Yet her sense of unfairness soon prevails and she decides to leave her own circle of friends and join Tommy in order to intervene. When she says 'Tommy, your nice shirt. You'll get it all messed up' (*NLMG* 10), it is not a rebuff or an attempt to claim possession of Tommy by including him in her own discourse. What her seemingly casual words signify is a readiness to make herself available to him and to accept responsibility. Without quite realizing this, Kathy is making an offer, which is always an incomplete project and necessitates ever-renewed effort. The contrast between her own response and that made by her friends – who 'fix' the boy in a cliché by calling him 'mad animal' (*NLMG* 11), or a 'layabout' (*NLMG* 9) – is crucial. Her spontaneous reaction not only helps Tommy, but also sets a pattern of sympathy and responsibility for the Other. This will, ultimately, lead to a conscious self-renunciation, the state when she no longer wants anything for herself (as once she wanted her lost tape). The growing maturity of self finds its natural expression and confirmation in her discourse. If the monologues of her fictional predecessors are often self-serving and pathetic, Kathy's matter-of-fact speech is addressed to the Other and has both clarity and authenticity. In contrast to her well-meaning teachers – who, like the doctors, have knowledge and power and cannot avoid a measure of complicity with the practices they oppose – Kathy stands out because she does not try to possess or dominate through language. Because of her concern for others, she avoids the traps of self-delusion and complacency into which her friends occasionally fall.

When the pupils leave Hailsham and begin a semi-independent life, they share the Cottages with slightly older 'students', whose origin and destiny are identical to their own. Kathy is disturbed to notice the artificiality of the language used by the 'veterans', who pick up expressions and gestures from television serials. Since they have never lived in a family, their only role models and linguistic models are people on the screen. Kathy's closest friend, the know-it-all Ruth, is quick to imitate what is already an imitation. She is anxious to produce a correct impression, and to present herself and Tommy as a couple, so she reproduces the mannerisms practised by the 'veterans'. To her, loving someone means to be seen by others as being in love. Through her speech she both produces a desirable self-image and reaffirms her own sense of herself as Tommy's lover.

It is evident from Kathy's account that, even as a child, Ruth was a dominant figure and strove to establish her position as a leader through her discourse. Accordingly, others awaited her self-confident opinions and instructions. Ruth's main strategy, and a source of her power, consisted in creating false impressions. She artfully suggested her superior position with respect to knowledge she allegedly possessed and an involvement in activities from which others were excluded. Moving carefully along the axis of inclusion/exclusion, she created her own privileged circle, whose members were allowed to share her secrets and fantasies. By deluding herself about her special role, she also managed to delude the others. Her self-confident speech persuaded her friends that she might succeed in breaking away from the deterministic pattern imposed on her as a clone and lead a life of her own.

Yet the identity she tries to construct must collapse at a critical point. Her hard-earned self-reliance makes her confrontation with the facts even more tragic. Weary of illusive comforts, she finally spells out what her friends have feared but dare not voice: 'We are modelled from *trash*. . . . If you want to look for possibles, if you want to do it properly, then you look in the gutter. You look in rubbish bins. Look down the toilet, that's where you'll find where we all came from' (*NLMG* 153). This speech marks a complete change of discourse. It also eventually leads to the dramatic confession Ruth makes shortly before her death. She admits that she deliberately misrepresented Tommy in order to separate him from Kathy. It was through lies that she created a false persona for him as someone who disapproved of casual sex:

> Well Kathy, what you have to realize is that Tommy doesn't see you like that. He really, really likes you. . . . But I know he doesn't see you like, you know, a proper girlfriend. . . . Tommy doesn't like girls who've been with ... well you know, with this person and that. It's just a thing he has. I'm sorry, Kathy, but it wouldn't be right not to have told you. (*NLMG* 183)

Apart from lying, Ruth assumes a false, pseudo-ethical stance. This places her as the exact opposite to Kathy, whose speech is characteristically to the point and free from hidden hints. Although Ruth, on the whole, avoids straightforward lies, she tries to create pockets of ambiguity. For example, years earlier, she implied that she may have received a gift from a favourite teacher at Hailsham. Having inspired curiosity and envy, she then maintained that she could not possibly tell where the pencil case came from: 'it's a mystery' (*NLMG* 58). Ruth's long-delayed transformation is achieved by admitting to selfishness and deception. This is when she finally speaks in a voice of moral awareness, cognizant of right and wrong. To Kathy, responsible maturity comes naturally and culminates in her uncomplaining acceptance of her situation and in the acceptance of Tommy's request made shortly before his death. He demands that she give up being his carer, so as to leave intact the image of him he wants her to retain.

Kathy's mode of speech, directed to the Other from the beginning, changes as she is growing up. As children, Hailsham pupils developed a unique semiotic and linguistic code. They had been gradually introduced by their guardians to euphemisms such as 'carers' or 'recovery centres'. In addition, there were certain subjects not mentioned and questions not asked – ostensibly for fear of embarrassment, but more probably out of self-protection. Unless they are named, things may be assumed not to exist. In the Hailsham days, the nearby woods became a symbol for an unfamiliar and undefined threat. In a way, a sense of impending destiny was often tamed and familiarized by integrating it into their daily activities. Jokes about health checks or about 'unzipping' (*NLMG* 85) and producing organs were meant to smooth the dangerous edge of teachers' talk about donations.

Whilst at Hailsham, Kathy's use of language conformed to this code, but her mode of speech changes in accordance with her personal development. Her growing maturity consists in gradually acknowledging the priority of her friends' welfare over her own. Her ethical stance becomes very consciously defined by placing priority upon the Other. She repeatedly makes herself available to successive donors during her twelve years as a carer. Focusing on others, she deliberately plays down the drama of her own existence and disregards her anxiety and exhaustion. It is through this other-directed mode of discourse, which expresses and confirms her identity, that she comes to achieve self-control and a detached, quietly stoical attitude.

Kathy's mode of speech places her at the opposite end of the scale of personal discourse used by her literary predecessors. Stevens, Ryder and Banks were all hidebound by Prufrockian deficiencies. Kathy's discourse refuses to play their narcissistic game of pretending to address others while they are really talking to themselves. It therefore possesses an ethical dimension impossible to achieve by those other selfish figures. By placing themselves at the centre of the world, Ishiguro's male narrators preclude potential dialogue and reduce their enunciations to a limited variety of monologues. Kathy expresses her commitment to the Other and is the only Ishiguro protagonist fully capable of entering into an ethical dialogue which goes beyond a verbal performance. Among a gallery of unconsoled and unconsolable characters, she is the only one who, having acknowledged the limits of existence and the corruption inherent in the self, can come to terms with the reality of her condition. She is capable of transforming the negativity of her circumstances into an ethical stance which opens up to the Other, and which consists in both finding and providing authentic consolation.

In Ishiguro's writing, unadorned language is correlated with honesty, whilst elaborate language is correlated with moral confusion. It is less clear, though, whether the discourse of his characters can be distinguished on the basis of gender. The marked differences between the male and female mode of speech are unlikely to be coincidental. But it would be rash to step beyond merely registering this difference by offering firm conclusions. Ono, Stevens, Ryder and Banks are, each in his own way, morally and intellectually immature. Their understanding of reality, and in particular of their place within it, is clearly deficient. In contrast to his female characters, they are cowardly creatures unable to face up to the challenges of existence. They are vain and constantly troubled by self-doubt. What they crave most is respect by others, which, paradoxically, their very speech and behaviour precludes. Their dreams of achievement, expressed in solemn and self-important speech, alienate them further from real accomplishment and render them mildly ridiculous, rather than dignified.[6] Yet, it would be a simplification to link their ambitions and self-centredness with the stereotype of the inflated male ego, in opposition to the common-sense practicality or capacity for empathy and self-effacement conventionally attributed to women. The two female protagonists (Etsuko and Kathy) are indeed shown as much stronger, unself-deceiving characters capable of dealing with the exigencies of life and of entering into an ethical dialogue with others. They neither think nor talk of dignity or self-respect. But the dignity and self-respect they possess comes naturally as a consequence of their behaviour and speech. Their language, unlike that of Ishiguro's dissimulating male narrators, is truly constitutive of their self and identity.

notes

1. The Saussurean linguistics which introduced the concept of structure into the study of language provided a model for anthropology as well as philosophy, psychology and literary theory. The pioneering works by Claude Lévi-Strauss (1904–2009), *Les structures élémentaires de la parenté* (1949) and *Anthropologie structurale* (1958), became an inspiration for the structuralist school of thought in the human sciences and critical theory, which included Lacan, Barthes, Genette, Foucault and others.

2. Lacan claimed that the relation between the signified and signifier as defined by de Saussure is essentially the same as the relation between the conscious and the unconscious. The suppressed element resurfaces in the form of errors, slips or incongruous elements of behaviour, which function as signifiers. The study of signifying chains as expressions of identity is revealing, especially in view of the controlling and restrictive role of consciousness. This perception throws additional light on the role language plays in producing and establishing the sense of identity.

3. This connection is explicitly articulated by another French linguist, Émile Benveniste, who claims that the self is realized through the speaking situation when the subject expresses himself to the Other and, through the speech act, constitutes his own identity and that of another speaker. According to Benveniste, 'it is in and through language that man constitutes himself as a subject because language alone establishes the concept of "ego" in reality, in its reality which is that of the being': *Problems in General Linguistics* (Coral Gable: University of Miami Press, 1971), p. 224. This idea is echoed by Lacan, who construes the role of the speaker engaged in a dialogue as constitutive of the self, of another speaker and of everything else (that is, the world).

4. Frank Kermode, 'Outrageous Game', *London Review of Books*, 21 April 2005, 21–2.

5. The concept of an 'ethical encounter' with the Other and the subsequent responsibility is crucial for Emmanuel Levinas, who is another important influence on modern literature and theory. Levinas maintains that it is through the encounter with the Other that one becomes aware of one's own identity as being different from something or someone else. This encounter is the origin of language and communication in the sense of being in relation with the Other, which is a profoundly ethical experience.

6. Ishiguro's presentation is not unsympathetic: he does stress their unhappy childhood and their difficult relations with parents as an exonerating factor.

part ii
the early, 'japanese', works

5

'putting one's convictions to the test': kazuo ishiguro's *an artist of the floating world* in japan

motoko sugano

summary

In Britain, Kazuo Ishiguro's fictions have been received favourably from the start of his career, and his reticent writing style has proved attractive to readers. However, in Japan the translation of An Artist of the Floating World *(1986) was quietly received.[1] Immediate responses to* Ukiyo no Gaka *(1988) were focused on the readability of the translation rather than on the novel itself: the paradoxical nature of 'retranslating' into Japanese the original English text's representation of Japan, and the transfiguration of Ishiguro's understated writing style. What this discussion of form 'repressed', however, was the fact that it was* Ukiyo's *uncomfortable subject matter that made the novel unpopular, because it confronted readers in post-war Japan with the debate about the 'war responsibility' of the nation.*

'english' and 'japanese' onos

Kazuo Ishiguro's second novel, *An Artist of the Floating World* (1986), was translated by Professor Shigeo Tobita, an established translator of English Literature, and published as *Ukiyo no Gaka* (hereafter *Ukiyo*) in January 1988. Tobita had translated a wide variety of works, including Joseph Heller's *Catch-22* (1955) and Kurt Vonnegut's *Mother Night* (1961). He has become known for producing translations with a deceptively simple and plain style, which would appear suitable for Ishiguro's subtle and intricate handling of language. Yet this particular translation

69

presents us with a number of representational issues that illuminate the problematic reception of his work in Japan.

Before looking in detail at the formal aspects of the Ishiguro translation, it is helpful to explain how the Japanese writing system works. Contemporary Japanese writing primarily uses five writing systems:

1. *Kanji* (Chinese ideographs);
2. *Hiragana*;
3. *Katakana*;
4. *Roma-ji* (Roman alphabet);
5. *Su-ji* (Arabic numbers).

Most of the *kanji* ideographs carry discrete meanings, whilst *hiragana* and *katakana* are syllabographs. *Hiragana* is used to indicate a conjugal ending for *kanji* and to write anything that *kanji* is incapable of expressing. *Katakana* is specifically used to describe loan words, onomatopoeia or expressions that the author wishes to emphasize in particular.

Ukiyo is entirely set in Japan and is narrated by a Japanese character, the painter Masuji Ono; all other characters are Japanese, too, and the novel works within the mode of realism. These narrative settings require the translator to present Ishiguro's work realistically and in a way that is readable for Japanese readers. The translator's decision on style, which would indicate whose point of view the novel represents, was clearly affected by this requirement. Instead of applying the norm of historical novels to reinforce the image of the pre-war educated elderly Ono, Tobita used the norm of contemporary novels to reflect the possible tone of voice that Ishiguro, in his thirties, might have spoken had he been writing in Japanese.[2] Thus the translation intends to reproduce not only Ishiguro's perfectly pitched and 'deceptively simple' writing style with an unaffected and plain prose which enables favourable access to his fiction, but also his contemporary point of view.

Ukiyo achieves readability by using *kanji* for proper nouns. Prior to *Ukiyo*, Ken Onodera, with the hint of a suggestion by Ishiguro, applied *kanji* to proper nouns in his translation of *A Pale View of Hills*.[3] As a rule, however, Japanese translators transcribe the syllables of proper nouns in foreign texts into *katakana*. This rule applies to Japanese-sounding names, as these are considered to be borrowed words which have no exact equivalent in Japanese. Names in Japanese create a range of homonyms whose meanings are often articulated by different combinations of *kanji*, because they carry specific meanings. As such, *kanji* ideographs are often used as a vehicle of characterization. To explain why he took a flexible approach towards the translation of Japanese names in *An Artist of the Floating World*, Tobita says that rendering the names of the characters or places in *katakana* obstructs the flow of reading.[4] *Ukiyo* prioritizes the readability of Ono's speech register rather than blindly following the convention of English–Japanese translation.

Even though reproducing names in *kanji* is an acceptable translation practice for both reinforcing readability and reproducing the characters' verbal register, the translator needed to exercise significant discretion over characterization in Japanese. The strategy deployed by Tobita is to choose the most popular or representative combinations of *kanji* for the names, in order to avoid undesirable or inappropriate connotations for the character or place. The translator associates Setsuko with the notion of restriction and discipline and the name of the actress in Yasujiro Ozu's *Tokyo Story* (*Tokyo Monogatari*, 1953), and Noriko with a historical chronicle and the heroine of Ozu's *An Autumn Afternoon* (*Sanma no Aji*, 1962). The translation of the name Ono loses the tragicomic implication of negation (Mr Oh-No, 'I'm in Denial') in English, and implies a 'small field'. The use of *kanji* for place names is also crucial for the readability of the translated text because Ishiguro's 'Japan' is full of fictional place names. For example, in the sequence where Ono rides the tram to Matsuda's place, four names – Arakawa, Tozaka-cho, Sakaemachi and Minamimachi – appear in one paragraph to trace the passing of the scenery (*AFW* 85–6). If these names were to be transliterated in *katakana*, the readability of the translation would have been seriously damaged. Tobita prioritizes readability over reproducing the sense of foreignness that the names in *An Artist of the Floating World* convey for the reader in English.

Tobita also rearranges the flow of speech. Ishiguro creates Ono as a spontaneous narrator who 'narrates-as-he-thinks' and who does not care much about the sequencing of what he relates. The opening of the novel demonstrates the difference between the texts:

> If on a sunny day you climb the steep path leading up from the little wooden bridge still referred to around here as 'the Bridge of Hesitation', you will not have to walk far before the roof of my house becomes visible between the tops of two gingko trees. Even if it did not occupy such a commanding position on the hill, the house would still stand out from all others nearby, so that as you come up the path, you may find yourself wondering what sort of wealthy man owns it. (*AFW* 7)

Ono's characterization as the narrator is moderated through a translation that places a priority on producing a smooth flow of voice and focalization. In Tobita's translation, Ono is more careful and self-conscious about how he presents his narrative:

> From one end of the small wooden bridge that is still referred to around here as 'Tamerai bashi' [the Bridge of Hesitation], there is quite a steep path leading to the top of the hill. On a sunny day, before walking very far up the path, the roof of my house between the tops of two soaring gingko trees will come into view. The house occupies the spot on the hilltop with a particularly good view, and the size of the house would appear overwhelmingly large if it were built on the flat ground. Those who climb the hill would probably wonder what kind of wealthy man is living in such a grand residence. (*Ukiyo* 4; my translation)

Tobita's translation breaks the first sentence into two distinct sentences, but, from the point of view of the Japanese reader, the flow of speech is improved. In his Postscript to the translation, Tobita asserted that the narrative finally read correctly when the opening phrase 'if on a sunny day' was placed at the beginning of the second sentence.[5] Compared to the zigzag movement of the original, the sentences are rearranged in order to direct more emphatically the reader's eye movement from low to high. The first sentence sets the focus on the bridge (the starting point), then moves upward to the top of the hill. In the translation's second sentence, the state of the weather ('a sunny day') is more closely linked to the view of the house from outside. The nuance of 'soaring' is added, whereby the translation registers the height of the gingko trees and prestigious standing of the house more clearly than in the original English text. In this example, Ono has a smoother train of thought and the structure of his narration is more accessible to the Japanese reader than that of the original English, whilst Tobita still manages to convey effectively the sense of Ono's elderly rambling.

Another important aspect evident in the quotation above is that the translator attends to Ono's repetitive use of the second-person pronoun ('you').[6] In English, this pronoun does not always address a particular person or a group of people. Ishiguro uses it ingeniously to dramatize what is behind Ono's intimate, yet aloof, tone of voice. His use of second-person address manifests Ono's spontaneous, rambling narration as well as his limited perception of audience that suits the condition of his old age.[7] For example, in the novel's first paragraph, the appearances of 'you' deliberately baffle the reader by creating the impression that we are plunged into the middle of unknown territory. This effect is toned down significantly in the translation, from which the second-person address is eliminated. Tobita follows the Japanese convention that avoids translating personal pronouns (such as 'I', 'you', 'he' or 'she') unless they affect meaning or address. In general, translating each of these personal pronouns creates an air of 'translationese', and is considered to be over-literal and unsophisticated. Tobita's translation creates naturalness in the Japanese prose and this provides a smooth introduction to the novel as it focuses on describing the location and view. Consequently, the sense of awkwardness generated by Ono's repeated yet empty use of the second person, which suggests his old age, becomes invisible in the translation. The alleviation of an incessant second-person address refigures his characterization but also renders the character more accessible to the Japanese reader.

The translation's readability is further enhanced by working on sentence length. In the original, Ono sometimes narrates in lengthy, formal sentences that reflect the older generation's haughty manner of address. In the scene where he lectures on his resistance to Mori-san's art, for instance, he packs his criticisms into one long sentence:

> All he [the Tortoise] would have recognised was that it represented a blatant disregard for Mori-san's priorities; abandoned had been the school's collective endeavour to capture the fragile lantern light of the pleasure world; bold calligraphy had been introduced to complement the visual impact; and above all, no doubt, the Tortoise would have been shocked to observe that my techniques made extensive use of the hard outline – a traditional enough method, as you will know, but one whose rejection was fundamental to Mori-san's teaching. (*AFW* 174)

Ono's use of semicolons creates an extended sentence that rhetorically disguises his simple logic with something more elaborate. Tobita breaks this sentence into five short sentences, as if to puncture Ono's disguise. This creates the effect of giving a list of reasons, with each reason becoming clearer and more 'reasonable' to the reader:

> He [the Tortoise = Kame-san] would have simply thought that Ono's painting impudently disregards Mori-san's taste. His painting abandons the effort made by the whole school to capture the fragile light from lanterns in the pleasure world. It makes strong use of the eye-catching technique of bold calligraphy. And what is more, Kame-san must have been shocked to recognise my extensive use of bold outlines. As it is known, this is just a traditional technique, but it was Mori-san's policy to reject it. (*Ukiyo* 235; my translation)

In the translation of foreign texts, breaking down long sentences into shorter ones is often used as a means of facilitating readability. It is a necessary remedy for coping with differences in linguistic function between English and Japanese. Japanese, for example, does not have an exact grammatical equivalent of conjunctions, such as the semicolon or relative pronouns. However, it affects Ono's characterization here by creating a clean, crisp rhythm. This rhythm contradicts the 'English' Ono, whose long sentences create a slower rhythm of voice than that of the 'Japanese' Ono. The articulation of the sentence structure also suggests that Tobita intended to recreate the voice of the young author, Ishiguro, rather than that of the rambling narrator.

Refiguring Ono's narrative is a crucial means of gaining readability in translation but, though justifiable in Japanese, it also affects Ishiguro's attempt to resist creating a linear, progressive narrative. In English, names in Japanese, Ono's manner of rambling speech, his repetitive use of vocabulary and his redundant sentence structure not only generate an awkwardness of language, but also prevent a smooth speech flow. The Japanese translation respects Ishiguro's own elliptical style, but some of Ishiguro's other manoeuvres in English are not attempted. Ishiguro's resistance to producing a continuous narrative is subtle; it is naturalized as the language spoken by an old man whose first language is not English. Ironically, elements that create a sense of displacement in the English text are not translatable as 'foreignness' in Japanese, and Ishiguro's challenge of linear narrative is therefore weakened.

In short, Tobita's translation attempts to transfer Ishiguro's reticent yet resonant writing style in English faithfully to Japanese. With particular attention to readability, the translation applies *kanji* to proper nouns, reorganizes the flow of Ono's speech by rearranging sentence length, makes Ono's diction more youthful and adjusts the repetition of pronouns. Tobita avoids too much of the 'translationese' of literal translation and exercises a norm which respects 'natural' and readable prose. Clearly, it was not Tobita's translation that produced the novel's muted reception: it was the subject matter, rather than formal issues, that hindered its popularity.

the topic of war and japanese responsibility in *ukiyo no gaka*

A review of *Ukiyo no Gaka* by Masashi Miura revealed his uneasiness over both Ono's unchanging faith in militarism during the war and Ishiguro's treatment of the topic.[8] His review exemplifies the idea that the historical or cultural referentiality of the translated text determines its acceptability amongst target readers. Although some English critics refer to the topic of Japanese imperialism and the issue of war in post-war Japanese history in *An Artist of the Floating World*, they may not be aware of the full ramifications of these issues to the Japanese reader. In early Japanese reviews, critics tended to avoid this topic altogether and Tobita's translation itself attempts to divert the readers' attention from the topic of war and responsibility in his translation. If they touched upon the representation of war in *Ukiyo* at all, critics would praise Ishiguro's courage for mentioning something that was still considered to be a taboo subject in Japan.

War, particularly in its relation to the issue of war responsibility, is an inherently ambivalent topic of exploration in post-war Japanese society. The difficulty in dealing with this subject matter is manifest in the way that the Japanese have found it difficult to formulate a communal body of memory that incorporates the history of the war in which the Japanese are accountable.[9] The debate pertaining to the history of war covers broad areas: the government's authorization of history textbooks (e.g. the 'Ienaga Textbook Trials', disputed from 1963 to 1997); the issue of 'comfort women' (still not settled); the dispute over the status of the Yasukuni shrine (likewise an ongoing issue); and issues of historiography concerning the fifteen-year war between China and Japan, which forms the historical background of *Ukiyo*. All these issues of war are extremely delicate and become complicated by the ideological positions of whoever presents the argument. Accordingly, to say something on the topic of war, even when related to a work of fiction, requires the speaker to articulate carefully his or her position. This explains why Tobita attempted to prevent *Ukiyo* from being read as an exploration of the topic of war and of Japan's responsibility.

Also to be considered was the controversy over the responsibility of artists for producing war propaganda paintings or what are called 'war record paintings'.[10] The collaboration of artists with the militarist government gradually intensified after the Manchurian Incident in 1931, which subsequently led to the fifteen-year war between China and Japan. State control over cultural activities was tightened under the National Mobilization Law of 1938, which forced the nation to contribute to the war effort. Artists, including high profile painters, were sent to the front to produce war-record paintings (see Illustrations 1–4). After the war, these paintings were confiscated by the occupation army and sent to the USA. They were returned in 1970 on an indefinite loan to the National Museum of Modern Art in Tokyo. The extremely delicate nature of these paintings is evident in the fact that only one or two of them could be exhibited at any time due to objections from neighbouring countries.[11] As the examples show, most of the war record

76

illustration 1 Ryushi Kawabata, *Capture of Luoyang* (1944). (c) Katsura Kawabata and Minami Kawabata, 2011. Collection of The National Museum of Modern Art, Tokyo (indefinite loan).

illustration 2 Saburo Miyamoto, *Surprise Attack of Naval Paratroops at Manado* (1943). (c) Mineko Miyamoto, 2011. Collection of The National Museum of Modern Art, Tokyo (indefinite loan).

illustration 3   Kakuzo Seno, *Charge* (1937). Collection of The National Museum of Modern Art, Tokyo (indefinite loan).

illustration 4   Takeshiro Kanokogi, *Triumphal Entry into Nanjing* (1940). Collection of The National Museum of Modern Art, Tokyo (indefinite loan).

paintings depict soldiers under military operations in the overseas war front, often on a large canvas. Though it is too simplistic to conclude that all the war record paintings unquestionably glorify the cause of the war, they represent the aggression that haunts the history of the post-war Japanese society.

In his review, Miura points out that Ishiguro refers to this history and resurrects the forgotten debate on artists' responsibility. In late 1945, a debate over artists' services to the war raged in the *Asahi Shimbun* news-paper between Tsuguharu Fujita, who justified his service to the coun-try, and Shigeo Miyata, who insisted that those artists who produced propaganda arts should refrain from practice for a while. Goro Tsuruta responded to Miyata and Fujita that the artists had no choice but to collaborate. Around 1950, as the country shifted its focus to economic recovery and advancement, the controversy lost prominence, apart from the occasional discussion in magazines amongst painters such as Saburo Miyamoto, Junichi Mukai or Kenichi Nakamura on their art and service during the war.[12] Although *Eyes to the Horizon* is a poster and not an oil painting, Ono's fate as a propaganda artist is similar to that of these painters. Ishiguro may touch upon this topic incidentally, for *An Artist of the Floating World* was written before The National Museum of Modern Art in Tokyo published the catalogue of war-record paintings in 1992. *Ukiyo* seems to operate within the reverberations of the very real and fractious debate surrounding the artists' responsibility during wartime.

The Japanese translation makes a couple of revisions for the sake of preventing the translated text from being associated with this topic of war responsibility. One major change, which was made after consulta-tion with Ishiguro, is the replacement of the statue of the Emperor Taisho in the Takami Garden (*AFW* 132–5) with the statue of the former Mayor Yamaguchi (*Ukiyo* 175–9). The effect of this change is significant. It transforms the history of the Takami Garden from a space of imperial commemoration to a memorial for a former mayor whose name sounds adequately generic to Japanese ears and whose career is not associated with the issue of war and responsibility. Moreover, in the English text, the statue of Emperor Taisho is surrounded by benches and described as a meeting spot for Ono, Setsuko, Noriko and Ichiro. Presenting such a statue as a place where citizens can chat and enjoy the sun does not fit particularly well in the Japanese context. The ideological position of the Emperor is an extremely delicate matter in post-war Japanese history, and Tobita's alteration can therefore be understood as a removal of a reference that might have caused embar-rassment among readers.

There is another, more subtle instance of avoiding the topic of wartime militarism: the translator sometimes adjusts Ono's militarist overtone. Towards the end of the novel, in the section to which Miura refers to in his review, Ono returns to the hilly areas in Wakaba province from which he could have a good view of Mori-san's villa:

> For, as he [Matsuda] pointed out himself, the likes of him and me,
> we have satisfaction of knowing that whatever we did, we did at the

time in the best of faith. Of course, we took some bold steps and often did things with much singlemindedness; but this is surely preferable to never putting one's convictions to the test, for lack of will or courage. (*AFW* 201–2)

The Japanese translation of this section reads as follows:

> For, as he himself was saying, the likes of Matsuda and I are aware that, whatever it was, we acted in accordance with faith, and take satisfaction in that fact. Of course, we at times did adventurous things, and too often charged ahead like carriage horses. But our attitude was far better than that of those who never even try to act on their convictions because they lack enough will and courage. (*Ukiyo* 272–3, my translation)

This section in the Japanese shows Ono's continuous faith in his past conduct, but it tends to alleviate militarist implications. In the second sentence, the phrase 'some bold steps' is replaced with the more abstract expression of 'adventurous things', and the word 'singlemindedness' is disarmed to become the figurative expression 'often charged ahead like carriage horses', which emphasizes a comical image of progress and advancement. Moderating militarist slogans, especially in the closing chapter of the novel, renders the section more palatable for the Japanese reader.

In the previous section, it was stated that Tobita's translation works within the mode of realism because it prioritizes readability in Japanese over simply inscribing foreignness by literal translation. Consequently, the Japanese translation might have lost the story's 'imaginative' quality to serve as a parable. Allusions to history in *An Artist of the Floating World* are fictionalized and displaced for the reader in English; however, when they are translated back to Japanese, there appears to be only a fine line of difference between a historical parable that aims to achieve universality and the 'real' history, which must be considered in this particular situation. As a response to those readers who attempt to 'translate' Ishiguro's imaginary Japan to the 'real' history, the translator writes that the theme of the book is not about responsibility during wartime. Tobita's Postscript notes that the book might be read as the story of a man who has collaborated in the war and regrets his actions on the surface, but in fact the real theme is the helpless (and very human) tendency of Ono to veer towards self-righteousness.[13] This explanation highlights the universal significance of the story and implies that Ishiguro did not intend to restrict its appeal to the Japanese

readers. Tobita's comment suggests that while the ambiguity inherent in
Ishiguro's novels allows for rich interpretations, it runs the risk of being
lost when interpreted in a particular context.

In conclusion, Ishiguro's prose style was introduced to readers in
Japan by Shigeo Tobita's translation, which recaptures in Japanese
the author's deceptively simple style. However, this strong introduc-
tory translation did not overcome the novel's thematic difficulty for
the target culture. The Japanese translation of *An Artist of the Floating
World*, therefore, attempts to navigate between the translated text and
the anticipated difficulties stemming from the book's allusions to the
history of Japan at war. The substitution of the statue of the former
Mayor Yamaguchi for the Statue of Emperor Taisho diverts the reader's
attention away from an unnecessary association with the topic of war
responsibility. However, the muffling of Ono's militarist discourse does
not achieve the intended effect. Despite the views expressed in the
translator's Postscript, the novel is still related to the war in Miura's
review. Even if the author does not write about 'real' or 'contemporary'
Japanese society, the historical matters with which *Ukiyo* confronts the
Japanese reader appear to bear 'unfortunate' resonances that invoked a
mild form of (self-)censorship. *Ukiyo*'s allusions to exactly these ideas of
responsibility and complicity in the Second World War resulted in its
limited success with its Japanese readership.

notes

1. Kazuo Ishiguro, *Ukiyo no Gaka*, trans. Shigeo Tobita (Tokyo: Chuokoron,
   1988).
2. Shigeo Tobita, 'Translator's Postscript', in Kazuo Ishiguro, *Ukiyo no Gaka*
   (Tokyo: Chuokoron, 1992), p. 317.
3. Kazuo Ishiguro, *Onna tachi no Toi Natsu*, trans. Ken Onodera (Tokyo: Chikuma
   Shobo, 1984).
4. Shigeo Tobita, 'Translator's Postscript', in Ishiguro, *Ukiyo* (1992), pp. 317–18.
5. Shigeo Tobita, *Honyaku no Giho* [*The Craft of Translation*] (Tokyo: Kenkyusha,
   1997), pp. 115–16. The first two sentences are broken into five short sentences
   in the paperback edition reissued from Hayakawa Publishing in 2006.
6. Ono also tends repeatedly to use the conjunction 'but'. His use of this word
   also elucidates his train of thought, which is locked in the same place. See
   p. 99 of *AFW*, for example.
7. Gregory Mason, 'An Interview with Kazuo Ishiguro', in Brian W. Shaffer and
   Cynthia F. Wong (eds.), *Conversations with Kazuo Ishiguro* (Jackson: University
   Press of Mississippi, 2008), p. 9.
8. Masashi Miura, 'Senchu no Shinnen wo tou [Interrogating his Faith during
   the War]', *Asahi Shimbun*, 4 April 1988, morning edition, 12.

9. Materials relevant to this topic include Masato Miyachi (ed.), *Nihonshi* [*History of Japan*] (Tokyo: Yamakawa Shuppansha, 2008); Yutaka Yoshida, *Asia Taiheiyo senso* [*The War in Asia and the Pacific*] (Tokyo: Iwanami Shoten, 2007); James M. Vardaman, *Nihon gendai shi* [*Contemporary Japanese History since 1945*] (Tokyo: IBC Publishing, 2006); Shinichi Arai, *Senso sekinin ron* [*War Responsibility*] (Tokyo: Iwanami Shoten, 2005); and John Dower, *Embracing Defeat: Japan in the Wake of World War II* (New York: W. W. Norton, 2000).

10. For the collection, see The National Museum of Modern Art, Tokyo, *Catalogue of Collections; Watercolours and Drawings/Calligraphy/Sculpture/Supplementary Materials/War Record Paintings* (Tokyo, 1992). For an article in English, see Kay Itoi and George Wehrfritz, 'Japan's Art of War', *Newsweek*, 4 September 2000, 44–8. In a narrow sense, war record paintings refer to those paintings produced between the first instalment of the Sacred War Art Exhibition in 1939 and the end of the war in 1945. Tano Yasunori and Akihisa Kawata, *Imeji no naka no sensou; from Nisshin/Nichiro kara Reisen made* [*War in Images; Paintings of War from the China-Japan War and the Russia-Japan War to the Cold War*] (Tokyo: Iwanami Shoten, 1996), p. 3.

11. 'Art Exhibition for Returned War Paintings Cancelled', *Asahi Shimbun*, 9 April 1970, evening edition, 10.

12. See 'Taisen wo Kaiko suru', *Sankei Weekly*, 19 August 1956; 'Ushinawareta Sensoga', *Yomiuri Weekly*, 18 August 1967.

13. Shigeo Tobita, 'Translator's Postscript', in Ishiguro, *Ukiyo* (1988), p.285.

6

'cemeteries are no places for young people': children and trauma in the early novels of kazuo ishiguro

caroline bennett

summary

Kazuo Ishiguro's early novels excavate traumas created by war and corruption, and one way of understanding the psycho-social behaviour and internal devastation of the adult characters is by tracing their relationships with children. Adults, such as Etsuko in A Pale View of Hills *(1982) and Ono in* An Artist of the Floating World *(1986), are unwilling to face up to the past and regress and behave like children as a strategic evasion of their responsibilities. This chapter argues that the divisions between their younger and older selves are often blurred, resulting in generational conflicts that can also be seen as an analogy for a post-war global politics in which the presence of the new, dominant power, such as the United States, has an infantilizing effect upon former imperial centres such as Japan and England.*

'all children have to be deceived'

In an interview to promote *Never Let Me Go* (2005) Kazuo Ishiguro stated the following about our relationship to children:

> To some extent at least you have to shield children from what you know and drip-feed information to them. Sometimes that is kindly meant, and sometimes not. When you become a parent, or a teacher, you turn into a manager of this whole system. You become the person controlling the bubble of innocence around a child, regulating it. All children have to be deceived if they are to grow up without trauma.[1]

Yet, rather than being purely innocent, the children in Ishiguro's fictions can often be viewed as troubled projections of the traumatized adult characters. Indeed, whilst his children behave in ways that are closely identified with adult behaviour, adults often behave as children in that they evade any sense that they should exhibit mature responsibility. For instance, the obsession of Boris in *The Unconsoled* with the 'Number Nine' football figure mirrors the recurrent thoughts of Ryder, his putative father, about the sport (*U* 54–7). In *When We Were Orphans*, Christopher Banks uses his magnifying glass to examine a Chinese woman whose leg has just been blown off. This scene is not only gruesome and disturbing, but is also a demonstration of how the detective reverts to childish behaviour when faced with brutal reality (*WWWO* 289). Ishiguro's early novels, in particular, demonstrate the power of the literary imagination to deconstruct archetypal images of adults as wise and 'fallen', and of children as innocent. Children, such as Mariko in *A Pale View of Hills* and Ichiro in *An Artist of the Floating World*, function as retroactive projections triggered by trauma and are constitutive of a self-defence mechanism constructed by adult characters. Conversely, adults such as Sachiko in *A Pale View of Hills* and Ono in *An Artist of the Floating World* regress subconsciously into childish and naïve behaviour in order to persuade themselves of their innocence. Ishiguro stated: 'I'm not aware of making any distinction between children and adults when I'm writing . . . We do not really say goodbye to our childhoods, to our pasts. They haunt us, they determine the way we look at life'.[2] This paradoxical role reversal of intergenerational projections are presented tentatively in *A Pale View of Hills*, but become increasingly visible in *An Artist of the Floating World*. Rather than showing a radical epistemological divide between the child and the adult, these novels suggest that the two roles are bound by degrees of unself-consciousness and knowledge.

'you see how our roles are reversing': *a pale view of hills*

In *A Pale View of Hills* the themes of trauma and adult–child relationships cluster around a small group of characters. Its narrator, Etsuko, is a middle-aged Japanese woman living alone in Surrey, England, who thinks back over the recent suicide of her adult daughter, Keiko. Niki, her surviving younger daughter, is visiting, but wants to get away from her mother as she finds this life and its surroundings restrictive. Etsuko recalls a summer in Nagasaki when she was expecting her first child, thus opening up an inner narrative of retrospection set in Japan in the years after the atomic devastation of 1945. She narrates the story of her life at that time, and that of her 'friend' Sachiko, a single mother with a daughter named Mariko. The subject of the death of Niki's elder sister, Keiko – or more accurately, her suicide – is brought up immediately. In the embedded narration, it is revealed that Etsuko lived in one of four blocks of flats built following the bombing of Nagasaki. Their block marked the end of the post-war rebuilding programme. Beyond lay a stagnant wasteland reaching down to the river (*PVH* 11), representing the limits of redevelopment and civilization.

In the course of narrating Etsuko's 'present' story of Niki and Keiko and her 'past' story of Sachiko and Mariko, there is a small but explosively significant slippage between the two strands. In a critical passage, Etsuko refers to Mariko as if she were her own daughter, as critics have noted.[3] There is therefore a blurring of the outer and inner stories. However, the extent of the narrator's self-deception remains unclear, although it is evident she is capable of deliberate deceit: for example, in concealing Keiko's death from Mrs Waters (*PVH* 51–2). Another blurring of the two narratives occurs when Etsuko mentions that 'Keiko was happy that day' when they went into the hills (*PVH* 182), thus contradicting the previously narrated statement that it was Mariko who was taken on the day out (at a time when Etsuko was still pregnant with Keiko). Etsuko/Sachiko has not been honest with herself, or with the reader, and is masking the truth. Either way, then, she has missed out the largest part of her own story, especially how she became Mrs Sherringham of Surrey. However, it cannot be simply assumed that Mariko/Keiko should be viewed as a victim and Etsuko/Sachiko as an impostor or fraud: both are victims of post-war trauma.

A Pale View of Hills shows Ishiguro already specializing in the psychology of reminiscence. The inner narrative reveals a seamless recollection within a recollection, of how Etsuko met Sachiko, a woman who had fallen on hard times and was living in the only ramshackle cottage remaining by the river. Her isolation and outsider status are symbolized in the landscape. Brian Shaffer provides a Stygian reading of the river across which, in Greek mythology, the souls of the dead were ferried into the underworld.[4] Despite their differences, the women become friends and Etsuko helps Sachiko gain employment in a noodle shop, a job somewhat beneath her station. Mariko is a deeply troubled and insubordinate child. She fights, does not attend school and returns home from days of wandering alone covered in mud. She often goes missing. Yet her mother does nothing to prevent it. Sachiko's ignorance of her daughter's character is revealed when she says that she is convinced Mariko will not venture over the other side of the river. But she does – frequently (*PVH* 38).

On one occasion, there is a heart-stopping moment when Etsuko and Sachiko find Mariko lying prone and they think she is dead. Her eyes have a 'peculiar blankness' (*PVH* 41), and there is a wound on the inside of her thigh that is never explained. She talks about a strange woman, seemingly a harbinger of death, whom Shaffer interprets as someone who is simultaneously to be feared, but also to be sought out.[5] Etsuko presses Mariko on whether she had been with someone, but Sachiko laughs it off. She claims: 'I know my own daughter well enough' (*PVH* 43). But, patently, she does not. She refers to her daughter's 'games' dismissively, yet it is Sachiko herself who is the one who plays games by going out to meet Frank, her American lover, and leaving Mariko alone in the unlit and unheated house for long stretches. Sachiko makes light of her own disappearances and the irresponsibility of her fiancé: 'Sometimes, you see, he's like a little child' (*PVH* 69). Having proposed to take Sachiko and Mariko to America to start a new life, Frank himself then goes missing.

In the outer narration, Etsuko and Niki are uneasy with each other, as is so often the case with Ishiguro's parent–child relationships. Niki cannot bear the thought of being a mother; and, when the conversation turns to unmarried mothers, Etsuko disapproves. However, she jokily accepts her daughter's censure of her time-frittering television habits, saying: 'You see how our roles are reversing, Niki' (*PVH* 49). When an acquaintance enquires ingenuously after Keiko, Etsuko's response – although evasive – gives the impression she is alive and well. The woman's initial mistaking of Niki for Keiko can be neatly wrapped inside Ishiguro's configuration of the interchangeability and doppelgänger-like qualities of the female characters. Niki and her mother are haunted by ghostly feelings, which are representations of guilt (*PVH* 174). On one occasion, when they are both in the kitchen at 5 a.m., unable to sleep, Niki complains that her father should have done more for Keiko, thus suggesting another paren-tal failure (though, in this case, it is a step-parent at fault). Etsuko says she knew it would not work out for Keiko. But Niki defends her, reas-suring her she could have done nothing more. She applauds her mother for taking action, although this is not what Niki herself is doing. She is drifting as her sister had done, extending her childhood and avoiding the responsibilities of adulthood. She objects to 'getting married and having a load of kids' (*PVH* 180). Dreams become significant in the exchanges between mother and daughter. Etsuko relates a dream she has had in which there occurred that most potent symbol of childhood and innocence, a little girl on a swing. However, the connotation of the image is skewed, as the girl is not suspended from a garden swing but is hanging from a noose (*PVH* 96).

There is, then, a significant traumatic voltage that charges the relationships of the two sets of mother-and-child in *A Pale View of Hills*. The subplot of the book develops further the theme of intergenerational conflict. Within the embedded narration, Etsuko is visited by Ogata-San, the father of her husband, Jiro. She enjoys light-hearted conversation with her father-in-law. However, Jiro and his father disagree when they discuss politics, democracy and personal values. Ogata-San attempts to manipulate his son over an issue concerning his teaching reputation. Although he attempts to be controlling and powerful, Ogata-San also has a childish side. One time, as he awaits Jiro's return from work so that they can play chess together, he admits to Etsuko: 'I feel like a small child waiting for his father' (*PVH* 56). The game becomes a symbolic representation of their relationship. On the chessboard, the battle of father versus son is enacted. Despite the appearance of civility, the predetermined moves of the pieces cannot disguise the fact it is a figurative battle to the death. Jiro gives up on the game, only to be accused by his father of childish defeatism and an inability to use strategy. When Jiro sulks, his father states: 'Children become adults but they don't change much' (*PVH* 131). Ogata-San does not realize how provoking he is by childishly insisting on continuing the game, despite the reluctance of Jiro, and by refusing to spare his son's feelings. The next morning Ogata-San criticizes a relative for being an old 'war-lord', oblivious to the irony, as he had effectively belittled his son the previous night (*PVH* 136–7). The elderly man projects his own immature behaviour onto his son.

In a discussion with his daughter about playing the violin, Ogata-San states that nothing you learn as a child is ever completely lost. His comments are also applicable to childhood traumas. However, this notion is undermined by the fact that the music has literally gone out of their lives. This is made clear when Ogata-San picks up the violin and Etsuko describes his playing as 'hideous' (*PVH* 56). Similarly, Etsuko refuses to play as she is hopelessly out of practice. Etsuko notes, jokingly: 'Father's like a child these days' (*PVH* 57); and, later, 'the little child is feeling guilty now' (*PVH* 58). She defuses awkwardness by introducing an affectionate tone of joshing into their dialogues. Etsuko's traumatic wartime experiences are never explicitly detailed, but the events that have traumatized Mariko are revealed indirectly when Sachiko relates a horrific incident in war-torn Tokyo. One night, she and Mariko witnessed a distressed woman drowning her baby in the canal. Her eyes 'didn't seem to actually see anything' (*PVH* 74). They later find out that the woman went on to hang herself. This recalls the dangers associated with Mariko and the child-murders by the river while foreshadowing Keiko's suicide. According to her mother, Mariko now sees the woman from Tokyo everywhere. Sachiko understands that her child is traumatized. Mariko's version of these strange sightings is not conveyed, perhaps because she is incapable of making sense of it, and nobody helps her to articulate her fears. Tension rises with concerns for the neglected and unschooled Mariko whose mother fails her. It may be true, as Sachiko claims, that children 'play at make-believe and get confused where their fantasies begin and end' (*PVH* 75). However, it is the parent, Sachiko, who is the fantasist, as she optimistically places all her hopes in the unreliable drunkard, Frank, and is unable to face the responsibilities of motherhood.

Part Two brings a sense of relief from these tensions with the trip by cable car into the hills of Inasa referred to in the novel's title (*PVH* 99). Even here, though, the troubled relationship between mother and child reveals a latent disturbance. During this day out, Mariko's lack of social skills become evident. She engages in conflict with an irritating boy and hurts him deliberately. Later, Mariko wins a box which she plans to make into a home for her kittens. When Mariko complains because Sachiko will not let her take the box home, she is told by her mother: 'Stop being so childish' (*PVH* 165). Yet her mother is far from mature, as we see when Sachiko later spitefully drowns the kittens. By destroying the only objects of her daughter's affections, she inexplicably and irrevocably condemns her daughter to a world of trauma. Shortly after, Mariko is described as having the expressionless eyes of the woman who drowned her own baby (*PVH* 166). What should have been an innocent day out in the hills has revealed deep tensions in the relationship between mother and daughter.

In the subplot of Part Two, Ogata-San visits Shigeo, author of an article questioning his pre-war teaching record in an educational journal, and the clash of the generations becomes more pointed. Shigeo accuses Ogata-San of promoting dangerous ideologies, and even uses the word 'evil' in relation to the old man (*PVH* 147). The former pupil is more loyal to his principles than to his old teacher. Ogata-San finds this impossible to understand, given that his unexamined cultural belief system derives from a Confucian ideology that champions loyalty to one's superiors as the greatest duty. Shigeo's criticism of the child-like, unquestioning acceptance of authority, which ultimately led to Japan's involvement in the war, suggests that at the time of open Japanese imperialism even adults were expected to be seen and not heard. To have a dissenting opinion was to be disloyal. This traditional creed is anathema to Shigeo, who believes it is what led Japan into the horrors of fascism and war. For an adult to be childishly innocent in the face of atrocity is to turn a blind eye to iniquity.

As we have seen, in psychoanalytic terms *A Pale View of Hills* presents a cornucopia of repressive symptoms such as splitting, dissociation, rationalization and projection. Wong analyses the novel in terms of psychological rupture, referring to Georges Poulet's theory of split selves. She notes that the narrator 'splinters her thinking and feeling selves'.[6] Etsuko represses feelings of guilt at the cruel neglect of her daughter. As it cannot be fully suppressed, the horror she has witnessed eventually forces its way through the flaws and cracks of the story of her 'friend' Sachiko. Etsuko lacks insight into her own impulses and characteristics, and cannot bear to think of herself as the mercenary woman who, in an implied reading, left her husband and ran off to England, thus sacrificing the happiness of her daughter.

'in combat with numerous invisible enemies': an artist of the floating world

The traumas and generational conflicts of *A Pale View of Hills* are pressed further in *An Artist of the Floating World*, a novel that also deals with the aftermath of the Second World War. As the devastated and occupied Japan seeks to rebuild itself, Masuji Ono, a retired and apparently well-known painter, is haunted by memories of his involvement in the rise of Japanese militarism. Like many of Ishiguro's narrators, Ono's apparently calm present is disturbed by nostalgia. Soon the reader becomes aware of the narrator's sinister acquiescence in fascistic ideologies before and during the war.

The four sections of this novel are demarcated by dates starting in October 1948 and ending in June 1950. These sections indicate a narrator writing and reflecting at different moments, and suggest that time may have helped him make some sense of his life and position. Ono, however, protests too much: he portrays himself as innocent, likeable and of good standing in the community, but unconscious slips in his discourse betray him. He starts off his narrative on a high note, recalling how he and his wife took part in an 'auction of prestige' (*AFW* 9) to acquire the house they wanted to buy. He is anxious to point out they had nothing to fear as their background was examined before the sale. In conveying this and other episodes, Ishiguro employs subtle techniques to create the impression of a consciousness that is gathering fragmented memories of the past to form a self-justifying narrative in the present. Yet the task is not easy. Ishiguro shows through this process that memory is not just fissured, but always in flux. In the course of Ono's recollections, the socio-political system of pre-war Japan is criticized, but Ishiguro is keen to avoid presenting his narrators as guiltless functionaries. Instead, he throws light on the individual's role in making up that flawed system and how, in later life, the adult's culpability is displaced by a child-like sense of irresponsibility.

In *An Artist of the Floating World*, Ishiguro charts the disruption of the generations and conflict between their competing ideologies wrought by defeat in the war. Ono's ideology and pride in Japan are no longer permissible in post-1945 Japan. Therefore, there is a collapse of ascribed identities and social hierarchies that involves the creation of a new self-imagining. Survivors of the old dispensation such as Ono are in denial and seek to exculpate themselves from past circumstances, yet lack a sound moral perspective. The Japan of the pre-war years was more sharply contoured and certain about its values. The younger generation's awareness of the expectations of their patriarchal elders is demonstrated by the young, ambitious Ono's response to his father's question regarding his career intentions: 'Your mother, Masuji, seems to be under the impression that you wish to take up painting as a profession. Naturally, she is mistaken in supposing this' (*AFW* 44). The boy feigns agreement. The undertone of latent disapproval, the parental heavy-handedness and casual disregard of his son's wishes speak of a time of subservience. These episodes prove that Ono was expected to be a subservient child. Yet, he refuses to comply, and eventually become an artist. The patriarchal Japanese society is already challenged before its infantilization on the global stage.

Indeed, later Ono does find himself in a position of subservience. His grown-up daughters often refer to him as if he was a child: 'You'll have to take father off my hands a little' (*AFW* 13), says Noriko to Setsuka, implying that he is a burden. When trying to explain why Noriko's marriage plans had fallen through, Ono is defensive and displays a child-like irresponsibility. He tries to rationalize his evasiveness and, in doing so, he exculpates himself. He has delusional tendencies regarding his fame and status as a renowned artist. He wrongly convinces himself that Noriko's suitor pulled out of the first set of marriage negotiations because their family was of too high a status for the groom. In this portrayal of vacillation, Ishiguro shows a sensitive regard for the complexities involved in the ephemeral nature of ideals. The generation that thought their values were timeless has, nonetheless, lived to see their values replaced and reviled.

The grandfather–grandson relationship of Ono and Ichiro is the most developed example of psychological projection in *An Artist of the Floating World*. Ichiro speaks to his grandfather in a manner that his mother thinks will offend. He seems to get his way, however, as he rebuffs the approaches of Ono: 'Can't you see I'm busy' and 'I can't play with you just now!' (*AFW* 29). At play on his own, Ichiro seems to be 'in combat with numerous invisible enemies' (*AFW* 29), just as the grand-father is in combat with others and with his sense of himself. When the elderly man tries to interest the boy in painting, the reader receives the first jolt with regard to assumptions about Ono's past. Ichiro asks his grandfather why he retired from painting, and declares: 'Father says you had to finish. Because Japan lost the war' (*AFW* 32). Ono dismisses this lightly, but then tellingly turns to a blank sheet from the pad, as if this is what he wishes to do with his life. He wants to be free from responsibility for his own actions and from the rules and restrictions laid down by his daughters and son-in-law. Later, the grandfather and grandson discuss going to see a film. In the exchange that follows, the boy says that the film might be too frightening for his grandfather (*AFW* 33). This could be a friendly gibe or it could be that the boy is disguising his own fears, but the two are bound in a juvenile conspiracy against the women, showing their desire for intimacy and solidarity. Yet, Ichiro shows maturity and an enquiring mind, asking awkward questions about why the composer of patriotic songs, Mr Naguchi, killed himself. He looks repeatedly at his reflection in the plate glass window. This hints that the boy is a good deal more reflective than his grandfather (*AFW* 154–5).

In his play time, Ichiro acts out imaginary scenarios as the Lone Ranger, an Americanization of the younger generation that Ono finds distasteful. The Lone Ranger is a clean-living, upstanding character and an icon of American values who never shoots to kill, only to disarm. One of the cowboy hero's most prominent signifiers is his mask, which contributes to a hidden and mysterious identity. Ono, too, assumes a mask – a mask of respectability – to disguise the fact that he is ruffled by his less-than-illustrious past. He is pained by the fact that his grandson does not choose Japanese warriors as his role models. Ichiro's identification with the white Lone Ranger recalls the cross-cultural identification that Frantz Fanon observed amongst young black boys from the Antilles in *Black Skin, White Masks*.[7] The characters of Ishiguro's post-war Japan are not colonial subjects, as such, but are infantilized by American's assumption of parental power after 1945.

Ichiro's behaviour in *An Artist of the Floating World* is a rebellion against the older generation. He does not see himself as subject to patriarchal authority. At the same time, he and his grandfather enjoy a conspiracy against the women whom they belittle, albeit in a jocular way. However, it is the women who succeed in holding sway. In Ono's case, this retreat back to childishness may be the start of a recuperative process. Wong describes Ono as 'resurrecting his former self as a process of self-bereavement, as a way of mourning that lost self'.[8]

Reformulations of identity are difficult, and it is not at all clear that Ono is willing to renegotiate his identity, as this may make a mockery of all that he stood for, did and thought. Ono is struggling to broaden his self-identity to make it elastic enough to accommodate his new situation. His storytelling is a discursive strategy that attempts to redefine his boundaries. It allows him to create a sense of order and coherence, and offers him the chance to test out different subject positions. Ono can be contrasted in this regard with Setsuko's husband who, for all his modern views, is domineering and has a rigid sense of self. He condemns the old Japanese ways, just as Jiro and Shigeo do in *A Pale View of Hills*. Ono is flexible enough to make allowances for this bluntness as he considers what his son-in-law must have suffered in Manchuria (*AFW* 50) during the conflict that followed Japan's invasions into China in the 1930s.

'kind of mental evasion'

Ishiguro's novels are excavations in mental territories which have been ravaged by war and corruption. They examine the psycho-social behaviours that result from such internal devastation. The protagonists of his early novels scratch at the surface of old wounds until they bleed. Trauma lies at the heart of *A Pale View of Hills* and *An Artist of the Floating World*: nowhere more so than in the figures of the children who inhabit the worlds and minds of adults. Conversely, the adults – who have lost their bearings, literally and morally – regress and behave like children as a kind of mental evasion. Their adherence to social minutiae and a culture of conformity temporarily mask the discomforts of moral and political change. Etsuko and Ono are unwilling to face up to the past, but the past has a story to tell, and it always insinuates itself back into the present. They are unreliable narrators, even to themselves: when they excavate their memories, they find them glossed with the patina of denial and forgetfulness. In doing so, the divisions between their younger and older selves are often blurred, and generational conflicts are revealed when they interact with children.

notes

1. Tim Adams, 'For me, England is a mythical place', *Observer*, 20 February 2005, 17.
2. Kazuo Ishiguro and François Gallix, 'Kazuo Ishiguro at the Sorbonne, 20 March 2003', in François Gallix, Vanessa Guignery and Paul Veyret (eds.), *Études Britanniques Contemporaines, Revue de la Société d'Études Anglaises Contemporaines*, 27 (2004), pp. 20, 11.

3. See Barry Lewis, *Kazuo Ishiguro* (Manchester: Manchester University Press, 2000), pp. 34–6; and Cynthia F. Wong, *Kazuo Ishiguro* (Tavistock: Northcote, 2005), p. 31.

4. Brian W. Shaffer, *Kazuo Ishiguro* (Columbia, SC: University of South Carolina Press, 1998), pp. 27–30.

5 Ibid., p. 30.

6. Wong, *Kazuo Ishiguro*, p. 37.

7. Frantz Fanon, *Black Skin, White Masks*, trans. Charles Lam Markmann (New York: Grove Press, 1967), pp. 146–7.

8. Wong, *Kazuo Ishiguro*, p. 43.

part iii
the remains of the day

7

'i can't even say i made my own mistakes': the ethics of genre in kazuo ishiguro's *the remains of the day*

meghan marie hammond

summary

Kazuo Ishiguro's The Remains of the Day *is, simultaneously, a travel narrative and road novel; an autobiography and apologia for a life's work; a struggle with the impulse to lie; a state-of-the-nation novel; a love story and a romance; and, sometimes, a confession. The ageing speaker, Stevens, moves through these various narrative modes in order to make sense of his memories of his days as a butler at Darlington Hall in the years before the Second World War. The tension, and sometimes slippage, between genres reveals Stevens's desire to communicate his life story and justify a lifetime of self-denial and role-playing. His inability to establish a stable narrative logic, however, also spells his failure as a narrator of selfhood. Ishiguro's novel poses a set of challenging questions about the nature and uses of genre in relationship to the ethics of narration. Ultimately, Stevens proves incapable of constructing an acceptable life story or of atoning for his past mistakes because he has passed his life refusing to self-narrate.*

inhabiting roles: mr stevens's narrative agency and atonement

Some critics of Kazuo Ishiguro's *The Remains of the Day* (1989) have been quick to conclude that much of Stevens's story is unconsciously communicated and that the text reveals a repressed emotional past of

95

which Stevens is unaware. Deborah Guth speaks of the 'hidden narratives' that 'dismantle' the tale of professional achievement that Stevens tries to tell and argues that Stevens's love for Miss Kenton can only be read through the 'series of enigmas, gaps, and dislocations' embedded within Stevens's narrative.[1] Kathleen Wall argues that Stevens unintentionally communicates the narrative of his 'fractured subjectivity' through 'verbal patterns or tics'.[2] Bo G. Ekelund explores 'the structural complicity of cultured forms that narrativise and defuse guilt even as they perform the service of exposing it'.[3] James Phelan calls Stevens's examination of his life 'almost unwitting'.[4] He states that the butler does not have 'conscious awareness' of his feelings,[5] and argues that Stevens's misremembering is a 'sign of his repression of feeling'.[6] Such Freudian readings are persuasive but run the risk of reducing Stevens's substantial narrative work to a web of symptoms. To label Stevens's engagement with the painful episodes of his past as unconscious robs him of what little agency he has, while absolving him from responsibility for his part in the infamous history of Darlington Hall.

On the contrary, Stevens is not the unconscious victim of psychic structures of repression, but rather a conscious speaker who has suppressed his emotional life. Ishiguro himself has suggested that the relationship between Stevens and Miss Kenton is about self-denial rather than repression.[7] Stevens is clearly aware that he has spent his life playing a role that strives to mask any traces of non-professional identity, as he demonstrates when he says that a worthy butler has to '*inhabit* his role, utterly and fully' (*RD* 169). For Stevens, the dignified butler can only cease to play his role when he happens to find himself completely alone (*RD* 169).

Stevens's self-knowledge is not so stifled that we must attribute his 'hidden narratives' to a repressed unconscious. In fact, upon his release from the material and mental confines of Darlington Hall, he actively tries to communicate his life story in a way that justifies decades of self-restraint and 'butlerian' role-playing. He wants to explain the events of his life in a way that validates his choices and confirms the correctness of his worldview, which depends on his own understanding of dignity. To this end, when offering explanations for the events of the past, he repeatedly uses phrases like 'demonstrate' (*RD* 25, 40, 70); 'clearly demonstrable' (*RD* 141); 'proved demonstrably' (*RD* 30); 'attributable/ attributed to' (*RD* 4, 15); 'accounts for' (*RD* 122, 169); 'evidence' (*RD* 140, 226); and 'no doubt' (*RD* 48, 66, 96, 121). At times his explanations seem unnecessary or spurious, but no matter what their status, they reveal continuously and subtly Stevens's desire to control his autobiography.

This desire for narrative power contends with the unreliability of his ageing mind, of which Stevens himself is aware. He states, for instance, that he has recently committed some 'small errors' in the course of his duties at Darlington Hall (*RD* 5). Later, his description of his father's descent into old age retrospectively echoes this early passage and prompts Stevens to admit that he cannot trust his own recollections. He recalls that Miss Kenton once confronted him about 'trivial errors' committed by the elder Stevens, saying that though he might once have been a superior butler, 'his powers are now greatly diminished' (*RD* 59). Stevens ends the passage with a correction, conceding that he cannot remember if it was Miss Kenton or Lord Darlington with whom he spoke that day (*RD* 60).

Stevens continues to make such corrections, always with some connection to Miss Kenton. His confusion and apprehension signal unresolved feelings for Miss Kenton and his attempts to order his tangled memory reveal a desire to understand her part in his life, but there is no certain evidence that he does not know that he loves her or that he does not recognize her departure as a personal loss. Stevens's fundamental problem is not his memory, then, nor is it the fact that he has suppressed the unpleasant realities of his life so as to have a more acceptable story – his difficulty is that he does not know *how* to tell that story. Stevens's search for a way to tell his desired story manifests in the shifting modality of his narration. He ultimately fails because he is unable to find the right rules of representation for the task.

The Remains of the Day is the record of a search for the form of telling that will allow Stevens to understand his past, assign value to his years of service and sacrifice, and share his story. His desire to communicate with another person is central to his narrative project, as we see in his concern for his unnamed listener's reception of the story. From the start, he worries about how his words will be interpreted and his actions judged, peppering his speech with references to the clarity of his meaning (*RD* 5) and expressing hopes that his character will not be misunderstood (*RD* 11). His anonymous addressee is another domestic servant, someone familiar with the duties of a butler, whom he addresses only in the confines of his own mind.[8] His particular 'you' shows his need to communicate to a receptive human being who can understand his personal history. Even if the listener is imaginary – just as Ishiguro himself has spoken of his ideal reader as a Norwegian – Stevens's creation of a fellow butler as his ideal reader grants insight into his goal.[9] We must note, however, that his imaginary act here is in fact a product of his *lack* of imagination – he must speak to somebody like himself because he cannot conceive of a receptive listener unlike himself.

Stevens must *create* a listener who mirrors his own mental state because of his social ineptitude and paralyzing difficulty with communication, which is most overtly demonstrated in his inability to banter. He explains that his new American employer, Mr Farraday, expects him to join in friendly banter *(RD* 14). When lodging in Taunton he tries, and fails, to participate in social banter. His response to a joke about the sexual activity of the landlord and his wife waking Stevens in the morning prompts an awkward scene in which he is greeted first with silence and then with pitying laughter *(RD* 130). Stevens is intensely preoccupied by his past and present difficulties with communication, as his continued concern about banter and the memories he shares show.

the narrative modes of *the remains of the day*

The seemingly associative nature of Stevens's verbal output suggests at first glance that he has no narrative resources or techniques at his disposal to plot his story consciously. However, he does have a strategy to answer his desire. He builds this strategy not around plot, but rather around genre. Unused to the role of author, he moves from one narrative mode to another. The first mode he uses to tell his story is that of the travel narrative, which is evoked by the diction of his opening sentence: 'It seems increasingly likely that I really will undertake the expedition that has been preoccupying my imagination' *(RD* 3). Here, 'really will' and 'imagination' posit his trip to the west of England as a journey into an undiscovered landscape, in the manner of Conrad's *Heart of Darkness* (1904). We later learn that he has been inspired by a series of (fictional) travel books called *The Wonder of England,* by Mrs Jane Symons. He explains that after Miss Kenton left Darlington Hall, he took to reading the volume on Devon and Cornwall, from which he gained a sense of the place where Miss Kenton had gone to live after her marriage *(RD* 11–12). News of her separation from her husband leads him back to the 'marvellous descriptions and illustrations' in the travel book, which fuel his excitement to 'actually undertake a motoring trip' to the same region of England *(RD* 12).

As Mr Farraday points out, Stevens has spent his life inside the walls of country homes *(RD* 4). The travel genre – and *The Wonder of England* in particular – has framed his knowledge and experience of the world outside Darlington Hall. Stevens feels that his reading of *The Wonder of England* has granted him some understanding of distant parts of his country and of the absent Miss Kenton. Andrew Teverson claims that Stevens's reading is 'flawed' because it excuses him from exercising his own vision.[10] Stevens, however, is not such a poor reader – he puts Mrs Symons's volume to its intended use by letting it guide his underdeveloped imagination, and he uses the genre's rules of representation to search for narrative stability.

Travel narrative organizes what is unfamiliar and confusing for the reader and presents an ordered product. Stevens adopts the antiquated tone and grand style of the travel books he knows on his journey into unfamiliar country. Speaking of his time in Salisbury, he describes visiting the cathedral eulogized by Mrs Symons in *The Wonder of England*: 'This august building was hardly difficult for me to locate, its looming spire being ever-visible wherever one goes in Salisbury' (*RD* 27). For him, this style produces a 'proper' mode of thinking for his trip, as we see in the first of his exalted descriptions of the English countryside, where he recalls the view from a hill on his first day as 'most marvellous' (*RD* 26). It is this recognition and labelling of the wondrous things he sees that leads him to feel he is fit for the task at hand: he says that it was when he looked out on that view that he started to take on the proper frame of mind for his motoring journey (*RD* 26). That journey is more than a sightseeing trip or professional visit – it is also a figurative journey into his past and the self, as we see when he uses his newly acquired skills as travel narrator to open a discussion of his profession. Returning his attention to the hilltop vista, he claims that the finest English landscapes possess a 'greatness' with which the exciting sights of other countries cannot compete (*RD* 28–9). He continues by rhetorically asking just what this 'greatness' is and where it can be found (*RD* 28). Then, making a sudden turn in his discourse, he says the question of greatness in the landscape is much like the question that has plagued his profession for years: 'what is a "great" butler?' (*RD* 29). Here he uses the appreciation for landscape that he has learned from travel narrative to make a case for greatness. He mistakes his contemplative judgement about the aesthetic qualities of the countryside for objective judgment, and believes that one can say with certainty that Africa is inferior due to its 'unseemly demonstrativeness' (*RD* 29). Similarly, an inferior butler can 'be proved demonstrably' to be lacking in greatness (*RD* 30). According to his logic, then, it follows that the superior butler can be proven to possess that greatness. While he admits the difficulty of finding that proof – anticipating that others will say his attempts to analyse 'greatness' are pointless (*RD* 44) – he nevertheless seeks to do so, unsuccessfully, in his narrative. While his journey does reach its destination, the narrative of his life fails to reach the conclusion he desires with Miss Kenton, and he himself remains unable to achieve the proof of dignity he craves.

Stevens's narrative also operates as 'oratorical autobiography', a form of narrative apologia in which, according to William Howarth, the writer 'pose[s] as an apologist, ready to defend his faith in a system, larger than himself'.[11] Stevens defends his profession, his father and his former employer in an attempt to create a narrative context that legitimates his past. He designs his own schema of the profession, using his father as the model of a butler. He is convinced that his father was, in his prime, 'the embodiment of "dignity"' (*RD* 34). In accordance with the apologetic mode, he offers anecdotal evidence to bolster his claim. He recounts a story in which his father shamed guests of his employer into behaving properly (*RD* 39), and another in which he served the man responsible for his eldest son's death (*RD* 42). He explains that he has corroborated both incidents, and hopes his listener will agree that each paints his father as the personification of 'dignity in keeping with his position' (*RD* 42). Here we see the continual importance of the addressee, who allows Stevens to engage in the defensive mode. He needs this addressee to function as a locus of validation for his narrative. We begin to recognize, however, that his attempts at objective apology may be insufficient when he resorts to defending faith in his beliefs. He closes his defence of his father's greatness, after so much time spent offering evidence, with a weak assertion that with butlers, as with the landscape, 'one simply *knows* one is in the presence of greatness' (*RD* 44).

Despite such forays away from logic, Stevens clings to the apologetic mode throughout his narrative, seeking also to defend his own actions. Although he has a 'wish to explain' (*RD* 50), what he discloses is his stifled emotional life, which he indirectly posits as necessary for the attainment of greatness in his field. After relating a terse scene in which he confronted his father about his waning professional ability, he expresses the fear that his addressee will think he treated the elder Stevens tactlessly. He defends himself, saying he had no option but to treat the situation as he did, and assures his listener that an explanation of the full context will absolve him of any filial disrespect (*RD* 70). The scene with his father occurred as the house prepared to host an informal international conference which, according to Stevens, was the moment when he first showed a capacity for dignity (*RD* 70). He attempts to reveal that capacity in his narrative by showing himself overcoming the difficulty of his father's death on the culminating night of the conference. He recalls that while he was serving drinks downstairs while his father lay in distress, Lord Darlington approached him and said he looked as if he had been crying. He goes on, 'I laughed and taking out a handkerchief, quickly wiped my face. "I'm very sorry sir.

The strains of a hard day"' (*RD* 105). Guth claims that Stevens portrays his past self in a seamless turn from bereavement to serving port, and is unaware of the 'pathos' of his story.[12] However, Stevens is cognizant of his story's emotional weight, and he aims to convey it. As Phelan claims, Stevens's 'report of the other characters' dialogue indicates that he expects his addressee to infer that he has been crying'.[13] He carefully narrates this scene to defend himself as precisely the kind of butler who is able to maintain his dignity in any situation, despite being a caring son underneath.

Stevens's defence of himself is dependent on the successful defence of his master, Lord Darlington. Mapping out his pre-war world, Stevens pronounces that the important debates and decision-making went on behind the closed doors of England's great houses. He describes his world as a wheel, 'revolving with these great houses at the hub, their mighty decisions emanating out to all else' (*RD* 115). Within this system, according to Stevens, one ought to be concerned with the moral status of one's employer (*RD* 114). Thus, it is imperative that he refute the charges of Lord Darlington's anti-Semitism and Nazism with complete authority (*RD* 145). However, his defence of Lord Darlington gradually falls apart and other modes of narrative take its place. He increasingly tempers the apologetic mode with revisions and claims of unquestioning commitment, perhaps in an attempt to escape the apologist's necessary burden of moral responsibility. Eventually, he admits that if a butler is to have any worth, he must stop seeking the perfect employer and simply tell himself that the one he has is noble and worthy of devoted service (*RD* 200–1). He posits this commitment of faith as the proper and logical act of a butler within the world as he understands it: thus, he can say that it is illogical for him to feel any shame or regret (*RD* 201). But he does feel regret and shame, which is why his defensive narrative is peppered with incidents that show him engaging in calculated evasions or lies.

His brief, spoken narratives of denial change as he travels. What starts out as simple rejections of unpleasant truth later evolve into attempts to create alternate truths. He denies having worked for Lord Darlington twice (*RD* 120, 123), and offers no better explanation than he wished to hear no derogatory remarks about his former employer (*RD* 126). These early slips betray little more than a desire to escape the truth. Later, his lies grow into a radical revisioning of his life as a dignified, worthwhile and necessary part of the wheel-structured system (*RD* 115) that he helps maintain. He performs this revisioning by carefully withholding information, using his listeners to help him create the untruth. Stuck in a rural inn with a group of villagers who mistake him for a gentleman, he awkwardly avoids the truth and leaves them to their own conclusions. Asked if he was ever in Parliament, he replies that he concerned himself with foreign policy rather than domestic affairs (*RD* 187). He also boasts that he knew many great men before the war and 'had their ear' on matters of importance (*RD* 188). Here, he voices a creative fantasy that fulfils his ideal of the butler's role. To borrow from Georges Gusdorf's thoughts on embellished autobiography, Stevens 'realizes himself in the unreal'.[14] There are two received narratives: the story of a gentleman, which the villagers hear; and the story of a butler doing his small part, which Stevens hears. When he asserts that he wished to do his part to secure world peace (*RD* 189), he designs a story in which he made a positive difference in society. This story, however, cannot stand against his own increasingly insistent knowledge that Lord Darlington, the centre of his wheel-based system, was a failure.

In trying to understand Miss Kenton's part in his story, Stevens must take an entirely different approach to narrating. For most of the novel, he insists that his relationship with Miss Kenton is strictly professional, which prompts Guth to say that theirs is 'the story of a love which he neither sees nor feels'.[15] However, Stevens is aware of his feelings. As we approach the end of the novel, it becomes increasingly clear that he wants to know exactly where his personal relationship with Miss Kenton went wrong. In this particular quest for evidence, he employs the mode of the romance novel, which first surfaces when we learn that he is secretly a reader of sentimental love stories. He recalls a scene in which Miss Kenton, curious to know what he is reading, prises a book from his hands. Before we discover what he is holding, his tone abruptly shifts: 'suddenly the atmosphere underwent a peculiar change – almost as though the two of us had been suddenly thrust on to some other plane of being altogether' (*RD* 166–7). In order to explain and examine his memories of Miss Kenton, Stevens – who, as far as we know, has never voiced his feelings of love – uses the language of the love stories he has experienced as a reader. He excuses his perusal of such novels as a means of bettering his vocabulary, but also asks why he should not find pleasure in tales of men and women who have romantic affairs and 'express their feelings for each other, often in the most elegant phrases?' (*RD* 168). The otherworldly moment he creates in narrating his confrontation with Miss Kenton is in keeping with such stories.

The experience of the reader is also one of shifting from one plane of being to another, as the atmosphere of the page undergoes an unexpected stylistic change. Stevens uses the romance novel mode to signal the significance of the pantry episode, which he later admits is one of many critical moments that may have put him and Miss Kenton on an 'inevitable course towards what eventually happened' (*RD* 175–6). The outcome was Miss Kenton's marriage, which Stevens describes as far more than a work-related loss (*RD* 171). He reflects that, all those years ago, it seemed that he had all the time in the world to 'sort out the vagaries of one's relationship with Miss Kenton', and he never suspected that 'small incidents would render whole dreams forever irredeemable' (*RD* 179). It is in this romantic departure from his standard tone of professionalism that he attempts to reconcile his past with Miss Kenton and to understand how he failed to voice his feelings. However, when he meets with Miss Kenton again – now Mrs Benn – he can still only access the mode of the sentimental, romantic, love story in his narration and not in actual conversation. Upon learning that she wonders what life they would have had together, he tells her not to let foolish thoughts rob her of deserved happiness (*RD* 240). Yet he confides to the reader, by using a cliché that is typical of the language of the romance novel, that when she spoke 'my heart was breaking' (*RD* 239). He cannot redeem his dreams of love by registering his heartbreak in conversation, and the schism between what he says to Miss Kenton and what he discloses to the reader only serves to prove that, by fulfilling his role as a butler, he silenced the life whose story he would have liked to recount.

As his narrative comes to a close, Stevens speaks in the confessional mode to another butler in Weymouth. Returning to the matter of professional errors, he admits that his time as a great butler is over. He explains that errors have crept into his work, and while they may seem negligible, for him they are fraught with meaning (*RD* 243). What these errors signify is that he can no longer inhabit the role for which he sacrificed the needs of his private life. Stripped of the role he spent so many years building, he realizes the futility of his search for proof of dignity. Bemoaning the fact that he trusted Lord Darlington's poor judgement, he tells his listener, 'I can't even say I made my own mistakes. Really – one has to ask oneself – what dignity is there in that?' (*RD* 243). Stevens confesses with crushing certainty that he did not embody his idea of greatness, even in his prime. His faith in Lord Darlington, around which he structured his worldview, turned out to be misplaced. It is at this point, when every mode of narration has failed to help him constitute himself as the subject he would like to be, that he surrenders to a final mode of speech: banter.

Stevens has no skill for banter and, until the end of his narrative, sees little point in participating in that expected form of speech. Listening to the banter of strangers on the Weymouth pier, however, he decides that it may not be the pointless pursuit he assumed it was. Banter may even hold, he thinks, the 'key to human warmth' (*RD* 245). He ends his narrative by affirming that he will henceforth take up bantering with enthusiasm. He vows to return to Darlington Hall and practise with increased effort while he awaits Mr Farraday's return (*RD* 245), thus hopefully greeting his American employer with the welcome surprise of pleasant banter.

Stevens's surrender to banter is neither a sign of progress nor a desperate attempt to restore normality. Rather, this final decision is the mark of his failure. Before Weymouth, each narrative form he employs is a narrative strategy meant to help him tell his own story. On the pier, however, he understands that the story he wants to tell does not exist. His total commitment to the role of butler has foreclosed the possibility of fulfilling his narrative desires. Banter takes him out of narrative, away from the attempt to tell his story to a listener and, in the process, justify his life. In banter, there is no meaningful teller–listener relationship, only a series of responses meant to elicit mild amusement. What remains of his day is empty dialogue that leaves no room for the narrating subject. Thus, for him, banter is the place of exile from narrative possibility, the place where we locate tragedy in *The Remains of the Day*.

'a palimpsestic private life'

Stevens's exhaustion of the narrative modes available to him (travel narrative, apologia, creative denial, romance novels) comes directly after he admits that even his mistakes were not his own (*RD* 243). Thus, his abandonment of the attempt to tell his own life story comes when he realizes that he did not *live* his own life. His present inability to tell and his past failure to live are inextricably connected, for he allowed his 'butlerian' role to impose upon him the story of a man without his *own* story. Life-long commitment to a profession that requires self-effacement has prevented him from developing the ability to self-narrate that promotes a sense of having led one's own life.

Stevens is exiled from the enacted subjectivity of a traditional novel or autobiography by the fact that he is not the protagonist of his own story and is not a modern subject in his own right. In fact, he fits perfectly Gusdorf's description of pre-modern, and pre-autobiographical, man:

> he does not feel himself to exist outside of others, and still less against others, but very much *with* others in an interdependent existence that asserts its rhythms everywhere in the community. No one is rightful possessor of his life or his death . . . Each man thus appears as the possessor of a role, already performed by the ancestors.[16]

If Gusdorf's understanding of pre-modern man strikes us as naïve, it is nevertheless helpful for understanding Stevens's plight in a rapidly changing society that no longer endorses loyal service to another individual as a legitimate purpose in life. Stevens is incapable of accessing any narrative framework that can help him with the ethical mess he must consider at the end of his days – he has no way to resurrect his long-forfeited capacity for self-narration and self-determination. Ultimately, his narrative efforts cannot undo the fact that he played a minor role in another man's dark biography. He can neither write over the tale of Lord Darlington, nor scrape away his part in it, to reveal a palimpsestic private life hiding underneath. By committing to his role he has inflicted irreparable violence upon himself – he has denied himself personal history.

notes

1. Deborah Guth, 'Submerged Narratives in Kazuo Ishiguro's *The Remains of the Day*', *Forum for Modern Language Studies*, 35 (2) (1999), 126, 132.
2. Kathleen Wall, '*The Remains of the Day* and Its Challenges to Theories of Unreliable Narration', *Journal of Narrative Technique*, 24 (1) (1994), 23.
3. Bo G. Ekelund, 'Misrecognizing History: Complicitous Genres in Kazuo Ishiguro's *The Remains of the Day*', *International Fiction Review*, 32 (1–2) (2005), 70.
4. James Phelan, *Living to Tell About It: A Rhetoric and Ethics of Character Narration* (Ithaca: Cornell University Press, 2005), p. 32.
5. Ibid., p. 35.
6. Phelan, 61.
7. Brian W. Shaffer and Cynthia F. Wong (eds.), *Conversations with Kazuo Ishiguro* (Jackson, MS: University Press of Mississippi, 2008), p. 149.
8. See Karl E. Jirgens, 'Narrator Resartus: Palimpsestic Revelations in Kazuo Ishiguro's *The Remains of the Day*', *Q/W/E/R/T/Y: Arts, Littératures & Civilisations du Monde Anglophone*, 9 (1999), 228. See also Wall, '*The Remains of the Day*', 24.
9. Shaffer and Wong, *Conversations with Kazuo Ishiguro*, pp. 145–6.
10. Andrew Teverson, 'Acts of Reading in Kazuo Ishiguro's *The Remains of the Day*', *Q/W/E/R/T/Y: Arts, Littératures & Civilisations du Monde Anglophone*, 9 (1999), 252–3.
11. William Howarth, 'Some Principles of Autobiography', *New Literary History*, 5 (2) (1974), 370.
12. Guth, 'Submerged Narratives', p. 129.
13. Phelan, *Living to Tell About It*, p. 52.
14. Georges Gusdorf, 'Conditions and Limits of Autobiography,' in James Olney (ed. and trans.), *Autobiography: Essays Theoretical and Critical* (Princeton: Princeton University Press, 1980), p. 43.
15. Guth, 'Submerged Narratives', 131.
16. Gusdorf, 'Conditions and Limits of Autobiography', pp. 29–30.

8

novelistic practice and ethical philosophy in kazuo ishiguro's *the remains of the day* and *never let me go*

lydia r. cooper

summary

Stevens, a butler and the narrator of The Remains of the Day, *and Kathy, a clone created to donate organs and the narrator of* Never Let Me Go, *describe their respective careers as evidence that they have achieved 'dignity'. The narrators directly address the reader, inviting sympathy, but the novels' narrative structures undermine the reader's ability to sympathize as the narratives provide evidence that Stevens and Kathy in fact became complicit in the atrocities committed by their respective societies. These two novels thus suggest that even in the most repressive, autonomy-denying, social systems, every individual still possesses the ethical obligation to stand against inhumanity by practising compassion.*

stevens and kathy as moral agents

In *The Remains of the Day* (1989), the butler Stevens travels to meet his former colleague Miss Kenton in the West Country, but, at the same time, he embarks on a mental journey intended to demonstrate that he has witnessed the 'best' of England and achieved his greatest goal in life: 'dignity' in his position (*RD* 115). Stevens bases these claims on his having served Lord Darlington, an influential gentleman possessed of an 'indisputable moral standard' (*RD* 123). Stevens's memories, however, reveal that Lord Darlington, with his fascist associations and anti-Semitic leanings, was hardly an 'indisputably' moral man. Yet Stevens himself is a sympathetic narrator. His social position places him at the margins of his society and restricts his capacity to express his own opinions or act on his own desires. So when he rhetorically asks, 'What is the point in worrying oneself too much about what one could or could not have done to control the course one's life took?' (*RD* 257), it is tempting to agree with his unspoken conclusion. *Never Let Me Go* (2005) presents a similar protagonist, Kathy H., whose unreliable yet sympathetic narration reveals a woman who is trapped in a system that denies her autonomy. Once more, there is an emphasis upon the importance of recognizing and acting on those few moral choices left open. Kathy H. is also a sympathetic narrator who presents her tale with disarming innocence. For example, she attempts to be humble in recording her life's accomplishments but then admits, 'Okay, maybe I *am* boasting now' (*NLMG* 3). Both Stevens and Kathy offer up their memories as evidence of the respective 'successes' of their lives within autonomy-denying social systems, and foreground that the narrator's capacity to determine his own actions and beliefs is limited. However, their reconstructed memories actually reveal their moral culpability, suggesting that it is precisely within autonomy-denying systems that the smallest choices may become radical expressions of humanity.

Neither Stevens nor Kathy are uncomplicated or simplistically immoral people. They express distress over the immorality of their social systems and yearn to lead meaningful lives worthy of respect. Stevens describes one man's lifelong commitment to dignity, while Kathy demonstrates a consistent desire for human connection. Yet these novels are disturbing precisely because the atrocities in them are not (and perhaps cannot) be named or identified. Both Stevens and Kathy 'boast' about attitudes that, upon closer reflection, indicate a systematic suppression of free will. In an interview, Ishiguro declares that his novels 'are about people who go wrong in life in some way, who take wrong turns in life. . . . And of course you make mistakes or you backed the wrong team; the challenge is all about having the right values in the first place and somehow having the strength of character to stick to them'.[1] So Stevens insists that a butler should not express his views to those with political power. Because he is powerless to change his society, he claims that he has therefore no moral obligation to question its beliefs. Yet his memories suggest that he was not entirely powerless. When Lord Darlington meets with the German ambassador, Ribbentrop, Mr Carpenter criticizes Stevens for watching 'his lordship go over the precipice like that' (*RD* 235). But Stevens insists that he 'trust[s] in his lordship's good judgment' (*RD* 236). He struggles with his dawning realization that Lord Darlington was not worthy of that trust, yet refuses to acknowledge his own complicity in his employer's mistakes. Even at the end of the novel, he insists that 'for the likes of you and me, there is little choice other than to leave our fates, ultimately, in the hands of those great gentlemen at the hub of this world' (*RD* 257). The appeal is unconvincing. His recollections have shown that the butler was a silently consenting participant in Lord Darlington's political machinations.

Kathy in *Never Let Me Go* also provides an incisive example of 'backing the wrong team'. As she recalls her childhood at Hailsham, an experimental school that educated cloned children humanely, she explains that they felt emotions inconsistent with their programmed roles as donors. But the children quashed these human instincts because they felt that having 'such needs' would be 'like somehow . . . letting the side down' (*NLMG* 73). The reader eventually realizes, however, that Kathy's acquiescence in the attitudes imposed on her by her society make her an enabler of the systematic murder of clones for their viable organs. Although in a dehumanizing culture that will ultimately kill her, Kathy nevertheless possesses the capacity to choose to internalize its pernicious attitudes or to reject them. Her narration, like that of Stevens, thereby demonstrates the crucial necessity of moral choices even when the choice itself is limited.

choice in autonomy-denying systems

The novels' argument for the necessity of resisting autonomy-denying social constructs is relevant to post-Holocaust ethical philosophy. In *Eichmann in Jerusalem* (1963), Hannah Arendt discusses the defence of Adolf Eichmann for his war crimes. Eichmann was no pawn but a major architect of the exterminations, yet he insisted that 'under the then existing Nazi legal system he had not done anything wrong'.[2] Blind duty and obedience, however, are dangerous values to uphold when such passive behaviour leads to atrocity. The Holocaust was achieved through the acquiescence of millions of ordinary human beings. The worst atrocities are accomplished by ordinary people who fail to speak out against social constructs and attitudes that create inhuman behaviour. Informed by this dark context, Ishiguro's work acknowledges the capacity of civilized humans and institutions to commit acts of incomprehensible terror, and focuses on particular moments and actions in which ordinary men and women make choices of terrible consequence.

To understand the ethical arguments made by Ishiguro's narrators, it is important to note how the structure of the novels in which they appear unmasks the role of personal responsibility in autonomy-denying systems. Such an emphasis is consistent with the insistence of post-Holocaust ethical philosophy that the individual remains responsible for rejecting unethical social systems. In his memoir about his experiences in Buchenwald, *Literature or Life* (1994), Jorge Semprún defines ethical philosophy as a worldview based on the assumption that 'freedom' is the human capacity to choose between the 'ontological equivalents' of 'Good' or 'Evil'. He defines 'radical Evil' (Kant's term) and its corollary, what he calls 'fraternity', as the respective rejection or practice of empathy.[3] Extreme autonomy-denying systems, like the concentration camps, distil the purest forms of inhumanity. Yet even within those systems, some individuals choose not to internalize the dehumanizing attitudes and instead act out empathetic and loving connections with other people. Thus the worst atrocities and noblest expressions of compassion begin in the smallest decisions. As an example, Semprún opens his memoir by considering the village just outside Buchenwald after the camp's liberation. He claims that he saw the camp as the villagers must have seen it: 'Because they did see the camp, for Christ's sake, they actually did see it, they had to see what was going on, even if they didn't want to know'.[4] According to Semprún, the villagers' ability to see without knowing derives from a radical lack of empathy and an ability to profess ignorance of what was happening inside the camps, even as years of crops died under layers of human ash. However, this lack of empathy outside the camps is juxtaposed with images of an equally radical fraternity within the camp. Semprún refers to the tightly knit group of fellow communists who banded together in the camps. These men practised an empathy so profound that each death was treated like a communal death, and the survivors later felt as if they 'lived for all the dead'.[5] He also describes how a German worker had written 'stucco worker' rather than 'student' on Semprún's intake card, thus sparing his life and acting out of a fraternal interest in another's welfare.[6]

Semprún suggests that, within autonomy-denying systems, all individuals bear a moral responsibility to choose to perceive and act upon the recognition of one's shared humanity with others. Not to do so is an ethical failure. It is a failure that Ishiguro's narrators reveal through their retrospective stories. Both *The Remains of the Day* and *Never Let Me Go* suggest that small withdrawals from responsibility can be radically inhumane actions. The only hope of redemption lies in 'fraternity', or what Stevens calls 'human warmth' (*RD* 245). He cites the loss of other 'fellows' – other butlers in great houses, people with whom he may have been able to create a fragile web of communication – as one of the causes for his inability to learn the art of light-hearted bantering (*RD* 17). At the end of the novel, Stevens overhears young couples bantering and wonders at their ability to create 'such warmth among themselves' (*RD* 257). His belated recognition of the value of 'warmth' contrasts with his lifelong commitment to dignity or doing one's duty without question, with 'calmness' and 'restraint' (*RD* 29). This even leads him to neglect his dying father and reject Miss Kenton's proffered love. His mistake, then, is that he 'backs the wrong team' by choosing dignity, with its requisite isolation and self-negation, over human fraternity.

Stevens and Kathy do not set out to become complicit in atrocity. Rather, since they have both arrived in the 'twilight' years of their lives, the impetus behind their narratives is to demonstrate that they have achieved 'dignity' and accomplished their work 'well' (*RD* 33; *NLMG* 3). Because both narrators deliver their texts with a confessional urgency, a careful examination of their explicitly defined audiences of sympathetic peers becomes critical to any interpretation of the novels' ethical philosophy. Readers who acknowledge the gulf between the values these narrators cling to and the reality they ignore can sympathize with them, whilst at the same time withhold approbation.

'obdurate blindness'

Adam Parkes proposes the idea that *The Remains of the Day* actually sets up two audiences. The first is a 'sympathetic, imaginary "you"' whom Stevens addresses, whilst the second audience comprises the readers of the novel, who are distanced from Stevens by recognizing the ironic gaps between memory and reality.[7] In other words, Stevens holds up his introspective narrative like a mirror, but that mirror permits Stevens only a distorted realization of what the reader sees clearly: that the dignity on which Stevens has based his life is 'hollow'.[8] It also becomes increasingly clear to the reader that the butler remains unaware of the ways in which his own life has failed. Stevens consistently presents memories that are supposed to support his self-valuations, but which in fact contradict them. For example, he defines 'dignity' as a quality of containment and internal quietude that, he says, gives 'we English' an 'important advantage over foreigners' (*RD* 44). His nationalistic assertion is troublingly naïve. He ignores evidence that qualities like 'dignity' and 'greatness' cannot be defined in simplistic nationalistic terms, yet he asserts that great butlers are by and large all 'Englishmen' (*RD* 44). The butler is blind to the racism lurking beneath such a sentiment.

Kathy, on the other hand, seems more self-aware than Stevens of the dualism between her experienced reality and that perceived by outside observers. Her emotional response to the revelation that she and the other Hailsham students are clones is that it was like 'walking past a mirror you've walked past every day of your life, and suddenly it shows you something else' (*NLMG* 36). However, Kathy's glimpse of external reality – the 'something else' – is limited. She continues to address only an audience of clones, peers who judge her life's value by the familiar rather than the unfamiliar image. Because of this short-sightedness, Kathy's remarks about her success as a carer sound empty by the end of the novel, much like Stevens's boasting. Kathy makes a final journey to Norfolk, after hearing that Tommy has died, but she claims 'I wasn't after anything in particular' (*NLMG* 281). This is disingenuous. She imagines seeing Tommy, who has been lost to her, coming through the mist and raising his hand in greeting. Kathy refuses to acknowledge the depth of her grief and that the real reason for going to Norfolk is to mourn Tommy. Like Stevens, then, Kathy's narrative creates two audiences: her imagined sympathetic audience, and the readers who note the widening gap between what she admits and all that she does not admit.

Parkes claims that Stevens's 'obdurate blindness' to his own failure is the unexplained 'deeper mystery' of *The Remains of the Day*.[9] However, the gaps between self-awareness and reality in both novels demand explanation. The novels' confessional technique compels readers to associate themselves with the 'you' that the narrators address. For example, Stevens presents his argument that he has achieved 'dignity' to a 'you' whom he compares to himself: 'the likes of you and I will never be in a position to comprehend the great affairs of today's world' (*RD* 211). Stevens assumes that his audience is a servant lacking autonomy like himself, yet, given that the novel sets up an elegiac image of an almost-disappeared world of 'Great Houses', it seems rather foolish of him to assume his audience is truly *like* him. In the same way, Kathy addresses herself to a 'you' whom she identifies as peers raised in another boarding school: 'I don't know how it was where you were' (*NLMG* 13) is a typical statement. Her boarding school programme, readers later discover, is a holding place for clones. So when Stevens addresses a servant-class 'you', and Kathy addresses an audience of fellow clones, the implied reader is imagined incorrectly.

While the imagined audiences of the narrations of Stevens and Kathy are not cognate with their actual audiences, the novels nevertheless presuppose that readers will be able to relate to the social systems in which Stevens and Kathy exist. In an interview, Ishiguro says that Stevens's assumptions about his life are 'slightly absurd and sad, but nevertheless there is . . . a shred of sound logic there. . . . I think that's what most of us do to dignify what we do in life'.[10] But, if 'most of us' can relate to Stevens and Kathy to some extent, then readers must know how to interpret accurately their narrative arguments. In particular, readers must follow how the dual audience construction works in order to adjudicate their pity appropriately. Both Stevens and Kathy demonstrate that they are complicit in the unethical systems, but their complicity derives from a fundamental empathetic failure. Stevens fails to act out compassion towards his fellow human beings, like the Jewish maids whom he fires without protest and like Miss Kenton and his father, whose tentative offers of affection he rejects. Kathy is both more compassionate and more acute in her perceptions, but she still fails tragically when she accepts her society's devaluation of her own humanity. The novels thus demand their audience's compassion and pity even as they require audiences to distance themselves from the self-deluded narrators. Stevens and Kathy aver that 'dignity' means accepting their own lack of autonomy, but both of their narratives are haunted by glimpses of a radical empathy that could undermine this very system.

Stevens and Kathy, in fact, present flawed arguments. Because they do not fully acknowledge the pernicious nature of their respective societies, their pride in fulfilling their proscribed roles is both tragic and troubling. Stevens ultimately denies his own culpability because he refuses to admit his role as an agent. He claims that he (and his imagined audience of fellow servants) will never understand the political machinations of the world around them, and, by extrapolation, therefore cannot be moral arbiters. However, Stevens's justifications are weak. For example, when he 'defends' Darlington's firing of the Jewish maids, he attempts to underscore his lack of autonomy by claiming that neither he nor Miss Kenton are in a position to understand – or to do – anything about their master's decree. Yet Miss Kenton does object, although she does not do anything about her concerns. Later she expresses regret over her compliance: 'Had I been anyone worthy of any respect at all, I dare say I would have left Darlington Hall long ago' (*RD* 161). Miss Kenton, in other words, may have limited autonomy, but she understands her complicity and is able to identify immorality and reject its corrosive attitudes.

Stevens concludes his memories by describing a triumphant night, the 'summary of all that I had come to achieve thus far in my life' (*RD* 239). Yet on the night in question, he has emotionally wounded the woman who loved him in order to stand silent while his master, Lord Darlington, furthered his policy of appeasement with Ribbentrop and the Nazi regime. Stevens's feeling of 'triumph' in fulfilling his role is disturbing. The ethical implications of Kathy's narrative are more subtle. She takes pride in her role as a 'carer' for 'donors' and begins her narrative by outlining how well she does her job (*NLMG* 3). Her acceptance of that role, however, is undermined by the recurring image of Tommy throwing a tantrum in defiance of his fate: 'raging, shouting, flinging his fists and kicking out' (*NLMG* 269). Indeed, Kathy's first recorded memory of her childhood at Hailsham is tainted by violence and complicity. When Tommy is goaded by bullies, Kathy and a few other girls stand around and watch. She feels an urge to 'do something', but since none of the girls standing around her move, she remains silent. They felt, she says, that 'whether we approved or not didn't come into it' (*NLMG* 7). Like the girls, Tommy is incapable of actually preventing his future death or successfully changing the inhumane world in which he lives, but at least he voices his disapproval. Tommy's tantrums are implicit rejections of the role to which he has been condemned and indicate an important level of autonomy. But the agency represented by Tommy's rages and Miss Kenton's guilt are overshadowed by Kathy's and Stevens's firm declarations of innocence. According to Stevens, Miss Kenton had nothing to feel guilty about, just as Kathy regards Tommy's rages with an almost embarrassed incomprehension.

'a warmer light': *anagnorisis* and moral choices

Although it is tempting for readers to identify with Ishiguro's narrators and with their interpretations of their own roles in society, the novels are structured in such a way that readers discern the flaws in their arguments. Both novels lay bare the narrators' failure to own up to their own ethical obligation to reject the dangerous attitudes of a repressive society. Moreover, both novels employ a systematic symbolism of light and dark, derived from classic Aristotelian poetics in which *anagnorisis* figures as a moment of insight or self-recognition that matches the narrators' good and bad moral choices. Moments of choice by Stevens or Kathy are often associated with a marked presence or absence of light. Stevens's memories of Miss Kenton are of her standing in some form of illumination, from her lighted parlour to sunlit windows. Stevens may have limited autonomy, but the light/dark imagery suggests that the butler has enough autonomy to choose between the small choices available to him. Stevens rejects the 'light' Miss Kenton offers, both in terms of her personal approaches to him and her moral reactions to Darlington's anti-Semitism. In believing himself to be entirely powerless, Stevens abdicates moral responsibility and so becomes ethically guilty of all that he does *not* do.

Stevens makes repeated claims that his social position required him to abdicate responsibility for his actions and to defer to his master's commands. This argument reaches an apex when he engages in a heated debate with the left-leaning Mr Harry Smith while staying at the Taylors' house. Their discussion takes place around a dining table lit by the 'low yellow light' of an oil lamp. Mr Taylor remarks that this is 'a warmer light' than that given by an electric lamp (*RD* 190). But Stevens isolates himself ideologically from the literal and metaphysical warmth of the

homely and intimate scene. The butler is pretending to be a gentleman
and he ratchets up his play-acting by insinuating to Smith that he played
an active role in politics during the years leading up to the Second
World War. Ironically, Smith assumes that Stevens is an aristocrat, and
so argues that dignity – which he defines in terms of autonomy – must
be available to all people. Stevens disagrees and states his belief that
dignity-as-autonomy is reserved for the upper classes, whilst for the
lower classes dignity means behaving 'in keeping with my position' (*RD*
233). Stevens finally escapes the awkward situation for the 'sanctuary' of
his room above (*RD* 203), a term that reminds us of his butler's pantry
at Darlington Hall. In her 'invasion' of his private space, Miss Kenton
castigates Stevens for reading by the light of an 'electric bulb' and claims
that the scene puts her in mind of 'condemned men spending their last
hours' in solitude (*RD* 174). So the artificial light in the butler's pantry is
linked with Stevens's isolation at the Taylors' house. In both instances,
Stevens's alienation is both unnecessary and unwise.

   In his final analysis of his life's success, Stevens questions the price
of remaining aloof. He stares into a gathering darkness that symbolizes
his loneliness and, perhaps, his blindness to the truly valuable aspects
of life. At the beginning of the novel, he describes Darlington Hall as
if it were a microcosm of the larger world. He argues that by being part
of this country house he has functioned as an 'insider' in the larger
machinations of the empire (*RD* 123). But that initial image dissolves as
the narrative's perspective widens with each retelling and Stevens's gaze
narrows. At last, Stevens reveals that he is nothing more than an exile
in both his own country and his own language. The butler, after understanding how much his lost autonomy has cost him, begins for the
first time to comprehend his own absolute alienation. And, with that
glimmer of knowledge, he sits in the darkening evening of Weymouth
pier. As the lamps come on, he feels that he must learn to speak all over
again, mastering a whole new form of language, namely bantering (*RD*
251–2).

   Stevens's role as an outsider effectively positions him in metaphorical
darkness. His attraction to light and to language at the end of the novel
suggests some measure of growing self-knowledge, but previously he
has demonstrated little awareness of any inconsistencies or contradictions in his perceived reality. Throughout the novel, his gaze is consistently narrowed until it focuses on Miss Kenton in 'the pool of grey
light' in the hotel's parlour (*RD* 244). Significantly, he comes closest
to breaking with his sense of dignity (an absolute denial of autonomy)
when he speaks with Miss Kenton: she is in a lighted room, he is standing in the doorway. When he rejects her, she shuts the door, leaving

him in a darkened corridor (*RD* 236). He spends the rest of the evening in literal darkness as he stands under an unlit arch at Lord Darlington's command. He remains in the dark, both literally and metaphorically.

Never Let Me Go also undermines Kathy's assertions of powerlessness through light and dark imagery. The novel consistently depicts the twin perceptions of the clones – as human and inhuman – through descriptions of light and dark, so that those moments – when Kathy is given a choice to either accept or reject her own humanity – are metaphorically illuminated. Light is associated with the humanity of the clones and darkness with their inhumanity. For example, early in the novel, Kathy describes how Madame would shudder when she brushed against one of the children on her infrequent visits to the school. The children felt as if 'we'd walked from the sun into chilly shade' (*NLMG* 35). The reality of the social system in which Kathy and the other cloned children exist is consistently associated with darkness and the 'dark and troubling' truth Tommy intuits (*NLMG* 35, 192). Near the end of the novel, Kathy, in her role as carer, deviates from a proscribed schedule in order to take her post-operative friends, Tommy and Ruth, to see an old beached boat. This scene is described in familiar light and dark imagery. The three stumble through a 'quite dark' wood until they come into an open marshland where a beached boat lies in 'weak sun' (*NLMG* 219, 220). Hailsham, originally created to prove that cloned children were capable of producing art and therefore had souls, has been shut down. Tommy claims that the frail sunlit boat reminds him of the wreck of the idealistic school (*NLMG* 220–1). Ruth, who is dying after her second 'donation', ends their idyllic moment by recalling them to the present with a reference to her frail state. Her frailty, however, is not a problem to her, but merely a fact. 'After all', she points out, 'it's [donations] what we're *supposed* to be doing, isn't it?' (*NLMG* 223). While no one voices an objection, Tommy, the only one to protest actively against their identity as organ-donors, remains for a moment staring at the boat, shading his eyes from the sunlight. Kathy's memories consistently illuminate minor attitudes and moments of resistance, indicating that she and the other clones have, at the very least, the autonomy to embrace their own humanity and to mourn their inevitable deaths.

The song that gives the novel its title, 'Never Let Me Go', symbolizes for the young Kathy a world of human intimacy and love. She plays it and dances in a shaft of light, holding a pillow that she imagines as the baby she will never have. Unknown to her, Madame stands in a dark hall and watches the child dancing in sunlight (*NLMG* 71). Later, Madame tells Kathy that she cried because she saw 'a little girl . . . holding to her breast the old kind world, . . . and pleading [with it], never to let her go' (*NLMG* 266). Yet Madame chose not to act on this recognition of Kathy's humanity. According to Madame, the purpose of Hailsham was to raise clones whose behaviour and sophistication would permit the outside world to view them as 'human', to '*prove you had souls*' (*NLMG* 255). Since Hailsham has been shut down, it is clear that the novel's clone-dependent society, like Madame, has decided to dismiss Kathy's humanity.

After they leave Madame, Kathy and Tommy drive down a dark road. Kathy imagines that the road 'existed just for the likes of us [clones], while the big glittering motorways with their huge signs and super cafés were for everyone else' (*NLMG* 267). Kathy's division of the dark and light precedes Tommy's tantrum. At his request, Kathy stops the car while Tommy gets out and walks into the darkness. Kathy, following him, finds him screaming in a field. She sees 'his face in the moonlight, caked in mud and distorted with fury' (*NLMG* 269). She calms him down and, for a brief moment, they hold onto each other 'because that was the only way to stop us being swept away into the night' (*NLMG* 269). However, after a few moments, they release each other and head down the 'dark road' towards the hospital centre where Tommy will soon be killed (*NLMG* 270). In this moment of fury and desperate love, Kathy and Tommy act out their own humanity, but they are forced to let each other go and be swallowed by the darkness.

In *Literature or Life*, Semprún claims that the essential experience of the Holocaust was a 'dark, shining truth: . . . the darkness that has fallen to our lot, throughout all eternity'.[11] The 'darkness' is the inescapable conclusion that all humanity is capable of such atrocity. Such situations are created by people who are not evil but, rather, are obedient to the attitudes and duties of evil systems. Both Stevens and Kathy exist in oppressive social systems and, for the most part, they are denied physical agency. The 'dark, shining truth' of these novels is that Stevens and Kathy are not, in the final analysis, entirely devoid of agency. Both narrators insist that they have done the best they could within systems that denied them autonomy. As marginalized individuals operating inside oppressive social systems, the narrators ask for and deserve readers' sympathy. But when Kathy and Stevens insist that they achieved 'dignity' through internalizing the attitudes of their social systems, they change from being objects of pity to being cautionary figures warning against the banality of complicity. Kathy ends her narrative imagining Tommy coming back from the dead, but quickly adds that, while she was crying, she 'wasn't . . . out of control' (*NLMG* 282). Her sense of dignity, like Stevens's, derives from her repression of her own autonomy, and, in this novel, literally her own sense of humanity. For this reason, Kathy's 'boastful' narrative fails to win its audience's approbation. Tommy's momentary crazed rage offers audiences a glimmer of hope because his fury suggests that, while the clones may not be able to control their physical destiny, they can control their emotional response. *The Remains of the Day* similarly undermines its narrator's argument by suggesting that an ethical reader cannot and should not take Stevens at his word. Stevens asks his audience to join him in his 'sense of triumph' at his life's accomplishments (*RD* 115). But he concludes his mental and physical journey weeping on a pier: 'What dignity is there in that?' (*RD* 256). In this heartbreaking question, readers recognize Stevens's crucial failure to value the 'warmth' of human connection as opposed to the 'dignity' of obedience to a morally corrupt social system.[12] In both novels, what the narrators fear above all is the indignity of raw human interaction, which Stevens pictures in terms of taking off one's clothes and which Kathy pictures in Tommy's rage. If such radical empathy is undignified, it is, paradoxically, also the only source of salvation of humanity in these darkly postmodern and, in *Never Let me Go*, post-human worlds.

notes

1. Cynthia F. Wong, 'Like Idealism to the Intellect: An Interview with Kazuo Ishiguro', *CLIO: A Journal of Literature, History, and the Philosophy of History*, 30 (3) (Spring 2001), 318.
2. Hannah Arendt, *Eichmann in Jerusalem* (London: Faber, 1963), p. 18.
3. Jorge Semprún, *Literature or Life* (London: Viking, 1997), pp. 89, 55. Originally published in 1994 in Paris by Gallimard as *L'Ecriture ou la vie*.
4. Semprún, *Literature*, p. 140.
5. Semprún, *Literature*, p. 122.
6. Ibid., pp. 289–303.
7. Adam Parkes, *The Remains of the Day: A Reader's Guide* (New York: Continuum, 2001), p. 41.
8. Ibid., p. 38.
9. Ibid., p. 41.
10. Brian W. Shaffer, 'An Interview with Kazuo Ishiguro', *Contemporary Literature*, 42 (1) (2001), p. 5.
11. Semprún, *Literature*, p. 88.
12. For other essays that discuss issues connected with Stevens and self-deception, see R. Atkinson, 'How the Butler Was Made To Do It. The Perverted Professionalism of *The Remains of the Day*', *Yale Law Journal*, 10 (1995), 177–220; and A. Z. Newton, 'Telling Others: Secrecy and Recognition in Dickens, Barnes and Ishiguro', in Adam Zachary Newton, *Narrative Ethics* (Cambridge, MS: Harvard University Press, 1997), 241–85.

9
kazuo ishiguro's *the remains of the day*: working through england's traumatic past as a critique of thatcherism

christine berberich

summary

Ishiguro's The Remains of the Day *examines the appeasement politics pursued by Britain in the 1930s and the popular support for the German and Italian fascists amongst the aristocracy. It does so with the benefit of a hindsight denied to Nancy Mitford and P. G. Wodehouse, who dealt with these trends in their fiction at a time much closer to the events they describe. Ishiguro uses his temporal advantage to present a subtle analysis of how appeasement flourished not just because of the active involvement of key players in large country houses, such as Lord Darlington, but also because of the passive acquiescence of the general populace, such as Stevens. Ishiguro's novel can also be read as a critique of mythologies about Englishness and how they operated in Thatcher's Britain of the 1980s.*

'we didn't know about buchenwald': british fascism and literary responses

The Remains of the Day (1989) could be taken as a celebration of England and its past 'Greatness'. It seems to foreground quintessential signifiers of Englishness: the nation's green and pleasant land, the country house with its mythical inhabitants, the upper-class lord and the duty-bound butler. A closer reading reveals that Ishiguro brings to the fore a dark chapter in British history: the involvement of the upper classes in pre-Second World War appeasement politics and the active collaboration of some members of the British upper classes with the German Nazis. The text raises painful, but necessary, questions about the nature of Englishness and its supposedly glorious past. It establishes *Vergangenheitsbewältigung* (a German term denoting the therapeutic process of 'working through' that allows the national psyche to come to terms with collective trauma). But the exploration of fascism contains also a cautionary subtext that criticizes and warns against the dangerous social and moral regression enacted by the Thatcherite celebration of Englishness and Victorian moral values and its refusal to acknowledge the nation's darker life of the mind.

The history and politics of twentieth-century British fascism in the 1930s centres on the founder and leader of the British Union of Fascists (BUF), Sir Oswald Mosley (1896–1980), who dabbled in politics from an early age. He was elected to Parliament as a representative of the Conservative Party in 1918, but crossed the floor and supported the Independent Labour Party in the 1920s. He resigned from Labour in 1930 and, a year later, founded the New Party. This was initially described as 'an uneasy truce between "a Socialism which is vestigial and a fascism which is incipient"'.[1] In 1932, after a tour of Mussolini's Italy, Mosley decided to model his party on the Italian example and unite the New Party with the already existing British fascist parties under the new name of the British Union of Fascists, with him as their acknowledged leader. The party gained much support, from key political figures of the future such as Aneurin Bevan and Harold Macmillan, as well as newspapers such as the *Daily Mail* and *Daily Mirror*. It attracted 50,000 members from the general public. It also gained the support of influential intellectuals, such as the writer Henry Williamson (1895–1970) and the military theorist J. F. C. Fuller (1878–1966). Mosley established a paramilitary protection corps that became infamous under the name of the 'Blackshirts'. Although created to protect Mosley and his party officials, the Blackshirts gained notoriety by instigating brawls and riots, especially with communists and Jewish groups. At their Olympia Rally in 1934, a mass riot broke out after Blackshirts forcibly removed hecklers, an action that lost the BUF most of its public sympathy. The party was unable to stand in the 1935 election. In 1936, Mosley and his Blackshirts tried to march through London's East End, an area in which the population was largely Jewish, but they were blocked by protesters drawn locally and nationally. In 1940, Mosley was arrested and spent the rest of the war in a private house in the grounds of Holloway Prison. After the war, he attempted to revive his political career but never drew substantial support. In the BBC's 2006 History Magazine poll, he was voted the 'Worst Briton'.

British sympathies for the German and Italian fascists (which led to imitation and, in some cases, collaboration) have been a fascinating topic for writers since the 1920s. Aldous Huxley's *Point Counter Point* (1928) stages a Mosley-like protagonist, Everard Webley, who forms a group of fascists, the Brotherhood of British Freemen. H. G. Wells's *The Holy Terror* (1939) analyses the psychology of modern dictators. In Elizabeth Bowen's classic wartime novel *The Heat of the Day* (1949) the soldier Robert Kelway is a fascist traitor passing on sensitive information to the Germans.

Two examples of novels that responded to British fascist sympathies in a comic mode are Nancy Mitford's *Wigs on the Green* (1934)[2] and P. G. Wodehouse's *The Code of the Woosters* (1937).[3] Mitford (1904–73) is mainly known as a middlebrow writer of romantic novels such as *The Pursuit of Love* (1945) and *Love in a Cold Climate* (1949). She also gained fame with *Noblesse Oblige* (1956), a satirical essay collection in which she analysed the difference between upper class and non-upper class use of language by coining the phrases 'U' and 'non-U' speak. Mitford's aristocratic family connections are important in this context. Her sister Diana became Mosley's second wife during a secret ceremony held in the private Berlin residence of Joseph Goebbels, at which Hitler was present.[4] She used her contacts to establish links between the BUF and the Nazis. Another sister, Unity, was a fanatical Nazi and fervent admirer of Hitler. It has even been alleged that she was his mistress and bore him a child.[5] Whatever the truth of this, she lived in Germany throughout the 1930s in close proximity to Hitler. Although Nancy became a staunch supporter of the socialist cause, she was intimately acquainted with British fascism through her sisters Diana and Unity. She attended Blackshirt meetings in 1934, including the infamous Olympia rally. This led her to state: 'I remember Prod [her husband Peter Rodd] looked so pretty in a black shirt'.[6]

In *Wigs on the Green* Unity appears thinly disguised as Eugenia Malmains, the wealthy daughter of a local Gloucestershire squire whose Fascist sympathies clash with local pacifists. Eugenia, an ardent supporter of 'the Colonel' (a figure modelled on Mosley), spends her time shouting fascist slogans and racial abuse on the village green: 'do you want your streets to run with blood, your wives to be violated and your children burnt to death? No? Then join the Union Jack defenders here and now – '.[7] Mitford satirizes the fact that there is nothing at risk in the rural idyll of Chalford. Eugenia denounces her own old Nanny as an 'enemy', labelling her 'a filthy Pacifist' in charge of a 'yellow razor gang'.[8] Mitford's novel suggests that much of British fascism originated in political naivety and the boredom of the aristocracy, and that some characteristics of the English identity are dangerous in their ambivalence. A statement made by Jasper, Eugenia's socialite adherent, emphasizes this: 'Thank God for our English eccentrics'.[9] The statement also shows that Eugenia's political struggle is not necessarily taken seriously, even by her supporters. Although *Wigs on the Green* is deemed a 'timely parody of Fascism and the British Unionist Party',[10] some consider the novel to be unaware of the threat of fascism. Mitford parodies fascists and fascism, but this strategy is also in danger of reducing them to a joke. In a post-war letter to Evelyn Waugh she admitted that 'we were young & high-spirited then & didn't know about Buchenwald' – rhetoric which echoed the excuses of German citizens after the war.[11]

P. G. Wodehouse created a parody of Mosley and the BUF in Sir Roderick Spode and the Movement of the British Black Shorts, which appeared in the Totleigh Towers saga. The first instalment, *The Code of the Woosters* (1938), contains many parodic descriptions of Spode and his Movement:

> 'Don't you ever read the papers? Roderick Spode is the founder and head of the Saviours of Britain, a Fascist organization better known as the Black Shorts. . . . 'Well, I'm dashed! I thought he was something of that sort. That chin . . . Those eyes . . . And, for the matter of that, that moustache. By the way, when you say 'shorts', you mean 'shirts', of course.' 'No. By the time Spode formed his association, there were no shirts left. He and his adherents wear black shorts.'[12]

Spode is depicted as a cowardly bully who tries to intimidate by sheer brute force whenever he can. Wodehouse had no sympathies for the Fascist movement. He goes further than Mitford's simple and potentially politically naïve ridicule. Wodehouse's portrayal of Spode is a full-blown satire that exposes its bullish fascist villain to potential social ruination. Jeeves, the butler who is a precursor of Mr Stevens, reveals to his master Bertie Wooster that Spode leads a secret life as 'Eulalie', founder and designer of a luxurious range of ladies' underwear.[13]

the remains of the day as analysis of british appeasement politics

Whereas Mitford and Wodehouse were writing in the midst of events, Ishiguro had the benefit of political and historical hindsight when writing *The Remains of the Day*. He used this temporal advantage to assess critically British appeasement during the interbellum in Britain. This culminated in Prime Minister Neville Chamberlain's signing of the Munich Agreement (1938). 'Appeasement' developed 'out of fears, anxieties and misplaced optimism',[14] but it had its origins in diverse movements. There was a great surge of economically motivated pacifist sentiment that followed the Great War. There was also a strand of 'social appeasement', which often emerged among members of the upper classes who were not normally politically active but who now felt threatened by radical social changes.[15] Many members of the aristocracy longed for a strong leader to take Britain back to her former imperial glory, but there was also the sense that the Versailles Treaty went against England's perceived principles of fair play. Among the early visitors to Darlington Hall is John Maynard Keynes (*RD* 74), one of the financial advisors at the Versailles Treaty who warned that German reparation payments were too high and might result in economic crisis and potential new conflict.[16] Lord Darlington notes that, traditionally, Britain did not treat the enemies it had defeated in battle so harshly (*RD* 71). He refers to traditional – though, at this point, rather obsolete – notions of gentlemanliness, honour and, potentially, *noblesse oblige*. He considers it his honour as a gentleman not to punish a defeated foe more than is necessary. This is reinforced when Darlington explains to Lewis that his position is specifically English: 'Most of us in England find the present French attitude despicable. You may indeed call it a temperamental difference, but I venture we are talking about something rather more' (*RD* 87). Lord Darlington feels impelled to stand up for the rights of Germany and its people out of a liberal reflex that leans towards appeasement. It eventually leads, however, to his involvement with the Nazis and fascists. His optimistic misjudgement of those regimes seals his political fate and turns him into an open anti-Semite.

The subtle trajectory of the novel's play with information and narration suggests precisely how the process of appeasement was able to regress into collaboration with the Nazis. It is Stevens's narration which forms a barrier between the reader and Lord Darlington. The truth about his employer is only gradually revealed and adds another layer to Ishiguro's analysis of British collusion with the Nazis. Whereas Lord Darlington is an easy target, Stevens's slippery narrative suggests a more subtle and malign parallel between fascism and the British tradition of relying too much upon social and cultural behaviour and discursive and linguistic strategies and coding.

At the outset Stevens gives us the archetypal image of the eccentric Lord: 'his lordship was persuaded to overcome his more retiring side only through a deep sense of moral duty' and 'he was a truly good man at heart, a gentleman through and through' (*RD* 61). Yet it is an aside that reveals that Lord Darlington's supposed political 'meddling' is not a mere fad, but is in fact a dedicated and systematic engagement at the highest political level that lasts throughout the entire interwar period: 'It is important to be reminded . . . that although Darlington Hall was to witness many more events of equal gravity over the fifteen years or so that followed, that conference of 1923 was the first of them' (*RD* 70). The list of influential figures that Stevens recounts as guests at Darlington Hall underlines this: Lady Astor, of Cliveden Set notoriety (*RD* 134); Lord Halifax, the infamous Foreign Secretary at the time of the Munich Agreement and one of the architects of British Appeasement (*RD* 135); Herr von Ribbentrop, Hitler's ambassador to London, successful at charming his way into the British upper classes (*RD* 135); and Oswald Mosley himself (*RD* 137, 145). This reading of Lord Darlington's political affiliation is supported by a comment made by Congressman Lewis during the 1923 conference at Darlington Hall, when he warns the French delegate Mr Dupont that he 'was being manipulated by his lordship and other participants at the conference' (*RD* 95). Despite Lord Darlington's apparently well-intended attempts to negotiate better treatment for a defeated foe, he eventually supports the fascist cause with a determination that challenges his position as an alleged 'amateur' politician.

The more pernicious collusion with the fascists in *The Remains of the Day* does not take place via the active support of Darlington, but through Stevens's unquestioning dedication to his master: 'A "great" butler can only be, surely, one who can point to his years of service and say that he has applied his talents to serving a great gentleman – and, through the latter, to serving humanity' (*RD* 117). Stevens's narrative shows that he always tried to support Lord Darlington to the best of his abilities – and not only out of a sense of duty but, possibly, with conviction. 'History could well be made under this roof' (*RD* 77) he tells his staff grandly, on the eve of the all-important conference of 1923. Even with hindsight he claims that 'to have served his lordship at Darlington Hall during those years was to come as close to the hub of this world's wheel as one such as I could ever dream to have come' (*RD* 126). His acceptance and endorsement of Lord Darlington's politics is nowhere more blatantly obvious than when he refuses to challenge the dismissal of the two Jewish maids to Miss Kenton: 'His lordship has made his decision and there is nothing for you and I to debate over' (*RD* 148). During the years of Lord Darlington's active involvement in right-wing politics, Stevens acts as his silent tool, uncritical of all that the 'great man' Lord Darlington does. The butler is blinded by his own ambition; and, also, by his self-importance. He rejoices in the fact that 'the state of the silver had made a small, but significant contribution towards the easing of relations between Lord Halifax and Herr Ribbentrop that evening' (*RD* 136). This silence, and Stevens's obvious pride in the role he played, show his willing participation in his master's agenda. His later claim that he only followed orders rings hollow.

Stevens's defence of Lord Darlington also shows some surprising insights. He is highly critical of contemporary society's lack of *Vergangenheitsbewältigung*. He states that the general view held after the war that Ribbentrop deceived the English gentlemen he visited in the 1930s is open to scrutiny. Indeed, the butler finds it 'rather irksome to have to hear people talking today as though they were never for a moment taken in by Herr Ribbentrop' (*RD* 136). Lord Darlington was far from alone in thinking Ribbentrop's intentions were honourable at that time. The German ambassador was a welcomed guest at many of the country houses belonging to the aristocracy, especially in 1936 and 1937. It is only hindsight that later allows these self-same people to criticize Lord Darlington for lapses of which they themselves were culpable.

This insight shows that Stevens's often repeated mantra that he has no political opinion or knowledge is incorrect. He knows and always knew what was going on around him. It also demonstrates a wider problem. Stevens, whose overall language is characterized by its restraint, shifts into surprisingly aggressive language during these reflections: the repeated use of 'irksome', in particular, reveals his riled emotions. While his diatribe attempts to exonerate Lord Darlington, he also succeeds in revealing the hypocrisy of a society that, in seemingly mutual agreement, closes its eyes to an inconvenient truth and makes one person into a scapegoat while many others share the blame. Ishiguro thus warns against mythification: the Nazis and their supporters were not only found across the Channel: their propaganda reached England's shores and also found (some) resonance within the country's establishment.

a 'certain kind of england': *the remains of the day* as criticism of thatcherism

The Remains of the Day questions appeasement politics in interwar Britain, but the novel can also be read as a criticism of the ways in which mythologies about Englishness are themselves used for shaping the contemporary national consciousness. Bruce King explains that

> the butler and England of *The Remains of the Day* are imitations of a mythic past when the nation was run by those who owned great country houses and were served by devoted employees willing to

forsake any other life for the privilege of doing their duty. With a few twists it could be a novel by Evelyn Waugh, or even P. G. Wodehouse. Such pastiche is also criticism. The social order it seems to celebrate is shown to depend on repression and exploitation.[17]

This statement is interesting for a variety of reasons. While Ishiguro's novel follows in the footsteps of literary precursors such as Waugh and Wodehouse, it does so in a manner that is a good deal more politically self-aware. Yet it also allows us to read the novel not as an exposé of England's dark past, but also as a criticism of the contemporary socio-political climate. Ishiguro stated in an interview:

I wished to set this book in a mythical landscape, which to a certain extent resembled that mythical version of England that is peddled in the nostalgia industry at the moment. This idea of England, this green, pleasant place of leafy lanes and grand country houses and butlers and tea on the lawn, cricket – this vision of England that actually does place a large role in the political imagination of a lot of people, not just British people, but people around the world.

I think these imaginative landscapes are very important. I felt it was a perfectly reasonable mission on my part to set out to slightly redefine that mythical, cozy England, to say that there is a shadowy side to it. In a way I wanted to rewrite P. G. Wodehouse with a serious political dimension.[18]

This quotation draws our attention to contemporary England, rather than its past. *The Remains of the Day* was published at the height of Margaret Thatcher's Tory government, when economic laissez-faire and elbow-politics were encouraged.[19] The Young Urban Professional (Yuppy) ruled supreme in London, as symbolized by the Docklands 'rejuvenation' project that created new and upmarket loft-living spaces for Thatcher's Yuppies at the expense of the working-class East Enders, who felt they were pushed out of their traditional habitat. On the international stage, the British Empire had all but disappeared and Britain was struggling to define her place in the world hierarchy. Effectively, then, the Thatcher government, along with the social groups that reflected and affirmed its ideology, also made use of repression and exploitation. They simultaneously celebrated not only their lifestyle, but also a more traditional manner of living.

The frame narrative of the novel is set in 1956, the year of the Suez Crisis, which saw the ultimate humiliation of Britain as an imperial power. In the 1980s, the Prime Minister Margaret Thatcher herself

seemed to bemoan the irrevocable end of the British Empire. She repeatedly called for a return to Victorian values. In her interview with the
Daily Mail on 29 April 1988, she railed against the damage wrought by
what she considered to be the overly permissive society of the 1960s
and 1970s:

> Permissiveness, selfish and uncaring, proliferated under the guise
> of new sexual freedom. Aggressive verbal hostility, presented as a
> refreshing lack of subservience, replaced courtesy and good manners.
> Instant gratification became the philosophy of the young and the
> youth cultists. Speculation replaced dogged hard work.[20]

Thatcher itemizes here three key concepts of the Victorian era, a time
when self-made men could hold their own among gentry and aristocracy through hard work, good education and impeccable manners. This
cemented the middle-class concept of gentlemanliness as a *moral* rather
than a status title.[21] The call for a return to the values of her forefathers
in light of the demise of Empire could be read as a single-minded denial
of history. Similarly, in *The Remains of the Day* Lord Darlington refuses to
see the inherent danger in dealing with the Nazis before the war. After
the war, Stevens denies his lordship's guilt and complicity – and through
him, his own – in a denial of history that is equivalent to Thatcher's.

Against these social, political and historical events, Ishiguro's novel
is set in what appears to be the tranquillity of the English country
house – one of the most traditional of all English environments.
Fittingly, Ishiguro's protagonist is a traditional, backwards-looking and
subservient butler, in awe and admiration of the lord he serves. Both the
figure of the butler and the upper-class lord are English national stereotypes, defined by Walter Lippmann as 'pictures in our head ... fed to
the public through the media'.[22] Notions of Englishness are very often
perpetuated by idyllic film and television adaptations. One only has to
think of Merchant–Ivory productions such as *Maurice* (1987), *Howards
End* (1992) and their adaptation of *The Remains of the Day* (1993). Then
there are the so-called 'white flannel dramas',[23] such as the Granada TV
adaptation of *Brideshead Revisited* (1981) or the hugely successful film
Chariots of Fire (1981).[24] Those films were particularly popular in the
1980s and 1990s. It was a time when Britain, as highlighted above, was
losing her influence in world politics. The politicians leading the country advised the nation to look back wistfully to an allegedly better and
'greater' past. This sudden rise in the number of period films glorifying a
mythical predominantly English past served a distinct political function
that needs to be examined in relation to the Prime Minister's longing

for Victorian values. These values included replacing the Welfare State with private philanthropy, promoting the concepts of self-reliance and a firm moral compass, and advocating the virtues of hard work. The tone of this agenda was set by her nostalgia for the glorious days of Empire and an intractable belief in the nation. Although Thatcher and her party repeatedly called for a return to the manners and morals of their forefathers, it could be argued that their own behaviour did not always adhere to those ideals. The free-market economy that Thatcher supported left little room for decency and honesty but, instead, gave rise to the 'greed-is-good' mentality of the Yuppie and the development of a social underclass. As Raphael Samuel has convincingly argued, Thatcher's evocation of Victorian values was nothing but a convenient, though misleading, campaign tool – 'modernization in mufti'[25] – that dispensed with Victorian ideals such as compassion and liberalism in favour of the worship of ruthless capitalism.

In writing *The Remains of the Day*, Ishiguro shows himself aware of the political spin that was put on England's past in the 1980s. In a 1993 interview with Allan Vorda, he explained:

> the kind of England that I create in *The Remains of the Day* is not an England *that I believe ever existed*. I've not attempted to reproduce, in a historically accurate way, some past period. What I'm trying to do here . . . is to actually *rework a particular myth* about a certain kind of England. . . . where people lived in the not-so-distant past, that conformed to various stereotypical images. That is to say an England with sleepy, beautiful villages with very polite people and butlers and people taking tea on the lawn. . . . The mythical landscape of this sort of England, to a large degree, is harmless nostalgia for a time that didn't exist. The other side of this, however, is that it is used as a political tool.[26]

Ishiguro shows that *The Remains of the Day* creates a mythical England that he wants to query and problematize. The text's subtle undercutting of imagery and myths of Englishness and 'Greatness' works against the artificial conservation of historical sites by heritage thinkers, not because Ishiguro finds that such sites are not worth preserving, but because their preservation implies the radical altering and disconnection of a historical reality. Such strategies are, however, at best ambivalent because of their association with an idealized but ultimately delusional notion about the nation's past.

According to Roger Fowler, '"Myth" and "mythical" have long been commonly used in contexts opposing them to "truth" or "reality"'.[27]

The Remains of the Day tries to highlight how 'myth' and 'mythical' are presented as 'truth' or 'reality'. What is ostensibly harmless nostalgia for the heyday of the English country house and other traditional institutions might, in fact, cover up dark secrets and unsavoury truths. Writing in the aftermath of the Second World War and the Holocaust, Frank Kermode is very much aware of the dangers of myths, and he posits fictions as an antidote:

> We have to distinguish between myths and fictions. Fictions can degenerate into myths whenever they are not held to be fictive. In this sense anti-Semitism is a degenerate fiction, a myth; and *Lear* is a fiction. Myth operates within the diagram of ritual, which presupposes total and adequate explanations of things as they are and were; it is a sequence of radically unchangeable gestures. Fictions are for finding things out, and they change as the sense-making changes. Myths are the agents of stability, fictions the agents of change. Myths call for absolute, fictions for conditional assent. Myths make sense in terms of a lost order of time . . . fictions, if successful, make sense of the here and now.[28]

Importantly, for the narrative of *The Remains of the Day*, the butler's memories concern not only his own, private life, but his entire country's past. Petry explains that in the novels of Ishiguro the 'main concern is the intermingling of one's personal past (biography) on the one hand (and especially how people try to cope with their past), and society's collective memory (history) on the other'.[29] As such, *The Remains of the Day* makes it clear that an individual's past must be read in the context of his or her country's past. By trying to come to terms with one's own past, one ought simultaneously to address one's (national) identity – and this is merely another form of *Vergangenheitsbewältigung*. In the case of *The Remains of the Day*, the text is a direct criticism of British engagement with fascism. It indirectly holds up a mirror to similar processes of mythologization and denial of changes in power structures that occurred during the Thatcher period. In doing so, Ishiguro not only produced a historical novel, but also a very contemporary one. It is a text that openly addresses the inherent dangers in a political regime that took great pride in advocating traditional values, whilst actually practising the exact opposite.

notes

1. Stephen Dorrill, *Black Shirt: Sir Oswald Mosley and British Fascism* (London: Viking, 2006), p. 163.
2. Nancy Mitford, *Wigs on the Green* (London: Thornton Butterworth, 1935).

3. P. G. Wodehouse, *The Code of the Woosters* (London: Vintage, 1990 [1937]).
4. Dorrill, *Black Shirt*, p. 393ff. All information on Diana Mitford is taken from Jan Dalley, *Diana Mosley* (New York: Alfred A. Knopf, 2000) and Anne de Courcy, *Diana Mosley* (London: Chatto and Windus, 2003).
5. Information on Unity Mitford is taken from David Pryce-Jones, *Unity Mitford. A Quest* (London: Weidenfeld and Nicolson, 1995). See also the TV programme 'Hitler's British Girl' broadcast by Channel 4 on 20 December 2007.
6. Nancy Mitford, 'Letter to Evelyn Waugh, 25 July 1955' in Charlotte Mosley (ed.), *The Letters of Nancy Mitford & Evelyn Waugh* (London: Sceptre, 1997), p. 366.
7. Mitford, *Wigs*, p. 237.
8. Ibid., p. 18.
9. Ibid., p. 26.
10. Laura Thompson, *Life in a Cold Climate. Nancy Mitford. The Biography* (London: Review, 2003), p. 116.
11. Mitford, 'Letter to Evelyn Waugh, 25 July 1955', p. 366.
12. Wodehouse, *Code*, p. 54.
13. Wodehouse, *Code*, p. 223.
14. Keith Robbins, *Appeasement*, 2nd edn. (Oxford: Blackwell Publishers, 1997), pp. 6, 49.
15. See here again the effects on, for example, Mosley's own family mentioned previously. Cannadine sums up Mosley's fascism as being 'deeply rooted in his own rootless experiences as a landed gentleman': see David Cannadine, *The Decline of the British Aristocracy* (London: Papermac, 1996), p. 549.
16. See www.bbc.co.uk/history/historic_figures/keynes_john_maynard.shtml for details.
17. Bruce King, *The Internationalization of English Literature. The Oxford English Literary History, Vol. 13, 1948–2000* (Oxford: Oxford University Press, 2004), p.168.
18. Kazuo Ishiguro in interview with Suzanne Kelman, 'Ishiguro in Toronto' (1989), reprinted in Brian W. Shaffer and Cynthia F. Wong (eds.), *Conversations with Kazuo Ishiguro* (Jackson, MS: University of Mississippi Press, 2008), pp. 45–6; originally published in Linda Spalding and Michael Ondaatje (eds.), *The Brick Reader* (Toronto: Coach House Press, 1991).
19. For previous accounts of how *The Remains of the Day* can be read as a critique of Thatcherism, see M. Griffiths, 'Great English Houses/New Homes in England?: Memory and Identity in Kazuo Ishiguro's *Remains of the Day* and V. S. Naipaul's *The Enigma of Arrival*', *Span*, 36 (1993), 488–503; and J. J. Su, 'Refiguring National Character: The Remains of the British Estate Novel', *MFS: Modern Fiction Studies*, vol. 48 (3), (2002), 552–80.
20. Quoted in Alan Sinfield, *Literature, Politics and Culture in Postwar Britain* (Oxford: Basil Blackwell, 1989), p. 296.
21. See, for example, Chapter Two in Christine Berberich, *The Image of the English Gentleman in Twentieth-Century Literature: Englishness and Nostalgia* (Aldershot: Ashgate, 2007).
22. Quoted in Susan Condor, '"Having History": A Social Psychological Exploration of Anglo-British Autostereotypes', in C. C. Barfoot (ed.), *Beyond*

Pug's Tour: National and Ethnic Stereotyping in Theory and Literary Practice (Amsterdam: Rodopi, 1997), p. 213.

23. See www.museum.tv/archives/etv/B/htmlB/bridesheadre/bridesheadre.htm.

24. For a Merchant–Ivory Filmography see www.merchantivory.com/filmography. html; for information on the 1981 Granada mini-series of *Brideshead Revisited* see www.screenonline.org.uk/tv/id/536563/; for information on *Chariots of Fire* see www.imdb.com/title/tt0082158/.

25. Raphael Samuel, *Island Stories. Unravelling Britain. Theaters of Memory, Vol. II* (London: Verso, 1998), p. 346.

26. Allan Vorda, 'Stuck on the Margins: An Interview with Kazuo Ishiguro', in Allan Vorda (ed.), *Face to Face: Interviews with Contemporary Novelists* (Houston: Rice University Press , 1993), pp. 14–15; emphases mine.

27. Roger Fowler (ed.), *A Dictionary of Modern Critical Terms*, revised and enlarged edn. (London: Routledge and Kegan Paul, 1987), p. 153.

28. Frank Kermode, *The Sense of an Ending* (New York: Oxford University Press, 1968), p. 39. Originally published in 1967.

29. Mike Petry, *Narratives of Memory and Identity: The Novels of Kazuo Ishiguro* (Frankfurt: Peter Lang, 1999), p. 7.

part iv
the unconsoled

10
into the labyrinth: kazuo ishiguro's surrealist poetics in *the unconsoled*

jeannette baxter

summary

The Unconsoled (1995) is Kazuo Ishiguro's most experimental novel to date. The kind of experimentalism at work in this novel, however, is not easy to pin down, vacillating between postmodernism, fantasy and realism. 'Surreal' and 'surrealist' have also been used as standard terms by reviewers and critics attempting to describe the spatio-temporal and experiential dislocations of The Unconsoled, *yet no critical move has been made to consider Ishiguro's surrealist poetics and politics. This chapter, therefore, situates* The Unconsoled's *experimental aesthetics within the artistic and intellectual tradition of surrealism.*

the surrealist labyrinth

In *The Unconsoled*, Ishiguro's representation of a nameless and unidentifiable urban labyrinth of displaced memories, dreams and desires boasts strong connections with surrealism's enquiries into the architectures of the unconscious. Following Sigmund Freud's delineation of the unconscious as a labyrinthine space of repetition, trauma and the uncanny, the surrealists adopted the labyrinth motif in their visual and literary investigations into the human psyche. As André Breton put it in 'The First Manifesto of Surrealism' (1924), the surrealist artist's exploration of the unconscious was akin to falling into a subterranean space of uncertainty: 'I would plunge into it, convinced that I would find my way again, in a maze of lines which at first glance would seem to be going nowhere'.[1] Like Alice falling down the rabbit-hole in Lewis Carroll's *Alice's Adventures in Wonderland* (1865),[2] Ryder's and Boris's descent into the city make the reader feel lost on a mysterious path to 'nowhere' (*U* 43). This gestures towards a second significance of the surrealist labyrinth as metaphor for a twentieth-century European landscape of shifting geographical borders and political divisions. This is perhaps most vividly explored in Georges Bataille's inter-war meditation, 'The Labyrinth' (1935), an indictment of the violent ascendency of fascism which was reducing the heterogeneous nation states of Europe to a pale and faceless 'NOWHERE'.[3] Politically and artistically out-of-place within an emerging fascist Europe, the surrealists underwent a double displacement when key members such as André Breton, Max Ernst and André Masson were forced to seek refuge in America during the Second World War. Rendered homeless, the exiled surrealists fled the 'nowhere' of Europe only to feel lost amongst cultural and political landscapes which were inevitably unfamiliar and disorientating.[4]

This chapter explores the ways in which *The Unconsoled* draws on the historical and intellectual legacies of surrealism in order to examine narratives of political and cultural dislocation in post-war Central Europe. It explores intertexts such as Carroll's *Alice's Adventures in Wonderland*; Giorgio de Chirico's *Hebdomeros* (1929); and the post-war surrealist tract 'The Platform of Prague' (1968), which responded creatively and critically to the Sovietization of post-war Central Europe. This leads to a discussion of Ishiguro's post-war history and politics, or, as some critics would have it, the absence of identifiable historical and political events in *The Unconsoled*.[5] Several previous readings of the novel have claimed 'a historical, *semi-realist* space' in *The Unconsoled* which has 'an intimated political counterpart in Central European History'.[6] However, this chapter reads *The Unconsoled* as a counter-historical, Surrealist space.

no place like home: an uncanny central europe

The aesthetic of nowhere haunting *The Unconsoled* is a useful starting point for rethinking those critical responses to the novel that either dismiss its unidentifiable setting as insignificant or criticize it for not being grounded sufficiently in recognizable spatial co-ordinates.[7] The consensus is that *The Unconsoled* is set in an unspecified city somewhere in the heart of Central Europe. Although not wholly reducible to it, the 'nowhere' setting of the novel, as Richard Robinson explains, gestures to a turbulent history of geopolitical transformation across Central Europe: 'For example, it was possible in the twentieth century to have lived under Austria, Poland, the Soviet Union, and Ukraine – while not moving an inch'.[8] It emerges that the overdetermined, labyrinthine space of Central Europe is a site of contesting identities, cultures and political histories. A 'nowhere [that is] the product of an excess of competing somewheres' is at play in Ishiguro's narrative.[9] The unnamed urban setting of The Unconsoled is not one city but a palimpsest of soft and malleable European cities that resist geographical fixity. Ishiguro's narrative is seemingly set in an amalgam of Hungary, Germany, Austria, Czechoslovakia, Scandinavia, Italy and Poland, while at the same time it is reducible to none of these places.

Ishiguro borrows this aesthetic of nowhere directly from the surrealist literary tradition and, more specifically, from de Chirico's little-known novel Hebdomeros. Written and published between the wars, this fiction opens in the middle of nowhere: 'And then began the tour of that strange building situated in a street that looked forbidding, although it was distinguished and not gloomy'.[10] The reader is plunged into an unspecified location. The text resists the need for orientation, however, and the reader is never grounded in any particular place. Instead, we accompany the eponymous protagonist on his wanderings through urban landscapes which not only shift and distend inexplicably, but which also resemble each other in unsettling ways: 'Hebdomeros found himself once more in the same town or, rather, he had the impression that it was the same because something had changed in the layout of the streets and the site of the castle'.[11] How are we to interpret this uncanny sense of déjà vu?

According to Freud, the unheimlich or uncanny can be understood as 'that class of the frightening which leads back to what is known of old and long familiar'.[12] The uncanny is a source of anxiety, fear and confusion because it exploits the ways in which the familiar is haunted by the unfamiliar (and vice versa). Hebdomeros may sense that he has 'already seen' the urban setting which he finds himself in, but, at the same time, he cannot be entirely sure. This feeling of déjà vu also dominates Ryder's arrival in the unspecified setting of The Unconsoled. Appearing out of nowhere, the celebrated concert pianist not only has no memory of where he has come from, but he also lacks any clear sense of why he is in the city in the first place. Ryder is more than a little bemused, for instance, by the desk clerk's constant mutterings about the preparations for the pianist's forthcoming public appearance: 'I simply nodded, unable to summon the energy to enquire into the precise nature of "Thursday Night"' (U 4).[13] Furthermore, the schedule with which Ryder is supposed to have familiarized himself remains frustratingly unfamiliar. Although a memory of studying the schedule on a 'long plane trip' begins to unravel like Ariadne's thread (Ryder can even remember the texture of the typing paper), it transpires that he could recall none of its contents (*U* 15). Neither can Ryder be certain whether he is, as it is generally supposed, familiar with some of the inhabitants of the city: his initial response to Brodsky – whose name means nothing to him (*U* 4) – is contradicted a few pages later when he has the feeling that the name is familiar (*U* 15). Disorientated, it is almost as if Ryder is lost in another kind of de Chirico text, namely the visual landscapes of 'The Enigma of Arrival and the Afternoon' (1912) or 'The Anxious Journey' (1913), in which the themes of arrival, confinement and escape are shrouded in such ambiguity.

It is striking that, like Hebdomeros, Ryder also appears to be homeless, moving repeatedly from one anonymous residence to another. Significantly, the sense of physical and psychological displacement that this kind of transitory existence engenders is made manifest in the uncanny or *unhomely* hotel-setting of the novel. Indeed, the hotel is presented as a labyrinth of tunnel-like corridors, concealed doorways and malleable rooms in which realist notions of spatial and temporal unity are shown to be inconsistent. Ryder's elevator ride to his room, for instance, takes a disproportionate amount of time to complete. This temporal disjunction is experienced in the real time of reading as we eavesdrop on Gustav's labyrinthine tale about the city's community of porters. Narrated over several pages, Gustav's story is so excessively detailed and digressive that even he loses his way and is forced, much to the frustration of Ryder and the reader, to retrace continually his steps. Other kinds of temporal ruptures occur whenever Ryder tries to go to sleep within the hotel. While Hoffman, the hotel manager, is repeatedly disconcerted by the length and apparent frequency of his guest's 'short naps', Ryder has the distinct impression that he is only sleeping fitfully (*U* 117). Time has a tendency to disappear within the hotel labyrinth.

Paradoxically, it is whilst he is trying to sleep in the unhomely space of the hotel that Ryder experiences a brief yet intense feeling of 'being at home'. Drifting between waking and sleeping, his experience of his environment is *heimlich*, meaning, quite literally, 'of the house': 'The room I was now in, I realised, was the very room that had served as my bedroom during the two years my parents and I had lived on the borders of England and Wales' (*U* 16). Although the room has altered in superficial ways and has different paintwork and decorating features, the ceiling is recognizably the same as that of his childhood. What is particularly notable about this episode is that Ryder's childhood bedroom is not represented on the level of simile or metaphor: the hotel room is not said to be *like* his old bedroom; rather, it *is* his old bedroom at the same time that it is not. The homely is therefore at once unhomely because the familiar has returned in a way which is unfamiliar, but not wholly beyond recognition.

A further significant feature of this episode is its insistent aesthetic of nowhere. For the two years in which Ryder and his parents were rendered homeless – a period of displacement which is never explained within the text – they occupied a site of 'competing somewheres', namely the border territories between England and Wales. Ryder, it emerges, has a history of moving through unidentified and unidentifiable places. This theme of displacement continues by Hoffman changing Ryder's location within the hotel at every given opportunity, never once allowing the guest to feel at home, as on the occasion he suggests a shift to Room 343 (*U* 122). This, again, affirms the potential threat to Ryder's mental architecture.

Another example of where the text invites moments of homeliness within the unhomely, only to reject them outright, occurs when Ryder meets Sophie for what he believes to be the first time. Sophie, we soon discover, is involved in a protracted process of house hunting for Ryder, their son Boris (although Ryder may not be the biological father) and herself. She states that if she can only find the right place, everything will improve. She believes that the place she has arranged to see next 'could be a turning point for us' (*U* 89).

Sophie's quest to find a home is shown to fail on every level, however. Promises of comfort, stability and a sense of belonging tantalize with every viewing, yet they also remain frustratingly elusive. This aesthetic of homelessness is suggested in an earlier scene. Ever-impatient to play at 'making home' in their rented apartment, located only a few minutes away, Sophie leads Ryder and Boris through a series of labyrinthine back streets lined with looming, dirty brick walls (*U* 40). As the urban maze grows more claustrophobic, Sophie becomes increasingly preoccupied with the time and races ahead, eventually leaving Ryder and Boris behind in the labyrinth:

> Up ahead of us, Sophie's figure vanished around a corner and Boris's grip on my hand tightened . . . Once we finally turned it, I saw to my annoyance that Sophie had gained even further on us . . .
>
> . . . Sophie had turned down a side-alley, whose entrance was little more than a crack in the wall. It descended steeply and appeared so narrow it did not seem possible to go down it. (*U* 40–3)

This passage is richly reminiscent of the opening chapter of *Alice's Adventures in Wonderland* in which Alice pursues the time-obsessed White Rabbit down the rabbit-hole.[14] In both texts, the characters travel on a downward trajectory (Alice falls, Ryder and Boris follow descending pathways) only to find themselves lost in a series of unhomely spaces. As Barry Lewis has pointed out, a significant difference between Ishiguro's and Carroll's surrealist texts is the way in which the main characters respond to their situations.[15] The pianist's chance encounter with Geoffrey Saunders, an old-school friend and avatar of Carroll's Mad Hatter, should be the source of much confusion, yet Ryder slips immediately into a vacuous exchange with him about the weather. Furthermore, Ryder fails to respond when Saunders chastizes him for not turning up to a series of tea parties which he had not actually been told about: 'So when I heard you were coming, I immediately popped out and bought a selection of tea cakes . . . But today, when you still hadn't called, I threw them away . . . So I went to the bakery and got some fresh cakes . . . But you didn't call' (*U* 45). Whilst Alice engages inquisitively with the Mad Hatter's humorous riddles, Ryder does not stir from his soporific state, and he falls conspicuously silent in response to the illogicality of Saunders's accusations.

Whilst we have the distinct impression that Alice is the only character who is out of place in Wonderland, the landscapes of *The Unconsoled* are littered with figures that simply do not belong. Indeed, without exception, every character in the novel appears as if out of nowhere and feelings of disorientation and displacement are rife amongst them. Sophie's unsuccessful quest to find a home is repeated with a difference, for instance, in the case of Geoffrey Saunders. Inviting Ryder to his rented room, Saunders imagines the following:

'We'll talk over everything, spend a nostalgic hour or two discussing schooldays and old school friends . . . Yes, it does look rather like the sort of room one might rent in England. Or at least might have done a few years ago. That's why I took it. Reminded me of home.' (*U* 51)

Notably, Saunders's room in the unspecified town is not the home he is so desperate to call his own but an unhomely version of it. Although the furniture is arranged symmetrically and the room resembles a welcoming and homely space, there is something unsettlingly anachronistic about it. First, the room is not only out of place in terms of its accentuated English style (the space tries too hard to recall an old-fashioned university study or a room in a gentleman's club), but it is also out of time. It belongs, as Saunders wistfully admits, to an imaginary and idealized England of the past. Nostalgia – deriving from the Greek *nostos*, which means 'return home' – is a form of longing for the home that Saunders appeals to as a compensatory strategy for his own experience of spatial and temporal dislocation. He frequently complains about how quickly time passes (*U* 45). Through fireside conversation and the exchange of shared memories, Saunders proposes a homecoming of sorts. Yet, this is a narrative of homeliness that the text ultimately rejects. Even the imaginary home that Saunders so hankers after is shown to be of a temporary nature as it, too, is rented. Saunders dreams of returning to a home that was never properly his to begin with.

lost in the labyrinth: the poetics and politics of disorientation

The Unconsoled is littered with references to being lost in one way or another. Ryder and Boris descend into the labyrinth in pursuit of Sophie, only to become trapped within its vertiginous structures: they are lost and do not know how to proceed (*U* 48). This echoes Freud's understanding of the uncanny as a space which 'one does not know one's way about in'.[16] Ryder's comment not only foregrounds the motif of being physically lost within the novel's disorientating landscapes, but it also resonates with the feeling of cultural loss that haunts the anonymous city. The city's cultural vacuity is the source of much frustration and anxiety for its inhabitants. Christoff, a concert cellist by trade and the city's appointed bastion of culture for nearly two decades, attempts to shape and develop the city's cultural activities through 'enlightenment and initiative' (*U* 98). But his ordered, rational and 'functional' (*U* 101) approach to the arts has resulted in an erosion of cultural diversity and a loss of communal cohesion. As various inhabitants of the town put it: 'We're lost, hopelessly lost' (*U* 126).

Milan Kundera has argued that the violent legacy of cultural deracination of post-war Central Europe has engendered a similar kind of 'lostness'. In 'A Kidnapped West or Culture Bows Out' (1984), Kundera takes the Soviet invasion of Hungary in 1956 as the cue for a tentative mapping of the geographical, cultural and political landscapes of Central Europe. What emerges is a space 'situated geographically in the centre [yet] culturally in the West and politically in the East'.[17] Kundera goes on to characterize Central Europe as a shifting surrealist space that cannot be located within exact geopolitical frontiers: 'Central Europe is not a state, it's a culture, or a fate. Its borders are imaginary and must be drawn and redrawn with each historical situation'.[18] He goes on to argue that Central Europe is the polar opposite of France: the former is dominated by visual arts and the irrational, whilst the latter is characterized by literature, philosophy and rationalism.

Surrealism has been, and indeed continues to be, a significant counter-historical and counter-cultural presence within Central and Eastern Europe. The formation of the Czech and Slovak surrealist group in Prague in 1934 was a response, in part, to the violent history of cultural repression to which this part of the world has been repeatedly subjected. Krzysztof Fijalkowski revealed: 'Caught . . . between the rise and overthrow of fascism and the installation of Stalinist socialism, the Czech surrealist group of the 1940s lost many of its key members through death or emigration'.[19] The post-war years continued to be equally dangerous and oppressive for this community of surrealist artists, and they were forced into 'almost entirely clandestine activity', operating by the 1960s under the 'deliberately blank title "System UDS"'.[20] Eventually, moments of cultural reprieve came in the mid-to-late 1960s when the 'gradual relaxation of censorship over the course of the decade' made way for the surrealists' first public event since 1948: an exhibition, titled 'Symbols of Monstrosity', which took place at the Gallery D in Prague in 1966.[21] This was followed during the 'Prague Spring' reforms of 1968 by a major collaborative event with the Paris surrealist group called 'Pleasure Principle' (1968), an international exhibition of surrealist creativity and critique that travelled across Prague, Brno and Bratislava.

Further collective activity between the Prague and Paris surrealists resulted in a political tract, 'The Platform of Prague' (1968). This was a vehement critique of, amongst other things, the homogenization and neutralization of language and consciousness by repressive cultural and political systems. According to the surrealists, Central Europe was being forced into a post-revolutionary, post-cultural era by homogenizing Soviet forces with their false politics of cohesion and oppressive aesthetics of homeliness (a view echoed by Kundera). Whilst the linguistic, cultural and historical diversity of Central Europe was being absorbed into the homely myth of Mother Russia, the political force of Central Europe's unhomely literatures (its underground reviews, journals and periodicals) was ruthlessly silenced. And so, eventually, were the dissonant voices of the surrealists. Following the invasion of Czechoslovakia by Warsaw Pact forces in 1968, there ensued another period of the repression of free speech and the censorship of art and literature (or any other form of cultural protest). As a result, many artists and intellectuals, including Kundera, were banished from their homelands. Those surrealists who remained behind were forced into a 'further two decades of underground existence'.[22]

The Unconsoled enacts analogous narratives of cultural repression and depletion. When Ryder first encounters Stephen, an ambitious young pianist and uncanny avatar of himself, he is briefed on the city's once rich cultural heritage. Boasting a diverse 'artistic and intellectual' (*U* 71) centre, the city was once home to renowned painters and musicians such as 'Paul Rosario, the surrealist' and Mrs Tilkowski, the city's most 'revered' piano teacher (*U* 71). Now these artistic figures are nowhere to be found. What remains, instead, are accusations of 'prevarication' (*U* 107) and a fractious community that is impatient to fight back against the increasing unhappiness at its heart (*U* 112). Indeed, consistent with Kundera's observation that, in the face of eradication, 'cultural life grows correspondingly more intense, more important, until culture itself becomes the living value around which all people rally',[23] the inhabitants of the unnamed city actively seek direction out of the 'dark corner' (*U* 100) of their cultural history. Hoffman has pledged to rehabilitate the Dionysiac Brodsky (Christoff's personal and professional antagonist) as a possible antidote to the city's cultural malaise. However, it is Ryder's presence that brings with it the promise of artistic and cultural revivification. One character admits to the pianist that all over the city the inhabitants can only talk of what will happen on Thursday night (*U* 114).

Yet, as various passages in *The Unconsoled* suggest, Ryder offers a specific brand of cultural rejuvenation: namely, a culture of celebrity that is more likely to feed the consumer/capitalist machine than to reignite the critical and cultural imagination. We learn this in the humorous encounter between Ryder and the scheming journalists who mock openly the pianist's narcissism and refer to him as 'a touchy bastard' (*U* 167). The joke is not only that Ryder eavesdrops upon the journalists as they rehearse their sycophantic lines – he is, in fact, sitting right next to them – but that he completely falls for, rather than questions, their disingenuous tributes. Seemingly indifferent to the strange and complex realities of the situation in which he finds himself, Ryder slips effortlessly into the role of the obliging performer. He emerges as the kind of narcissistic artist whose only real concern is, as Hebdomeros observes,

> to wait until the curtain suddenly goes up; to appear behind the footlights, violently lit from above and below, in the hope that a wild ovation will greet their arrival and that later a delirious crowd will carry them in triumph to the doors of their hotels under the amused glance of porters and bell-boys.[24]

One of the reasons why, according to Kundera, the eradication of culture in Central Europe went unnoticed is because Europe's own identity was disappearing. He states: 'For culture has already bowed-out. Its disappearance, which we experienced in Prague as a catastrophe, a shock, a tragedy, is perceived in Paris as something banal and insignificant, scarcely visible, a non-event'.[25] This loss of cultural and critical perspective is foregrounded repeatedly throughout *The Unconsoled*. Unlike Hebdomeros and Alice, the interrogators of enigmas who work so hard to uncover meaning hidden behind the familiar and the unfamiliar, Ryder is part of a lazy critical collective who 'can see, hear or read things which are totally obscure to them without feeling upset'.[26]

Ryder's lack of critical perspective is perhaps nowhere better articulated than at the novel's conclusion. Completely unaffected by Sophie's final rejection of him, he settles down on the tram and prepares to eat a magnificent breakfast. He is content to exchange small talk with an electrician who distracts him with elaborate tales about his parents (*U* 532). He finds comfort in the acritical and 'homely' space of the tram as it travels round and round in circles. The habitability and hospitality which this over-ground (and, by extension, safe) conscious space offers him provides a stark and welcome contrast to the destabilizing and fragmenting spaces of the 'unhomely' surrealist labyrinth. It even allows the pianist some uninterrupted time and space to indulge in some reassuring stories of his own: 'Whatever disappointments this city had brought, there was no doubting that my presence had been greatly appreciated – just as it had been everywhere else I had ever gone.' (*U* 534)

Ryder's final assessment of his visit to the unidentified city leaves the reader feeling frustrated and deflated. His soothing fictions merely serve as shields against the traumas of dislocation and loss that haunt the physical and psychological landscapes of the novel. The consoling narrative of homeliness that Ryder starts to construct for himself, then, is one which we have ultimately to reject. It is precisely within the context of the homeliness/homelessness dialectic and its relationship to twentieth-century Central European history, politics and culture that Ishiguro's appropriation of the surrealist labyrinth has such resonance. Speaking to the state of 'out-of-placeness' which defines the surrealist space of twentieth-century Central Europe, and indeed the surrealist experience within twentieth-century Europe, Ishiguro's narrative can only leave the reader feeling unconsoled. But the suspicion remains that it is only out of this state of readerly disquiet that we can enter into the labyrinth of post-war Central European history and culture in a way that just might be critical and meaningful.

notes

1. André Breton, 'The First Manifesto of Surrealism' in Richard Seaver and Helen Lane (trans), *Manifestos of Surrealism* (Ann Arbor: University of Michigan Press, 1972 [1924]), p. 21.

2. Lewis Carroll, *Alice's Adventures in Wonderland* [1865], (London: Penguin).
3. Georges Bataille, 'The Labyrinth' in Allan Stoekl (ed.) and Allan Stoekl with Carl R. Lovitt and Donald M. Leslie, Jr. (trans), *Visions of Excess: Selected Writings, 1927–1939* (Minneapolis: University of Minnesota Press, 1994 [1935]), pp. 171–7 (p. 176).
4. See Martica Sawin, *Surrealism in Exile and the Beginning of the New York School* (Cambridge: Massachusetts Institute of Technology, 1995).
5. See Amit Chaudhuri, 'Unlike Kafka', *London Review of Books*, 8 June 1995, 30–1; Cynthia F. Wong, *Kazuo Ishiguro* (Tavistock: Northcote House, 2000), p. 67; James Wood, 'Ishiguro in the Underworld', *Guardian*, 5 May 1996, 5.
6. Richard Robinson, 'Nowhere, in Particular: Kazuo Ishiguro's *The Unconsoled* and Central Europe', *Critical Quarterly*, 48 (4), (2006), 110.
7. Ibid., 107.
8. Ibid., 113.
9. Ibid., 114.
10. Giorgio de Chirico, *Hebdomeros,* trans. Margaret Crosland (London: Peter Owen, 1964 [1929]), p. 10.
11. Ibid., p. 39.
12. Sigmund Freud, 'The "Uncanny"', in *Art and Literature*, The Pelican Freud Library, vol. 14, trans. James Strachey (London: Penguin, 1985 [1919]), pp. 339–76 (p. 340).
13. This and subsequent in-text quotations, abbreviated to *U*, refer to: Kazuo Ishiguro, *The Unconsoled* (London: Faber and Faber, 1995).
14. See Lewis Carroll, *Alice's Adventures in Wonderland*, p. 15.
15. See Barry Lewis, *Kazuo Ishiguro*, (Manchester: Manchester University Press, 2000) p. 124.
16. Freud, 'The "Uncanny"', p. 359.
17. Milan Kundera, 'A Kidnapped West or Culture Bows Out', *Granta*, vol. 11 (1984), 96.
18. Ibid., 106.
19. Krzysztof Fijalkowski, 'Invention, Imagination, Interpretation: Collective Activity in the Contemporary Czech and Slovak Surrealist Group', *Papers of Surrealism*, 3 (Spring 2005), 2.
20. Ibid.
21. Ibid.
22. Ibid., 3.
23. Kundera, 'A Kidnapped West', 97.
24. Ibid., 109–10.
25. Ibid., 117.
26. De Chirico, *Hebdomeros*, p. 10.

11
'waiting for the performance to begin': kazuo ishiguro's musical imagination in *the unconsoled* and *nocturnes*

gerry smyth

summary

Kazuo Ishiguro shares a preoccupation with music common amongst his generation of writers, but he is unusual in his awareness of the representational problems that occur when writing about music. In The Unconsoled *(1995), the traditional power of music as a consoling discourse that can heal the traumatized subject is deflated because in the modern world consolation resides not in the consummate moment of artistic performance, but in the multitudinous moments that comprise everyday life. The 'album' of interrelated stories* Nocturnes *(2009) may likewise be located within a tradition of fiction in which music is a key consideration at a thematic and formal level.* Nocturnes *is a profoundly musical text that functions as a subtle exposition and an affirmation of what it means to be 'human' in the modern world.*

music and contemporary british fiction

It is hardly daring to claim that music represents an important aspect of Kazuo Ishiguro's artistic imagination. His writing, as well as his comments on his writing, reveals him to be an author for whom the legend of music looms large. *Never Let Me Go* (2005) is named after a song from the so-called 'Great American Songbook' – a repertoire of twentieth-century

144

jazz-tinged standards. It may seem initially to be a strange choice on Ishiguro's part, as the song's protagonist displays levels of dependency and passion – even psychosis – that are at odds with the nuanced atmospheres characteristic of his fiction.[1] It is interesting, nonetheless, that such a song becomes a key point of reference within Ishiguro's narrative, as if the author is invoking emotional relationships denied to his characters. Both Kathy H. and Madame 'hear' (by which I mean understand) the song in terms of their own desires and experiences. The former translates the term 'baby' from a sexual to a familial idiom, and hears the song as a plea from a mother to her child (*NLMG* 69–70). The latter understands the song as a metaphor for the political dispensation in which she is complicit (*NLMG* 266). In each case, Ishiguro invokes the power of music as a salient cultural form through which people attempt to understand the world and themselves in relation to it.

Ishiguro's profile as a writer for the cinema also has a musical dimension. Although his screenplay for *The Saddest Music in the World* (2003) was significantly altered before filming, the original idea remained: namely, the question of music's ability to embody emotion and the central role it plays in people's emotional lives.

We should acknowledge immediately, however, that in this regard he is typical rather than unusual: a glance at the landscape of modern British fiction reveals that music has emerged as a central preoccupation for the current generation of writers.[2] Two possible reasons for this are pertinent in the present context. The first concerns the formative influence of popular music upon late-twentieth-century British writers. Many of the individuals acknowledged as serious contemporary writers grew up during a period in which popular music was emerging as a unique means of engaging with and responding to the world. After the breakthrough of the first generation of rock musicians in the 1960s, the punk 'revolution' of the 1970s confirmed the absolute centrality of music for a significant proportion of the younger population, many of whom went on to make telling contributions to subsequent British culture in a range of artistic and cultural fields. We should probably not be surprised that writers such as Ishiguro have attempted to exploit the musical experiences of their youth, nor that many have attempted to effect a rapprochement between their primary means of artistic expression (writing) and a medium to which they are both sentimentally and intellectually sensitized.

A second reason for the prominence of music as an influence on contemporary British writing concerns the revolutionary changes wrought upon national culture as a consequence of globalization, and the impact of digitalization upon traditional cultural practices. Put simply, the ways and means by which the world may be experienced have changed utterly within the course of a single generation, and this has had an influence (in ways that are still emerging) upon established forms of subjectivity. Nowhere has this influence been felt more than in that cultural medium which, above all others, claimed to embody the core values and attributes of the modern human subject: art music.[3] The condition of art music, therefore, offers itself as a salient metaphor through which to explore the changes overtaking contemporary British culture, and it is an offer of which many British writers have availed themselves.

Ishiguro's interest in music appears to arise in the first instance from his personal experience; like many young men of his generation, his earliest attempts at artistic expression were through the medium of the guitar-based song. It was only when he felt that he had reached 'the limits of what [he] could do as a songwriter' that Ishiguro turned seriously to fiction.[4] However, artistic expression, and especially musical expression, has remained prominent throughout his *oeuvre*.

Ishiguro remains more or less unique amongst contemporary fiction writers, however, in as much as his fascination with music does not manifest itself as an uncritical transposition of one medium onto another. The fact is that music and literature function as ways of representing the world that, although related, are different in a number of key respects. The attempt to incorporate music into a literary text, or to replicate musical effects in such texts, will always be flawed, in so far as it ignores these fundamental differences. Ishiguro's 'music' acknowledges such differences; it does so, moreover, with reference both to the thematic significance of music within the narrative and to the formal organization of the text.

music and the everyday: *the unconsoled*

Ishiguro's musical imagination was first fully engaged in *The Unconsoled* (1995). One of the principal recurring strategies of the 'music novel' is the introduction of music as a palliative effect in a range of crisis situations. As Stephen Benson puts it: 'music is valued for its singular powers of affect, and by these means, its powers of consolation. Put simply . . . music has the potential to heal, to make things better'.[5] Music's role in the text is to allude to kinds and levels of experience that can find no expression in established linguistic discourses. Its entry into the text invariably signals a shift in the emotional economy of the plot; eventually it comes to symbolize (sometimes to offer on a thematic level) forms of resolution and redemption which are not available in the 'real' world of the narrative. This composite effect is, moreover, categorically subject-oriented: music's significance always comes into focus as a means to modify the perspective (and thence the identity) of a character with whom the reader identifies to a greater or lesser extent. The promise is clear: music can change your life – its job is 'to heal, to make things better'.

The role afforded music in this kind of novel is the product of a pact of bad faith shared by the author and the reader. This is because such literary music is always intended by the author, or understood by the reader, to stand for something beyond itself, and this for the very simple reason that in a medium restricted to written language *music cannot stand for itself*. Different writers have developed different strategies to cope with the necessary silence of literary music – by the use of figurative language (especially metaphor), for example, or by incorporating musical references which have an existence outside of the literary text (such as the song 'Never Let Me Go'). The fact remains, however, that the typical music novel realizes a necessary silence – the silence of a sonic medium when transferred into a non-sonic medium.

This was the dilemma faced by Ishiguro when he came to essay his own 'music novel'. The story is narrated by an internationally renowned pianist named Ryder who, as the text commences, has just arrived in an unidentified European city to play a concert. This plausible scenario is soon belied, however, by a series of bizarre episodes in which Ryder encounters various people (including his own wife and child) while also finding himself caught up in a civic dispute regarding the relative value and suitability of different musical traditions.

The Unconsoled is both uncomfortable and difficult to read and several critics have described the novel as 'Kafkaesque' to account for the novel's disturbing fusion of the ordinary and the fantastic.[6] The distortion of familiar phenomena is unsettling, while Ryder's increasing estrangement very rapidly communicates itself to the reader – a subject whom Ishiguro constantly risks alienating by the introduction of long passages, the relevance of which to the 'main' story seems at best tangential. Benson discerns something else: '*The Unconsoled* is pervaded by sadness and disappointment and therein resides the promise of its narrative: the enactment of consolation'.[7] This picks on something explicitly invoked in the text itself, when the conductor Brodsky refers to music as a 'consolation' for a wound that will not heal. What this particular wound might be is not specified. However, when Ryder suggests that Brodsky might expect to be healed by his romantic love interest, Miss Collins, he replies: '"She'll be like the music. A consolation. A wonderful consolation. That's all I ask now. A consolation. But heal the wound?" He shook his head … "A medical impossibility. All I want, all I ask for now is a consolation."' (*U* 313).[8]

Every character in the novel, including the narrator Ryder, is 'wounded' in some manner and they are all searching for relief from this shared human inheritance of pain and sadness. They are all in search of some form of experience or perspective that will enable them to carry on despite the 'wound' that each must bear. As Brodsky affirms, music traditionally offers such an experience and such a perspective: it presents the listener with a sense of resolution and closure, 'consoling' them in various ways; at the very least, it maintains the possibility of consolation. Certainly, in terms of its constituent forms (sonata form, for example) and devices (key signatures, for example), Western music of the Classical and Romantic periods might be regarded as a 'consoling' discourse, offering narrative shapes and types through which the listening subjects could assert a sense of identity and thus become 'real' to themselves. The live concert features as yet another element of this discourse. The performance of such music by artists of greater or lesser excellence represented perhaps the consummate 'consoling' opportunity – a narrative in which the vision of the composer and the genius of the interpretation combine to offer a sonic experience which wards off (albeit temporarily) the silent terror with which the human subject is otherwise surrounded.[9]

This model of musical consolation is at odds with a Modernist conception of subjectivity as fundamentally alienated from itself; and this is where the echoes of Kafka in Ishiguro's novel begin to clarify. The text's principal plotline sees Brodsky's Romanticism opposed to Christoff's Modernism, with different elements within the town supporting one or the other, and Ryder the performer stuck in the middle. All this is beside the point, however, and for two reasons. Firstly, there is the problem that music, when represented through a non-musical medium, can never be satisfactorily reconciled with its object; literature, to put it figuratively, cannot 'console' music, because they are categorically estranged. Secondly, the final consoling performance, in relation to which all the different models of music affectivity might be evaluated, never in fact arrives. The resolution that Ryder's concert promised throughout the narrative is not forthcoming, and the reader in search of meaning – of the book and of themselves in relation to the book – is, in this sense, left 'unconsoled'.

Ishiguro's novel ends with a hellish image of Ryder, recently estranged from his wife and child, sitting on a tram going round and round the city, eating an apparently never-ending breakfast and swapping commonplaces with a stranger sitting opposite. Things are not quite as bad as they seem, however. The musician retains positive memories of sharing a recent bus journey with his son when they were both happy and enjoying each other's company. The food and conversation he shares with his new acquaintance offer an equally positive image of the universal human faculty of empathy, as well as people's capacity to find comfort and pleasure in ordinary things and everyday situations. There is a kind of music in the everyday, opposed to the notion of the consummate musical performance, and it is this which Ryder and his companion 'play' in the closing pages of the narrative. The pianist knows that he will at some point have to disembark to prepare for a flight to Helsinki and yet another concert date; in the meantime he is happy to ride the tram, talking and eating with his new friend. The promise of artistic consolation has been compromised in the (post-)modern world, it would seem: consolation resides, if anywhere, not in the consummate moment of the artistic text (either musical or literary), but in the multitudinous moments which together comprise everyday life – not in the arrival, that is to say, but in the travelling.

This interpretation is supported by what amounts to a song version of the same episode written by Ishiguro for jazz singer Stacey Kent and included as the title track on her album *Breakfast on the Morning Tram* (2007). Like Ryder, the protagonist of the lyric is alone and unhappy in a foreign European city (Amsterdam, in fact); and like the fictional pianist, this character ends up on a city tram where he is cheered up by a stranger while partaking of the breakfast fare and watching the city slowly come to life.

It is fascinating to compare the literary and musical treatments of this scene in the light of Ishiguro as, in some senses, a 'frustrated' songwriter and at the same time a novelist who, as we have just observed in relation to *The Unconsoled*, disdains the traditional consolations of literary music. Clearly, the formal properties of the novel and the song lyric are very different. Amongst the many points of comparison one might make, however, the most compelling concerns the sense of 'consolation' found in each. Ryder's sympathetic companion at the conclusion of *The Unconsoled* is recalled by the people in 'Breakfast on the Morning Tram', whose concern for the unhappy foreigner speaks of a shared humanity in the face of universal disappointment. The song itself, moreover, represents a form of 'consolation' for the absence of music in *The Unconsoled* – an absence that was both formal (the reader could not have heard the music invoked in a novel, even if the author had attempted to describe it) and thematic (Ryder never performs his concert). Having withheld the possibility of musical consolation in his

book, Ishiguro's lyric for 'Breakfast on the Morning Tram' offers us a
sense of that very possibility – transposed, no doubt, into a different
idiom but composed from the same matrix of (musical and thematic)
sensibilities.

Each of Ishiguro's four contributions to Kent's albums, in fact, functions in a similar manner. Besides the title track, the lyrics of 'The Ice
Hotel', 'I Wish I Could Go Travelling Again' and 'So Romantic' attempt
to create certain moods by the subtle use of language and imagery. The
listener's entire engagement with the song may be modified by unusual
diction or syntax, for example, or by what might seem like an odd
choice of metaphor. These lyrics concern adult relationships in various states of functionality, and they describe worlds in which (unlike
those inhabited by the protagonists of various kinds of popular music)
straightforward emotional experiences are, by and large, unavailable.
In many ways, in fact, they anticipate the worlds inhabited by the characters in *Nocturnes* (2009), a text in which, as its title suggests, Ishiguro
continues his engagement with the role and representation of music in
contemporary culture.

organic resonance: *nocturnes*

Ishiguro's collection *Nocturnes* is subtitled 'Five Stories of Music and
Nightfall'; while the former term clearly refers to a theme that recurs
throughout the text, the latter is less straightforward. Although many
of the characters featured in the stories are advanced in years, in this
instance 'Nightfall' does not represent a particular age conceit whereby
characters are approaching the 'nightfall' of their lives – a theme
Ishiguro explores most overtly in *The Remains of the Day* (1989). It
appears to refer, rather, to the existential landscape in which people live
out their sense of self: when the hopes and desires which animate our
'day' may succumb all too soon to the disappointments of 'nightfall'.
Nocturnes seems a particularly apposite title, as each of the stories in
Ishiguro's collection depicts characters inhabiting musical landscapes
which are compromised in some manner, or to some degree.

Like all Ishiguro's work, a slightly surreal or uncanny atmosphere
pervades this collection, manifested in the partial echoes and parallels
the reader discerns throughout the stories. Scenarios and relationships
are repeated so that they appear familiar, but then are subtly altered so
that the reader's expectations are being constantly disrupted. All the
stories have first-person narrators, although in each case these characters figure differently in relation to the action. While some are fully
implicated, others are more detached. The narrator of the first story

(Janeck, a Pole) and the unnamed narrator of the last story are very similar. They both play in Italian cafe orchestras, for one thing, while the former also shares an Eastern European background with Tibor (a Hungarian), the main protagonist of the final piece. Likewise, the first three stories repeat the pattern of an outsider becoming involved in a troubled relationship, while unpredictable, slightly hysterical women feature in all five stories – sometimes, as in the opening and closing pieces, in very similar contexts (summer holidaying in Italian cities).

This unsettling atmosphere is underpinned by the rather flat, unanimated prose in which each story is written. A similarity of tone and diction pervades the collection; each narrator is resolutely middlebrow, and this makes for a certain evenness of style which, given the diversity of the settings and characters, again appears rather odd. The singer-songwriter narrator of 'Malvern Hills' is just as likely to introduce a cliché ('exciting interlude', N 89) as is Raymond, the put-upon narrator of 'Come Rain or Come Shine' ('We were especially pleased ...', N 38). When the narrator describes how he 'spotted' (N 189) Tibor in the piazza in 'Cellists', it is a direct echo of Janeck's description of how he 'spotted' Tony Gardner in 'Crooner' (N 3). Windows, both closed and open, recur throughout (N 25, 85, 93, 144, 173, 201) – symbolizing different things in the context of each story, but also helping to link each story to every other. The text is a web of images, references and locutions, and one can understand why Ishiguro was resistant to allowing any of the individual stories to be published independently. Although they stand alone, *Nocturnes* only fully resonates when the reader begins to track elements across the individual components of which it is composed.[10]

The uncanny impression created by slightly unfocused repetition extends to the representation of music. Again, examples proliferate. Janeck plays guitar, like the narrator of 'Malvern Hills', although it is clear that each subscribes to a very different musical world. 'Crooner' brings together the 'light' classical music performed by Janeck and the 'light' jazz associated with Tony Gardner, and both styles are revisited in each of the following stories. Accordionists are casually mentioned in 'Crooner' (N 9) and 'Cellists' (N 189); the Beatles are referenced in the former and again in 'Malvern Hills' (N 110). The effect creates an organic text in which meaning resonates both within and between the individual elements, and in which the reader – in so far as they can 'spot' or discover connections – becomes an active agent in the creation of meaning.

Note that 'crooner' and 'cellists' are iambs beginning with the same letter; although the stories with these titles are connected in a myriad of ways, they are also linked at a material level – that is, at the level of the signifier. Likewise, the cafe called 'Florian' (*N* 3) on the first page of the first story is recalled by the accordionist called 'Fabian' (*N* 189) on the first page of the final story. They are not exact replications, but as dactyls beginning with the same letter there is enough of a similarity in the material form of the word to suggest parallels to the alert reader. On a purely linguistic level, simply to say 'crooner' is to acknowledge the proximity of 'cellists'; to say 'Florian' is to admit the presence of 'Fabian'. Although each term 'contains' a musical significance, in other words – *standing for* this or that particular musical meaning (a certain kind of singer, a music venue, and so on) – these terms already possess a musical significance in so far as they look and sound similar.

What this also suggests is that besides being *about* music, *Nocturnes* is also *in itself* a musical text because it 'utilizes or attempts to imitate musical forms and/or compositional procedures within a literary context'.[11] Ishiguro himself likened the text to an album (see note 10), and there may indeed be a case for considering it as a species of 'concept album', a musical form which came to prominence during the era of progressive rock. Less fancifully, it could also be suggested that the features noted above – repetition with variation, evenness of tone, the manipulation of meaning at the material level of the signifier – function with reference to common musical properties and effects.[12] If Ishiguro's imaginative techniques are approachable in terms of music, moreover, then so too is an understanding of the pleasures afforded by his writing. It is probably going too far to claim that *Nocturnes* offers as much to the listener as to the reader; something is certainly lost, however, if the musical element of the text itself remains unengaged.[13]

For our purposes, 'Cellists' is the key story in *Nocturnes* because it resonates most clearly with the issues broached in this chapter. The narrative is relatively simple. In an unnamed Italian city (although not the Venice of 'Crooner') towards the end of the summer season, a talented but callow Hungarian musician named Tibor ekes out a living whilst trying to decide his future. After a poorly attended recital, he meets Eloise McCormack, a middle-aged American woman, who is apparently on vacation in Italy. Eloise claims to be a virtuoso cellist and she offers to instruct the young musician. Only after numerous lessons does she confess that she has never actually learned to play the instrument – the reason being, she claims, that she was afraid of 'damaging' (*N* 214) her gift. Prompted by the arrival of Eloise's fiancé from the USA, Tibor decides to take up a position as a chamber musician in an Amsterdam hotel. The story is narrated seven years later by an unnamed member of one of the local cafe orchestras.

The image of a woman whose musical 'expertise' is *virtual* – limited to secondary (verbal) representations rather than a primary (performative) realization – is a comic exposure of the tendency to attempt to describe music using a resource (language) which, given its secondary (denotative) rather than primary (performative) nature, is radically unsuited for the task. This is a tendency which anyone who has ever attempted to describe a piece of music – which is just about everyone, including musicians – confirms. In the everyday world, that is to say, we all have a smack of Eloise McCormack; we like to speak about the music that appears to speak to us and for us – at least speaks to and for the people we believe or would wish ourselves to be. By taking it to a new, albeit ridiculous, level, Ishiguro exposes an important element of the ideological work to which music is put in the modern world.

It is only when it is formalized in particular modes or contexts that the significance of the discrepancy between music and language begins to emerge. As mentioned in the introduction to this chapter, literary history reveals that writers of fiction have been especially susceptible to this tendency. Whether out of envy towards a form which they believe to be more in touch with the essence of humanity; out of suspicion regarding the expressive limitations of their own medium; or out of fear of aesthetic (and intellectual) redundancy; the fact is that a wide range of writers since the eighteenth century have attempted to implicate themselves in the musical imagination.[14] Music – its pleasures, its insights, its terrors – is at the heart of the human adventure; writers from every generation, whose task it is to cast that adventure (or at least episodes from it) in narrative form, have felt the force of music bearing down on them, and have attempted to accommodate it in a variety of ways.

Nocturnes may be located within a tradition of fiction in which music is a key consideration, not only at a thematic level, but in terms of its provision of a space for the negotiation of the human. Ishiguro's uniqueness, however, lies in the extent of his understanding of the flawed relationship between music and literature, and it is in this context that 'Cellists' must be approached. If Eloise McCormack represents a general human tendency to attempt to understand (and use) music through language, she also represents a very specific tendency which claims allegiance with the emotional complexity of music, even though the musical performance itself is, by necessity, absent (she does not play). She is, in other words, the vehicle through which Ishiguro articulates his own position as a writer about a form of emotional energy that is categorically unavailable (the reader cannot hear the music described in the literary text). Eloise's air of assumed authority, the determination with which she insinuates her way into Tibor's life, and the ease with which she ejects him from hers when material security is at issue, is in effect an allegory of the writer's engagement with music. Each claims to know the truth about music, but each is in fact detached from its mysteries – aware of the essential energies tapped by music, but unable or unwilling to access those energies.

performing our humanity

Music offers Ishiguro a means through which to address some of humanity's most deeply held convictions: that nature can be articulated in cultural form; that each individual operates an economy of emotional and intellectual energy; that our lives are essentially narrative-shaped; that love redeems us from our evolutionary inheritance. By introducing a subject about which so many people in the modern world feel (or claim to feel) so strongly, he is able to explore that world in a unique way, for music offers a unique arena for the rehearsal, and ultimately for the performance, of our humanity.

The message from *The Unconsoled* and *Nocturnes* is essentially the same: the grand performance – that breakthrough moment in which some aspect of truth will be revealed – is, by and large, absent. Music promises us a return to some primordial moment in which emotion and intellect, enunciation and meaning, will be united, as they were, perhaps, before our fall into knowledge (which is a fall that each generation makes in its turn and in its own particular mode). That promise, however, is very, very rarely honoured. And so, Ryder's concert never happens; the musicians and music lovers of *Nocturnes* are all compromised to a greater or lesser extent, obliged to accommodate their musical impulses alongside much more mundane fears and desires. If music represents the highest aspirations of the species – the means through which we approach the Godlike – it is at the same time a signal of our routine, frequently ignominious, failure.

While this accounts for the air of frustration and regret that pervades Ishiguro's fiction, it is not the case that hope is entirely absent from his artistic vision. As mentioned in relation to the conclusion of *The Unconsoled*, there is a music of the everyday – a music relieved of the weight of expectation, removed from the grand search for truth. This form of music is created by ordinary people interacting and by the dynamics of everyday exchange. 'Music' promises us narrative, drama and climax, whereas this music of the everyday is comprised of banal moments of *partial* insight and *partial* understanding. The turn towards music as a key to human experience is in essence a Romantic gesture;

what we find in Ishiguro is a version of postmodern reality in which human experience modifies received notions of what music is and what it can achieve. The music of the everyday is not enshrined in the performance; rather, it is everything that surrounds the performance – the myriad moments of anticipation and disappointment, love and betrayal, fear and desire, of which ordinary life is composed.[15]

The five stories featured in *Nocturnes* are 'about' music in some form: musical experiences, musical practices and musical meanings. The reader turning to this text for confirmation of the life-affirming power of music (as encapsulated in the performance) is bound to be disappointed, however. For Ishiguro, music is what happens while we are waiting for the performance to begin.

notes

1. See my book *Music in Contemporary British Fiction: Listening to the Novel* (Basingstoke: Palgrave Macmillan, 2008) for an extended study of the trend.
2. Amongst the better-known contemporary British writers who have essayed the 'music novel' we may include Peter Ackroyd, Jonathan Coe, Louis de Bernières, Michel Faber, Janice Galloway, Nick Hornby, Jackie Kay, Hanif Kureishi, Ian McEwan, David Mitchell, Andrew O'Hagan, Ian Rankin, Salman Rushdie, Zadie Smith, Rose Tremain, Alan Warner, A. N. Wilson and Jeanette Winterson.
3. For a brief overview of the changes overtaking the institutions and practices of art music, see Nicholas Cook, *Music: A Very Short Introduction* (Oxford: Oxford University Press, 1998).
4. This quotation is from the interview at www.guardian.co.uk/books/2009/apr/27/kazuo-ishiguro-interview-books in which the author talks at length about his early attempts at song-writing and his attitude towards music in general.
5. Stephen Benson, *Literary Music: Writing Music in Contemporary Fiction* (Aldershot: Ashgate, 2006), p. 146.
6. See for instance Richard Bradford, *The Novel Now: Contemporary British Fiction* (Oxford: Blackwell, 2007), p. 215.
7. Benson, *Literary Music*, p. 147.
8. Kazuo Ishiguro, *The Unconsoled* (London: Faber and Faber, 1995).
9. On the relationship between music and silence see Smyth, *Listening to the Novel*, pp. 189–200.
10. Ishiguro stated: '[I've] always said I don't want them published separately, I don't want them split up. I think that's a bit unreasonable of me because they would probably work alone, but I personally always thought of them as a single book. It's just a fictional book that happens to be divided into these five movements . . . I don't like these musical analogies, because it sounds wildly pretentious. Maybe it's better to say it's more like an album, and you

don't sometimes want a track released as a single.' www.guardian.co.uk/
books/2009/apr/27/kazuo-ishiguro-interview-books

11. William E. Grim, 'Musical Form as a Problem in Literary Criticism', in Walter
Bernhart, Steven Scher and Werner Wolf (eds.), *Word and Music Studies:
Defining the Field* (Amsterdam: Rodopi, 1999), p. 238.

12. In the interview cited in notes 4 and 10, Ishiguro likened *Nocturnes* to a
particular classical form: 'It sounds very pretentious, but you know in some
music forms, like sonatas, you get five what seem like totally separate pieces
of music but they go together.' On the relationship between fiction and
sonata form see Smyth, *Listening to the Novel*, pp. 44–8.

13. An unabridged audio reading of *Nocturnes: Five Stories of Music and Nightfall*
(London: Faber and Faber, 2009) is narrated by Trevor White, Ian Porter,
Julian Rhind-Tutt, Adam Kotz and Neil Pearson.

14. See Smyth, *Listening to the Novel*, pp. 59–93, for an overview of the role and
representation of music in the British novelistic tradition from Laurence
Sterne to Anthony Burgess.

15. This may be what Barry Lewis is referring to when, with direct reference
to Ishiguro, he writes: 'quality writers will manage to make music out of
the most mundane matter'. See *Kazuo Ishiguro* (Manchester: Manchester
University Press, 2000), p. 43. In the light of the current chapter, however, it
is important that the idea of 'music' referenced in such a comment should not
reintroduce the Romantic discourse of music as a consummate revelation on
the part of the privileged individual subject, a danger which is not altogether
avoided by the use of terms such as 'quality'.

12
'into ever stranger territories': kazuo ishiguro's *the unconsoled* and minor literature

tim jarvis

summary

While writing The Unconsoled *(1995), Kazuo Ishiguro was frustrated by critical approaches to his earlier work that centred on its purported 'realism'. This chapter explores how* The Unconsoled *fulfils his intention to journey into ever stranger territories by focusing on the novel's engagement with the work of the canonical modernist writer Franz Kafka.* The Unconsoled *is an exploration, partly allegorical, partly direct, of the crisis facing a major, established artist who wishes to pursue an experimental aesthetic. Gilles Deleuze's and Félix Guattari's concept of 'minor literature' informs the discussion.*

the unconsoled and kafka

In their discussions of Kazuo Ishiguro's most 'difficult' work, *The Unconsoled* (1995), critics often refer to the work of Franz Kafka. Ishiguro has acknowledged the influence of this hyper-canonical modernist writer to whom he had turned due to his frustration with critical approaches to his earlier work that centred on its purported verisimilitude: 'Kafka is an obvious model once you move away from straight social or psychological realism'.[1] Indeed, the novel's allusions to Kafka's corpus are extensive. Ishiguro's setting resembles Kafka's in its lack of spatio-temporal specificity, its mysterious atmosphere and the sudden contiguity of places that are geographically far apart. *The Unconsoled* shares with Kafka's novels a somnolent protagonist who is unable to comprehend fully what is happening around him, yet is strangely willing to accede to the demands of others. It also has in common with Kafka's corpus a macabre, antic comedy – seen, for example, in Brodsky's accident and the amputation of his leg (*U* 447), which the reader only subsequently learns is a prosthesis (*U* 464). Furthermore, *The Unconsoled*'s atmosphere of incompletion, the sense that its ending is arbitrary and open, and that narrative resolution could be forever deferred, recalls Kafka's three longer works.

There are several areas of direct overlap with Kafka. The Sattler Monument, which Ryder describes as reminiscent of 'a single turret' of 'a medieval castle' (*U* 182), and which is situated on the top of a hill, is a direct evocation of the eponymous castle of Kafka's final novel, *The Castle* (1926). The strange potency which music possesses in *The Unconsoled* resonates with moments in Kafka's work. There is Grete's entrancing violin playing in 'Metamorphosis' (1915); the eldritch music described in the short story 'Investigations of a Dog' (1922); the piping of Josephine the singing mouse; and Karl Rossman's piano playing in *The Man Who Disappeared* (1927; the novel also known as *Amerika*). Finally, two of the porters mentioned in *The Unconsoled* who attend the gatherings in the Hungarian Café, Josef and Karl, are named after the protagonists of *The Trial* (1925) and *The Man Who Disappeared*, respectively.[2]

The general critical response to *The Unconsoled* addresses these Kafka-like aspects and concurs that the novel fails because it does not, in Amit Chaudhuri's words, 'allow its allegory to be engaged, in any lively way, with the social shape of our age' in the way Kafka's fictions do.[3] Barry Lewis notes the legacy, but his discussion of it is in the context of an argument about the 'fuzzy' fictional space of *The Unconsoled*.[4] Gary Adelman discusses Kafka primarily to demonstrate the ways in which *The Unconsoled* departs from a Kafkan model, mobilizing these differences as evidence for an argument that the artistic aim he ascribes to *The Unconsoled*, namely that of projecting the interior of a character outwards through the device of doubles, is a radically new one.[5] In one of the seminal essays within Ishiguro criticism, Richard Robinson confers on the placelessness of the unnamed city of *The Unconsoled* a haunting aesthetic rootedness, that of Kafka's central Europe. For Robinson, the Kafkan inheritance is primarily formal and spatial: 'with its Kafkan meta-language, *The Unconsoled* borrows its setting from a second-hand literary-cultural map'.[6]

Such readings arise from a particular interpretation of Kafka's work, one that attempts to circumvent early critical trends that focused solely on the psychoanalytical or metaphysical aspects of Kafka's novels. Kafka is read with a prominent political-ideological bias, one which privileges the symbolic politics of Kafka's writing and the lively engagement with the social shape of the age Chaudhuri finds wanting in *The Unconsoled*. Whereas Kafka's writings are read as parables of bureaucracy, capitalism, fascism and communism, Ishiguro's novel is deemed an 'empty' experiment in formalism because the novel does not allow itself to be re-inscribed easily into a particular historical moment, such as the post-Cold War uncertainty of the 1990s.

The critical response that reads *The Unconsoled* in political-ideological terms, and sees it as lacking value in those terms, is a considered and valuable one. However, I would like to propose that it is possible to recuperate the novel and demonstrate it is a text that articulates something very powerful about the nature of culture, by means of a different approach. In our assessment of *The Unconsoled* it is important to understand the intricate relationship between content and form. In order to assess Ishiguro's evocation of Kafka's profoundly political aesthetic, which explored contemporary political and social issues at the level of form, it is necessary to read the novel differently. In order for Ishiguro to produce the qualities associated with Kafka's work – its disorientating effect and its auguring of coming evils – it is necessary for the novel to deploy Kafka-like tropes in new, amplified ways. The horrors that Kafka's modernist fictions portended had come to pass and there were a new set of concerns to grapple with. For instance, where Kafka's work expresses an alienation arising from the disenfranchisement and isolation of the individual under oppressive regimes, Ishiguro's novel is grappling with an estrangement caused by the post-national and transcultural consciousness of the age of globalization. This leads to comic misunderstanding, at the very least, and at worst leads to a wholesale failure of communication. Ishiguro is writing against a state in which the aesthetic object has been stripped, to a degree, of its intensity (this is the cultural situation depicted in the novel). *The Unconsoled*'s engagement with Kafka's writings is therefore not tangential, but lies at the heart of our journey 'into ever stranger territories' (*U* 492).

minor literature and *the unconsoled*

The provocative work of Gilles Deleuze and Félix Guattari has recently proven a rich source for redirecting classic literary analyses and conventional perceptions of man and the world. Their subversive project aims to destroy traditional ways of understanding society that are reliant on using reason and rational arguments. *Anti-Oedipus* (1977) and *A Thousand Plateaus* (1987) are key works in their canon; they attack conventional, Freudian psychoanalysis and the culture of therapy which supports a capitalist system that produces a schizophrenic subject.[7] Their *Kafka: Towards a Minor Literature* (1986) is particularly useful in providing a critical framework which enables a reading of *The Unconsoled* as a novel producing radical aesthetic effects that have a political significance: Claire Colebrook calls this 'the politics of style'.[8] The idea of 'minor literature' which Deleuze and Guattari formulate in their book offers a way of engaging with Ishiguro's text as an experimental work by a writer attempting to free himself from a restrictive popular conception of his writing.

Minor literature has a number of specific characteristics. First, a 'minor literature doesn't come from a minor language; it is rather that which a minority constructs within a major language'.[9] Deleuze and Guattari note that Kafka's work is interesting because it exemplifies a linguistic deterritorialization that is related to geographic displacement. Kafka is a Czech Jew writing in a major language, German, and Ishiguro, Japanese by birth, writes in a lingua franca, English. There is no reason to suppose that Ishiguro felt oppressed by a major culture, but his frustration with the critical reception of his earlier books indicates that *The Unconsoled* is an attempt to minoritize himself.

One of the most striking features of *The Unconsoled*'s experimental style is the distortion of the conventions of first-person narration. The protagonist, Ryder, is granted sporadic periods of limited omniscience, or clairvoyance, when he has access to the thoughts of other characters, and is able to describe in minute detail events at which he is not, or has not been, present. For example, Ryder narrates an encounter and conversation between Stephan and Miss Collins (*U* 56–63), which takes place in 'a large white apartment building [several] stories high' (*U* 55), while Ryder himself waits outside in a car.

This deliberate narratological impossibility, this flouting of traditional realist rules of representation, foregrounds the idea that minor literature is a syncretic, inclusive category which opens up language as a space where the oppressed may inscribe themselves. It is this feature that makes this form of literature 'great' for Deleuze and Guattari. Claire Colebook notes: 'all great literature, for Deleuze and Guattari, is minor in this sense: language seems foreign, open to mutation, and the vehicle or the *creation* of identity rather than the *expression* of identity'.[10]

A 'second characteristic of minor literatures is that everything in them is political. . . . its cramped space forces each individual intrigue to connect immediately to politics. The individual concern thus becomes all the more necessary, indispensable, magnified, because a whole other story is vibrating within it'.[11] For minoritarian groups in particular, the private world is never disconnected from the public world: the two are always connected. Therefore, the personal is always profoundly political. This is something Ryder learns in *The Unconsoled*: though he attempts constantly to sever himself from the city's intrusive, pushy population, the novel's trajectory leads to his becoming at one with the traumatized body politic.

This political dimension is related to another feature of minor literature, which is that 'everything takes on a collective value' because 'there isn't a subject; *there are only collective assemblages of enunciation*'.[12] Although the trained reader is used to framing Ryder as a singular protagonist, he soon becomes a 'conductor', or like the seer Tiresias from T. S. Eliot's *The Waste Land* (1922), who channels the discourses and utterances of an entire city. Indeed, from his second encounter, with Gustav the hotel porter (*U* 4), the first-person narrator is forced to voice other characters' tales, a process of deterritorialization that erodes Ryder's sense of selfhood. Indeed, a radically disturbing power lies in Ishiguro's use of narratological ambiguity. The reader is never actually sure whether Ryder is relating the innermost concerns of other characters or merely projecting his own anxieties onto them. In addition, at the moments when Ryder is acting as a third-person narrator, disturbances in his immediate physical environment can arrest his omniscience. The narratological impossibility discussed above is cut short when he hears Boris shift behind him (*U* 61). It is as if he can only sustain an immersion in the collective assemblage so long as nothing reminds him of his subjectivity.

The third criterion of minor literature is that its 'language is affected with a high coefficient of deterritorialization', which undercuts the oppressive language of hegemony, whose purpose is to categorize and enforce stasis.[13] Language, for Deleuze and Guattari, is not primarily communicative, but is a means to impose and preserve traditional ways of organizing the world. Writers of minor literature can enact an escape from these constrictions in their texts by offering one of two creative procedures. The first artificially enriches language by making it swell up through excessive symbolism and submerged significations. The second procedure goes in the opposite direction by creating an arid language that is deliberately stripped bare and thereby made more intense. Deleuze and Guattari count Kafka among the proponents of the latter approach (another is Samuel Beckett, an important figure in their writings). While the method that enriches language will ultimately fail because it tends towards a high coefficient of deterritorialization, that which desiccates is more successful.

Ishiguro's poetic technique in *The Unconsoled* introduces a tension and ambiguity in its creative procedures. The novel's language is affectless;

and symbolic imagery that would lure the reader to traditional, Freudian psychoanalysis – that would help to 'decode' or 'explain' Ryder's condition – is largely absent. Its prose has a Kafkan sobriety, and its tone is set through stark description, not figurative language. However, the novel conforms in other ways to the 'majoritarian' model, which artificially enriches language. *The Unconsoled* contains a number of situations drawn from common dream scenarios. A good example of this is Ryder's accidental exposure of himself at the banquet in honour of Brodsky. Another is the imposing entrance that turns out to be 'the very thing [Ryder] had most feared', namely a broom cupboard (*U* 278). The novel also imbues a number of material objects and things – including music, football and wounds – with symbolic resonance.

This ambivalence is potent. In *Kafka* Deleuze and Guattari argue that the 'becoming collective' of a narrating singular subject is a key feature of minor literature:

> When a statement is produced by a bachelor or an artistic singularity, it occurs necessarily as a function of a national, political, and social community, even if the objective conditions of this community are not yet given to the moment except in literary enunciation. From this arises two principle theses in Kafka: literature as a watch that moves forward and literature as a concern of the people. The most individual enunciation is a particular case of collective enunciation.[14]

Ishiguro's attempt to produce a strange and idiosyncratic novel certainly indicates a striving towards artistic singularity, yet Deleuze's and Guattari's reference to bachelorhood also implies an antinomy between creative barrenness and fertility. Whereas Kafka's stalled aesthetic production and his inability to complete a novel are signs of his inability or unwillingness to create a bounded work of art (and, by extension, an enclosed image of man), Ishiguro writes a very long book that, despite its cyclical structure and the open-endedness of its 'conclusion', is manifestly complete.

The Unconsoled appears to flout, or transgress, the criteria that define minor literature. However, in a later essay, 'Literature and Life' (1993), Deleuze argues that 'writing is inseparable from becoming', a Deleuzian concept which again moves us away from the singular and static to a vision of man and the world that emphasizes plurality and diversity, and that is always in the process of metamorphosis.[15] The figure of the bachelor is key to minor literature because the condition of bachelorhood – a singular, male position – implies a denial of the female, and therefore offers the potential for becoming. In Western cultures, the female gender has commonly occupied a position of subservience; male writers are goaded and shamed into 'becoming female' due to their 'superior' status, or lured into it by lusting after the desired stigmatized term. *The Unconsoled* can be read as the 'becoming minor' of an author ashamed of the mainstream status resulting from the success of *The Remains of the Day*, as Ishiguro acknowledges in the Interview at the end of this book.

The novel dramatizes the analogy between the male–female and major–minor positions in the way in which Ryder engages with the curious legacy of Max Sattler. Early in the novel, two journalists trick the pianist into having his photograph taken in front of a memorial to the maligned figure of Sattler. The monument is atop a steep hill, and described as 'a tall cylinder of white brickwork, windowless apart from a single vertical slit near the top. It was as though a single turret had been removed from a medieval castle and transplanted here on top of the hill' (*U* 182). Its verticality, whiteness and lack of windows suggests flight, the blankness of fugue and the delirium of sexuality. However, its celebration of phallic power appears to be cancelled out by the symbolic castration effected, in the same scene, by a gust of wind that blows Ryder's tie over his shoulder (*U* 182). *The Unconsoled*'s reader is simply unsure what the Sattler monument means because traditional, Freudian psychoanalysis as a model for producing meaning does not work. This suggests a correspondence between the Sattler legacy and minor art.

The reader realizes that the journalists' attempt to get Ryder to pose before the monument is intended to discredit him, though he is strangely oblivious to the mockery barely concealed behind their fawning manner. However, when he thinks back on the incident later, he asserts that 'it had seemed the most telling way of sending out an appropriate signal to the citizens of [the] city' (*U* 371). Later, when the pianist discusses Sattler with Pedersen, he is told that for many in the city this figure had represented the possibility of positive change, but that, in the councillor's opinion, 'it is simply not in the city's nature to embrace the extremes of Sattler' (*U* 375). Within the novel, the Sattler legacy is an example of minor art which, for Ryder, becomes a model representing positive transformation and progression – a process of 'working through' the trauma causing the city's tragic condition of stasis. Characters in positions of power with a vested interest in maintaining things as they are believe the Sattler monument to be a potentially dangerous and destabilizing force within the community; Ryder, as a major artist who experiences the minoritarian work, comes to understand the imaginary and creative power of the ambiguities that it represents.

'running on a continuous circuit': linguistically proliferating figures

Deleuze and Guattari argue that the 'assemblage' of a work of minor literature can only be 'explained' if it is first disassembled and then its component parts (and the connections between them) examined carefully. They discover in *The Trial* and *The Castle* 'proliferating series' that effectively open up situations that had led to stalemate in Kafka's previous works.[16] The key terms of the impediments that exist in the other fictions are trios and doubles. The individual is either trapped in the triangular father/mother/child relationship of the family or 'doubled' by discourse, as subject of both enunciation and statement. This also leads to entrapment, for either one of the subjects remains stationary and delegates movement to the other; or both move, implying a third individual directing their actions and, therefore, a return to the familial triangle.

The Unconsoled is filled with doublings of the protagonist. As Gary Adelman notes: 'every encounter is Ryder encountering ego projections of himself, Ryder refracted'.[17] Throughout the novel, this schizophrenic doubling falls back upon familial triads. Ryder and his avatars (in particular, though not exclusively, Boris, Stephan and Brodsky) seem always enmeshed in triangular formulations. Yet although the Ryder/mother/father triangle seems to draw us back into the Freudian psycho-geometry which has at its heart the family, there are many other triangulations – such as Boris/Sophie/Ryder; Stephan/Christine/ Hoffman; and Brodsky/Miss Collins/the chimerical pet – which suggest a proliferation of configurations that destroy the stable, original model of psychoanalysis.

In *The Trial* and *The Castle* the triangular relations multiply until 'a central figure [starts] proliferating directly'.[18] In both novels, Josef K.'s proliferation is such that every component part of the textual assemblage contains a version of K., destroying conventional conceptions of character in literature and, more importantly, a unified image of man. This process enables the subject to 'overflow its own segments . . . spread over the line of escape and expand over the field of immanence'.[19] In *The Unconsoled*, however, the meaningless, deterritorializing teeming that Deleuze and Guattari discuss in relation to Kafka's novels does not occur. Ryder's proliferation and doubling is still partly tied to the idea of the unitary coherent subject. He meets other selves that represent him as he was, or will be, at key moments of his life, and a rationale governs the multiplication.

The novel's protagonist, Ryder, is deemed to be one of the finest concert pianists in the world and would therefore seem to represent a major artist. Despite this apparently central position in cultural life, the novel's experiment expresses the disintegration of his identity. However, despite the radical aesthetic, the novel does produce a traditional *catharsis* that partially recuperates a sense of self and re-establishes a consolatory restoration. Ryder ends up trapped by the tram's continual circuit, and indeed seems to welcome this position: the novel ends with Ryder making his way back to his seat, at one with the social body. It is as if his strategy of creating and identifying doubles provides sufficient impetus to break free of the familial triads and the orders that govern human life which they represent – but not enough to escape their pull completely. The escape effected by Ryder is only partial, unlike that of K.'s. After all, the tram Ishiguro's protagonist finds himself in at the end of the novel is 'running on a continuous circuit' (*U* 534). Therefore, Ryder's deterritorialization, like that of the novel as a whole, is incomplete because this final image suggests a bounded whole or the trajectory of an orbiting body.

It is Leo Brodsky who does achieve deterritorialization, a point of disequilibrium, a flight or escape that is diagonal to the constricting forces of language and society. Brodsky is regarded as a possible saviour of the community. Early in the novel the councillor, Pedersen, describes to Ryder a gathering of the city's elite at which the idea is advanced that a number of the problems besetting the place could be solved if only Brodsky was rehabilitated and restored to the peak of his musical powers. This would 'put into reverse the spiral of misery gaining ever greater momentum at the heart of [the] community' (*U* 112).

At the climactic concert on Thursday evening, Ryder describes how the conductor pushes the musicians of the orchestra 'into ever stranger territories': 'He was almost perversely ignoring the outer structure of the music . . . to focus instead on the peculiar life-forms hiding just under the shell' (*U* 492). In this passage, Brodsky is burrowing beneath the standard aesthetic pleasures offered by the piece to seek the strange, the discomfiting, the minor. It illustrates that Brodsky is carried away by the delirium of his desire, which he is unable to resist; he is becoming a minor artist, whose being is deterritorializing, in a process of becoming. The piece he is conducting is Mullery's *Verticality*, a name suggestive of flight and vertigo.

As is often the way with minor aesthetics, Brodsky's ideas prove too radical and alienating. The musicians become incredulous, distressed, even disgusted (*U* 494). Then, in the middle of the piece, the conductor collapses. He has gone too far along the line of flight and 'ascends a few inches into the air' before crashing down (*U* 496). There does remain a final chance for recuperation and reterritorialization, however.

Miss Collins goes over to Brodsky and seems, tentatively, to be considering a reconciliation. Then he self-indulgently mentions his wound, a signifier of his artistic minority, but also its cause: it was due to the pain it gives him that he turned to drink. Miss Collins's response is anger and revulsion: '"Your wound," Miss Collins said quietly. "Always your wound. . . . You're going somewhere horrible now . . . Go on your own with that silly little wound!"' (*U* 498–9).

Brodsky will not let go of the pain that he believes to be the source of his creativity: he has succumbed to the well-worn notion of the tormented artist. But, as Deleuze notes, 'illness is not a process but a stopping of the process ... the writer as such is not a patient but rather a physician, the physician of himself and of the world'.[20] In turning to his wound, Brodsky has interrupted his artistic process.

Deleuze notes that the final end of transformation, the apotheosis of minor writing, is a 'becoming mortal', which essentially means to relinquish any dreams of omnipotence associated with the Freudian configuration of the subject.[21] Brodsky does not die, though he nearly does succumb, recalling the warning of Deleuze and Guattari that 'the lines of flight always risk abandoning their creative potentialities and turning into a line of death, being turned into a line of destruction pure and simple'.[22] We are to assume Brodsky will 'see out his days as the town drunk' (*U* 522), as a socially and culturally invisible man, while Ryder will continue to be the master artist that he is reputed to be.

Still, that he survives his collapse would suggest a victory of the minor mode; Deleuze describes the minor artist as one who possesses 'an irresistible and delicate health that stems from what he has seen and heard of things too big for him, too strong for him, suffocating things whose passage exhausts him'.[23] He is taken to the 'St Nicholas Clinic' (*U* 522), the name of which is significant, as 'Nicholas' derives from the Greek for 'victory of the people' and the saint, Nicholas of Myra, who was famed for his unconditional generosity. Brodsky has bestowed a gift on the community, that which the minor aesthetic offers: an intimation of how to achieve liberation from oppressive strictures.

This hint averts the community's dreary fate. Ryder observes, following the fiasco of the concert, that 'clearly the evening's events had made [the city's inhabitants] reassess themselves and their community in some profound way, and the resulting mood, for whatever reason, appeared to be one of mutual celebration' (*U* 523). Mark Wormald argues that art can 'console individuals and communities for losses and wounds, whether real or imagined'.[24] Yet it is the radical, delirious and minor aesthetic that facilitates this consolatory power, whereas Christoff's art, with its 'formalised restraints' and its 'sense of structure', does not appear to possess it (*U* 201, 502). It is the unsettling nature of *The Unconsoled*'s aesthetic extremes that enhances our readiness to be moved by the wounded citizens and, above all, by Ryder's opposite, Brodsky.

However, Ryder's feeling at the end that 'things had not, after all, gone so badly' (*U* 534) might not be completely unfounded. Ryder has been the catalyst for Brodsky's transfiguring performance. When he first arrives in the unnamed city, he hears the conductor sitting at a piano, 'playing a single short phrase [from *Verticality*] over and over in a slow, preoccupied manner' (*U* 4). Brodsky is trapped, and Ryder's presence facilitates his liberation. While K. and Brodsky flee and deterritorialize, and Ryder remains trapped in his liminal state, it is Brodsky's intervention as a 'conductor' that enables his flight and heals the community's crisis.

The problem probed by *The Unconsoled* is the popular resistance to the liberating potential of minor art. The solution offered is that of a major artist confronting his audience with a minor artist, in the way that Ishiguro presents Kafka through the resonances in *The Unconsoled*. The major artist alerts his audience to the strictures that fetter them, but sacrifices a personal flight, as the less experimental novels that Ishiguro subsequently published demonstrate. This is not to suggest that *The Unconsoled* is a failure in Deleuze's terms. In dramatizing the dilemma facing the bestselling and critically acclaimed writer who seeks to open up a larger audience to a revolutionary minor writing, Ishiguro has produced a novel that, though it does not wholly achieve minority, is extremely powerful. It enacts a 'minorization' of major literature by producing a text that approaches the intensity of minor literature. This is a formidable achievement, especially in the light of Deleuze's judgement that 'among all those who make books with a literary intent . . . there are very few who can call themselves writers'.[25] *The Unconsoled*'s is a plangent music, yet with a note of hope, which aims to rouse readers from their torpor and show that aesthetic artefacts can still move and disturb, interrogate and probe. It strives to call into being a community of people who care that such works exist. It is art in the throes of becoming, and it is from this that its power derives.

notes

1. Maya Jaggi, 'Kazuo Ishiguro talks to Maya Jaggi', *Wasafiri* 22 (1995), 21.
2. References in this paragraph are to Franz Kafka, *The Castle*, trans. Willa and Edwin Muir (London: Vintage, 1999); 'Metamorphosis', in *Metamorphosis and Other Stories*, ed. and trans. Malcolm Pasley (London: Penguin, 2000); 'Investigations of a Dog', in *Metamorphosis and Other Stories*, trans. Willa and

168 *the unconsoled*

Edwin Muir (London: Minerva, 1992); 'Josephine the Singer, or the Mouse Folk', in *Metamorphosis and Other Stories*, ed. and trans. Malcolm Pasley (London: Penguin, 2000); *The Man Who Disappeared*, trans. Michael Hofmann (London: Penguin, 1996); and *The Trial*, trans. Idris Parry (London: Penguin, 1994).

3. Cited in Richard Robinson, 'Nowhere, in Particular: Kazuo Ishiguro's *The Unconsoled* and Central Europe', *Critical Quarterly*, 48 (4) (2006), 110.

4. Barry Lewis, *Kazuo Ishiguro* (Manchester: Manchester University Press, 2000), p. 128.

5. Gary Adelman, 'Doubles on the Rocks: Ishiguro's *The Unconsoled*', *Critique: Studies in Contemporary Fiction*, 42 (2) (2001), 178.

6. Robinson, 'Nowhere, in Particular', 126.

7. Gilles Deleuze and Félix Guattari, *Anti-Oedipus – Capitalism and Schizophrenia*, trans. Robert Hurley, Mark Seem and Helen Lane (New York: Viking Press, 1977 [1972]) and Gilles Deleuze and Félix Guattari, *A Thousand Plateaus – Capitalism and Schizophrenia*, trans. Brian Massumi (Minneapolis: University of Minnesota Press, 1987 [1980]).

8. Clare Colebrook, *Gilles Deleuze* (London: Routledge, 2006 [2002]), p. 117.

9. Gilles Deleuze and Félix Guattari, *Kafka: Towards a Minor Literature*, trans. Dana Polan, Theory and History of Literature, vol. 30, 7th edn. (Minneapolis: University of Minnesota Press, 1986 [1975]), p. 16.

10. Colebrook, *Deleuze*, pp. 103–4.

11. Deleuze and Guattari, *Minor*, p. 17.

12. Ibid., pp. 17, 18.

13. Ibid., p. 16.

14. Ibid., pp. 83–4.

15. Gilles Deleuze, 'Literature and Life', in Daniel W. Smith and Michael A. Greco (trans.), *Essays Critical and Clinical* (Minneapolis: University of Minnesota Press, 1997), p. 1.

16. Ibid., p. 53.

17. Adelman, 'Doubles on the Rocks', 168.

18. Deleuze and Guattari, *Minor*, p. 55.

19. Ibid., p. 87.

20. Deleuze, 'Literature', p. 3.

21. Deleuze and Guattari, *Minor*, p. 2.

22. Gilles Deleuze and Félix Guattari, *A Thousand Plateaus*, trans. Brian Massumi (London: Continuum, 2004), p. 558.

23. Deleuze, 'Literature', p. 3.

24. Mark Wormald, 'Kazuo Ishiguro and the Work of Art', in Richard Lane, Rob Mengham, and Philip Tew (eds.), *Contemporary British Fiction* (Cambridge: Polity Press, 2003) pp. 234–5.

25. Ibid., p. 6.

part v
when we were orphans

13
'in the end it has to shatter': the ironic doubleness of kazuo ishiguro's *when we were orphans*

christopher ringrose

summary

This chapter investigates those many different forms and layers of irony in Kazuo Ishiguro's When We Were Orphans *(2000), arguing that Ishiguro's use of ironic doubleness, which highlights the way in which Christopher Banks's triumphs are haunted by disaster and humiliation, prevents any closed reading. The counterpointing of Banks's successes and failures, and the text's ironic contradictions, remains challenging to the end, offering a profound uncertainty about the limits of knowledge in the modern world.*

when we were orphans: a critical archaeology

Kazuo Ishiguro's *When We Were Orphans* (2000), the story of the 'orphaned' detective Christopher Banks, who returns to Shanghai in 1937 to investigate the mysterious disappearance of his parents when he was a child, has generated many appreciative readings, but each of them has found it difficult to accommodate all its enigmatic elements. There is, for example, Banks's disorientating combination of fame and failure, as his own assertions about his successes – 'my first public triumph was a heady one . . . invitations poured in from entirely new sources' (*WWWO* 19) – are undermined by Uncle Philip's dismissal of his life's work: 'A Detective! What good is that to anyone?' (*WWWO* 294). Then there is the novel's reticence about the exact nature of those 'triumphs' of detection, as well as the paradox of an apparently lonely and isolated hero who ends his narrative by stressing that he and the young woman he cares for 'understand each other's concerns instinctively' (*WWWO* 310). In many ways, the novel is Ishiguro's most ironic work – one that tests the reader's capacity for double-reading even more than his previous novels. Ishiguro's commitment to irony in this text recalls the provocative nineteenth-century thinker Søren Kierkegaard, who stated that 'just as scientists maintain that there is not true science without doubt, so it may be maintained with the same right that no genuinely human life is possible without irony'.[1] The difficulty with *When We Were Orphans*, as with Kierkegaard's own work, is in deciding when – if ever – the ironies cease and stability of reference takes over.

Naturally, each critic of *When We Were Orphans* has placed one aspect of the text at the centre of their reading. Gillian Harding-Russell's early essay chimed with many reviews in seeing the book as being concerned with misprision, unreliable narration and a provisional truth which cannot be apprehended completely, but only found piecemeal among various memories. Her perceptive approach focuses on Christopher Banks's capacity for self-delusion and the extent to which he is both sympathetic and flawed.[2]

Katherine Stanton, as with other critics, compared Christopher Banks to the butler Stevens in *The Remains of the Day* (1989), as 'yet another study of a painfully deluded character who allows his work (and his childhood traumas) to sabotage any chance he has for love and romance, and thus for a truly meaningful life'.[3] Here Stanton offers Banks's relationship with Sarah Hemmings as a 'lost' normative ending to the novel, in a way that seems too certain. However, for Stanton the book's crucial encounter is in Part Six – Banks's concern for the fate of the Japanese soldier at the hands of his compatriots, who seem to regard him as a traitor. Banks asks if he can see him again. This she sees as 'a brave extension of his willingness to differently imagine his attachments' and a counterpoint to the strident nationalism of the Japanese officer who compares Japan's imperial ambitions to those of nineteenth-century England.[4]

Brian Finney draws parallels between Ishiguro's artistic journey away from realism and his representation of Shanghai as an imperial centre and a battleground.[5] He agrees with other commentators, such as Timothy Weiss, that *When We Were Orphans* challenges realist readings: 'Ishiguro's strategy in this book is to progressively break the reader's dependence on the conventions of traditional fictional realism'.[6] But he is strangely compliant with such conventions himself in his summary of the conclusion of the book:

> The novel ends with Banks finally at peace with himself and the world, once he has abandoned the attempt to live out the fantasies

of his literary predecessors and childhood self. He has at last come to recognize the universality of his orphaned state, to adopt (with the reader) a metaphorical understanding of his circumstances and his world. In typically ambiguous fashion, he concludes that for most of us 'our fate is to face the world as orphans, chasing through long years the shadows of vanished parents' (*WWWO* 313). Whether this observation represents a deep insight into the workings of our collective psyche or a palliative for Banks's own wasted life is, as always in Ishiguro's skilfully polished work, impossible to determine.[7]

This acknowledges the ambiguity in Banks's summing up, but takes his final reflections (and Uncle Philip's revelations) as non-ironic and stable, assuming that, whereas the 'reunion' with Akira is mistaken, the sense of failure (Banks's, the West's) is definitive, and can be summed up as a life that has been wasted.

When We Were Orphans is both under-determined and over-determined. The novel is receptive to any number of different theoretical and critical approaches, but none of them in the end subsume its possibilities, and all are themselves subject to ironic undercutting. The approach through genre and parody is a case in point. In his neatly titled 'Sherlock Holmes – He Dead', Tobias Döring analyses extensively Ishiguro's ironic subversion of the detective story. Döring locates that genre's origins in imperial, Victorian Britain and its 'cracking and yielding' in the postcolonial era.[8] *When We Were Orphans* thus deconstructs myths of Englishness and stands as a reproach to and marker of the end of Colonial dreams: '[Christopher's] Sherlock Holmes identity . . . shatters'.[9] In this context, Uncle Philip's brusque dismissal of the sacrifice of Christopher's mother has postcolonial overtones: 'Your mother, she wanted you to live in your enchanted world for ever. But it's impossible. In the end it has to shatter. It's a miracle it survived so long' (*WWWO* 294). However, irony destabilizes the text here, as at many other points, for the reader is unlikely to have registered Banks's tentative, insecure world in England as altogether 'enchanted'. Like many readings of *When We Were Orphans*, Döring's essay interprets the book in a plausible way, without being wholly convincing. For the book to interestingly 'disenchant the figure of the English detective',[10] we would have to have more details about Christopher Banks's career, to place him within the tradition of English crime fiction. In the event, Ishiguro deliberately omits from the narrative any details about the cases that have made Banks famous. Nevertheless, Frederick M. Holmes comes to a similar conclusion to Döring, seeing Banks as a detective who 'will suffer disillusionment and defeat . . . a ridiculous figure with a simplistic, childish understanding of the nature of good and evil'.[11] He is able to cite Ishiguro's own words in support: 'he had this magnifying glass, and he would investigate high society crimes. By the end [he is] doing the same thing in war zones trying to find out who the murderer is'.[12] Ishiguro refers here, incidentally, to one of the least artistically satisfactory moments in his novel, when Banks, in his nightmarish journey through the ruins of the Shanghai battle zone in 1937, uses his magnifying glass to examine the exposed bone of a dead Chinese woman whose 'stump looked peculiarly clean' (*WWWO* 272). For Holmes, Banks is a ridiculous figure; but if his character is so easy to read, how is it that *When We Were Orphans* 'mirrors the complexity of the contemporary world'?[13] The answer may be that the world is indeed complex, but so is Banks's relation to it.

ironic doubleness in *when we were orphans*

This complex relation makes it possible to link the mercurial, teasing persona of the Danish nineteenth-century philosopher Søren Kierkegaard with the measured narrators of Kazuo Ishiguro's fiction. Radical irony and repetition are central to both authors' working methods and worldview, to the extent that it is impossible to consider the fiction of Kazuo Ishiguro without dwelling on the nature of irony – verbal, situational and 'dramatic'. Claire Colebrook provides useful distinctions between these levels:

> Dramatic, cosmic and tragic irony are ways of thinking about the relation between human intent and contrary outcomes. This sense of irony is related to verbal irony in that both share a notion of meaning or intent beyond what we manifestly say or intend. In dramatic and cosmic irony the other meaning is plot or destiny. In verbal irony the other meaning is either what the speaker intends or what the hearer understands; but how do we know what this other meaning is?[14]

Two Ishiguro passages provide reference points for his handling of verbal irony. In *An Artist of the Floating World*, the narrator, artist Masuji Ono, describes pre-war social drinking sessions with his students at an establishment called the 'Migi-Hidari' – 'a large sprawling place with an upper floor and plenty of hostesses both in Western and traditional dress' (*AFW* 24). The nuances in this episode are characteristic of the book: the concern with status within a masculine group; the formality of Ono's utterance, which offers stock phrases and their time-honoured reassurance and affirmation of established meanings; the underlying sense of Ono's self-justification and the question of how far he is aware of, and concerned to pre-empt, possible alternative readings of his account – readings that might reference his complacency, snobbishness, tendency to play favourites and so on. The discourse is at once emphatic and vulnerable.

A similar unease and irony shapes the first page of *When We Were Orphans*. Christopher Banks, newly graduated from Cambridge, invites an old school friend, James Osbourne, to his newly acquired flat in Kensington, which contains an antique sideboard and an oak bookcase containing crumbling encyclopaedias, 'all of which I was convinced would win the approval of any visitor' (*WWWO* 3). On Osbourne's arrival, he and Banks talk about the workers' unions and debate German philosophy, which enables them to display to one another 'the intellectual prowess' they had gained at their respective universities (*WWWO* 4). The word 'convinced' is not wholly persuasive. There is again the slightly stilted reference to the pleasures of intellectual discussion, and the use of phrases like 'intellectual prowess' that appear performed, ventriloquial. Banks goes on to refer to 'the higher walks of life' (*WWWO* 5), of 'blending in perfectly' (*WWWO* 7) and 'encountering points of custom' (*WWWO* 11). His use of such phrases, and his remembered pleasure at 'the way [his] voice came out' on a social occasion (*WWWO* 20) is one of the things that lead Katherine Stanton to see 'orphaned', displaced Christopher, as 'a mimic man who, despite his diligent efforts, "has never really felt at home" in England'.[15] In terms of Kierkegaardian/Ishiguro irony, that may not be a bad thing. For both writers, ethical life is characterized by a contest between the desire to play out a role and the inability of roles to contain identity – hence the mixture of self-assertion and vulnerability that generates verbal irony in Kierkegaard's *Either/Or* (1843) as well as Ishiguro's *An Artist of the Floating World* and *When We Were Orphans*. If *When We Were Orphans* existed simply to show the limitations of Banks's self-perceptions (and, by implication, those of his class and nation), the book would be less intriguing. These limitations are there but, in the spirit of Kierkegaard, they represent not resting points but starting points for further irony, some of which may undermine the reader's confidence in his or her original judgements.

The retrospective narratives of *A Pale View of Hills*, *An Artist of the Floating World* and *The Remains of the Day* lead the reader into assessing misjudgements, doubleness of meaning and apparent contradictions. Almost any concept highlighted in these novels – love, trust, loyalty, esteem, pride, to give some examples – is in danger of being ironically undercut. (The difference in *When We Were Orphans* is that such concepts may be discarded, but then reinstated.) This scepticism stems in part from Ishiguro's position as a postmodern writer, for whom such absolutes are destabilized, but it also arises because, as Claire Colebrook says, 'there can never be a position of pure saying. All speech is haunted by irony. Not only can we question whether what is said is really meant; any act of speech can be repeated and quoted in another context, generating unintended forces'.[16] Colebrook here approaches Kierkegaard's restless prioritization of a sense of irony in his early work *The Concept of Irony, with Continual Reference to Socrates* (1841):

> Irony [is] the infinite absolute negativity. It is negativity, because it only negates; it is infinite, because it does not negate this or that phenomenon; it is absolute, because that by virtue of which it negates is a higher something that still is not. The irony established nothing, because that which is to be established lies behind it. . . . Irony is a qualification of subjectivity.[17]

Irony and ironic humour thus operate as a 'boundary zone' between the aesthetic, ethical and religious spheres. Kierkegaard argues that while the ethical sphere involves taking due account of the seriousness of one's actions and thoughts, a shift to the ironic may bring in a perspective of humour, a sense of the ridiculous. Clare Carlisle glosses this shift in Kierkegaard as 'arising from the insight that human existence is at once unbearably heavy and ultra-light; full of significance and yet pretty insignificant'.[18]

Kierkegaard's invocation of religious feeling in relation to irony is provocative. A more common literary sense of the ironic mode is that it flatters the reader through the kind of *de haut en bas* tone associated with Evelyn Waugh's *Decline and Fall* (1928). It is certainly possible to read *When We Were Orphans* as a history of ironic failure. Apart from the verbal ironies that feature in Christopher Banks's narrative, there is hardly any level of meaning in the book that is free from structural irony. These include: the detective whom we never see solving a crime or puzzle (Banks); the lover who forgets his beloved and leaves her stranded when he should be running way with her (Banks and Sarah Hemmings); the man who seeks to rescue his parents, but who has already been rescued by his mother (Banks again); the Englishman who is never 'at home' in England (Banks); the ethically driven interventions in world history that peter out into insignificance (those of Sir Cecil Medhurst and Banks himself); the life-blighting mystery that is resolved in five minutes of revelations (from 'Uncle Philip'); the forgiveness for a crime that was never committed (Banks's mother Diana Banks); the celebrity who is both mocked and admired (Banks); the disaster that becomes a (minor) triumph (the trip to Shanghai in 1937); and the self-esteem that is corroded by doubt.

It is tempting to read *When We Were Orphans* as a narrative where ten pages of Chapter 22 represent a hard, direct revelation of facts surrounded by 303 pages of misunderstanding, misreading and conjecture. In those pages, 'Uncle Philip' tells Banks about the fate of his parents. Banks's father ran off one day with his lover and died of typhoid in Singapore two years after. His mother insulted a Chinese warlord, Wang Ku, and was taken by him into a form of slavery, to be used as a concubine in Hunan province, where she was often whipped in front of his guests. Furthermore, the father ran away because he loved Banks's mother too much: Wang Ku 'found her spirit . . . highly attractive', enjoyed 'taming the white woman' (*WWWO* 294) and provided the money for Banks's upbringing and education. Furthermore, Uncle Philip colluded in the mother's abduction because he desired her himself, but could not bring himself to proposition her after her husband's disappearance, since she respected him as someone decent.

It is worth emphasizing the perverse nature of Uncle Philip's disclosures. In an embarrassing revelation and breach of convention, he declares to Christopher that the idea of his mother being 'conquered' excited him: it gives him pleasure to imagine 'what was happening to her' (*WWWO* 296). In this compressed, brutal and distressing way, sexuality and desire, which have been suppressed throughout Banks's narrative, redefine the relationship between four of the major figures from his childhood: mother, father, uncle, patron. There is an additional dimension to these revelations. The colonial power and financial nexus that Banks believed all along to have been behind the disappearance of his parents proves to be significant. The opium trade, deriving from India, was promoted by the British because they liked the Chinese to be in chaos, drug-addicted and 'unable to govern themselves properly' (*WWWO* 288). The trade was guarded by warlords like Wang Ku and opposed by Diana Banks on ethical and political grounds. Yet it provided funds for Christopher's education and tormented his father because of the moral demands of his principled wife. In fact, the overall control of this trade by the Chinese communist regime blighted Christopher's own life and turned him into an orphan. Commentators such as Cunningham[19] and Sim[20] have examined *When We Were Orphans* as a replaying of the plot of Dickens's *Great Expectations* (1861), with Wang Ku playing the Magwitch role of hidden benefactor to Banks's Pip. However, Pip was not forced to imagine his mother being humiliated and sexually assaulted or fantasized about in bizarre and brutal versions of the Oedipal triangle involving three father-competitors: Wang Ku,

Uncle Philip and Banks's father. This is the scenario Christopher has arrived at thirty years too late to put right.

Christopher thus comes face to face late in the book with revelations that might end his journey. He is tortured by this account of his own parents' sexuality and vulnerability, and betrayed by a trusted guardian who had aided and abetted the kidnapping of his mother. It is too late for him to save those he loved, and there is little hope of closure through marriage or a close relationship, even though his ward Jennifer asks in the book's closing scene, 'How about *you* getting married? . . . You're always mentioning your lady friends' (*WWWO* 309).

Banks never marries, but his narrative does trace his significant relationships with women, all of which are related in different ways to his sexuality. While all three relationships might be seen as ending in failure, a Kierkegaardian ironic reading might see them as all representing some capacity for virtue and achievement. Banks, characteristically, apologizes for each of them. When he finally finds his mother in a nursing home in Hong Kong, he says to her that he's very sorry it's taken him so long: 'I've let you down badly' (*WWWO* 305). She has been through three phases in his imaginative development: as the adored, lost, brave mother of an only child; as the object of desire embodied in Uncle Philip's narrative; and finally as the amnesiac, de-sexed creature who 'forgives' him.

The second apology is made to Jennifer, the orphan he had adopted and brought into his home as a child: 'I should have done more for you, Jenny. I'm sorry' (*WWWO* 308). She had been introduced to him by Lady Beaton the philanthropist, who knew an orphaned girl who was miserable and 'so misses England' (*WWWO* 129). Banks's offer to take her in is at first mistrusted, presumably on sexual grounds: 'Perhaps I should not hold it against her that [Lady Beaton's] first reaction was to recoil with a look of suspicion' (*WWWO* 129). Although the adoption is later entered into with good will, Banks's account of this arrangement, and of his decision to leave her behind for a period of time (*WWWO* 133), is set in the context of three mysterious verbal exchanges that undermined his self-esteem. These are as follows:

(1) The words of the police inspector in Somerset when Banks is working on the investigation of child murders. Banks and the inspector agree that there is something particularly horrifying about the murders, an 'even more ghastly' truth that makes them feel that they are looking into the depths of 'the darkness' (*WWWO* 135). The exact nature of this crime and of the darkness is not revealed. There are a number of implications: that sexual abuse is involved,

or that other children committed the murder, or that family members were involved. Banks responds by quoting the words of his boyhood friend Akira on 'holding strong' but is disconcerted by what he takes to be the accusatory tone of the policeman when he demands that Banks use his status to go to 'the heart of the serpent' and attack the evil.

(2) The incident at the Royal Geographical Society when Canon Moorly insists that, of all people, Christopher Banks should realize that the heart of the modern crisis of the 1930s lies in Shanghai, spreading 'its poison over the years further across the world, right through our civilisation' (*WWWO* 138). Here again, the speaker is emphatic but cryptic, and Banks does not gloss what they take to be the nature of the evil: could it be opium addiction?

(3) The incident at the Draycoats' wedding when the red-faced man, brother to the groom, takes exception to what he sees as the ragging and discourteous treatment accorded to Banks by a group of young men: 'It's barbaric behaviour. You're a guest, just as they are, and if they can't be civil, they'll have to go' (*WWWO* 141). Again, the exact nature of the offence is omitted, and eventually Banks's narrative returns to the source of these memories of discomfort: the feeling that in departing for Shanghai and 'the challenge of [his] responsibilities' (*WWWO* 149) Banks is abandoning and betraying young Jennifer: a point made strongly by Miss Givens (*WWWO* 146). The ironic doubleness of *When We Were Orphans* is apparent here: in assuming his 'responsibilities' for the family mystery and for global catastrophe, Banks is betraying his guardianship of a child, and in a way replaying his own experiences. Furthermore, taking the orphaned Jennifer into a bachelor establishment had been itself both a self-indulgent and a humane gesture. In the three memories that are provoked by his leaving Jennifer, three interlocutors – the policeman, Canon Moorly and the wedding guest – highlight the way in which Banks's triumphs are haunted by disaster and humiliation – a pattern that persists to the end of the novel in an ironic compound of success and failure.

Banks's success? Few commentators apply the term to the narrator of *When We Were Orphans*. The Kierkegaardian irony of his relationships with women is, nevertheless, that they are successes of a kind, despite Brian Finney's dismissal of Banks's 'wasted life'. Banks *does* find his mother, and takes some consolation from her confused words. Jennifer, who says to Banks 'I owe you everything' (*WWWO* 308) – admittedly a characteristically double-edged phrase – is a troubled soul, who offers him the honorary position of uncle to all her future children (*WWWO* 309). Even though the prospect of finding such a 'home' remains remote at the end of the book, this is not a cheap irony – two ruined people clinging together and lying to each other – but a rich one touched by tenderness.

Readers of *The Remains of the Day* will be alert to the sacrifice of Banks's relationship to the third significant woman, Sarah Hemmings, on the altars of reticence and obsession. A key conversation, potentially momentous and relating to Christopher's emotional life, occurs in Chapter 16 when Sarah asks him to run away with her and for them to become a couple. In a manner akin to Uncle Philip, she offers him a solution. He has never had a profound emotional attachment; for all we know he is a virgin; now he can go to Macao and acquire a lover in her. Sarah even offers him the promise of a ready-made family unit with Jennifer, considerations for whose welfare might otherwise have been an obstacle to their union. Like many others in *When We Were Orphans*, this conversation is hard to decode, from Sarah's brittle encouragement – 'We could go to South America, run away like thieves in the night. Wouldn't that be fun?' (*WWWO* 212) – to Christopher's half-hearted assent: 'yes, I'll go with you. I'll go with you, we'll do as you say. Yes, you might be right. Jennifer, us, everything. It might turn out well' (*WWWO* 214). At this point, the novel offers us two solutions to the sense of melancholy and gloom that hangs over it. Uncle Philip presents life's great mystery as already solved and faded: a pair of intrigues that revolve around sex and power and parents; Sarah presents romance and human contact, sex and scandal as an answer to the sense of repression and displacement that surrounds Banks. Banks himself recognizes Sarah's proposition as an offer of escape. Three times he refers to the sense of release generated by his decision to run away: he experiences the sort of giddiness when coming suddenly out into 'the light and fresh air after being trapped in a dark chamber' (*WWWO* 212); he could feel a 'massive weight' lifting off him (*WWWO* 214); and it was as if a 'heavy burden' had been removed (*WWWO* 215). Yet a sense of doom has been cast over their relationship by Sir Cecil's perverse drunken confidence some nights before. In words anticipating Uncle Philip's reflections on Christopher's mother, Sir Cecil betrays his wife in her hearing and speaks of his perverse pleasure in imagining that strangers in Shanghai might take her for a whore: 'I like people to mistake my wife for a harlot' (*WWWO* 172). If Sarah goes off with Christopher to Macao she will (in conventional eyes) confirm this misrecognition and mimic Christopher's mother: the respectable educated sensitive woman who becomes a harlot. Alternatively, Christopher would be repeating his father's history. They will become displaced wanderers – as do, eventually, Sarah and her French companion Monsieur de Villefort (*WWWO* 311).

In one sense, the outcome of this liaison with Sarah is the triumph of a delusion – Banks neglects his appointment with her in his determination to track his missing parents to a residence opposite the house of the famous blind actor Wei Chin. Both practically, and in terms of Banks's preoccupation with his parents, however, the decision is the right one, and the alliance of two orphans would not necessarily have compensated for past losses.

The conclusion of *When We Were Orphans* suggests a paring down of meaning, and appears to offer an end to ironies, in the form of clear-sighted single vision. Uncle Philip takes the mystery that fuels Christopher's quest and lays it bare in love and betrayal. Sarah's offer of love and escape dwindles into companionship, internment and death. Mother's few final words about Puffin are erected by Christopher into a testament of enduring love (*WWWO* 305–6). Jennifer's loneliness spins slowly around Christopher's own, and the promise of homeliness, parenthood and childhood seems flimsy. On the final page Christopher offers his own muted version of the end of *The Great Gatsby*: beating on, a boat against the current, he sees himself as chasing for a long time 'the shadows of vanished parents' (*WWWO* 313).

My preference would be to decline this offer of closure, with its too-precise distinction between the knowable and the unknowable, and its pessimistic 'realism' about the orphaned. Significant historical context is omitted from these pages dated 14 November 1958: the terrible price paid in 1945 for Japanese imperialism – if Japan is to become a great nation, like England 'it is necessary' (*WWWO* 278) – for the Chinese Revolution and for the increase in the number of migrants and orphans between 1937 and 1958. Banks's narration, too, is as open to ironical reading here as it was on the opening page. For a book so concerned with historical forces and moments, his reference to 'our fate' (which is 'to face the world as orphans') presents, as something learned through bitter experience, the fact that compulsions cannot be overturned. This summary implies the getting of wisdom but sits oddly with the last paragraph, where chasing of shadows is not much in evidence. The conclusion acknowledges the friendship with Jennifer (*WWWO* 310), but sets aside Banks's sharper insights and the achievements of himself and others in the previous pages. These would include: his bitterness at the lack of 'shame' in the expatriate Shanghai community (*WWWO* 215); his mother's bravery in opposing the opium trade; the mixture of fidelity and hubris that characterizes his own return to Shanghai;

his concern for the fate of the Japanese soldier; his belated realization that 'many things aren't as I supposed' (*WWWO* 277); and Sarah's magnanimity in her letter to him. The counterpointing of successes and failures, and ironic contradictions, in *When We Were Orphans* remains challenging to the end, as does the problematic reference dropped quietly into the penultimate sentence, in which Banks declares that London has come to be his home, though there are times when an emptiness fills his days, and he continues to give Jennifer's invitation 'serious thought' (*WWWO* 313). One's first reaction might be to register this as a verbal irony. Banks seems aware that his contentment could be seen as smug, but in seeing either London or Jennifer's place in the country as 'home', he is surely deceiving himself: he is a perpetual exile and orphan who has no home except childhood memories. After all, he said as much to 'Akira' in 1937 (*WWWO* 256). On a deeper level of irony, however, the ending remains characteristic of the gaps in this text that cannot be closed. Here they exist as the gap between affection and bonding with Jennifer, and the emotional needs that the relationship cannot quite fulfil; and the gap between a resignation to living out one's life in certain places, and the need to be at home, fully and intuitively.

notes

1. Søren Kierkegaard, *The Concept of Irony, with Continual Reference to Socrates*, trans. H. V. Hong and E. H. Hong (Princeton: Princeton University Press, 1989), p. 326.
2. Gillian Harding-Russell, 'Through the Veil of Memory', *Queens Quarterly*, 109 (1) (2002), 95–101.
3. Katherine Stanton, *Cosmopolitan Fictions: Ethics, Politics and Global Change in the Works of Kazuo Ishiguro, Michael Ondaatje, Jamaica Kincaid and J. M. Coetzee* (London and New York: Routledge, 2006), p. 79.
4. Ibid., p. 80.
5. Brian Finney, 'Figuring the Real: Ishiguro's *When We Were Orphans*', *Jouvert: A Journal of Postcolonial Studies*, 7 (1) (2002), paras.1–32. Finney observes: 'Banks's journey through the inferno of the Japanese–Chinese warfront is both a personal rite of passage and a vivid confrontation with the death and destruction produced by the commercialism and imperialism of the industrial nations prior to the War, death that inevitably adds heavily to the number of children left orphaned. Just as Banks's protected childhood was bought at the price of his mother's servitude to a Chinese warlord, so the protected and privileged existence of the wealthy community living in the International Settlement was bought at the cost of widespread opium addiction and poverty among the Chinese population . . . Banks, like Ishiguro, is a transnational torn between two countries and cultures' (paras. 26–7).

6. Timothy Weiss, 'Where Is Place? Locale and Identity in Kazuo Ishiguro's *When We Were Orphans* and Ricardo Piglia's *La ciudad ausente*', in *Translating Orients: Between Ideology and Utopia* (Toronto: University of Toronto Press, 2004), p. 142.
7. Finney, 'Figuring the Real', para. 32.
8. Tobias Döring, 'Sherlock Holmes – He Dead: Disenchanting the English Detective in Kazuo Ishiguro's *When We Were Orphans*', in Christine Matzke and Susanne Mühleisen (eds.), *Postcolonial Postmortems: Crime Fiction from a Transcultural Perspective* (Amsterdam and New York: Rodopi), p. 63.
9. Ibid., p. 81.
10. Ibid., p. 82.
11. Frederick M. Holmes, 'Realism, Dreams and the Unconscious in the Novels of Kazuo Ishiguro', in James Acheson and Sarah C. E. Ross (eds.), *The Contemporary British Novel* (Edinburgh: Edinburgh University Press, 2005), p. 20.
12. Ishiguro cited in ibid., p. 24.
13. Ibid., p. 20.
14. Claire Colebrook, *Irony* (London: Routledge, 2004), p. 15.
15. Stanton, *Cosmopolitan Fictions*, p. 80.
16. Colebrook, *Irony*, p. 165.
17. Kierkegaard, *The Concept of Irony*, p. 262.
18. Clare Carlisle, *Kierkegaard: A Guide for the Perplexed* (London: Continuum, 2006), p. 83.
19. H. C. Cunningham, 'The Dickens Connection in Kazuo Ishiguro's *When We Were Orphans*', *Notes on Contemporary Literature*, 34 (5) (2004), 4–6.
20. Wai-chew Sim, *Globalization and Dislocation in the Novels of Kazuo Ishiguro* (Lewiston, Queenston and Lampeter: Edwin Mellen Press, 2006), p. 224.

14
'shanghaied' into service: double binds in *when we were orphans*

alyn webley

summary

This chapter looks closely at the psychological state of the main protagonist of When We Were Orphans, Christopher Banks. *It suggests that his distur-bance is a direct result of the social and economic contradictions he and his family experienced whilst living in Shanghai in the early part of the twenti-eth century (Banks's father worked for Morganbrook and Byatt, a firm that supplied opium to the Chinese and against which his mother campaigned). By using Gregory Bateson's concept of the double bind, Webley casts light on both Banks's obsession with the disappearance of his parents and his subsequent vocation as a detective.*

the child is the father to the man

When We Were Orphans features a central protagonist who is, simul-taneously, both a child and a man. Christopher Banks's father and mother disappear mysteriously when he is a boy living in Shanghai's International Settlement in the early decades of the twentieth century. Thus orphaned, the remainder of his upbringing takes place in England, but he returns to the Chinese city as an adult in the late 1930s. By this stage he has established himself as a well-known detective and his quixotic mission is to track down his parents. There is a shift in the mode of the book, between realistic narrative in Part One to something bordering on the surreal and irrational in Part Two. Ishiguro explains these transformations as follows:

> What I was trying to do is to paint a picture of what the world might look like if it ran according to the less rational emotional logic that we often carry within us . . . [for instance] when Christopher Banks goes around declaring that his parents must be holed up somewhere, even after all these years, and he must free them, and this is the most important crucial thing in stopping the war, people don't do a double take. Because he still lives in the childhood vision of the world that's frozen since the time that he lost his parents when he was a little boy, it's remained arrested at that point and now it's applied to the adult world that he encounters.[1]

So Banks sustains his childhood worldview into adulthood, with disastrous consequences. But what impelled this peculiar state of affairs? This chapter will argue that it was the stressful double binds in which the Banks family were enmeshed whilst living in Shanghai that brought about his disturbed psychological state.

Ishiguro's novel analyses the 'schizophrenic' effects that imperial capitalism can impose upon private and public life.[2] It explores the contradictions that are engendered on a number of levels: psychological, social, political, economical and cultural. In an effort to resolve or relieve these pressures, Banks forges an identity as a detective and submerges himself in his work as professional problem-solver. However, as with the protagonists of Ishiguro's other novels (such as Stevens the butler in *The Remains of the Day* and Ryder the musician in *The Unconsoled*), Banks's adherence to a vocational imperative ultimately masks the true nature of the problems he wishes to solve.

banks's contradictory childhood

In *When We Were Orphans*, Banks recalls the early childhood experiences that gradually resulted in a decision to pursue his vocation as a detective. These recollections give a far more direct and extended account of his childhood experience than that of other characters from Ishiguro's novels. Banks's narrative, therefore, gives a clear demonstration of how the subject is formed and how the child becomes (or, rather, fails to become) an adult. Banks was brought up in Shanghai at a time when the self-governing enclave of the city known as the International Settlement was home to the British and American concessions in China. The house in which Banks lived with his mother and father is described in Chapter 4 as 'a huge white edifice with numerous wings and trellised balconies' (*WWWO* 51). Although he admits that his memory might be exaggerating to a degree, the picture he paints is one of colonial affluence. It was in the large white house, and its garden with its manicured lawn and elm trees, that the young Banks spent much of his time playing games with the Japanese boy next door, Akira. Their world of childhood was safely inoculated against the harsh reality that surrounded them. Just a few miles away was the warren, a labyrinth of back-to-back slums separated by small alleys and home to thousands of impoverished Chinese factory workers.

Although the Banks's house seems to be an emblem of wealth and status, it does not actually belong to them: it 'was the property of Morganbrook and Byatt, which meant that there were many ornaments and pictures around the place I was forbidden to touch' (*WWWO* 51). This admission about the actual condition of the family's life somewhat undercuts the superficial image of affluent independence first presented. In fact, the family's prosperity was dependent on the whims of the imperial trading firm for which Banks's father worked. His father was, in effect, a professional servant. In Ishiguro's construction of Banks's background, his continuing fascination with the problems of professional identity is visible. *When We Were Orphans* unravels fully the repercussions of the invasion of corporate values into the realm of private life. The social power relationships affecting Christopher's parents shape the relationships established within the family. They form the cultural backdrop that eventually leads to the arrest of Christopher's personal development and the maintenance of the world view he formed as a child into adulthood.

It emerges that the relationship of Morganbrook and Byatt to the local population is an exploitative one. In addition to its legitimate trading activities, the company inflicts immense suffering on the Chinese by importing cheap opium from India into Shanghai. With the help of local warlords for distribution purposes, the firm profits from the addictions that they themselves had created. The British had a long history of such exploitation stretching back to the so-called Opium Wars of 1839 and 1858. It is estimated that by 1909 a quarter of the entire Chinese population were addicts.

The extent to which the illicit concerns of Morganbrook and Byatt interfered with the Banks's family life becomes clear on one of the many occasions that a company health inspector calls round to the house. He is there to check not only the state of the building and its furniture, but also the family and the domestic staff, all of whom are considered as the property of the company. On this particular occasion, the health inspector recommends to Christopher's mother that they dismiss the Shantung servants. This is partly because of doubts about their hygiene and health, but also because of suspicions about their honesty. When pressed by Christopher's mother for an explanation, the inspector replies that the rampant opium addiction in Shantung can force the servants into becoming thieves. Christopher's mother is exasperated and points out that this problem was being caused by the company itself. She tells him 'that the British in general, and the company of Morganbrook and Byatt especially, by importing Indian opium into China in such massive quantities had brought untold misery and degradation to a whole nation' (*WWWO* 60). Morganbrook and Byatt, as an arm of British imperialism, had set up a relationship with the local population that was a no-win situation for the Chinese. The poor people of Shantung had become addicted to opium thanks to the company. In order to pay for their habit, they were forced into cheap labour as servants for Morganbrook and Byatt. Because they are not given sufficient wages, some of them stole from their employers. If they are sacked, they will turn to opium as a source of consolation and the cycle will begin again. In other words, they were caught within a double bind.

double binds in family and society

The anthropologist Gregory Bateson first put forward the theory of the double bind. It can be defined briefly as 'social interactions in which the individual is repeatedly exposed to conflicting injunctions, without having the opportunity to adequately respond to those injunctions, or to ignore them (i.e., to escape the field)'.[3] In this formulation, it is a means of understanding the adverse impact of the communication of contradictory messages on the psychological state of individuals within a family. However, the theory has much broader implications. *When We Were Orphans* presents an institutional double bind in the relationship between an imperial capitalist company, Morganbrook and Byatt, and the indigenous population of Shanghai. The imposition of the necessity for servile work on the poor people of Shanghai, combined with the importation of large quantities of opium, created the perfect conditions for mass addiction. At the same time, this condition was used as a criterion for the refusal to employ them, thus further increasing their poverty and the likelihood of dependence on opium. As Banks's mother puts it, Morganbrook and Byatt 'not only liked the profits very much, they actually *wanted* the Chinese to be useless. They liked them to be in chaos, drug-addicted, unable to govern themselves properly. That way, the country could be run virtually like a colony, but with none of the usual obligations' (*WWWO* 288).

In this scenario, Ishiguro emphasizes the inherent contradictions in the relationship of imperial capitalism to its victims. It is a relationship in which exploitation 'must not be seen as such. It must be seen as benevolence. Persecution preferably should not need to be invalidated as the figment of a paranoid imagination, it should be experienced as kindness'.[4] The insistence of Banks's mother in pointing out the contradictions inherent in the company's relationship with the people of Shanghai undermines this attempt to promote exploitation as benevolence and persecution as kindness. *When We Were Orphans* thus establishes this institutional double bind as the backdrop to Banks's childhood experience. The argument over the opium trade politicizes Christopher's childhood by placing it on the knife-point of conflicting political and commercial interests. Even as a boy, he is embroiled in the socio-political structures and discourses that shape his world.

This impossible situation is the cause of the family conflicts that eventually deprive Banks of both parents. The devolution of this conflict from the social environment into a personal conflict between Banks's mother and father ensures that the narrator is pushed out into a position of political, as well as personal, marginality from the outset. Excluded from occupying a central space in the family by his parents' conflict, Christopher's development was arrested. His future shift from the family into society was diverted onto a course that was outside the usual dynamic of social integration. He was, in effect, doomed to spend much of his adult life attempting to recover his lost parents in order to continue his growth.

Banks's mother was in a particularly difficult position within this tangle of allegiances. On the one hand, she wished to remain loyal to her husband. On the other hand, he was an employee of Morganbrook and Byatt, a company whose exploitative practices in relation to the Chinese population perturbed her religious principles. Yet she, too, is indirectly involved in the opium scandal as she is living in the company house on company money. She takes her verbal protests to the health inspector one step further by organizing luncheons for the wives of other employees at which they can address the duplicity of Morganbrook and Byatt. Having successfully converted a few women to her cause, she then holds more serious meetings with them in the presence of a clergyman or diplomat and Christopher's Uncle Philip. These activities are in direct opposition to the activities of Christopher's father in his role as employee. The issue was a volcano waiting to erupt.

Banks recalls one particular occasion on which he overheard his parents quarrelling in the dining room. His mother berated his father, asking him if he was not ashamed to be in the service of this company: 'How can your conscience rest while you owe your existence to such an ungodly wealth?' (*WWWO* 70). Christopher admits that this kind of argument between his parents was a frequent occurrence. The source of the shame felt by Christopher's mother is that their livelihood is owed 'to such an ungodly wealth'. In a rather cowardly fashion, his father had come to a resigned acceptance of his own complicity in the activities of his employers.

As a good Christian, Banks's mother considers the building of the British Empire as an essentially civilizing activity. But at the same time, her criticism of the company's trade as 'sinful', and its profits as 'ungodly wealth', also issues from her religious conscience. So her own material circumstances place her in a highly ambiguous relation to such wealth. Whether she likes it or not, her position as the wife of a company employee means that she is part of the machinery of empire. This is an 'enormously complex machinery: a machinery dedicated to the continuance of European rule, the exploitation of natural resources, and the spread of European culture as an accompaniment to the continued subordination of native peoples'.[5] Diana Banks's Christian sensibilities are caught up in this process of subjugation. Her sense of religious mission supplements the establishment and preservation of colonial power.

Banks's mother is, therefore, caught in a situation every bit as binding (albeit, not as crushing) as that of the opium-dependent Chinese. The religious stance that she adopts to support her resistance to the activities of Morganbrook and Byatt is the very same one that is habitually used as a cover for the establishment of the brutal economic forces that she is fighting. The option of leaving the company was not open to Banks's father. Christopher recalls having overheard part of a conversation between his parents concerning the possibility of leaving Shanghai and returning to England. His father admitted that a return would financially ruin the family: 'Without the firm, we're simply stranded' (*WWWO* 86). So, despite the wish of Christopher's mother to return home, the constraints of the family's economic situation prevent it. The whole family, it might be said, has been 'shanghaied' into the service of imperialism at its most destructive and corrupt.

painful choices

It is worth returning at this point to the double bind, particularly the expansion of the concept by so-called 'anti-psychiatrist' R. D. Laing to the subjective embodiment of power relationships. In *The Politics of Experience* (1967), Laing is concerned with the issue of why certain people become permanently labelled as 'schizophrenic'. He looks closely at disturbed patterns of communication within families and the double binds they often generate. His suggestion is that it is prolonged exposure to contradictory messages from parents and other relations in childhood that leads to the condition of schizophrenia. Laing does not limit his observations to the family unit. He places this dynamic of contradiction within the larger context of the civic order of society and the ways that institutions can exercise control and power over large numbers of individuals. The power relationships at work in society can reach such an intense pitch that they not only disrupt normal family relationships, but also have the capacity to pervert cultural development.

At first glance, *When We Were Orphans* may seem to be far removed from such concerns. However, as Banks's disconcerting account of his past life progresses, it discloses the role that the political order of society has played in setting the trajectory of his existence. In terms of double bind theory, the family's economic situation can be seen as the restriction which does not allow them to resolve their no-win situation or leave the field of conflict. The arguments between Banks's parents, therefore, are repeated endlessly. Christopher claims to have been unaffected by these arguments: 'I was well used to such periods and never concerned myself unduly with them. In any case, it was only in the smallest ways that they ever impinged upon my life' (*WWWO* 71). But is this plausible? It is almost always the case that when Ishiguro's narrators seek to gloss over an issue that they are at their most unreliable. Furthermore, one side-effect of repeated exposure to a double-bind situation is flattened affect, or an unwillingness to acknowledge the emotional upheaval experienced in a situation of conflict. In any event, Banks's unfolding of his personal development reveals tacitly that these arguments did, indeed, have a deep psychological impact.

By illustrating how Banks was a frequent witness to the arguments of his parents, *When We Were Orphans* adds a further layer of familial contradiction to the institutional knots of Shanghai. The emotional damage caused by these disruptions affects Banks in a very complex way. Bateson et al. suggest that the double-bind situation is one which generally involves 'two or more persons. Of these we designate one, for purposes of definition, as the "victim". When a person is caught in a double bind situation, he will respond defensively in a manner similar to the schizophrenic'.[6]

The formation of Banks's identity as a victim follows a path which is carved from his exposure to these double binds. Not only is he conflicted by the relationships with his mother and father, and his parent's own dilemmas, but he is also damaged by his family's paradoxical role as part of the wider social network. The conflicts in the family begin with the position of Christopher's father as a functionary of the company that makes contradictory demands upon him. These contradictions, in turn, are the source of the arguments between Christopher's parents. Christopher could only attempt to find a solution to the problem of his parents' relationship based on the narrow parameters of his childhood world. The young boy was subjected, via the arguments in the family, to the duplicities of Morganbrook and Byatt. At the same time, he was trying to evolve his own identity by acquiring Englishness through emulation or mimesis. He recalls a question that he once asked his Uncle Philip: 'Uncle Philip, I was just wondering. How do you suppose one might become more English?' (*WWWO* 76). Such pressures were an integral part of his family's life and unconsciously mediated through the young boy. Banks's childhood self has internalized his parents' quarrels as personal conflict.

The most painful moment in this whole nexus of conflict comes when Christopher is asked to choose between his parents. Banks recalls that he was placed in this impossible situation on the occasion when Uncle Philip suggested that they all go to the racecourse for the afternoon. His father replied that he would excuse himself from this trip because he had a lot of work to do. At the same time, however, his mother expressed her enthusiasm for such a trip, saying that it would do them all some good. Christopher realizes that it all depends on him, but that, whatever he decides, one of his parents will be hurt. He is aware that he is offered a choice to either go out to the racecourse or to stay at home with his father, and he understands the deeper implications. If he chooses to stay in, his mother would refuse to go to the racecourse in Uncle Philip's company, so their outing depends on his going with them. Banks notes: 'Moreover I knew – and I did so with a calm certainty – that at that moment my father was desperately wishing us not to go, that for us to do so would cause him huge pain' (*WWWO* 84).

This episode further reveals the depth of the impact of the family's difficult condition on their personal relationships. The increasing strain on the marriage of Mr and Mrs Banks (complicated by the presence of Uncle Philip) and their precarious socio-economic situation were being increasingly ingested by Christopher as time went by. The boy describes his clear recognition of the deeper dynamics of this situation, of his father's true feelings and of the fact that his father is dependent upon

Christopher to save the situation. Christopher's intense awareness of the conflicting emotional dynamic generated by his mother's wishing to go on the trip and his father's wishing to stay put him in a no-win situation.

The pressure of choosing between his father and mother had been accumulating in the background of Christopher's life for some time. Through the steady build-up of arguments and issues of contention, *When We Were Orphans* demonstrates how the institutional double binds created by Morganbrook and Byatt flow into the private sphere of the family and disturb the equilibrium of Banks's childhood. In the racecourse incident, the young boy takes it upon himself to save the situation. However, the dilemma is brought to an end by his mother, who tells him to get ready quickly. He obeys instantly, and with alacrity, though with a false show of enthusiasm. Ultimately, the choice was taken out of his hands.

Banks's childish tendency towards an over-inflated sense of responsibility later became a significant aspect of Banks's adult life. His determination to acquire Englishness as a solution to his parents' conflicts is mirrored in later years by the grandiose role he assigns himself in the global fight against evil. It is his anxious childhood, then, that can be proposed as the psychological origin of Banks's vocational imperative and submersion of identity in his persona as a detective. There is one further twist, however, which both exacerbates his struggles and develops his deluded conviction in the redeeming powers of his chosen vocation. This is related to, first, the disappearance of his father and, then, not long after, the abduction of his mother.

watching the detective

One day, on returning to the house after playing in the garden with Akira, Christopher discovers his mother in conversation with Mr Simpson, from Morganbrook and Byatt, and two policemen. His father had not turned up for work and had not been seen since he had left the house that morning. Trying to reassure her son, his mother says: 'what we have to appreciate . . . is that the city's very best detectives have been assigned to the case . . . We have to be hopeful. We have to trust the detectives' (*WWWO* 108). Banks wonders if the detectives are too busy, however. In this short exchange lies the seed of how Christopher sought to solve the family dilemmas created by their various double binds. He decided he would have to become a detective himself to find his father. The young boy's anxiety and bloated sense of responsibility would not allow him simply to leave the job to the professionals.

The games he played with Akira began to reflect this mission and always followed a particular pattern: 'My father was held captive in a house somewhere beyond the Settlement boundaries. His captors were a gang intent on extorting a huge ransom' (*WWWO* 110). Christopher played the parts of both his captive father and one of the rescuing detectives.

Banks's aspiring identity as a detective is further consolidated when his mother goes missing, despite his efforts to keep a vigilant watch over her and prevent her from being abducted, too. Under the pretence of going to buy a piano accordion, Uncle Philip takes the young boy into Shanghai and abandons him there, leaving him to find his own way home. By the time he returns, his mother has already disappeared. With no idea why his parents had gone missing, Christopher is placed in the care of an aunt in Shropshire and sent to boarding school. Before journeying to England, Christopher protests that he would rather stay in Shanghai because according to him the best detectives in Shanghai are working hard to find his mother and father. However, his relocation goes ahead. These passages underline how Banks's vocational aspirations are founded on a type of pathogenic effect induced by the conflicting and traumatic experiences of his childhood.

Banks's recollections of his childhood in Shanghai contains an elucidation of how his early experiences affected the way in which he became integrated into society. These memories, however, are interwoven throughout *When We Were Orphans* with a parallel narrative of how he came to be an actual detective within the broader social context of his new life in England. As a young child transplanted to a country that was both familiar and alien to him, Banks is acutely aware of his 'otherness'. His attempts to integrate with his new environment are shaped by his pre-existing dispositions and cultural references. The writings of Conan Doyle about the formidable Sherlock Holmes assume a particular importance in helping to fuse together the discourse of the detective and the discourse of Englishness in Banks's young mind. These literary references also underline the imaginative process by which Banks constructs his identity. He models himself on the fictional detective, just as he observes and copies carefully the manners of his school friends in order to fit in with new norms and protect his fragile sense of self.

In England, Banks continues to play a solo version of the detective games he used to play with Akira, much to the consternation of his aunt. His desire to become a detective is recognized by his school friends in two specific incidents. The first is on the occasion of his fourteenth birthday, when his friends present him with a magnifying glass. He is delighted with the gift and goes on to use it as an adult when he investigates the Mannering Case and the Trevor Richardson affair.

The second moment of epiphany occurs when he is in the Lower Sixth and his friend Roger Brenthurst refers to him as 'Sherlock' (*WWWO* 9–10). Although seemingly trivial, these incidents represent a continuing deepening of Banks's identity as a detective. They emphasize the unification of function and person which remains the central cause of tension throughout the text. Christopher is left with little option but to shore up his own sense of identity as problem-solver as a bulwark to the painful family conflicts to which he has been subjected. To this extent, his entire career as a detective is a necessary delusion. He, too, has been 'shanghaied' into service.

no ending to madness

In *When We Were Orphans*, it is possible to trace how the institutional double binds inflicted by Morganbrook and Byatt in Shanghai, combined with the contradictions and conflicts internal to the Banks family, launched Christopher into a false identity. As Lewis notes, Banks's 'childhood obsession of solving the mystery of his parents' disappearance drives his adult enquiries, and brings him to the point of madness'.[7] This 'madness' may only erupt in the second half of the novel, but its aetiology is clear from the opening chapters. The text describes the processes by which the power constellations of society establish themselves in the minds of its individuals. Banks's obsession with his vocational identity can be interpreted as a schizophrenic reaction to the double binds to which he and his family were subjected. Contradictory and hypocritical activities, that are political and economic expedients for those institutions occupying the dominant strata of the social order, were translated into internalized conflict. Banks's identification with the role of the great detective is complete and leads to considerable social success, until a series of disclosed betrayals eventually make the maintenance of his vocational imperative untenable. He is deceived by his Uncle Philip, who conceals the truth of the disappearance of his parents both from the young boy and from the adult detective. It is only much later that all is revealed. Banks's father, it transpires, ran away with another woman, whilst his mother was enslaved as a concubine by the warlord Wang Ku (with the aid of Uncle Philip) as a form of sadistic revenge for being personally insulted by her.

The ending of the novel may be a little contrived (deliberately so, given its nods to *Great Expectations* by Charles Dickens), but the novel as a whole portrays convincingly how vast commercial institutions and their ruthless money-making practices can maintain adults in an aggravated, childish mindset. The conflict in the relationship of Banks's parents was bound up with their different stances towards the political order of which they were a part. Christopher was himself, as a child, caught up in complex double binds. The impossibility of finding a solution to the contradictions with which he was faced fuelled an intense sense of anxiety. The sudden disappearance of both his parents intensified his vulnerable psychological state and led to a vocational commitment that bordered on the delusional. In the light of this background, and with the aid of the concept of the double bind as expounded by Bateson and Laing, it is easier to comprehend why Banks carried forward his childhood vision of the world into adulthood.

notes

1. Cynthia F. Wong, *Kazuo Ishiguro* (Tavistock: Northcote House, 2005), p. 89.
2. It is therefore aligned with theoretical works such as Fredric Jameson, *Postmodernism; Or, The Cultural Logic of Late Capitalism* (London: Verso, 1992) and Gilles Deleuze and Félix Guattari, *Anti-Oedipus: Capitalism and Schizophrenia*, trans. Robert Hurley, Mark Seem and Helen R. Lane (London: Viking Press, 1977).
3. Mathijs Koopmans, 'Schizophrenia and the Family: Double Bind Theory Revisited', available at www.goertzel.org/dynapsyc/1997/Koopmans.html.
4. R. D. Laing, *The Politics of Experience* (London: Penguin, 1967), p. 49.
5. David Punter, *Postcolonial Imaginings: Fictions of a New World Order* (New York: Rowman and Littlefield, 2000), p. 2.
6. Gregory Bateson, Don D. Jackson, Jay Haley and John H. Weakland, 'Toward a Theory of Schizophrenia', *Behavioural Science*, 1 (1956), 251–3.
7. Barry Lewis, *Kazuo Ishiguro* (Manchester: Manchester University Press, 2000), p. 7.

part vi
never let me go

15
the concertina effect: unfolding kazuo ishiguro's *never let me go*
barry lewis

summary

This chapter explores Kazuo Ishiguro's Never Let Me Go *and its artful deployment of memory in structuring the 'pleated' shape of its narrative. Although superficially about clones, the novel's true concerns are those of mortality and value. By looking in detail at the passages concerning the Judy Bridgewater cassette, the chapter will demonstrate the novel's 'concertina effect', or the way that Kathy's memories fold into each other and gradually unfold as the story progresses. This narratological process mirrors the compressed lives of the protagonists, whose reduced life-span stands in a metaphorical relationship to that of normal human beings.*

the concertina effect: a brief introduction to narrative compression

Kazuo Ishiguro's novel *Never Let Me Go* (2005) appears to be a novel about clones. It features an alternative recent past, an England of the 1990s in which advances in genetic engineering have revolutionized medical affairs. In this parallel world, many illnesses and conditions are treated successfully by exploiting human clones as a source of tissues and organs. Scientific progress in this area has resulted in the establishment of organ farms, where clones are reared in order to provide 'donations' for non-clones. Not everyone is happy with this state of affairs. Benevolent institutions such as the Hailsham School have been set up to provide at least the semblance of an ordinary human existence for these enforced organ donors. Nevertheless, the brutal truth remains that the clones are little more than educated cattle. Like cows, pigs and sheep, they are so inured to their fates that the thought of escape never crosses their minds.[1]

However, cloning is a mere pretext for other concerns. M. John Harrison observes:

> This extraordinary and, in the end, rather frighteningly clever novel isn't about cloning, or being a clone, at all. It's about why we don't explode, why we don't just wake up one day and go sobbing and crying down the street, kicking everything to pieces out of the raw, infuriating, completely personal sense of our lives never having been what they could have been.[2]

Never Let Me Go, then, can be construed as a work that meshes the science fiction and dystopian genres in the manner, say, of John Wyndham's *The Chrysalids* (1955) or Margaret Atwood's *The Handmaid's Tale* (1985). Like these novels, *Never Let Me Go* is not hard-core sci-fi, but rather a tale that borrows certain themes and trappings of the genre to explore perennial issues about the human condition. Ishiguro's own account of what the novel addresses underscores this:

> When I am writing fiction I don't think in terms of genre at all. I write a completely different way. It starts with ideas . . . I guess it [the compression of the life span of the clones] was a useful kind of metaphor for how we all live . . . I just concertina-ed the time span through this device. These people basically face the same questions we all face . . . What are the things you hold on to, what are the things you want to set right? What do you regret? What are the consolations? And what is all the education and culture for if you are going to check out?[3]

In order to sound out these grand themes, the novel follows the fortunes of three clones – narrator Kathy, and her closest friends Ruth and Tommy – as they grow up together at Hailsham and the Cottages. It charts their hapless destinies as 'carers' and 'donors' when they leave the cosy confines of school and college. Although clones are its literal topic, Ishiguro's novel is also about death and the human condition.

Ishiguro's novel is particularly interested in exploring the relationship between memory and mortality through the story of the clones, and especially through narrator Kathy H.'s 'concertina-ing'[4] of remembered time within the novel, which recreates the compression and expansion of events as they are recounted. Close textual analysis of two large portions of the novel, in which Kathy unfolds her compressed memories, makes the 'pleatedness' of the narrative visible, whilst thwarting any simple explanation of the novel. Summarizing is never innocent: it always involves an element of interpretation, through the selection (or omission) of events and their combination with other events. It is not coincidental that both the lexemes 'explain' and 'explicate' arise from roots that mean 'unfolding'. The verb 'explicate' comes from the Latin 'explicatus', a variant past participle of 'explicare', meaning to 'unfold, unravel, explain'. This connects up with our modern word 'explicit'. In fact, 'explicitus' was written at the end of medieval parchments as a shortened version of the phrase 'explicitus est liber' – meaning, 'the book is unrolled'.

Ishiguro concertinas time in *Never Let Me Go* by reducing the life expectancy of the clones to around thirty years. This foreshortening is not connected with their unusual genetic constitution: their lives end abruptly as a consequence of the organ donations they undergo. The 'donors' may be asked to yield a liver, a kidney or a pancreas – in some cases, all three. The scientific implausibility of this is a detail that does not concern Ishiguro, whose interests do not lie in cloning per se but in its metaphorical potential.

The idea of squeezing time in this manner is striking. In a sense all fictions concertina time to their advantage, but there are a few novelists who stretch or compress time in extreme ways in order to draw attention to how it can be manipulated. Authors such as Laurence Sterne and Nicholson Baker play such games with time in *Tristram Shandy* (1760–67) and *The Mezzanine* (1988). Ishiguro's concertina-ing of time is principally a defamiliarization device. In *The Unconsoled*, he experimented with duration by crowding a large number of events or long speeches into a short segment of time. The classic example, at the beginning of the novel, is the rambling monologue of Gustav the porter that is delivered in the brief interval that it should take for an elevator to move between a few floors. In *Never Let Me Go*, the temporal shortening enables us to look anew at the human lot, by compressing the three-score-and-ten years, the normal expected life span for a healthy Westerner, into roughly half that passage of time. It is effective in cajoling us to meditate upon the brevity of our own lives and brings several matters sharply into focus. For instance, it seems odd that the clones devote so many of their childhood and teenage years to education, when what they are taught has little bearing upon their subsequent fates. How can George Eliot's *Daniel Deronda* (1876) possibly help them come to terms with the grisly business of organ donations? This may prompt us to consider the aptness of our own experiences at school, college or university.

Another way, however, in which time is concertina-ed or compressed throughout the novel is through memory. *Never Let Me Go*, like Ishiguro's other novels, features a first-person narrator who is trying to order his or her memories. Kathy – like Etsuko, Ono, Stevens, Banks and others – returns to the past to understand her present. At the opening of her narration, she is thirty-one years old, and is ready to give up her role as a carer to which she has devoted almost twelve years of service. The donors she has looked after and seen through to 'completion' – the chill euphemism for the final operation that leads to the death of the 'donor' – include Tommy and Ruth, her best friends from schooldays. Kathy sifts through what she remembers to help her make sense of what transpired between the three friends:

> I've been getting this urge to order all these old memories. . . .
> I realise now just how much of what occurred later came out of our
> time at Hailsham, and that's why I want first to go over these earlier
> memories quite carefully. (*NLMG* 37)[5]

What Kathy particularly wants to determine is what happened to the triangular relationship between herself, Tommy and Ruth, after they left Hailsham and the Cottages, drifted apart and then met again years later in very different circumstances. To understand that topic fully, she needs to go into their time at Hailsham, as it was at this school that they sowed the seeds of their friendship. Her memories, then, involve different layers of experience. Although these strata are associated with particular times and places, they cannot be easily separated from each other. Naturally, memories do not remain static in ordered sediments but are revised, refined and reframed through subsequent experiences. As Kathy notes, early events can seem more significant in hindsight than they were at the time (*NLMG* 77).

To look at the past in the light of later events, from the vantage point of a present that will inevitably itself become something remembered, is an extraordinarily difficult enterprise. It took Proust over three thousand pages to capture something of this complex to-and-fro of memory in *Remembrance of Things Past* (1913–27). *Never Let Me Go* simulates a similar effect without resorting to Proustian prolixity. A simple model may help us to appreciate the rendering of memory in Ishiguro's novel. Like all models, it is reductive, but it can provide us with a convenient and elegant mechanism for describing an intricate set of operations.

This model is based upon folds. When we fold something, such as a piece of paper, we bend it over on itself so that one part of it covers another. Memories are also a kind of fold, with this difference: they fold in time rather than in space. There is the present moment, in which the act of remembering takes place, and the past moment that is remembered. These two moments fold together so that the present and the past touch or 'cover' each other. This is to say no more than that every memory has at least two contexts: the conditions pertaining to the content of the memory itself and the circumstances in which it is remembered. For example, in Chapter 3 of *The Remains of the Day* the butler Stevens rereads the letter he has received from Miss Kenton. This takes place in the present time of the narration (1956) as he wakes in Salisbury, during his journey through the south-west of England. The letter refers to a specific memory of watching Stevens's father from a second-floor bedroom window of Darlington Hall as the elderly servant paced on the summer lawn with his eyes glued to the ground. The reason why Stevens Sr was retracing his steps is that, several days earlier, he had stumbled on some flagstones whilst serving refreshments. The memory, then, is linked with two associative fields: a summer evening several decades ago, when Stevens and Miss Kenton observed the pacing of Stevens Sr; and its present context, the guesthouse in Salisbury where Stevens peruses the letter recalling this episode.

The process does not end there. Each memory can be recontextualized any number of times, threatening a Proustian infinite regression that Ishiguro refers to in the Interview at the end of this book. Also, memories invoke other memories and become folded into themselves in many layers. Each layer has its own associations that criss-cross and overlap with each other. Such foldings can be multiplied almost indefinitely. Furthermore, the memories themselves change in the act of recollection, and these complexities cannot be adequately accounted for by this model.

However, the model is still useful. If we return to the analogy with paper, a single piece can be folded and refolded many times to produce a fan shape that opens and shuts like a concertina. This is known as a concertina fold. Such an arrangement is undoubtedly too neat to be mistaken as a faithful representation of memory. Nevertheless, it captures something important about our consciousness and the way that we process experiences. The alternating movement of compression and expansion is the means by which memories are folded together and unfolded. Memory is continually elided or elaborated. This concertina effect is useful for considering both the movement of remembering and how it structures Kathy's narration in *Never Let Me Go*.

Besides narratology, we find the concertina effect is active in several fields of knowledge, and is a common trope for figuring various cognate ideas. In economics, Friedrich Hayek uses it to describe fluctuations in the money cycle, suggesting that demand and supply would be in perfect equilibrium if it were not for the banking system.[6] It is money, supplied and withdrawn by the banks according to fluctuations in the market, which introduces disequilibrium. Consequently, when the economy contracts, there is a shortening of the period of production. In other words, there is a fall in the amount of capital goods production relative to consumer goods, although both sectors decrease output. Conversely, when there is an expansion of the economy, there is a lengthening of production. The production of capital goods rises relative to consumer goods, but both sectors increase output.[7]

How can we deploy this model of the concertina effect as an analogy for the way that memory functions in *Never Let Me Go*? Hayek's formula can be adapted for narratology if we borrow its terms. Economics is concerned with the flow of currency or units of exchange, whether in the form of cash, credit or capital. Value transfers from one agent to another in the nexus of goods and labour. What, though, is the main currency of *Never Let Me Go*, or indeed of any fiction? Most narratives trade in the linguistic capital of meaning or significance. This is their unit of exchange. That is why sequences of events are recounted in the first place. They are not told just for the sake of recitation. They tell a story and gesture towards some underlying pattern, moral, conclusion or perception of value. Events can be linked horizontally, as they occur in chronological sequence; or in a vertical fashion, when memory associates the present with the past through flashback or recall. The third option is prolepsis, when the present foreshadows the future.[8]

From the point of view of the reader and the author, then, the demand for meaning and the supply of meaning are the two forces that traverse the field of narrative. They are the equivalent of currency in Hayek's economic model – though, of course, they cannot be measured objectively. Meanings are exchanged either explicitly (through telling, or diegesis) or implicitly (through showing, or mimesis). Both of these result in explanation: a word that has its roots in the Latin 'ex plane', or 'to unfold'.

If a narrative exhibited a perfect balance between event and explanation, there would be no suspense or surprise. Each happening would be self-explanatory, with no hidden or delayed meanings. Indeed, there would hardly be a story at all, but a concatenation of isolated incidents: A + B + C. The possibilities for meaning multiply if causation is introduced into the equation. 'C' is no longer an independent unit, but can only be understood with reference to 'A' or 'B' (or both). It can itself become the trigger for later events. This interdependency opens up space for conflict, ambiguity, interpretation and misinterpretation – the reading process.

Within a novel such as *Never Let Me Go*, one predominant factor creates disequilibrium between the demand and supply of meaning. It is memory, or rather the process of remembering, that frustrates explanation. It does so by delaying the point at which explanations are provided and by introducing the possibility of multiple causal linkages between events. As Kathy goes further into her memories, the process of deriving significance from her account lengthens. This is what leads to a feeling of frustration on the part of the reader. Meaning is constantly deferred. The linear progress of the story is constantly interrupted by jumps back to the past through memory. Each memory leads to another memory, which prompts yet another memory; there are more and more contexts and circumstances to be explained; and we are forever zigzagging through the past, never quite arriving at a present that is satisfactorily accounted for. An infinite regress is set in motion that would not be out of place in a short story by Borges. Ruth's mistaken childhood belief that all the pieces in chess move in an 'L-shape' (*NLMG* 48) provides us with a pertinent image. This is how things move in *Never Let Me Go*, too: crabwise, with peculiar shuffles, swerves and hesitations, as the close textual analysis below demonstrates.

rewinding kathy's cassette tapes

The impact of the concertina effect in *Never Let Me Go* becomes particularly clear in a cluster of episodes surrounding the cassette tape by the (fictional) singer Judy Bridgewater. There are actually three tapes in the plot: (a) the Bridgewater tape that Kathy finds in a Hailsham sale and then loses; (b) the tape Ruth gives Kathy as a replacement for this, titled *Twenty Classic Dance Tunes*; and (c) the Judy Bridgewater tape found in a Cromer second-hand shop and bought for Kathy by Tommy. From the moment of their introduction, the tapes connect with many memories of both the Hailsham schooldays and the trip made to Norfolk whilst the students were at the Cottages. The two sets of events are pleated together in Kathy's memory:

> The album's called *Songs After Dark* and it's by Judy Bridgewater. What I've got today isn't the actual cassette, the one I had back then at Hailsham, the one I lost. It's the one Tommy and I found in Norfolk years afterwards – but that's another story I'll come back to later. What I want to talk about is the first tape, the one that disappeared. (*NLMG* 64)

So Kathy leaps from the circumstance of the losing of tape (a), follow-ing the pencil case incident, and then to the significance of tape (b), the Norfolk cassette. The fact that Kathy refers to the three tapes in the space of about six lines shows how compressed these memories are. In the course of the next few chapters, they are gradually expanded.

It is useful to remind ourselves of how the narrative progresses. Kathy acquires the original Judy Bridgewater cassette, tape (a), at Hailsham, a month after an episode featuring a different treasured item. Ruth's pencil case, with its shiny tan sheen, red dots and pom-pommed zip triggers envy amongst the young schoolgirls. It is likely that she acquired this at one of the school's sales. However, Ruth pretends that it is a special gift from their favourite teacher, Miss Geraldine. Kathy threatens to expose this deception, but eventually relents. She even comes to Ruth's rescue when her secret is almost revealed in public. These events are seem-ingly trivial, but they foreshadow the dangers that ensue from Ruth's tendency to make things up. They also fold into the story of the lost Judy Bridgewater tape, as we shall see shortly.

Before we find out anything more about the cassette, though, we zigzag into a digression concerning an in-joke amongst the Hailsham pupils about the 'lost corner of England' (*NLMG* 167). The origin of this expression lies in Miss Emily's geography lessons, where she illustrated the counties of England with pictures from calendars. She has no image for Norfolk, however, and on one occasion the teacher referred to the county as 'something of a lost corner' (*NMLG* 60). This amuses the pupils as Hailsham has its own 'Lost Corner' – a room on the third floor where lost property is kept. The association of Norfolk with things that are missing gains significance through repetition of the joke, until the thirteen-year-old Ruth and Kathy come to believe that anything that is lost will end up in that tucked-away county.

This sets the scene well for the story of how Kathy came to lose the tape. Once again, however, there are two further digressions or unfold-ings of the concertina-ed memories that zigzag us back to the past. First, Kathy describes the cassette cover, which shows Judy Bridgewater in a slinky dress, smoking in a louche South American bar, complete with waiters in white tuxedos and the obligatory palm tree decor. The cigarette sparks a reflection upon the taboo surrounding nicotine at Hailsham. Even Sherlock Holmes stories were banned because of the sleuth's passion for pipe smoking. The reason for the general prohibi-tion against smoking is obvious (though not, at the time, to the pupils): the donors need to keep their organs free from damage.

Kathy's second digression features one of the most important symbolic episodes of the novel. This anecdote concerns the time when Madame accidentally saw Kathy dancing in her dorm at Hailsham to 'Never Let Me Go' by Judy Bridgewater. As she waltzed around the room, Kathy held a pillow close to her, believing that the lyrics are about a female who cannot have babies (*NLMG* 70). Madame sobs. When Kathy later tells Tommy about the incident, he surmises that Madame was upset because she knows that the clones cannot have babies. The sight of the young girl clutching the pillow was especially hurtful to her. After many years have passed, Kathy has a chance to ask Madame directly if this is what she was thinking that day. It turns out to be incorrect. Madame interpreted the girl hugging the pillow more generally as a metaphor for a crueller, harsher world replacing 'the old kind world' (*NLMG* 267).

After these various delays, we finally reach the story of the disappearance of tape (a), an event that occurred some two months after the incident in the dorm with Madame. When Kathy discovered the cassette was gone, she asked her room-mates if they had seen it. Nobody had, and it does not turn up. Ruth tries to help Kathy by searching for the tape. It is still not found, but a fortnight later Ruth gives Kathy a present: it is another cassette entirely. She offers *Twenty Classic Dance Tunes* as a compensation for the lost Bridgewater tape. Although the schmaltzy orchestral music is not to Kathy's taste, the gift makes her very happy. It returns the favour she had extended to Ruth during the pencil case incident, and glues the two friends closer together.

The tale of the missing cassette, then, turns out to be a rather convoluted one. And here we should pause: it should not surprise us to find out that the adjective 'convoluted', along with its cognate 'involuted', is derived from a Middle English term meaning 'enfolded' or 'entangled'. Once again, narrative is linked with the notion of folding, and the unravelling of this coiled series of episodes helps us to become more involved – another word related to folds – in Kathy's world.

The story of how Kathy came to possess a second copy of the Judy Bridgewater cassette, tape (b), is equally involved or concertina-ed. Again, it is important to set it into its context. The tape is found when Kathy, Ruth, Tommy and their friends, Rodney and Chrissie, visit Cromer in Norfolk. The purpose of the trip is to check out a sighting of Ruth's 'possible', the original person from whom she was cloned – although this could be one of the many myths that circulate at the Cottages. When they reach the office where the woman works, however, it becomes clear that they have made a mistake. Ruth is upset and goes off in a huff with Rodney and Chrissie to visit their acquaintance, Martin, who lives nearby. Tommy takes this opportunity to get closer to Kathy. He tells her that earlier, when they were in Woolworth's, he had looked for a copy of the Bridgewater tape. He did not find it there as it is not a new release. Therefore, they decide to hunt for the tape in the second-hand shops of Cromer. After all, they are in Norfolk: the place where, as the Bible puts it, that which is lost shall be found. The idea pleases Kathy immensely. The search is successful, too, as – after rummaging around several charity shops – Kathy strikes lucky. Tommy is a little disappointed that he did not find the tape, but suggests that he buys it for Kathy. As with Ruth's gift of the orchestral music cassette, this helps bring the two friends closer together.

The episode concerning the finding of tape (c) is folded tightly into subsequent events. Kathy does not tell Ruth about finding the cassette in Cromer. She keeps it a secret between herself and Tommy. So, several months later when Ruth spots the tape, there is an uneasy moment when she asks why it was not mentioned to her. The awkwardness seems to pass and soon they are laughing together at the absurdity of Tommy's animal drawings. Several days later, Ruth exacts her revenge when the three of them are lolling under a willow tree in a churchyard close to the Cottages. She reveals to Tommy that the two girls cannot take his animals seriously and treat his animals as a joke (*NLMG* 192). This is a shock to Tommy, because he places a great deal of importance upon his artwork as a means of procuring a deferral of his operations. In fact, he had confided to Kathy about his plans for the drawings after they had found the cassette tape in Cromer. Ruth's revelation therefore drives a wedge between Tommy and Kathy. The division is made wider shortly after when Kathy and Ruth talk in an old bus shelter. Kathy wants to clear the air about what happened in the churchyard. Under the guise of friendly candour, Ruth reveals that Tommy could never contemplate seeing Kathy as a 'proper girlfriend' (*NMLG* 183), because she has had sex with other boys. Not only does this betray Kathy's trust, as she had told Ruth of her one-night stands in confidence, it is also hypocritical. Many years later, Ruth herself admits to having also slept around while at the Cottages, but keeps quiet about it during their tête-à-tête.

As we have seen, Kathy has different emotional investments and memories associated with the cassettes. She values tape (b) because it was Ruth's present and, when her friend passes away, it becomes a souvenir of their friendship. Otherwise, in itself, it is just a bare object. It does not concertina memories into itself: 'I still have it now. I don't play it much because the music has nothing to do with anything. It's an object, like a brooch or a ring, and especially now Ruth has gone, it's become one of my most precious possessions' (*NLMG* 75). Contrast this with both copies of the *Songs After Dark* cassette, tapes (a) and (c). The original tape that Kathy lost at Hailsham and the replacement tape that Tommy bought for her in Cromer are both densely associated with significance. Here is Kathy discussing the latter cassette and the memories it compresses.

> It was only later, when we were back at the Cottages and I was alone in my room, that I really appreciated having that tape – and that song – back again. Even then, it was mainly a nostalgia thing, and today, if I happen to get the tape out and look at it, it brings back memories of that afternoon in Norfolk every bit as much as it does our Hailsham days. (*NLMG* 171)

By carefully 'rewinding' the stories of Kathy's tapes, then, it can be seen that the cassettes serve two antithetical purposes: they are responsible for both helping to knit Ruth, Tommy and Kathy closer together and, ironically, are the cause of their splitting apart.

Ishiguro's *Never Let Me Go* contains many convolutions and repays careful rereading. The novel is susceptible to many unfoldings. As the narrator, Kathy, tells her story, she refrains from commenting upon many of her experiences and is very restrained concerning what she does reveal. She is thus in line with Ishiguro's other circumspect narrators, such as Etsuko in *A Pale View of Hills* (1982) and Masuji Ono in *An Artist of the Floating World* (1986). Her memories are not recounted in any kind of chronological sequence, but zigzag back and forth, with an emotional logic that is true to the way our minds actually work. Like Ishiguro's other novels, *Never Let Me Go* is about large issues: time, relationships, life and love. It is partly about clones, too, but the clone theme serves as a convenient pretext for these wider concerns.

It is a novel about missed opportunities, memory and, above all, mortality: what T. S. Eliot, referring to the dramatist John Webster, called the 'skull beneath the skin'.[9] In one of the final scenes of the book, Tommy rages in a field in the middle of nowhere after finding out that their hopes of a 'deferral' have been dashed. Kathy's description of how she hugged him is made poignant by her knowledge of the short amount of time we all have in which to concertina our lives: 'we were holding on to each other because that was the only way to stop us being swept away into the night' (*NLMG* 269).

notes

1. Contrast this with Michael Marshall Smith, *Spares* (London: HarperCollins, 1996) and *The Island*, director Michael Bay (Dreamworks, 2005). Both of these feature futuristic organ farm settings from which clones attempt to escape.
2. M. John Harrison, 'Clone Alone', *Guardian*, 26 February 2005, 26.

3. Ishiguro quoted in John Freeman, 'Ishiguro Novel Explores Theme of Memory', *The New Zealand Herald*, 'Life and Style', 21 March 2005.

4. For the sake of orthographic simplicity, from this point this word and its derivatives will be used without quotation marks.

5. This and subsequent in-text quotations, abbreviated to *NLMG*, refer to: Kazuo Ishiguro, *Never Let Me Go* (London: Faber and Faber, 2005).

6. See Nicholas Kaldor, 'Professor Hayek and the Concertina Effect', *Economica*, 9 (November 1942): 359–85.

7. The alternation between periods of contraction and expansion links Hayek's ideas with other concertina effects. In cardiovascular medicine, for example, the term is relevant to the breathing process. During the systolic phase of the beating of the heart, its muscles contract in order to pump blood into the arteries. In the diastolic phase, the muscles relax, allowing the chambers of the heart to fill with blood. Thus, the compression and expansion of the arteries play a crucial role in facilitating blood flow. Similarly, the concertina effect is also invoked in studies of facial ageing. Lines form as the skin loses its elasticity through time, again because of the alternation between contraction and expansion.

8. For a discussion of Ishiguro's use of prolepsis in *Never Let Me Go* see Mark Currie, 'Controlling Time', in Sean Matthews and Sebastian Groes (eds.), *Kazuo Ishiguro: Contemporary Critical Perspectives* (New York and London: Continuum, 2009), pp. 91–103.

9. T. S. Eliot, 'Whispers of Immortality' in *Complete Poems and Plays: 1909–1950* (New York: Harcourt, 1952), p. 32.

16
'something of a lost corner': kazuo ishiguro's landscapes of memory and east anglia in *never let me go*

sebastian groes

summary

This chapter shows that Kazuo Ishiguro's depiction of landscapes evokes questions about the relationship between personal and collective memory, knowledge and consciousness, time and trauma. His landscapes present the tragically limited protagonists with a means to gain self-knowledge, which they never actually achieve because there is a gap between traditional forms of knowledge and a modernity in which gaining knowledge is increasingly problematic. After situating Never Let Me Go *in a tradition of writing East Anglia, this chapter demonstrates how Ishiguro aims to bridge this divide. It ends by pointing out that buried within* Never Let Me Go's *East Anglia we find a dense layering of dark images drawn from hypercanonic modernist writers such as T. S. Eliot and Samuel Beckett.*

'a frame of mind appropriate for the journey'

Kazuo Ishiguro's *Never Let Me Go* (2005) tells the story of a group of clones created to provide vital organs for the inhabitants of an alternate England in the 1990s. The novel contains complex ideas about memory, identity and the imagination that are revealed in, and reinforced by, the symbolic representation of the flat, East Anglian fenlands. For instance, Chapter 19 (*NLMG* 214–32) describes the clones' second outing to a decaying boat abandoned in what we presume are East Anglia's marshes. No definite location is given, but the descriptions echo those of their first excursion to Cromer, located on the north Norfolk coast. There is

'a lot of sky reflected in the windscreen' and Kathy, Tommy and Ruth
drive 'into open, featureless countryside and travelled on along a near-
empty road' (*NLMG* 216). They continue 'across the empty countryside'
(*NLMG* 217) and enter woods that lead to open marshland:

> The pale sky looked vast and you could see it reflected every so
> often in the patches of water breaking up the land. Not so long ago,
> the woods must have extended further, because you could see here
> and there ghostly dead trunks poking out of the soil, most of them
> broken off only a few feet up. And beyond the dead trunks, maybe
> sixty yards away, was the boat, sitting beached in the marshes under
> the weak sun. (*NLMG* 219–20)

The image of the stranded boat crumbling away in the marshes gives us
an image of historical time eating away at all material structures and of
the earth swallowing up all evidence of human existence. It is a vision
of decline, death and meaninglessness in the face of time's destruction
of human memory. Although the individual sentences that make up
the novel move us forward in a linear fashion, the actual narrative
composition is one of retrospection, downwards and backwards into
Kathy H.'s personal memory, a movement that also conveys the retro-
gressive pull of history. Whilst walking towards the boat Kathy notes
that her feet are sinking into the soil (*NLMG* 220). We are symbolically descending back into geological history and archaeological deep
time, becoming spectators sinking away into this ghostly, Gothicized
prehistoric morass. The passage becomes a poignant comment on,
and reworking of, ideas about evolutionary regression, a typically
nineteenth-century concern as expressed in the proto-modernist
work of the later Dickens. *Our Mutual Friend* (1865), for instance,
parodied Social Darwinism by presenting images of evolutionary
regression rather than progress.[1] George Eliot was also influenced by
Darwin and interested in Social Darwinism, and Kathy H.'s reading of
Daniel Deronda (1876) at the Cottages (*NLMG* 120) becomes an ironic
comment on the function that this underclass of clones fulfil in the
late capitalist society. The passage's stress on regression as opposed to
progress becomes a comment on the unnatural, barbaric break with
biological evolution that they represent. Having been raised within
the confines of a cunning pedagogic machine that has systematically
withheld and manipulated information in an attempt to limit their
ability to understand their situation, the clones also misinterpret the
significance of the moment they are experiencing. They misread this
panorama as unveiling an aesthetic sublime rather than a moment of

darkness that reveals their role in the social and ethical break in the evolutionary chain they represent.

As this passage demonstrates, Ishiguro's representation of place evokes a set of questions about the relationship between personal and collective memory, knowledge and consciousness, time and trauma. His work explores universal and timeless subject matter through plot and character, and, just as the historical background in which his narratives are embedded seems arbitrary, place also functions as a seemingly accidental decor. Cities such as Tokyo, London and the unnamed European city in *The Unconsoled* (1995) have featured as the backdrops to his stories and symbolize modern life's complexities, while giving us an image of the ways in which the mind and memory operate. In *When We Were Orphans* (2000), for instance, Shanghai's 'warren' (*WWWO* 235) stands as a metaphor for Christopher Banks's inability to circumnavigate the labyrinth of his personal – and his home nation's – traumatic past. The countryside also functions as a mythological landscape in which inner and outer space are intricately intertwined. *The Remains of the Day* (1989) portrays the West Country, described as 'the English landscape at its finest' (*RD* 28), as a symbol of a mythical Englishness which is radically renegotiated in the post-war period.

Ishiguro's conception of place and space foregrounds a dialectical struggle between the myths and fictions that shape our perception of the world, and the extent to which our experience of the world matches our conception. This dialectic forms, however, a device that allows readers to trace the mental state of the characters. In *The Remains of the Day*, Stevens drives towards Salisbury, a journey which translates into a classic metaphor for the life he is about to narrate. When the surroundings grow unrecognizable and Stevens notes that he 'had gone beyond all previous boundaries' (*RD* 24), he takes a walk to relieve himself of the anxiety evoked by the unfamiliar territory. The butler is accosted by a Virgil-like figure, 'a thin, white-haired man in a cloth cap, smoking his pipe' (*RD* 24), who is at pains to convince Stevens that he should climb a footpath (*RD* 25). When he walks up the path Stevens experiences an epiphany:

> What I saw was principally field upon field rolling off into the far distance. The land rose and fell gently, and the fields were bordered by hedges and trees. There were dots in some of the distant fields which I assumed to be sheep. To my right, almost on the horizon, I thought I could see the square tower of a church . . . it was then, looking on that view, that I began for the first time to adopt a frame of mind appropriate for the journey before me. For it was

then that I felt the first healthy flush of anticipation for the many interesting experiences I know these days ahead hold in store for me. (*RD* 26)

The use of 'principally' suggests that the landscape is transformed into an image of the sublime, a moment of abstraction that potentially serves as a mental map which allows him to structure his life into a narrative. His vertiginous suspension over the landscape temporarily casts him into the role of Author-God, which opens his mind to his possibility of growing self-knowledge, of understanding his past, and to achieve redemption by connecting his life narrative with those of others, and embed it within a wider historical and national framework. As the reference to borders suggests, Stevens acknowledges he has been imprisoned in the fenced-off world of Darlington Hall, but it also stresses the importance of ordering as a sense-making device.

This scene is repeated almost verbatim throughout Ishiguro's *oeuvre*[2] and his use of the footpath is a staple Ishiguro symbol, or Eliotic objective correlative, that forms a vital contribution to a distinctive structure of feeling. The opening of *An Artist of the Floating World* (1986) foregrounds this set piece to suggest Masuji Ono's inability to acknowledge his complicity with a dangerous nationalistic discourse that supports the war effort. Ishiguro states of his use of symbolism:

I thought it helped strengthen this mental landscape mapped out entirely by what Ono was conscious of, and nothing else. . . . To a large extent the reason for Ono's downfall was that he lacked a perspective to see beyond his own environment and to stand outside the actual values of his time. So the question of this parochial perspective was quite central to the book. . . . Ono is fairly normal; most of us have similar parochial visions. So the book is largely about the inability of normal human beings to see beyond their immediate surroundings, and because of this, one is at the mercy of what this world immediately around one proclaims itself to be.[3]

One way of reading Ishiguro's mental landscapes and the footpath symbol is as a classic literary and philosophical device analogous to Plato's allegory of the cave, in which the acquisition of (self-)knowledge stands for the possibility of a move out of the world of shadows. In Ishiguro's writing, this fallen world is represented by the repeated images of pale views, misty fields or shadowy streets. Ishiguro's interest in organic and anthropomorphic metaphors suggests that the literary concepts outlined in Aristotle's *Poetics* are similarly appropriate: in particular *anagnorisis*, the hero's transcendent moment at which the truth of the situation is revealed, is relevant.

Ishiguro's harnessing of mental landscapes is rooted in the humanist, proto-modern tradition exemplified by, for instance, Dante's *The Divine Comedy* (1314–21) and John Milton's *Paradise Lost* (1667), both of which contain scenes in which the lost protagonist climbs a hill to reach a view and plunges into the mental depths below.[4] This Dantean and Miltonic pattern is also a model for the (mental) journey of Ishiguro's protagonist. Yet in Ishiguro's work this promise of enlightenment is undercut by a nagging darkness. The moment of revelation promised by these views is always a limited and temporary one. In *A Pale View of Hills*, Etsuko is unable fully to recover from the damage done by the loss of family and nation; in *The Remains of the Day*, Stevens achieves a partial acknowledgement of his complicity with fascism, but it is too late to change his character; in *The Unconsoled*, Ryder does not give his grand, healing performance; in *When We Were Orphans*, Banks reconciles himself with London as a home of sorts, but he never fits in; in *Nocturnes*, the musicians never reach their ambitions. Ishiguro seems sceptical about the possibility for the subject, trapped in 'parochial visions', to achieve self-knowledge. This moment never fully arrives because in a modern context the very act of gaining knowledge is questioned – as both the means of gaining knowledge, as well as traditional epistemological structures themselves, are in question. In the more experimental novels, such as *The Unconsoled* and *When We Were Orphans*, the vertiginous glimpses across these landscapes collapse into a meaninglessness from which the protagonists do not recover: modernity is an abyssal experience. Quieter works such as the early novels and *The Remains of the Day* foreground the limitedness and partiality of all structures of meaning, of knowledge and of language.

Thus, paradoxically, knowledge is still experienced in classical terms, as a vertiginous ascent to heaven or descent into hell, and Ishiguro's novels attempt to recreate this sensation of falling because it triggers a Platonic form of remembering which allows him to inscribe his readers with moral lessons and knowledge about ourselves and the world. Ishiguro's work exploits the tension between the impossibility of achieving a transcending moment of insight into the self and collective history, and the ability to recuperate such knowledge via an effect of ethical redemption. Such a redemption might come from the perfected aesthetics offered by the successful work of art in which the depiction of mental landscapes forms an important artistic dynamo.

this nowhere-landscape: a brief history
of writing east anglia

Nowhere is Ishiguro's engagement with place as a mental condition more deeply and more urgently felt than in *Never Let Me Go*, where the fictional boarding school-cum-concentration camp where the clones grow up, Hailsham, and Norfolk feature centrally. The narrator, Kathy H., notes that whilst driving around England she sees things that remind her of Hailsham, such as a large house or poplar trees: 'and I'll think: "Maybe this is it! I've found it! This actually is Hailsham!"' (*NLMG* 6). Hailsham has been destroyed so that Kathy is never able to regain its materiality; however, it is a loss that resonates in the depiction of the empty landscape.

The novel's representational problems are dramatized by a series of symbolic passages in which the East Anglian landscape, and Norfolk in particular – repeatedly described as 'featureless' (cf. *NLMG* 216, 281) – are prominent. In fact, it is the absence of detailed description itself that becomes a poignant comment on the regressive consciousness of the clones and the undifferentiated landscape. Miss Emily's geography lesson, which includes a calendar of England showing the different counties and pictorial representations, draws attention to the significance of the novel's setting. The calendar does not have an image of Norfolk, and Miss Emily states: 'You see, because it's stuck out here on the east, on this hump jutting out into the sea, it's not on the way to anywhere. People going north and south . . . they bypass it altogether. For that reason, it's a peaceful corner of England, rather nice. But it's also something of a lost corner' (*NLMG* 65).

A realistic reading is justified by the fact that the clones are not given a pictorial representation of Norfolk because this would allow them to identify and locate the scene of the crimes committed against them. Yet Ishiguro's choice for East Anglia as a place that produces the flat, nostalgic landscape of Kathy H.'s memory also fits neatly into the highly specific yet ambivalent significance that East Anglia occupies within the English imagination. In 'Norfolk' (1953), John Betjeman (1906–84) notes that 'These Norfolk lanes recall lost innocence,/. . . Time bring back/The rapturous ignorance of long ago'. Ishiguro's East Anglia is also a landscape of melancholic longing for lost innocence and love; yet in Ishiguro's novel, 'ignorance' is more painfully and ironically exploited in the sense that Kathy H. and her friends are deliberately kept in the dark about what they truly are.

In post-war fiction, East Anglia continuously figures as a paradisiacal place that has been left behind. Ali Smith's *The Accidental* (2006) depicts

Norfolk as 'this boring nowhere', for instance.[5] Angus Wilson (1913–91) notes that East Anglia has a magical dimension:

> I came to East Anglia fortuitously, seeking an immediate refuge in which to write. I have stayed here nearly thirty years. Without realising it, East Anglia has given to me a world of continuing enchantment – enchantment subtle and in depth, which slowly and secretly becomes a part of one's very being. It is, I think, above all, a transfusion one receives of changing lights and shapes.[6]

In *Never Let Me Go*, East Anglia also features as a refuge that has magical associations in the sense that here everything lost re-emerges; and the way that the landscape becomes 'a part of one's very being' is explored in Ishiguro's landscapes of memory. As a geographical backwater, this slow, peripheral territory becomes a signifier of the nation's lost innocence.

Added to these innocent connotations is a darker reputation of East Anglia as a place whose remoteness makes it particularly suitable for secret scientific and military experimentation. In Daphne du Maurier's Gothic science fiction story 'The Breakthrough' (1966), a computer engineer, Stephen Saunders, is relocated to the fictional town of Saxmere on the east Norfolk coast, where a crackpot scientist, Mac, is attempting to trap the life-force, or soul, at the point of death. It is described as a deserted landscape where 'stretching into infinity, lay acre upon acre of waste land, marsh and reed' whilst the laboratory itself 'looked more like a deserted Dachau than ever'.[7] In *Never Let Me Go*, Hailsham too functions as a concentration camp of sorts, and Madame and Miss Emily also try to capture the clones' souls via their artistic output. In J. G. Ballard's short story 'Storm-bird, Storm-Dreamer' (1966), 'the cold Norfolk marshes' are littered with the dead carcasses of man-size cormorants and black-headed gulls after 'new growth promoters used on the crops in East Anglia [have created] extraordinary and unforeseen effects on the bird life'.[8] Du Maurier's and Ballard's fantasy of Norfolk are projections into a dystopian future of elements that are conventionally associated with this county: it is an agricultural area, dominated by the growth of crops and pig farming, but one that is also associated with experiments in biology and genetics. It is a national myth that the population of Norfolk is inbred – 'Normal for Norfolk' is a derisory expression – to which, more recently, experiments with genetically manipulated crops (called 'Frankenstein Food' by protesters) have been added. The combination of these two aspects makes the region highly ambiguous: it is an Eden, a pocket where British history and personal memory are stored, whilst it also forms a dark place where knowledge and secrets are hidden.

Never Let Me Go is directly in dialogue with *Waterland* (1983), written by Ishiguro's close friend, Graham Swift. The novel tells the story of a history teacher, Tom Crick, who grew up in the Cambridgeshire Fens of East Anglia, which are repeatedly described as 'fairy-tale land', 'an empty wilderness', a 'nowhere' and as 'this nothing-landscape'.[9] By tracing how the silt – 'which demolishes as it builds; which is simultaneously accretion and erosion; neither progress nor decay' – formed the fens, Swift's novel creates an archaeological impetus that becomes a metaphor for the slow, arduous and ambivalent process of human history itself.[10] The safe, but incomplete, knowledge of historical narrative is slowly replaced, or supplemented, by a composite of stories that include fairy tales, legends, myth and speculation, suggesting that the past can only be understood if we include unofficial narratives in our investigations.

All these elements return in *The Rings of Saturn* (1995), a novel by W. G. Sebald. This narrates an epic walk through coastal East Anglia. The erosion of the landscape – from the sea's unceasing eating away at cliffs and turning human structures into ruins to the deforestation leading to the shaping of 'that melancholy region'[11] – comes to stand for a universal history of man's destruction at the hands of time. On his journey, the nameless narrator makes curious but insightful connections between seemingly disparate events in history which, rather than being narrated in a hierarchically ordered fashion, are connected into mesmerizing, anecdotal trains of thought that resemble a flattened-out, network-like structure. The effect is phantasmagoric and uncanny, as if we occupy 'an imaginary position some distance above the earth'.[12] Sebald's novel gives us 'vertiginous perspectives'[13] of history as a drawn-out and inexorable process of gradual decline resulting in 'a glimpse of the land now being lost forever'.[14] Although Ishiguro is focused more on human relationships than historical events in which people play but an accidental part, the atmosphere of melancholy and lament are drawn from the same source of inspiration: the East Anglian landscape.

never let me go: zigzagging through an east anglia of the mind

Never Let Me Go fits into this tradition but also forms a 'turn of the representational screw' for Ishiguro. Although this tradition is dependent on the real Norfolk 'out there', the clones have no sense or experience of the materiality of the outside world at all. Whereas Stevens's understanding of England is preconditioned by his reading of Mrs Jane Symons's *The Wonder of England* (*RD* 11), the clones have no means of knowing what the outside world looks and feels like at all, nor are they able to understand how representation works, or how to interpret meta-phors or symbolism. Hailsham forms a closed circuit, the absolute 'real' of the clones' experience, and the pedagogic doctrines of the school prevent them from accessing the 'real': 'This might all sound daft, but you have to remember that to us . . . any place beyond Hailsham was like a fantasy land; we only had the haziest notion of the world outside and about what was and wasn't possible there' (*NLMG* 66). This sparks the Norfolk mythology in which they literalize Norfolk through a wildly misconstrued analogy: they have a 'Lost Corner' where all lost and found property is kept, and someone 'claimed after the lesson that what Miss Emily had said was that Norfolk was England's "lost corner", where all the lost property found in the country ended up' (*NLMG* 65).

Hailsham's pedagogic system of indoctrination and the denial of the social nature of personality trigger the logic in which they translate the outside world into a version of this cruel, closed circuit. The ironic inversion of Plato's allegory of the cave – the world of the shadows is mistaken for the idealized Hailsham – points out the dangers of the break with the humanist tradition that the experiment represents. The literature that the clones read (including Shakespeare, George Eliot and James Joyce) is useless without experience of the human community from which these works sprang.

Never Let Me Go is an investigation, and criticism, of the destruction of imagination, memory and language. The impact of the clones' inability to verbalize complex thought and construct long-term memories upon their curious perception of the reader's world is highlighted by small examples scattered throughout the novel. When the clones finally confront Madame and Miss Emily towards the end of the novel, Kathy resorts to a mnemonic aid. She resorts to a plan whereby she memo-rizes some key lines and then draws 'a mental map' of how she would go from one point to the next (*NLMG* 146). But during the confronta-tion her preparation turns out to be 'either unnecessary or completely wrong' (*NLMG* 247). Without the capacity linguistically to formulate a coherent real to which representation refers, imagination – the human capacity to project hypothetically a situation into the future and to predict its outcome – breaks down. Yet this destruction of their prospec-tive abilities obliterates memory as well. Kathy points out a particular hoarding with an advertisement of an open-plan office with smiling people that reminds her of the office they 'found on the ground' (*NLMG* 225) in Cromer. Both Tommy and Ruth cannot remember much of this trip, after which the clones decide they could have attempted to figure out the nature of their situation.

The novel can be read as a criticism of the modern condition in which we are divorced from a 'real' and in which our experience of a perpetual present prevents a coherent logic. In *A Pale View of Hills*, the phrase 'looking forward' (*PVH* 111–12) is repeated eight times over two pages, stressing that it is necessary for Etsuko to move on, whilst also suggesting that looking back is a painful yet necessary act of working through trauma. In the passage from *Never Let Me Go* in which Ruth and Tommy discuss the lost opportunity of investigating the possibility of a deferral, the phrase 'looked into' is repeated five times on one page (*NLMG* 226). This suggests that the absence of a meaningful connection with the outside world forms another version of the epistemological rupture that leads to another 'inward turn' associated with modernist literature.

This adjustment to Ishiguro's earlier representational model echoes throughout *Never Let Me Go*, the narrative flatness of which is mirrored by Ishiguro's choice of landscape. This aesthetic of horizontality can be located on a number of levels, such as Kathy H.'s voice and her use of language. The exhausted vocabulary, uncomplicated sentences and inability to express complex emotions suggest spiritual vacuity. As Kathy H. notes, that is why there was 'a kind of emptiness to our talk' (*NLMG* 278). In the conveyance of knowledge, too, we find horizontality embedded within the narrative. Kathy H.'s main preoccupation is spending days on the road, a form of therapeutic busy-work that keeps her mind off her traumatic experiences. Due to the pedagogy of indoctrination that is imposed on the clones, their knowledge is not structured according to the most basic form of Western tradition, that of the causal, linear chain. After Madame cries over Kathy's imagining having a baby and her Judy Bridgewater tape subsequently disappears, Kathy tells us she never linked the two events (*NLMG* 73). Whereas narrators such as Stevens and Banks were able to achieve a partial insight into the wider structure of the world and their role in it, Kathy H. never gets any closer to realizing her plight.

The novel foregrounds its attempted approximation of narrative horizontality by a reworking of Ishiguro's objective correlative during the students' outing to Cromer, when they visit a cafe built on the cliff edge. Kathy H. notes that they 'were virtually suspended over the sea' (*NLMG* 146). During their conversation they discuss the importance of deferring donations, which seems to open Kathy's consciousness to understanding their predicament. When she pays for her meal, she states: 'I watched them through one of the big misty windows, shuffling about in the sunshine, not talking, looking down at the sea'

(*NLMG* 153). However, at the opening of the next chapter, the excitement had 'evaporated completely' (*NLMG* 154). Kathy finds a moment of insight – which is tied to her liminal position of vertical suspension over, and transition between, solid ground and the sea – mid-way through the novel, yet its potential for an *anagnorisis* is immediately compromised and deflated by the 'misty windows' that obscure her vision. Kathy is not (and never will be) able to understand the tragic evolution of which she is part; nor will she be able fully to understand basic aspects of human life such as 'love' and 'death'; nor is she capable of recovering the human world and its manifold meanings.

The novel confirms that later by subverting the objective correlative of the footpath. When, after lunch, Kathy and Tommy stroll through Cromer, they 'began going up a steeply climbing path, and we could see – maybe a hundred yards further up – a kind of viewing area right on the cliff edge with benches facing out to sea. It would have made a nice spot in the summer for an ordinary family to sit and eat a picnic' (*NLMG* 171). Halfway up the path, Tommy puts forward the theory that there could be a special arrangement, a deferral of donations, for couples who are 'truly in love' (*NLMG* 173). This leads to legitimization of other curious goings-on at Hailsham, such as the 'Lost Corner'/Norfolk relationship and the Gallery. For Kathy, this is an epiphanic moment: 'But something was coming back to me' (*NLMG* 173). Tommy's 'theory' of the clones' work of art for the Gallery being used as evidence for the suitability of couples is, for Kathy, a revelatory moment whose consequences are negative and traumatic. The 'logic' of this means that she and Tommy cannot become a couple as he has never submitted work to the Gallery, so she holds back and plays down the theory (*NLMG* 175). This second moment of potential insight is another red herring for the protagonists: the point is that Tommy's theory is wrong in the first place.

Within this overwhelming horizontality, however, Ishiguro has carved a zigzag movement into his novel, which becomes a metaphor of Kathy's evasion of *anagnorisis*, or perhaps a strategic inability to articulate the truth behind the programme in which they are involved.[15] If we return to the cafe scene in Cromer, there is a key phrase that illuminates Ishiguro's strategy. When Kathy and her friends walk to the cliff edge, she notes a road carved into it (*NLMG* 146). At first, it seems like a drop down to the beach, but once she leans over the rail, she sees zigzagging footpaths leading down to the sea-front (*NLMG* 146). This image is important because it establishes continuity and discontinuity with Ishiguro's previous work: just as in *A Pale View of Hills*, in which the path 'rose up the mountain in zig-zags' (*PVH* 108), we again have the

footpath, but this time it leads downwards and, metaphorically, away
from an *anagnorisis*. At the same time, the vertiginous glimpse into the
abyss – a potential collapse into meaninglessness – is recuperated in the
reader's experience of the complex zigzag of the novel's representation
of Kathy's inadequate and evasive memory.

The apparent absence of verticality and overwhelming horizontality
of the narrative forms a criticism of the various forms of flatness that
we are experiencing in modernity. It is in the complex dynamic associated with personal memory and collective history, with the imagination
and the critical faculty, that we find a mindful and meaningful engagement with the world. *Never Let Me Go* recuperates the sensation of this
deep structure by using a zigzag movement that bores down below the
surface and delves into archeological time and into literary history, and
attempts to recover the deep structures of humanism lost under the late
capitalist culture of surfaces.[16]

'modelled from *trash*': ishiguro's modernism

Never Let Me Go's mental landscape opens East Anglia's horizontality up
to the vertiginous sensations of mythical memory and history, which is
part of a distinctly modernist legacy that haunts the novel. Ishiguro notes
that East Anglia is the opposite of the green and pleasant West Country
we find in *The Remains of the Day*: 'But it's not a beautiful English countryside, it's bleak and cold and grey'.[17] This vision is aligned with that
of hypercanonic writers of High Modernism such as T. S. Eliot, Kafka,[18]
Joyce and Beckett. The influence of Eliot on Ishiguro's imagination in
Never Let Me Go is particularly strong, and we find references to *The
Waste Land* (1922) everywhere. When Tommy and Kathy return from
their unfinished ascent, they retrace their steps down the slope, but she
knew 'we still had time and didn't hurry' (*NLMG* 175). This sentiment
is repeated two pages later when Tommy notes: 'Well, I suppose we've
got time. None of us are in a particular hurry' (*NLMG* 177). This repetition is an inversion of the famous pub scene in the second part of *The
Waste Land*, 'A Game of Chess', in which the ordinary announcement
of drinking up time, 'HURRY UP PLEASE IT'S TIME', becomes a darkly
ironic comment on the bodily decay of the two gossiping women and
on Western civilization's decline in general.[19] The scatological imagery
at the ending of *Never Let Me Go* – when Kathy sees trees with 'strange
rubbish' such as torn plastic sheeting and carrier bags (*NLMG* 292) – also
recalls *The Waste Land*'s foregrounding of excremental imagery in 'the
brown land' and the Thames carrying 'empty bottles, sandwich papers,
/ Silk handkerchiefs, card board boxes, cigarette ends' and sweating 'oil

and tar'.[20] Ruth notes that it is the clones themselves who are 'modelled from *trash*' and that they should look in the gutter and rubbish bins for their possibles (*NLMG* 164). The 'strange rubbish' flapping in the wind, then, is analogous to, and a metaphor for, the clones themselves: it is their dead, used-up and 'unzipped' bodies that Kathy sees flapping about in the wind, caught in the trees; the plastic forms are their empty skins, carrier bags from which the organs have been removed. This excremental language criticizes a late capitalist system of endless mass-production in which their bodies have become the object of commodification and consumption, signifiers of, in Maud Ellmann's words, 'what a culture casts away in order to determine what is not itself, and thus establish its own limits'.[21]

Just as important in this final, haunting image is the resonance of Beckett's work. The rubbish-strewn trees by which Kathy waits for Tommy in the deserted landscape at the ruins of time recalls *Waiting for Godot* (1953), in which Vladimir and Estragon are forever waiting besides a dead tree in a 'bog', trapped in a dim world constructed out of half-remembered memories.[22] Yet, Kathy's world is a place without relieving humour, without catharsis and without hope for human salvation. It is the reader's task to recuperate humanity and restore memory on behalf of her.

notes

1. See Victor Sage, 'Dickens and Professor Owen; Portrait of a Friendship', in Pierre Arnaud (ed.), *Le Portrait* (Paris: Presses de l'Université de Paris–Sorbonne, 1999), pp. 87–101.
2. See (*PVH* 103–20); (*U* 365); and (*N* 104).
3. Kazuo Ishiguro interviewed by Gregory Mason, *Contemporary Literature*, XXX, 3 (1989), 341.
4. See Dante, *Inferno*, Book II, line 142 and John Milton, *Paradise Lost*, IV, 172–4.
5. Ali Smith, *The Accidental*, (London: Penguin, 2006), p. 23; first published by Hamish Hamilton in 2006.
6. Angus Wilson, 'Introduction', *East Anglia in Verse and Prose* (London: Secker & Warburg, 1982), p. 1.
7. Daphne du Maurier, 'The Breakthrough', *Don't Look Now and Other Stories* (London: Penguin, 2006), pp. 230, 232; originally published in 1966.
8. J. G. Ballard, 'Storm Bird, Storm Dreamer', *The Complete Collected Short Stories* (London: Flamingo, 2002), pp. 697, 700.
9. Graham Swift, *Waterland* (London: Picador, 1992), pp. 3, 17, 52; first published by William Heinemann in 1983.
10. Ibid., pp. 8–9.
11. W. G. Sebald, *The Rings of Saturn*, trans. Michael Hulse (London: Vintage, 2002), p. 169; first published in English in 1998 by Harvill; originally published as *Die Ringe des Saturn* by Vito von Eichborn Verlag, 1995.

224   *never let me go*

12. Ibid., p. 83.
13. Joanne Catling, 'Gratwanderungen bis an der Rand der Natur: Landscapes of memory', in R. Görner (ed.), *The Anatomist of Melancholy: Essays in Memory of W. G. Sebald* (München: Iudicium, 2003), p. 22.
14. Sebald, *Rings*, p. 296.
15. I owe this insight to Barry Lewis who provided insightful comments on the paper – presented at the Kazuo Ishiguro conference held at Liverpool Hope University, June 2007 – which forms the basis of this chapter.
16. This reminds us of the words of a poet associated with the 1930s, W. H. Auden (1907–73), who, whilst living in the Malvern Hills, wrote poems on the area, including 'The Malverns' (1950), which 'combines millennia of geological time with the millennial myths of the Grail legend whose progenitor is Eliot's *The Waste Land*'. Auden also wrote two poems called 'Nocturne' (1951; 1972). Auden was very much interested in the horizontality–verticality dynamic, writing in *Look, stranger!* (1936): 'Here on the cropped grass of the narrow ridge I stand,/. . . England below me'. And in 'Shorts' (1929–31), Auden writes that we should honour 'the vertical man' although we in fact only value 'the horizontal one'. W. H. Auden, 'Shorts', *Collected Poems* (London: Faber, 1991), p. 53.
17. Kazuo Ishiguro, 'I Remain Fascinated by Memory', in *Der Spiegel*, 10 May 2005, www.spiegel.de/international/0,1518,378173,00.html, accessed 3 June 2009.
18. See Mark Currie, 'Controlling Time', in Sean Matthews and Sebastian Groes (eds.), *Kazuo Ishiguro: Contemporary Critical Perspectives* (London and New York: Continuum, 2010), pp. 92–3.
19. T. S. Eliot, *The Waste Land*, 141; 152; 165; 168; 169.
20. Ibid., 175; 177–8; 267.
21. Maud Ellmann, *The Poetics of Impersonality* (Brighton: Harvester, 1987), pp. 93–4.
22. Samuel Beckett, *Waiting for Godot* (London: Faber, 2006), p. 7; first published in English by Faber in 1956.

17

'this is what we're supposed to be doing, isn't it?': scientific discourse in kazuo ishiguro's *never let me go*

liani lochner

summary

Kazuo Ishiguro's Never Let Me Go *(2005) can be read as a criticism of the potentially pernicious influence of scientific discourse and the Enlightenment tradition on notions of the human within contemporary culture. Raised at Hailsham, the clones' separation from shared social structures dehumanizes them in the view of the rest of society while the carefully orchestrated manipulation of language and knowledge result in a fatal lack of self-determination. Exploring love, friendship and community against a suggested background of biotechnology, Ishiguro posits the novel itself as a form of culture that can recuperate 'the human' from science's purely mechanistic and materialistic definitions.*

science and the subject

Kazuo Ishiguro's *Never Let Me Go* (2005) presents an alternative history of an England that might have existed by the late twentieth century if the post-war scientific breakthroughs were in biotechnology rather than in nuclear physics.[1] The narrator, Kathy H., and her friends are clones, products of genetic engineering, and created as part of an organ harvesting programme. They grow up in an environment isolated from mainstream society and, it is suggested, die at around the age of thirty. Based on this plot summary, reviewers were quick to categorize the novel as, on the one hand, a 'meticulous dystopia'[2] and, on the other hand, 'as sci-fi because of [Ishiguro's] use of clones'.[3] Yet, whereas the aim of the

225

literary dystopia is to caution against false optimism and the devastating effects of a scientific 'utopia' by projecting present developments imaginatively into the future – classic novels such as Aldous Huxley's *Brave New World* (1931) and George Orwell's *Nineteen Eighty-Four* (1949) spring to mind – Ishiguro deliberately avoids this paradigm by setting his novel in the recent past.

Ishiguro himself has on several occasions revealed that he drew inspiration for *Never Let Me Go* from current debates on cloning, but he warns against a reductive reading of the novel as a 'prophecy or a warning', stating that the story has 'clear metaphorical links with the way we all live as human beings'.[4] Kathy's exploration of her relationship with her friends Ruth and Tommy and their school days at Hailsham, a mythical campus where they grow up, underscores Ishiguro's interest in universal humanist themes such as individual agency and fate, and the individual's social responsibility: 'I was interested in the human capacity to accept what must seem like a limited and cruel fate'.[5] This emphasis, as well as the novel's disregard for scientific details, seems to suggest the divide between science and culture proposed by scientist and novelist C. P. Snow's 'The Two Cultures' lecture, first published in 1959, in which he argued that 'the intellectual life of the whole of western society is increasingly being split into two polar groups',[6] each with its own specialist vocabulary not understood by the other. However, as Gabriele Griffin argues, the 'contemporary cultural landscape' is marked by a more intertwined relationship between science and culture. Thus, the 'absence of signifiers of "acute science" – portraits of scientific procedure, specialist vocabulary, and so on – signals the breakdown of the boundaries between science and the everyday'.[7]

Science gained prominence in society during the Enlightenment when it was lauded as having the power 'to improve indefinitely the state of human knowledge, health and welfare'.[8] At the centre of this Age of Reason worldview was the belief in a human rational intelligence capable of 'pure science', the idea 'that the scientific mind . . . could register nature like a perfect mirror reflecting an extrahistorical, universal objective reality'.[9] As John Carroll puts it, 'for the first time the scientific method was abstracted from non-rational interests: the study of facts, as Hume urged, was separated off from values, theology, aesthetics and metaphysics'.[10] The leading figures of the movement unambiguously enshrined 'the autonomous rational individual as the central unit of society'[11] and the world. However, according to Carroll, the Enlightenment was 'rather narrow-minded, naïve about human motivation, about society and about politics, in danger of barricading itself inside an arid and abstract intellectualism' and, as a result 'the deification of Reason leaves much in human nature in the dark'.[12]

In a post-war context the biggest challenge to science's 'intrinsic moral neutrality, not to say its unlimited powers of benign progress',[13] came from the development and subsequent use of one of its ambiguous triumphs – nuclear technology. This created a new sense of the possible dangers of science and its vulnerability to political appropriation. Furthermore, increasingly in the twentieth century, concerns were raised about the impact of unlimited scientific development on human nature itself. Richard Tarnas explains:

> Technology was taking over and dehumanizing man, placing him in a context of artificial substances and gadgets rather than live nature, in an unaesthetically standardized environment where means had subsumed ends, where industrial labor requirements entailed the mechanization of human beings, where all problems were perceived as soluble by technical research at the expense of genuine existential responses.[14]

Yet during the late twentieth and early twenty-first centuries it has been the second scientific revolution in biotechnology that has resulted in new, vigorous debate across all sectors of society, aimed at convincing the public to either endorse or to reject these technologies. In these debates, the promise of a future where it would be possible to create a supply of donor organs, to eradicate genetic diseases or to end infertility is contrasted with fears that human cloning will lead to 'designer babies' with genetic traits selected by their parents and the creation of a 'genetic underclass'.[15] The risks, according to those opposing reproductive cloning, are that clones will be viewed as artefacts 'created as the means to fulfil the desires of another person: the clone generator',[16] and be subject to exploitation and commercialization through, for example, 'the sale of human bodies or body parts'.[17] Possible psychological harms to cloned humans have also been outlined, including a diminution or disturbance of identity.

While *Never Let Me Go* cannot be read as an explicit commentary on the ethics of biotechnology – it contains virtually no scientific details – the norms and discourse of science form a powerful undercurrent that shapes both the characters and the narrative. Ishiguro does not demonize scientific creation; rather, the text's critical focus emphasizes the naturalization of instrumentalist ways of seeing the world, its impact on social relations and on the very conceptions of what it means to be human. More critically, Ishiguro emphasizes the role of scientific discourse in the processes by which a culture, on the one hand, creates and sustains belief in itself, and, on the other, interpolates individuals as subjects in the dominant ideology. Ishiguro maintains an unresolved tension between the clones' preternaturally calm resignation to their physical fate and their concurrent desire to live. The mechanistic and materialistic determinism of the scientific universe which reduces the human to the body and its parts is contrasted with human values of love, friendship, family and community, which find their most intricate articulation and representation in the novel form.

Created for a medical purpose they will serve once they reach adult-hood, the clones' lives are bracketed by science. One of their teachers tells them that their lives are already mapped out for them and that, when they are old enough, they will fulfil their function by donating their organs (*NLMG* 80). The central concern of the novel is how the clones negotiate the terms of their foreclosed futures; this gives rise to a question never explicitly addressed: why do they never try to escape? Ishiguro's repeated use of the word 'fate' in interviews – even though the term is never used in the novel itself – becomes significant in this context. The clones' acquiescence to their own exploitation can be understood through Pierre Bourdieu's notion of *habitus*, which explains how consciousness is generated through a dialectical relation between the individual and his or her social context. These conditions of exis-tence create 'durable, transposable dispositions' which structure future actions and decisions in differing social contexts without it being 'in any way the product of obedience to rules . . . [or] the product [of] the organizing action of a conductor'.[18] Furthermore, because the relation to what is possible is a relation to power, 'the sense of the probable future is constituted in the prolonged relationship with a world struc-tured according to the categories of the possible (for us) and the impos-sible (for us), of what is appropriated in advance by and for others and what one can reasonably expect for oneself'.[19]

the sum of their (body) parts

At the heart of *Never Let Me Go* is the role that language and discourse play in our conception of the world. The reader's curious relationship to the novel's first-person narrator is set up in the opening line, when she introduces herself as 'Kathy H.' (*NLMG* 3). The familiarity suggested by the use of the first name is unsettled by the lack of a surname, which underlines the clones' otherness by pointing to their anonymity. As laboratory creations they have no family relations and, as they cannot procreate (*NLMG* 94), there is no possibility of passing on a family name. Similarly, the tone of Kathy's narration generates a sense of intimacy – 'I've heard it said enough,' she says about rumours that as a Hailsham student she has the special privilege of choosing the donors she cares for, 'so I'm sure you've heard it plenty more . . .' (*NLMG* 4) – which is undercut when she attempts to share memories that the reader cannot identify with, such as the fact that the guardians at Hailsham imposed a severe no-smoking rule (*NLMG* 67). Her account starts out on recognizable terrain – the dangers of smoking has formed part of our public discourse for years – but then veers onto strange ground, revealing how lessons would grind to a halt and books were banned if any reference to cigarettes were made. Earlier, when relating a story about an encounter between her and Tommy on the stairwell while waiting to see Nurse Trisha, she mentions almost in passing that the students at Hailsham had a weekly medical check (*NLMG* 13). While the reader's knowledge of her life is dependent on what Kathy chooses to divulge, the absences reveal most about her reality. For the reader, the above would constitute an undue emphasis on physical health; Kathy's throwaway comments, however, signal an unquestioning acceptance and establish it as an ordinary part of her day-to-day existence.

The clones' acceptance of the predetermined progression of their lives – becoming a carer and then an organ donor – is encoded in their desire to perform well in each of these stages. Kathy takes great pride in her proficiency as a carer and there is no overt acknowledgement of the suffering of the clones involved, nor of the emotional impact that witnessing their deaths might have had on her. When she comments on the death, or rather the murder, of a donor, she is more upset because she sees it as a professional failure, while the events leading to the clone's demise are revealed with consummate understatement: 'it had been a particularly *untidy* operation – but I wasn't feeling great all the same' (*NLMG* 99, my emphasis).

The reader's gradual understanding of the curious relationship between the clones and their bodies has led several reviewers to describe the novel as disturbing.[20] The affective response elicited in the reader is in stark contrast to Kathy's matter-of-fact observations, her use of euphemism and understatement. While the latter can be seen as a coping mechanism, other events in the novel suggest that for the clones there is a disconnection between the self and the body. When Tommy has an accident that leaves him with a gash on his elbow, some of the students decide to play a joke on him by pretending that his body can unzip like a bag (*NLMG* 83–4). The story becomes a grotesque mythology that desensitizes the clones to their bodily purpose: 'The idea was that when the time came, you'd be able just to unzip a bit of yourself, a kidney or something would slide out, and you'd hand it over' (*NLMG* 86). The dehumanized and instrumentalized view they have of their bodies touches on a key issue in the debate over the ethics of gene patents. While one group maintains that 'it is unacceptable to treat humans as a commodity', the other side disagrees 'that genes hold special symbolic value or that gene patents are a particularly problematic form of property'.[21] As Timothy Caulfield and Roger Brownsword explain, 'it is not so much the legal status of the human person that is at issue as it is the status of the body and body parts. The two are not necessarily the same'.[22] The latter argument seems to be the general consensus among the scientific community. In contradistinction, the novel's narrative tension resides in the conflict between the instrumental value of the clones as the hosts of healthy organs and the basic moral value of each individual as singular and irreplaceable.

In the society represented in *Never Let Me Go*, instrumentalist ways of seeing the world have already triumphed. People's discomfort over the clones' existence is outweighed by their fear at the loss of their own loved ones. As Miss Emily explains, the general population tried not to think of the clones at all. When they did, they thought of them as subhuman. In a world requiring clones to donate 'there would always be a barrier against seeing [them] as *properly* human' (*NLMG* 258, my emphasis). Even though the clones are exact genetic copies of humans and, therefore, human, the world has actively to construct them as members of a 'genetic underclass' – through their isolation, by calling them clones – in order to continue with the donations programme.

In current scientific discourse, cloning is sometimes considered an 'enhancement technology'. 'Genetic enhancement' techniques could be used to produce individuals who are resistant to certain types of viruses or to manipulate height and intelligence. This is a contentious topic of debate since, compared to reproductive cloning, genetic enhancement entails actually changing the human genome. However, scientists do not have the same qualms when it comes to manipulating the genes of animals to give them commercially desirable genetic traits such as 'high milk production, excellent meat marbling or quick growth'.[23] In *Never Let Me Go*, Scottish scientist James Morningdale's attempt to offer people the possibility of children with improved capabilities reminds them of a fear they always had. As Miss Emily claims, 'It's one thing to create students, such as yourselves, for the donation programme. But a generation of created children who'd take their place in society? Children demonstrably *superior* to the rest of us? Oh no. That frightened people. They recoiled from that' (*NLMG* 259). Cloning is acceptable if the 'product' is less, and not more, than human.

The clones' otherness is situated purely in their scientific origin; they are beings that were created through artificial means and are therefore not considered human, but artefacts. Madame articulates this view during the meeting with Kathy and Tommy about the possibility of a deferral, that is, of postponing their donations by proving their relationship. She refers to them as 'poor creatures' (*NLMG* 267). Ishiguro's choice of the word 'creature' is significant. It suggests a perspective in which the subjugation and exploitation of these beings is justified. While the aim of the Hailsham project was ostensibly to demonstrate that it was possible for the clones 'to grow to be as sensitive and intelligent as any *ordinary* human being' if they were reared in a humane environment, it was really just an attempt to improve the conditions in which the clones were raised, not to abolish the programme altogether. The wheelchair-bound Miss Emily herself, it is further suggested, is about to benefit from the donations programme (*NLMG* 251). This explains her reluctance to critique a system from which she stands to benefit.

no desire to escape

Like Frankenstein's monster, the clones are confined to a shadowy existence; however, while he rebels against his 'fate' and seeks revenge, the clones do not act even after their true position in society is revealed. Furthermore, apart from the mysterious 'they' that Kathy refers to, who seem to communicate with letters to inform the clones when they are to become carers or start donating, there is no enforcement of the donation programme. The clones' passivity can be explained only partially by their reification in a social system where they are literally sacrificed in the service of a medical science from which others will benefit. One of the arguments most often used against human cloning is that it will be detrimental to human dignity as 'an engine of individual empowerment, reinforcing individual autonomy and the right to self-determination'.[24] The creation of a human to serve the purposes of another – such as to serve a medical need – imposes an arbitrary restriction on the clone's individuality and 'therefore violates its autonomy, its freedom and dignity'.[25] Yvette Pearson claims that this reasoning is reminiscent of genetic determinism – that is, 'it holds that the physical and mental traits and behaviour of an individual are ultimately determined by his or her genotype'.[26] Pearson thus states that 'it is not cloning that restricts the autonomy of the clone', but rather the social factors of the environment in which the cloned individual grows up in.[27]

Pearson fails to recognize the irony of this comment in the context of the novel. The clones are aware that at some point each of them was copied from 'a normal person', which would suggest that 'somewhere out there' they would be able to find the person from whom they were modelled. They call these their '"possibles" – the people who might have been the models for you and your friends' (*NLMG* 137), and look out for them at every opportunity. Even though Kathy's statement thus suggests an affirmation of individual agency in determining the direction of their futures, her own actions trying to explain her sexual urges and the attempts of the clones to find their 'possibles' indicate otherwise.

Pearson's interpretation is based on a curtailed quotation; the sentence originally reads as follows: 'It was up to each of us to make of our lives *what we could*' (*NLMG* 138, my emphasis). This phrase asks for a more nuanced approach to the question of genetic determinism. Neither Kathy and her friends' futures, nor their acceptance of it, is determined by their genetic blueprint. Rather, it is their knowledge of who they are and what they have been created for that sets the limits on their lives. As Margaret Atwood states, 'there's the feeling that as the expectations of such a group are diminished, so is its ability to think outside the box it has been shut up in'.[28] This illustrates the extent to which *habitus* generates dispositions that are compatible with social conditions and in a sense pre-adapted to its demands: 'the most improbable practices are therefore excluded, as unthinkable, by a kind of immediate submission to order that inclines agents to make a virtue of necessity, that is, to refuse what is anyway denied and to will the inevitable'.[29] The clones see the purpose they have been created for as their *fate*; that is, they misrecognize their conditions of existence as a natural order. Consequently, even though there are no concrete constraints on the clones' freedom, they are unable to conceptualize a self-determined future.

The roots of the clones' lack of agency lie in their years at Hailsham. According to Ishiguro, the boarding school setting is 'a clear physical manifestation of the way all children are separated off from the adult world, and are drip-fed little pieces of information about the world that awaits them, often with generous doses of deception, kindly meant or otherwise'.[30] The setting enables Ishiguro to explore the importance of material structures for the ways in which the clones imbibe a worldview to the extent that certain objectionable norms and values become normalized. The irony of Hailsham is that the greatest harm to the clones results from its very efforts to shelter them. It represents an idyllic environment compared to the government schools in other programmes where clones are 'reared in deplorable conditions' (*NLMG* 255). That clones have tried to escape from some of these institutions is suggested by Miss Lucy's comment during a lecture that the fences surrounding them are electrified (*NLMG* 77). The government schools are repressive; they function through violence, which is 'liable either to provoke a violent riposte from the victim or force him to flee (that is to say, in either case, in *the absence of any other recourse*, to provoke the annihilation of the very relationship which was intended to be exploited)'.[31] In contrast, the 'soft violence' exerted by Hailsham results in a 'more effective, and in this sense more brutal, means of oppression'.[32] All the talks, videos, discussions and warnings to prepare the clones for their futures reproduce their submission to the rules of the established order and determine the parameters of their consciousness. These rules include the assumptions that go without saying – what Bourdieu calls the *doxa* of the field, shared by all its social agents – which determine the limits of the doable and the thinkable.[33]

Consequently, the Hailsham clones have no desire to escape. Even when they leave the school, living at the Cottages without supervision and driving freely across the country as carers, the clones submit to what Hailsham taught them to be their purpose. Within the limits of their predetermined futures, the clones therefore try to give some meaning to their lives by fulfilling what appears to be a very abstract conception of duty. Ruth tells Kathy and Tommy, 'I think I was a pretty decent carer. But five years felt about enough for me. I was like you, Tommy. I was pretty much ready when I became a donor. It felt right. After all, it's what we're *supposed* to be doing, isn't it?' As Kathy observes, 'it was the sort of thing you hear donors say to each other *all the time*' (*NLMG* 223, my emphasis). By repeating what they perceive to be their *duty*, the clones constantly affirm as natural an ideology of which they are the victims. In the end, it can be suggested, Kathy becomes an organ donor not only because she considers it her fate but also because this was the outcome for Ruth and Tommy, the people closest to her. The power of her identity as a Hailsham student is such that she cannot envision a different future. Ishiguro discloses that he wanted to create 'the sense that it was comfortable for her to resign herself to what everybody else had done already. That it feels normal to her, that it's her duty'.[34] Kathy's ultimate sacrifice reveals the extent to which her social conditions, her friendships and her loyalties, have determined her perception of a possible future; they constitute 'symbolic violence', 'the gentle, invisible form of violence, which is never recognized as such, and is not so much undergone as chosen'.[35] A few weeks after Tommy's death Kathy stands looking over an empty field in Norfolk, imagining that if she waited long enough he would appear on the horizon.

In current debates on the ethics of human reproductive cloning, the argument of genetic determinism is powerfully countered by emphasizing the role of both our genetic blueprint and our interaction with the social environment in our development as unique individuals. In *Never*

Let Me Go, however, Ishiguro shows that it is precisely this environment and the naturalization of the values of science in public discourse that can produce some of the feared effects of cloning. Kathy's subjectivity as a clone with a foreclosed future results in a loss *not* of her individuality, but rather her *sense* of individuality. By dislocating scientific discourse from its abstract environment and employing it in a cultural and social context which the novel is uniquely suited to explore, Ishiguro foregrounds its instrumentalist ethos and demystifies its claim to be value-free. Furthermore, the emotional content of Kathy's narrative points towards an affective remainder that lies outside of science's purview, challenging purely scientific notions of what it means to be human.

notes

1. James Butcher, 'A Wonderful Donation', *The Lancet*, 365 (9 April 2005), 1300.
2. Tim Adams, 'For Me, England is a Mythical Place', *Observer*, 20 February 2005, observer.guardian.co.uk/review/story/0,6903,1418284,00.html, accessed 14 February 2007.
3. Nicholas Wroe, 'Living Memories', *Guardian*, 19 February 2005, books. guardian.co.uk/departments/generalfiction/story/0,,1417665,00.html, accessed 12 January 2007.
4. Kazuo Ishiguro, quoted in Christina Patterson, 'Kazuo Ishiguro: The Samurai of Suburbia', *The Independent*, 4 March 2005, enjoyment.independent.co.uk/ books/features/article4537.ece, accessed 12 January 2007.
5. Kazuo Ishiguro, 'I Remain Fascinated by Memory', *Der Spiegel* Online, 5 October 2005, www.spiegel.de/international/0,1518,378173,00.html, accessed 12 January 2007.
6. C. P. Snow, 'The Two Cultures and the Scientific Revolution', *Encounter*, 69 (June 1959), 17.
7. Gabriele Griffin, 'Science and the Cultural Imaginary: The Case of Kazuo Ishiguro's *Never Let Me Go*', *Textual Practice*, 23 (4) (2009), 645–64, 657.
8. Richard Tarnas, *The Passion of the Western Mind: Understanding the Ideas that Have Shaped our World View* (New York: Ballantine Books, 1991), p. 355.
9. Ibid., p. 364.
10. John Carroll, *Humanism: The Wreck of Western Culture* (London: Fontana Press, 1993), pp.117–18.
11. Ibid., p. 124.
12. Ibid.
13. Tarnas, *Passion*, p. 364.
14. Ibid., p. 362.
15. Jane Perrone and Derek Brown, 'Human Cloning', *Guardian Unlimited*, 18 January 2002, www.guardian.co.uk/world/2002/jan/18/qanda.derekbrown/ print, accessed 13 January 2007.
16. Christof Tannert, 'Thou Shalt Not Clone: An Ethical Argument Against the Reproductive Cloning of Humans', *EMBO Reports*, 7 (3) (2006), 240.

17. Timothy Caulfield and Roger Brownsword, 'Human Dignity: A Guide to Policy Making in the Biotechnology Era?' *Nature Reviews*, 7 (January 2006), 72.
18. Pierre Bourdieu, *The Logic of Practice*, trans. Richard Nice (Stanford: Stanford University Press, 1990), p. 53. Also see Karl Maton, 'Habitus', in Michael Grenfell (ed.), *Pierre Bourdieu: Key Concepts* (Stocksfield: Acumen, 2008), p. 51.
19. Bourdieu, *Logic*, p. 64.
20. See Adams, 'Mythical Place'; and Butcher, 'A Wonderful Donation', p. 1299.
21. Caulfield and Brownsword, 'Human Dignity', p. 74.
22. Ibid.
23. Elizabeth Weise, 'FDA: Cloned Animals' Meat is Safe', *USA Today*, 27 December 2006, www.usatoday.com/news/health/2006-12-27-fda-cloned-meat_x.htm, accessed 13 January 2007.
24. Caulfield and Brownsword, 'Human Dignity', 72.
25. Tannert, 'Thou Shalt Not', 240.
26. Yvette Pearson, 'Never Let Me Clone? Countering an Ethical Argument Against the Reproductive Cloning of Humans' *EMBO Reports*, 7 (7) (2006), 657.
27. Ibid.
28. Margaret Atwood, 'Brave New World: Kazuo Ishiguro's Novel Really *is* Chilling', *Slate*, 1 (April 2005), www.slate.com/id/2116040/, accessed 12 January 2007.
29. Bourdieu, *Logic*, p. 54.
30. Kazuo Ishiguro, 'A Conversation with Kazuo Ishiguro', Random House, 2007, www.randomhouse.ca, accessed 12 January 2007.
31. Pierre Bourdieu, *A Theory of Practice*, trans. Richard Nice (Cambridge: Cambridge University Press, 1977), p. 192.
32. Pierre Bourdieu and Terry Eagleton, 'Doxa and Common Life', *New Left Review*, 191 (January–February 1992), 115.
33. Maton, 'Habitus', p. 59.
34. Brian W. Shaffer and Cynthia F. Wong (eds.), (Conversations with Kazuo Ishiguro Jackson, MS: University of Mississippi Press, 2008), p. 215.
35. Bourdieu, *Theory*, p. 192.

18
kazuo ishiguro's *never let me go* and 'outsider science fiction'

andy sawyer

summary

The term 'outsider science fiction' is used with increasing frequency to describe those novels that draw upon some of the themes, settings and imagery associated with the genre in order to explore issues more commonly associated with mainstream or literary fiction. Kazuo Ishiguro's Never Let Me Go *(2005) can be classed as an example of such 'outsider science fiction'. Indeed, it was shortlisted for the 2006 Arthur C. Clarke Award. This chapter considers how Ishiguro's novel operates within a science-fiction register and creates the kind of 'cognitive estrangement' associated with the genre.*

the genesis of *never let me go*

Kazuo Ishiguro's *Never Let Me Go* (2005) is set in an 'alternative' England of the late 1990s. The world it presents is similar to our own except in one crucial respect: scientific development since the Second World War has centred not on nuclear technology, but on advances in biogenetics. Specifically, the novel imagines a setting in which the rearing of clones to provide body parts for non-clones has become commonplace and socially acceptable. Institutions such as Hailsham produce students who will ultimately become donors. Few, if any, survive after four 'donations'; some die after two. Some, such as narrator Kathy H., survive for a time as 'carers', helping others to recover from the loss of their organs until it is time for their turn to donate.

Never Let Me Go thus presents a parallel world that uses motifs and ideas familiar from science fiction in order to produce the effect of 'cognitive estrangement' that is one of the genre's main characteristics.[1]

Darko Suvin's explanation of this term is bound up with the reader's recognition that the world a fiction presents is not our own world, but the world presented in such a radically different way that we cannot help but view it from the perspective of an outsider. There is a sense, of course, in which all novels present alternative realities: what is important here is the degree of difference between our own world and that of the fiction. Moreover, in science fiction, the difference that is at stake is created by what Suvin calls a 'novum': this is the new element of the narrative world that dictates plot, character and setting. It cannot be any old difference, but must be one that is scientifically plausible – or, at least, empirically possible in an alternate past, present or future state of affairs.

Kazuo Ishiguro demonstrated an awareness of this distinction in an interview for a science-fiction journal. He suggested the following about how to classify *Never Let Me Go*:

> these labels [e.g. 'science fiction'] don't worry me too much . . . you can call it science fiction if you like, in that I've used a scientific framework, or landscape, in which there are scientific possibilities that don't exist right now . . . I've just imagined a world where there have been breakthroughs in science that haven't in fact taken place. I worry less about genres and categories. I use whatever I can.[2]

Ishiguro's technique, which he describes in the interview as placing the reader into a position similar to that of the young children of the novel, equates exactly to that sense of estrangement a science-fiction narrative imparts: '[the readers] sense that this isn't like a realistic novel, there's some kind of strange landscape and they don't know what the rules are'.[3]

According to Ishiguro's description of the composition of *Never Let Me Go*, he never originally intended the novel to be science fiction as such. It was only when he heard a radio discussion about biotechnology that a way of writing the story fell into place. Ishiguro suggests that he has little interest in futuristic technology except as metaphor, and that he finds writing futuristic fiction uncongenial: 'I was never tempted to set this story in the future. That's partly a personal thing. I'm not very turned on by futuristic landscapes'.[4]

'Outsider science fiction' is a popular term to describe those works by mainstream writers who are not adherents of the genre, but who nevertheless use science-fiction motifs, settings or concepts to convey their ideas. *Never Let Me Go* clearly falls into this category. Other examples include Margaret Atwood's *The Handmaid's Tale* (1985) and *Oryx and Crake* (2003); Cormac McCarthy's *The Road* (2006); Sarah Hall's *The Carhulian Army* (2007); Jeanette Winterson's *The Stone Gods* (2007); and Michael Chabon's *The Yiddish Policeman's Union* (2007). Some of these have won, or been shortlisted for, awards in the field of science fiction. Most of them have been praised by journalists and critics who dislike using the term 'science fiction'. Some of these authors have happily accepted the term 'science fiction' as being part of their creative vocabulary; others reject the genre as a description of their work.

The term is surrounded by a series of category confusions. Among these are the assumption that some authors who may appear to be writing science fiction are not actually doing so. What looks like an example of the genre is actually some original, distinctive or separate mode. This ignores the fact that what seems like a speculative idea or a conscious allusion to the genre may, in fact, be received as a cliché to an audience versed in what critics such as Damien Broderick and Farah Mendelsohn call the science fiction 'megatext' or 'conversation': 'the community of science fiction writers has developed a tool kit, the absence or recreation of which is usually the hallmark of outsider science fiction (fiction written by professional writers which either claims to have invented a new genre, or which vigorously denies its categorization of science fiction)'.[5] The appearance of these devices in the mainstream may be because literary writers turn innocently to themes and ideas thinking that they are new, not realizing that have been used in the science-fiction field for decades. Yet science-fiction images are now part of a common stock of recognizable literary emblems.

Distrust of the term science fiction is at the very heart of the field. In the 1950s, Robert A. Heinlein first championed 'speculative fiction' as a more accurate term for the genre. John Wyndham claimed that what he wrote was more 'logical fantasy' than science fiction. For critics, the creative approach is to consider how science fiction is read rather than how it is labelled. Darko Suvin's definition of 'science fiction' is deliberately formal and structural: '[it is] a literary genre whose necessary and sufficient conditions are the presence and interaction of estrangement and cognition, and whose main formal device is an imaginative framework alternative to the author's empirical environment'.[6] Rather than focusing upon the nature of the alternative frameworks, this definition highlights the questioning, critical, even satirical, nature of the reflection upon our reality implied by 'cognition'. This arguable distinction has an advantage for the literary taxonomist. It concentrates upon what the text does, rather than the context in which it does it (e.g. a science-fiction magazine or a literary novel). It allows us to concentrate on the very real difference between someone being an orthodox science-fiction writer, such as, say, Arthur C. Clarke or Stephen Baxter, and a writer of occasional science fiction such as Atwood or Ishiguro.

never let me go in context

Deliberately oblique – even the geographical location of the principal setting, Hailsham, is never disclosed – *Never Let Me Go* is a work by a mainstream writer that draws upon science-fiction motifs, settings and concepts. Much has been made about its reluctance to be scientifically plausible: Ishiguro does not explore the 'how' of the technology, or what Darko Suvin calls the 'novum', of his fiction. But this is not Ishiguro's modus operandi in any case. However, his detached and estranging style in *Never Let Me Go* conveys a sense of what it might be like to live in a different world. The children of Hailsham are organ donors. Organ donation is a frequent occurrence in present-day medical practice. What makes Ishiguro's invented world particularly chilling is the fact that vast numbers of children are cloned and reared specifically to give up their kidneys and livers for the remainder of the population. What is more, the children themselves only gradually become aware of the dire fate that awaits them. A 'science-fictional' reading of the book would centre around their own discovery of their place in their world: which is a mystery to them, but not to the alert reader, especially one who is well-versed in the standard genre trope of cloning.

These clones are brought up in isolated environments akin to certain types of boarding school. Hailsham, where Kathy, Tommy, Ruth and their friends are educated, is the kind of progressive/liberal establishment exemplified by Bedales or Summerhill. There are, it is hinted, somewhat nastier environments where clones are reared. The clones know who they are and what their fate is. Crucially, they accept their circumstances almost unquestioningly. Keith McDonald, writing on *Never Let Me Go* as 'speculative memoir', declares that 'Kathy H.'s passivity and acceptance of her lot is at times enraging'.[7] However, he also goes on suggest that it is possible to find heroism in her attempt to recount her experiences. Kathy is engaged with understanding her place in a world in which she and her friends exist, but which is fundamentally not theirs. As one character says, they have not actually been deceived, but have been 'told and not told. You've been told, but none of you really understand' (*NLMG* 79). This results in fantasies about finding their 'possibles', the originals from which they have been cloned, at large in the world beyond Hailsham. It also leads to hopes of 'deferring' their final donations. The art that they were encouraged to produce at school and college is potential evidence for a deferral to be granted. If a couple can persuade the authorities that they are worthy, they can be given a few years of life together. Tommy and Kathy track down Madame, who selected their art work for her Gallery, and are told the brutal truth: Hailsham was a privileged enclave which was closed down after a scare produced by an attempt to develop superior clones. The emphasis on art was not so much to prove that some of the children had developed enough inwardly to be allowed to live together, but to persuade the authorities and the public that these clones were human at all. And this project, Miss Emily tells them, failed.

The boarding school environment – and the sense that the surrounding society does not see these children as human – recalls Wyndham. He was educated at Bedales School and his novel *The Midwich Cuckoos* (1957) is also about eldritch children who are both 'us' and 'not-us'. Ishiguro's short-lived clones serve as analogues for our own awareness of mortality and are reminiscent of Philip K. Dick's artificial creations in *Do Androids Dream of Electric Sheep?* (1968). More accurately, they recall the 'replicants' in the film adaptation of Dick's novel, *Blade Runner* (1982), one of the movies cited in Ishiguro's *Interzone* interview. Dick's kaleidoscope of shifting identities, however, paradoxically provides a more affirming narrative than that of *Never Let Me Go*. By foregrounding empathy or kindness as the heart of the 'human', Dick offers a way out of our distrust of otherness. This empathy, to Dick, is what separates humanity from the unfeeling androids. But for Dick, the 'human' has little to do with physical form. The androids that Rick Deckard hunts down and 'retires' are physically indistinguishable from humans. He is more concerned with the capacity to see the 'other' as part of a universal community. As Dick himself puts it: 'A human being without the proper empathy or feeling is the same as an android built so as to lack it, either by design or mistake'.[8] Dick's novels make us question our own humanity. His characters constantly question their own realities, as in the episodes where Deckard is not sure whether or not his colleague Phil is an android.

Dick's androids are programmed to exist for a mere four years, rather than the thirty or so implied for the clones in *Never Let Me Go*. Ishiguro's text is therefore less consoling. The novel uses creativity and art as a (failed) attempt to assess the 'humanity' of people like Tommy, Ruth and Kathy. The numerous instances of empathy shown by Kathy (especially to the manipulative Ruth and the angry Tommy) make a fascinating, if heavily ironic contrast, with *Do Androids Dream of Electric Sheep?* Both Dick's fiction and the film adaptation lead us to the same conclusion that the revelation at Madame's house in Ishiguro also gives us: that authenticity is not the same thing as originality. A deeper level of irony and poignancy is reached when we realize that Hailsham's art is, and never was, anything to do with proving humanity. Being human lies in another plane entirely from being creative.

But Ishiguro, unlike Dick, noticeably avoids playing with the implications of technological constructs such as 'android' or 'replicant'. Ishiguro is far removed from Ridley Scott's world of special effects or even Dick's complex and sombre interplay of alternative realities. The extrapolated future is eschewed for *Never Let Me Go*'s domestic English landscape. The distancing effect here is powerful because it is very much from within. If the novel is science fiction, it nevertheless avoids the magic tricks of faster-than-light travel or time machines. Yet it is undoubtedly a richly imagined world. One of science fiction's most interesting effects is the dynamic between the cosmic and the local: a detailed, invented environment that seems as complex as our own, but is definitely not ours. We really see very little of the world of *Never Let Me Go*, but when we do, it seems consistent with ours. Kathy, presumably, interacts with non-clones on her travels. The shopping episode in Norfolk suggests that the clones can mingle with ordinary humans. Madame, knowing that the schoolchildren are clones, finds them frightening, but in the ordinary non-clone environment they seem only slightly different: 'Are you art-students?' asks the woman in the Art Gallery (*NLMG* 161). However, the uncanniness of its main characters is present on every page. Despite the fact that the clones read a lot and experience ordinary human emotions and dilemmas, their response to each other seems strange. Students who leave the Cottages are hardly referred to, almost as if there were a taboo against it (*NLMG* 130). Is this a coping mechanism? They know, after all, that they too will eventually be used up and die.

There is no reference in Kathy's narrative to her having read any newspaper account of the development of cloning and the controversies that clearly surround it, but this may be because her early education was highly controlled. Or it could be because Kathy, like many of Ishiguro narrators, is neither telling us all she knows nor (possibly) allowing herself to reflect on the fact that she knows it. This represents another variation on the idea of the unreliable narrator. Kathy is less self-deceiving than, say, Stevens in *The Remains of the Day* (1989) or Christopher Banks in *When We Were Orphans* (2000): yet her entire world is unreliable. We cannot assume that just because the world of *Never Let Me Go* is like our world in most respects, it is like it in all respects. By presenting us with a world we cannot trust, Ishiguro emphasizes our affinity to Kathy and our own inability to understand our place in our own world. If *Never Let Me Go* were a realistic account of student angst, or a fully fledged alternative science-fiction world, our engagement with Kathy's perceptions would be less involved and less poignant. We are on the threshold between genres here. This world has motorways and Norfolk and Art Galleries and porn magazines – but what else does it have that is not disclosed?

Those who are alienated often fantasize about their origins. Kathy and her companions do likewise with their romantic search for 'possibles', as they search for lookalikes in magazines. The realization that their origins lie in the gutter suggests their true status in their world: 'We're modelled from *trash*. Junkies, prostitutes, winos, tramps' (*NLMG* 164). Clones are living tools, simply one step down from the underclass we prefer not to think about. They are 'not-human' because their function is to define those who receive the donations as 'human'. One wonders if this version of England has a race problem, given that it has already effectively created an 'other' to take on the role of soul-less alien.

The technology that has created this situation is neither fetishized in *Never Let Me Go* nor used as an excuse for a thriller plot. The novel presents the development of a technology without detailing it in practical terms. It is also concerned with the issue of how we can call ourselves human. To call the world of *Never Let Me Go* a dystopia is ambiguous. It deals with an ethical problem the way we often do, by ignoring it; or, in Miss Emily's case, by trying to give the clones better lives. Has knowledge of the truth actually affected Tommy and Kathy? Madame's designation of the clones as 'you poor creatures' (*NLMG* 9) may not even be appropriate, despite Tommy's anguish. He and Kathy disagree about whether his tantrums were a sign that he knew, unconsciously, about his fate. These individuals exist; their lives go on. What matters is Kathy's insistence that there are 'good carers' (*NLMG* 276) and that the reader can map the anguishes and consolations of the clones onto our world.

speculative spaces

Ishiguro's *Never Let Me Go* can be compared with a similar treatment of cloning that appears in *Spares* (1996) by Michael Marshall Smith. Smith's novel is more recognizable to the genre-fixated reader as bona fide science fiction. Unlike *Never Let Me Go*, *Spares* has many of the trappings that we all recognize as belonging to the genre. It is set in the future and begins with a description of the 'MegaMalls', airborne structures that transport the rich from one part of the globe to another while keeping them in the same environment of lavish consumption. This process goes wrong when one MegaMall remains stranded on the ground and becomes a microcosm of this technologically advanced, corrupt and gang-ridden future. This is science fiction in the grotesque mode. It is vivid, imaginative and unsettling. In this world, the super-rich have exploited cloning technology to create the Spares (which, despite the title of the novel, turn out to be somewhat tangential to the plot).

The horror of Smith's world is obvious. Thrown out of a corrupt police force, and with his wife and daughter brutally murdered, Jack Randall takes the only job he can on a Spares farm. He observes at first-hand the side effects of a society where (if you are wealthy enough) it hardly matters what you do to your body, because somewhere you have a Spare you can rely upon for replacement organs or limbs. Smith describes the place where the Spares are reared with gruesome relish:

> In the blue the bodies staggered and crawled like blind grubs, disturbed by the periodic moans of the spare who'd had part of his face ripped out. The body nearest the window looked up suddenly, a motion that was random and meaningless. She had only one arm, and the skin on the left side of her face was red and churned where a graft had been removed. Her eyes flickered across the window and her mouth moved silently, and worst thing was that her face and body were not sufficiently destroyed to hide how attractive her counterpart must be.[9]

Never Let Me Go is far removed from this extrapolated hell. Despite a motif and setting which we would find science fictional, *Never Let Me Go* is more centrally a novel of contemporary identity. It is about how we unquestioningly accept the lives our parental, educational and political authorities give us.[10] But the trope that Ishiguro uses, in comparison to the potential choices he could have made about how to render this particular story, has its own dynamic. We read the 'fantastic' differently.

By establishing a 'fantastic' telling of the story of Kathy H. and her companions which relates (however mutedly) to other fantastic discourses, the tale of Kathy is more than a parable or analogue for the reader's existential anxiety. The alienated and alienating setting calls for its own interpretation. Neither *Spares* nor *Never Let Me Go* is, of course, centrally about the technology or even the ethics of human cloning: technology that can only implicitly (and may never) exist in the real world. The reluctance of some readers to view *Never Let Me Go* as science fiction is quite rightly based upon the reductive nature of the kind of reading which concludes that human cloning is a 'bad thing'. However, we should be reluctant to impose an equally reductive humanistic reading by which the short lives of the clones merely function as metaphors that prompt us to contemplate our own mortality.

The speculative space opened up by Ishiguro and Smith allows us to explore the impossible in order to shed light upon the possible. The clone/human relationships are certainly powerful symbols for how we live in the world, but the imagined worlds of the novels are even more powerful metaphors for how we construct the world. It is therefore mistaken to force a 'realistic' reading upon Hailsham and the world in which it exists. The novel does not place the reader in a position of superiority to its characters. Rather, it coaxes the reader into a greater empathy with them because we, too, do not understand its setting. Knowing less about this world than Kathy does, we watch ourselves trying to make sense of it as we read. By understanding and second-guessing her place in it, we realize that this is exactly the relationship we have with our world. Immersed in a fantastic 'secondary world' which parallels ours, we are impelled to make sense of it, even if we have no clues other than the words on the page.

Such an immersive fantasy, according to Farah Mendelsohn, is one that allows us to experience the world along with its characters:

> We do not enter into the immersive fantasy, we are assumed to be of it: our cognitive dissonance is both entire and negated. The immersive fantasy must be sealed, it cannot, within the confines of the story, be questioned . . . the fantastic is embedded in the linguistic excesses of the text, or in the interaction between the setting and the protagonists, thus in the immersive fantasy, character and landscape become crucial. In the immersive fantasy, the plot may be the least fantastical element.[11]

This produces something similar to the cognitive estrangement noted by Savin. By establishing a secondary world of the fantastic – particularly one that partakes of the extrapolative, rational alternative that we find in science fiction – an author can establish a means of examining and criticizing the real world from which it springs.

Setting, or the relationship between interior and exterior landscape, becomes particularly important with this type of fiction. We have to understand their fantastic landscapes to follow what the characters are telling us. We need to explore the nature of their difference to understand precisely what is troubling them. Only then can we read their predicament back onto our own world. Setting allows us to explore a whole range of interpretations of 'otherness'; or, rather, to allow these interpretations to hover at the edge of interpretative awareness. In the works of Ishiguro, setting is usually subordinate to characters, relationships and ideas. As mentioned earlier, he has described how the setting of *Never Let Me Go* arose long after the story was embarked upon. The alternative-history, science-fictional thread of *Never Let Me Go* is thus Ishiguro's method of encouraging the themes behind the story to emerge. While this explanation is sufficient, it is also certainly possible to see *Never Let Me Go* as one of those rare but essential science-fiction texts that offer us an alternative world from the inside. It establishes one novum – namely that a technology has been developed which means that certain elements common to science fiction novels are present – and then explores the consequences. Although we would no doubt find it discomforting to live in a world where clones are reared to donate organs, it would come to be seen as natural and normal. In the same way, we all abhor car crashes, yet find it normal and natural to live with a mode of transport that kills or injures tens of thousands of people a year. In other words, *Never Let Me Go* is an alternative history involving a technology that most people, including those most intimately involved with it, never even stop to think about. They live with the moral results of this set-up as if there were no ethical questions arising from it. It is easy to be appalled by the world of *Spares* through descriptions similar to the one quoted above and to heap blame upon its super-rich exploiters. *Never Let Me Go* is less brutal and more insidious. The question of who is taking advantage of the 'donors' is unclear, but Ishiguro's novum seems far more embedded in his society than Smith's, as it is universally accepted by those who are complicit with it.

Never Let Me Go works as science fiction because it makes its interior metaphor real. In this reading, the world its characters live in is as important as the characters themselves. The novel is firmly about change, as is most science fiction, even though it refuses to do more than distrust that change. By not assuming that its technology is to be distrusted, and by the absence of the kind of rebellion that mars many lesser dystopias, *Never Let Me Go* neatly sidesteps two of the stock options of science fiction. Instead, it establishes a constructed 'otherworld', extrapolated from ours, which we take for granted as a reasonable analogue of our own.

In conclusion, *Never Let Me Go* is as much science fiction as any other text cited in this chapter. Ishiguro (and, in a slightly different vein, Michael Marshall Smith) write stories in which there are familiar science-fiction elements of plot and theme. In comparing *Never Let Me Go* with other acknowledged science-fiction writers such as Dick and Smith, we can also see that the idea of what a science-fiction novel is can be broader and deeper than that held by many critics and reviewers, both from within and outside the field. The question of whether or not Kazuo Ishiguro intended to write science fiction might, in the end, be irrelevant.

notes

1. See Darko Suvin, *Metamorphoses of Science Fiction* (New Haven: Yale University Press, 1979), pp. 7–10.
2. Rick Kleffel, 'Interview with Kazuo Ishiguro', *Interzone* 198 (May/June 2005), 62–3.
3. Ibid., p. 63.
4. Kazuo Ishiguro, 'Future Imperfect', *Guardian*, 25 March 2006.
5. Farah Mendelsohn, 'Introduction' to Edward James and Farah Mendelsohn (eds.), *Cambridge Companion to Science Fiction* (Cambridge: Cambridge University Press, 2003), p. 5.
6. Suvin, *Metamorphoses*, pp. 7–8.
7. Keith McDonald, 'Days of Past Futures: Kazuo Ishiguro's *Never Let Me Go* as "Speculative Memoir"', *Biography*, 30 (1) (Winter 2007), 74–83, 81.
8. Philip K. Dick, 'Man, Android and Machine', in *The Dark-Haired Girl* (Willimantic, CT: Ziesing, 1988), pp. 201–2.
9. Michael Marshall Smith, *Spares* (London: HarperCollins, 1996), pp. 42–3.
10. See M. John Harrison, 'Clone Alone', *Guardian*, 'Features and Reviews', 26 February 2005, 26.
11. Farah Mendelsohn, 'Towards a Taxonomy of Fantasy', *Journal of the Fantastic in the Arts*, 13 (2) (2002), 175–6.

the new seriousness: kazuo ishiguro in conversation with
sebastian groes

Sebastian Groes: When you started out as a writer in your twenties, did you already then have a sense of an authorship that would have a clear, organic trajectory, or did that only emerge later, if at all?

Kazuo Ishiguro: I only became aware of that after *The Remains of the Day*. Before *The Remains* I was taking it just one book at a time. I wasn't really serious about writing until I did the UEA Creative Writing course when I was aged twenty-four. Now people are very ambitious and they try to get into a prestigious Creative Writing course to help their career. But back in 1979, the UEA Creative Writing MA was the only one in the country, a prototype, and most people were highly sceptical about it. I'd have been mad to think it would help with a career. I was doing it largely because I could get a grant to do an MA. I'd been working in London with home-less people and it seemed rather an idyllic idea to spend twelve months at the expense of the state writing a few pages of fiction.

SG: And you got to work with Angela Carter as well.

KI: I hadn't even heard of Angela Carter when I first met her. Angela was a fairly obscure writer in those days; just a few people were in the know about her. It was difficult to track down her books, because they'd come out in hardcover and then gone out of print. Her work wasn't even available in paperback.

I met her in spring 1980. She had recently come back from Japan which had been very important for her, both as a writer and as a person. She kept alluding to a wild and strange past. She was a very different writer from, say, my other tutor, Malcolm Bradbury, who was university-based, a professor, a novelist and television playwright. Angela was someone who'd moved around the world, lived on the edge and often wrote stuff that nobody would publish. In a way, it's odd to think she's now become so revered, but then again it's not odd if you consider what she was writing. Angela was very different from what was going on at the time, particularly among female writers. There was good literary fiction around then, usually realist work engaging with the contemporary – Edna O'Brien, Margaret Drabble. But Angela's work was completely different from that.

SG: Carter's interest in Japan made you two click immediately, I suppose?

KI: Yes, there was a bond from the very start. We would sit in her house in Clapham, and have rambling conversations. It was all associative. I was a beginning writer at that point, and all the things I was interested in, she'd already explored. We talked about Japanese culture, and how it differed from British culture, in literature, film, behaviour and everything else. Angela was fascinated by Japanese things and at that point I was focussed on excavating my Japanese memories and trying to do something with my Japanese past.

We were both interested in pushing realism, finding alternatives to realism. For ages I didn't show her anything of what I was writing. She'd just read four short stories I'd done before her arrival at UEA, which at that point were ready to come out in *Introductions 7: Stories by New Writers* [Faber, 1981]. I remember conversations about how much one should satisfy realist concerns. There was a certain short story of mine. She said that although this particular character is the narrator, you don't say anything about her family: doesn't that matter? We'd often have these conversations about how you move out of realism; how you're in a realist mode but perhaps not in a realist mode; what you could and couldn't do; and to what extent an audience would follow you. To what extent it was okay to *not* satisfy certain expectations, such as giving the back-story information.

SG: Critics have often noted that there is a Gothic strand within your writing. In the early work, protagonists are haunted by ghosts from the past. The description of the country house in *The Remains of the Day* [1989] sometimes feels a bit 'Gothicky', and in *Nocturnes* [2009] you seem to be engaging with a literary tradition that represents Venice as a place associated with death. Did you get this Gothic interest via Carter?

KI: I don't think Angela influenced me in that kind of way. In fact, it's pushing it to say there's a Gothic element in my writing at all. Certainly not in Angela Carter's Poe-esque way or in the Romantic literature kind of sense. In my early work, such as *A Pale View of Hills* or 'A Family

Supper'[1983], there was a fascination with the supernatural. But it's an eerie Japanese supernatural, which is different from the Gothic.

I was going for understatement, with a calm surface and emotions beneath the surface. A kind of solicitor's report style that I was developing, and which ended up as the butler's style in *The Remains of the Day*. Angela, by contrast, was writing things like 'The Bloody Chamber' [1979] and was going for a Poe-esque high style, expressing emotions in a very elaborate way, with a deliberately oversensitized relationship to the world. She had a voice that was burlesque, stagey and circusy; it would sometimes mimic bawdy people on the Jacobean stage.

I respected Angela deeply, both as a writer and as a person, but I also felt that I didn't want to be influenced in a direct way by her writing. She has always been an enormous influence on the way I *think* about writing. Because she'd lived so long as a neglected writer earning her income as a left-wing journalist for *New Society*, she was able to teach me a lot about what it took to be a writer. She remained a mentor figure right up until the time she died. She also introduced me to my agent, Deborah Rogers, and to *Granta* magazine. She took me to my first literary party, for the literary magazine *Bananas*. There were all these little things she taught me, about how to behave towards these literary people, how seriously you need to take this or that person.

SG: In the light of your remarks about pushing realism, was that decision part of a subversive, independent-minded attitude towards your authorship?

KI: I didn't think of it as subversive. Today a lot of people think that being a novelist is glamorous. You come out of university as a bright young thing and turn into Zadie Smith. In my day that wasn't the case. More commercially successful writers than Angela or Malcolm still did other jobs, like journalism or teaching or the civil service. They weren't seen to be glamorous. They were shabby, dusty but highly respected figures. I thought writing was a kind of marginalized hobby. My wanting to be a literary novelist in the early eighties was like a young person today saying he wants to be a jazz bassist.

I remember there were people going around saying that if you wrote in a social-realist manner, you automatically supported the Tory government. I could never work that one out. My political instincts were always to the left anyway; I'd grown up on the left and had always done leftish work. I didn't ever buy into this idea that with your literary style you could cause a revolution or that you could bring down the establishment by doing something with the infinitive or by not having commas.

SG: So we shouldn't read the darker aspects of *The Remains of the Day* as a criticism of artists or production companies whose work was reinforcing Thatcher's glorification and mythification of England's Victorian heritage and morality?

KI: No, I was never consciously addressing the government of the day. In *The Remains of the Day*, I was conscious of the heritage industry and the English attitude towards Englishness, but perhaps more of how the world outside England viewed England. If I was trying to subvert or distort anything, it was the romanticized tourist vision of England, rather than anything to do with the Thatcher government.

   If there is anything that reflects my relationship with politics in *The Remains* and *An Artist of the Floating World* [1986], it's in the unease about the extent to which you can invest your own energies in some political cause. In both of those novels, the narrators feel it isn't good enough to just do their job for its own sake. They're anxious to put their work to a political purpose. Mr Stevens should be satisfied with butlering for butlering's sake, and Ono with art for art's sake, but they're not. They go one step further by saying 'My art is serving a greater cause', and that's where it starts to go wrong. That reflected my personal position at the time, having grown up in a much more politicized atmosphere compared to the one the younger generation are growing up in today. Everyone went around with lapel badges and when you met new people, you first had to figure out what their political positions were. There'd be this little coded thing about what kind of bread you bought, or which London listing magazine you read. This would tell you whether or not the person was SDP, which was a renegade centre-left party that had betrayed the Labour movement.

   Over the years, I became wary of political commitment. On the one hand I thought it was valuable to make up your mind and commit to one political end. On the other hand I saw so many people unthinkingly declaring themselves to this or that cause simply for tribal reasons. It reminded me of my parents' generation, who were very wary of political affiliation. They'd seen what had happened in the Second World War.

SG: You have written in women's voices on several occasions and have written them well. Etsuko and Kathy H. come to mind as convincing voices of women. When you write, there doesn't seem to be a great difference between children and adults. You've said you don't make a distinction between the two, because adults retain a part of their innocence through memories of their childhood. Can you tell me something about how you go about writing across gender, and whether a similar process is in operation?

KI: I don't pretend to be an experienced or seasoned writer of female characters. There are female characters in my books, as there are in any male author's work. An important breakthrough for me was the first story I ever published, which was narrated by a Japanese woman in late middle age. Also my first novel, *A Pale View of Hills* [1982], which was a grander version of that story. I built my confidence and first successes on being locked inside the head of a Japanese woman, so I was almost afraid of writing from any other perspective than that of middle-aged Japanese women.

I didn't think of whether this was dangerous. I was confident partly because I was a beginner and partly because I felt knowledgeable about the debates that were going on about feminism in my generation. I was listening to these debates every day; they were happening right in front of me. Or I would reach out a hand and there'd be magazines such as *Cosmopolitan* or *Company*. In those days, these were serious and interesting cultural magazines where these debates took place from a female perspective. I knew a lot of often quite radical women with badges and strange haircuts, who'd have these ferocious arguments with each other and with men, so I felt quite well-versed about the arguments.

In the early 2000s, when I started to write *Never Let Me Go* [2005], I didn't feel this same confidence about being able to tiptoe my way through this territory safely. I felt several stages removed from those rooms where these arguments and debates were taking place. People around me were talking instead about property prices and the latest Royal Shakespeare Company production.

With the children–adults opposition, the general rule for me is in life as in books: if you treat a character as a human being first and foremost, you tend not to run into trouble. Whether a character is male or female I assume they have the same human emotions that I, or people I know well, do. That's the only thing I work from.

SG: We all know what it's like to be young, to grow up and become an adult. But an adult man has never been a thirteen-year-old girl, so some feminists might not agree with that position.

KI: I don't say men and women are identical, and obviously I would not have the same emotions as many men. We all come from very different places and we occupy different positions in society. It's ridiculous for me to say that I understand someone who has grown up on a council estate or someone from the Caribbean. I just feel that if I have an instinct for understanding a fictional character that I create, the sex shouldn't be a barrier. Fundamentally, the emotions aren't that different.

SG: In her essay 'A Room of One's Own' (1929) Virginia Woolf states that the great artistic mind is androgynous, in the sense that the male and female parts of the mind are in harmony with one another. She mentions Shakespeare, for instance, as a writer who transgresses this apparent divide. Would you be able to explain your ability to represent both men and women's voices through such an idea?

KI: I don't know if I'd want to make such a claim for my work. It'd be good to be in such a position. It's more to do with the fact that the kind of writing I do is not – in the simple, direct sense – autobiographical. If you write autobiography in the straightforward, obvious sense, gender becomes more of an issue, because part of the exercise is that the author is exploring how his own emotions relate to his own history. If you then apply certain ideas to a female character, someone might find that presumptuous. It's not for you to do this exercise on someone who must have necessarily had a different set of experiences.

But take the model of Shakespeare. He wrote for a stage company, with a gallery of characters, and you have to make them work through your actors. If there's an autobiographical element, it's not embodied by any one character. It comes through in the story, in the drama. If you're working in that mode, it's easier and the exercise is less loaded. You're not writing from the point of view of a woman because she *is* a woman, but because one of the characters just happens to be a woman. I don't know if it's any more loaded than that. If you look at Wordsworth, it's difficult to get away from the self: the big subject is Wordsworth. But if you're in the Shakespeare tradition it's easier to write from the point of view of character, which involves different sexes, different ages and different classes.

SG: This issue of difference also resonates, perhaps, in your choice of Golders Green as a place of residence. Whereas some of your contemporaries, such as Martin Amis, Ian McEwan and Julian Barnes, live quite close to the centre of London – the geographical and literary centre of their world – you've chosen a more peripheral location. A location that's more in line with J. G. Ballard, who distanced himself deliberately from what he called 'those literary people'. Did you choose this territory deliberately as a way of distancing yourself from the centre of London?

KI: The place you choose to live in reflects your priorities, your tastes, but also your needs and what you can afford at a particular time. After living in south London, we moved to Golders Green eighteen years ago when my wife – who worked as a social worker – got a job with

Camden Social Services. I was never comfortable in south London. A writer was a very unusual thing there because it was basically a working-class community. Nobody understood what I did. I didn't realize what a relief it would be until I moved to north London, where there are a lot of writers. We looked at Hampstead, which would have been a more writerly place to live, but we realized we could buy a detached house with a big garden for the same price as a flat in Hampstead. The priority for us was to be near nice cafes. We like to sit outside in the sun and have a nice coffee, ice cream or quality cakes. This area was the best for coffee and cake.

I've been very happy with the distance from the centre of town. I have more of the American mentality. The centre of the city tends to be grotty and dangerous and dirty. What you want is quiet and detachment. Most people in Golders Green don't know who I am. I don't like an environment where I feel I'm being watched. I want to be anonymous. I like the J. G. Ballard model, although I wouldn't fancy Shepperton.

SG: In your work, place is never specific, but it functions as a backdrop for the story and characters. London is present in novels such as *When We Were Orphans* [2000], but we never get beyond anonymous public spaces, such as the tearooms in fancy hotels. In his fictional autobiography *Youth* [2002], J. M. Coetzee writes about his time in London and the frustration he experiences at his inability to 'master' the city. Don't you ever have the desire to master the place in which you live by capturing it in your writing?

KI: I'm not interested in the physical place. Essentially, I don't have a strong journalistic instinct in my writing. I'm not interested in nailing what London or Africa is like here and now. I'm interested in abstract things. London happens to feature as a backdrop in the novel I'm writing at the moment, but it's just incidental. London is there because it's useful for the themes I'm exploring.

SG: There are basically two literary traditions of London writing. The first is the journalistic, factual strand which describes the material city. You find this city in the work of Smollett and Thackeray. Then there is the mythical London you find in the work of Blake, Conan Doyle, Dickens and T. S. Eliot.

KI: [Cuts in] What would you say London stands for, thematically? London is something I cannot do because I've no kind of socio-historic interest. I'm not interested in describing London in a hard, journalistic sense, or looking at the Muslim families or the Cypriot community or at the parliamentarians. But if somebody threatened to kneecap me and burn down my house unless I wrote a London novel, I would need to ask myself what kind of myth and metaphor London is.

SG: You could look back to the tradition of Blake and Dickens who, in a London context, were interested in the metropolis as a place where rampant industrialization resulted in social injustice, the commodification of the human body and a crippling of the human spirit.

KI: London does not stand for that today. London stands for this strange world of funny money. Today, you wouldn't necessarily single out London for all the evils, but cities in Brazil and India, where you see horrific differences between rich and poor, with desperate poverty and crime. London is half a century into the welfare state. Of course there are huge discrepancies between rich and poor here. But compared to the average American city, that's not the thing that comes to mind.

What London does signify for people around the world is that it's a strange place full of foreigners. When politicians try to make something positive of Britain they often point to London and say it's a successful multicultural community. And right-wing people use it as a negative harbinger of the society to come, with every town and every village full of people from all over the world drifting through. You could live in a Shropshire village and it'd be dominated by Russians, who'd all suddenly leave and be replaced by Brazilians. I can't think of an overwhelming idea that London is an icon of today. You've been thinking about this for some time. Is there something about London that is an overwhelming metaphor for you?

SG: London still has a huge proportion of illegal immigrants without whom the entire city would grind to a halt. A great number of hotel staff, especially the invisible ones, are underpaid and overworked. Some parts of London resemble a Third World city. One interesting question that your juxtaposition of London and England's villages raises is whether London is still representative of England, of Britain. It probably isn't. The City and Canary Wharf have become city states, completely divorced from us and London itself, as was highlighted by the credit crunch.

KI: I think you're onto something there. London is perhaps no longer a single entity at all, but a series of little satellites that connect up to other worlds. Basically, each capsule connects to a bigger one that links up somewhere else in the world. We [writers and academics] don't know much about the financial world. Someone who works in that capsule knows about what's going on in New York and Tokyo, but he won't know what's going on a few streets away in London. Many aspects of

London are like that. Virtual worlds are living on top of each other. London is just insulated bubbles that link up to other bubbles.

SG: Blake and Dickens would probably say that in the end we are all connected.

KI: I don't know if we *are* necessarily connected. The world's changed so much since Blake and Dickens. You might want to point to the 7/7 bombings, when we were all terribly connected. But I know people in London who were more affected by 9/11 than by 7/7 because they had colleagues or friends who were in the twin towers. 7/7 happened in the next street.

If Blake and Dickens were around today they would not be writing about London, but about the rich West and the poor world. The point is that we think we're not connected, whilst we are. This is true not just of London citizens, but of people in the West in general, who don't realize that they're connected to Africa. The cholera epidemic in Dickens would be replaced by AIDS, or a plague that respects no boundaries between rich and poor. Where the parallel comes now between the world of the Dedlocks and the world of Joe the Chimney Sweeper – I may be mixing up my Dickens and Blake here – is the difference between people who buy clothing from Chanel in Paris and London and Wichita, and people who live in Rwanda, Ethiopia or Somalia.

SG: Changing the topic, research into the behaviour of memory shows that homesickness occurs twice for emigrants and exiles: just after they have left their native countries, and bouts of nostalgia when they grow older. When you were young and you started out writing about Japan, did you anticipate a return to this territory in later life?

KI: I've noticed this phenomenon anecdotally. People who left their home country and seemed to have settled abroad experience a nostalgia that suddenly comes on in late middle age. English people who live abroad start turning up in London during the summer, but they have to go back to America, China or wherever it is they've made their lives. I've noticed that, as these émigrés get older, they seem to desperately want to come back, but returning is too difficult. It starts to matter after a long time, when before it didn't. Also, people who seem very firmly settled in England, feel they need to return in later life, sometimes to uncomfortable countries. It's something Lorna and I have been very aware of, this homing instinct, which comes in an almost atavistic way. I've always been interested in this question because of my parents, who were originally only coming to this country for a few years – but then stayed and stayed. I'd always wonder, when they'd get older, whether they'd get this desire to return.

SG: That same research has also shown that when émigrés move to a new country, they first dream in their native language; then they adapt to the new environment, mentally and linguistically; but in old age, they start to dream in their native language again.

KI: When my father was dying, he seemed to have great difficulty understanding English. We had to interpret to the hospital staff. They actually asked us: 'Does he speak any English?' He'd been living in England since 1960. Apparently that is common, when people get ill. He didn't get senile, but when he did get very ill in the last few weeks, he was 'confused', as they say. He became more and more Japanese, and not just linguistically. He did seem to think he was back in Japan.

SG: Can you say something about the way in which you've drawn on your own past as a model for representing memory? In the story 'Malvern Hills' the narrator is a guitar player with a particular attitude to life. His failure as a musician suggests that this is a version of Kazuo Ishiguro, the artist as a young man. I was wondering whether, as you got older, this is a sign that you are indeed returning to specific parts of your past?

KI: In novels such as *When We Were Orphans* and *Never Let Me Go*, I have looked at my own memories of being young. The children playing in *When We Were Orphans* are drawn from memories about how I used to play imaginary games with my friends when I was a little boy. In *Never Let me Go* I tried to remember how I experienced that kind of hinterland period between being an adolescent and being an adult in post-student times. To some extent I'm sketching from life – but that's not the same as creating autobiographical characters.

In 'Malvern Hills', what I tried to remember was the self-centredness of being that age, when you're not sure whether you're still allowed to indulge in fantasies. Only a few years before the age of that character, when you're ten or eleven, you are allowed to say you want to be an astronaut, the president of the United States or a detective. When you say this a few years later, you're accountable. So you're at that point when you're no longer sure whether you are allowed to pursue your ambitions or not. What should be your strategy in facing life? And how do you cope with disappointment? When is it appropriate to be angry and frustrated? And when are you just having a tantrum? The story is looking at different models. With the older Swiss couple, I wanted to see two opposing strategies for coping with the usual disappointments of life. Their dreams have not come out quite the way they wanted them to come out. They've taken incompatible strategies and cancelled each other out, because they're together; if both of them were in denial, or if both of them were irate with life, that might work out, but one keeps getting furious and the other is in denial.

Typically, my starting point is abstract. I didn't want to write a story about hills – I only went to the Malvern Hills in 2006 – or about when I was young and attempted to be a rock'n'roll star. I heard a country and western song on the radio by a guy called Tim McGraw, and the chorus went: 'Why are you so angry all the time?' This kind of contented American saying to his wife: 'Why are you so angry all the time, we've got nice kids, nice neighbours, I don't understand why you're so angry all the time.' I thought that's a really interesting song.

But perhaps it is true, that as you get older you become more fascinated with memories of when you were younger.

SG: The point of this research is that it was a particular period in one's life, the late teens and early twenties, that one remembers best. People who are eighty or a hundred years old don't remember much of events after their thirty-fifth birthday. But the period between their fifteenth and twenty-fifth birthday is densely crowded with memories. It's called the 'reminiscence bump'.

KI: Most people I observe are very keen on this period of their lives, and it could be that you are in a different country at that age: it's intensified, accentuated, more conspicuous. But I've noticed that people beyond their mid-forties who studied at Oxford and Cambridge talk a hell of a lot about their university days, and at the drop of a hat. This is very odd, and it seems to be some kind of arrested development. There is something very special about that period when you're just becoming an adult, and when you're forming as a person. It doesn't matter whether you're ten years or fifty or even further away from your childhood memories – childhood memories have a special quality. Unless very traumatic things happen to you, life tends to get less dramatic. People do experience incidents and trauma in later life, but I don't know whether that can be the subject of memory in the same way.

When you reach a certain point in your career the learning and achievement curve aren't so steep. In fact, much of the struggle is to maintain the standard you used to take for granted – as with jogging, for instance. There comes a point when you look back with fascination, if not nostalgia, at a time when you seemed to have all this power to absorb and learn. You think, how did I make so much progress in just two years? What kind of creature was I in those days that I was observing so much and moving so fast? There is something exciting about remembering that point when you had that capacity to learn, to develop. With hindsight, of course, you know it was all in front of you. At the time, you don't know anything that's in front of you. For all you know the best bit, university, has gone by already. Only with hindsight you realize what a wonderful thing it is to be young. Not because you're doing hedonistic things, but because you had this capacity to grow and learn. You envy the young person you used to be for that quality alone, and for a certain recklessness to explore fearlessly and go into new territory.

SG: How has the texture of memory changed for you, now that you have more time and history behind you and perhaps less time ahead of you? And how does that translate into your novelistic practice?

KI: I was using memory as a technical device. Around the time of when I was writing *The Remains of the Day* and *The Unconsoled* [1995], I was fascinated intrinsically by memory. I just wanted to enter a world of memory. It gave me a thrill, to be in this kind of mode when a narrator would say he or she couldn't quite remember. It's almost like *Rashômon* (Akira Kurosawa, 1950), which has several different, subjectively perceived versions of the same story. There was a one man *Rashômon* going on in my early work.

When I was younger it was easier to point to the terrain of memory. There was less of it, there were fewer places that qualify as memory. I left my country and spent a lot of time thinking about the place that I left, and then the motives of memory are very clear. You have more motivation to remember . . .

But as you get older, the whole thing becomes more complex and you start to do strange sums sometimes. You surprise yourself when you learn that the distance between when you were at university and when you were five is less than fifteen years. If I go back fifteen years from now, it doesn't seem like anything. What felt like distant memories when I was in my twenties wouldn't qualify as that today. Going back fifteen years now doesn't have the romantic haze or the texture of memory. It's fairly banal. I remember sitting in this same room fifteen years ago doing an interview, about different books. It doesn't belong in the land of distant memory at all – none of this does. There's stuff that happened relatively recently, but in some ways it could legitimately claim to be memory, and it is being distorted and manipulated in a way that I don't realize. I suppose as one gets older, one doesn't get exactly arrogant about things that happened in the past, but there's an illusion that they're more under your control.

SG: After your first three novels, which were extremely tightly composed, you seemed to reach a peak in your virtuosity when it comes to handling memory in *The Unconsoled*. What we get there, in a way, is the texture of memory proper. Similar to the way in which Joyce's *Ulysses* [1922] was an attempt to replicate experience, *The Unconsoled* gives us an image of the complexity of how consciousness operates. Together with Ryder, the reader is lost in a landscape that has lost all material qualities and has become pure thought.

KI: At particular stages in my career, I've written novels that consciously address memory and I have subsequently talked about that process. I can now remember remembering. Sometimes I'm not sure whether I'm remembering the original thing or I'm remembering the concretized image that I remembered, say, twenty years ago. It's parallel to when you have a memory of an image and you're not sure whether your memory is actually just the memory of the photograph. At various crucial points in my life I've self-consciously tried to remember things, and firmly set things down in writing and pressed the print button in my head. Now I'm no longer sure whether I'm looking at the original raw material or if I'm remembering the thing I remembered and printed out in my mid-twenties or mid-thirties. This happens more as one gets older: it becomes harder to distinguish between memories and memories of memories.

SG: Is *Never Let Me Go* some kind of culmination of this? I wouldn't want to use the word 'simulacra' for fear of invoking Baudrillard, but the clones are doubles of originals somewhere out there in the 'real world', and their consciousness is linked to an original being lost, which they attempt to retrieve. Kathy then subsequently (mis)remembers the events.

KI: There certainly wasn't a conscious relationship when I was writing *Never Let Me Go*. I've only just now come to express the uncertainty of my original memories. It's something I've only thought about clearly now. I remember reading Proust, years ago. In one of his throwaway passages, he writes that he remembers a moment when he was seven, sitting in a library, remembering when he was three. It's a hall of mirrors effect, and just a little flourish, but I see there's a real truth in that now.

Whilst writing *Never Let Me Go*, I hadn't linked the business of Kathy and Co. looking for who they're modelled from with memory. I wanted to express their longing for a parent. They know they don't have parents in a literal sense, so they can't miss individuals, but I wanted to show that in some way that need for a parent is there. Not just the need for parental love or the practicalities of parenting, which in some ways they get. At some deep human level they need to feel they belong to some sort of genetic line. They feel they belong in the tides of humanity's generations. In this strange world, they want to belong in a profound sense which mattered to them emotionally.

But if we return to your earlier description of *The Unconsoled* as some kind of representation of the mind or consciousness, for me that novel is something that I hadn't finished properly. The first three books were like a single project whereby one book moved into the next. After *The Unconsoled* I felt as if there needed to be two more *Unconsoled*s or something in the same vein. When I finished *The Unconsoled* I couldn't do it anymore, and although I'd been permanently affected and elements of that mode were in the next novel, I experienced a certain distancing. After *The Unconsoled* I felt freer and more confident about how I might move away from realism. Nevertheless, *The Unconsoled* was something I had started, but I hadn't moved on to the next stage. The work I'm doing right now is almost like going back to the mid-nineties, when I finished *The Unconsoled*. It's the first time I feel ready to carry on some of the things I was doing then. I don't think that *When We Were Orphans* or *Never Let Me Go* are really continuations of *The Unconsoled*.

SG: But the end of *When We Were Orphans*, when Christopher Banks returns to Shanghai, collapses back into estranging territory similar to the *The Unconsoled* . . .

KI: Yes, it's almost like an infection. I thought the antibiotics had cleared it, but after a hundred pages it rears itself up again! It takes over. It pervades *Never Let Me Go* in a low-grade 'virusy' kind of way. I've always had in the back of my mind that I really need to get back to this thing that I was doing. There were certain issues and things that I'd always said to myself I'd work out. I feel it's time I went back to the things I was majorly concerned about when I was writing *The Unconsoled*. It's not just about concrete things, but a certain way of doing things, a certain approach to things.

It is possible that non-literary things influenced me as well. I have this awful choice: if I really want to, I can write bestselling novels. I can sell a million copies. I'm ashamed to say so, but when I look back it's possible that I didn't continue with *The Unconsoled* project in the way I might have done because I acknowledged that that would necessarily serve a smaller readership. *The Unconsoled* is, by some way, the novel that sold the least. But it's not just the commercial sales. I feel a certain kind of relationship with my readership. There is a readership out there that will follow you into all sorts of interesting places. Particularly today, there is this highly sophisticated mass-readership out there. They won't reject something just because it's not straightforward. *Never Let Me Go* is not a straightforward book at all, but it's been popular.

I don't share the cynicism about the dumbed-down audience. There's an audience out there that's literate in many kinds of ways. Not just in terms of books, but in all kinds of things: music, cinema, modern communications. It's a very sophisticated audience. There are people like Murakami and Roberto Bolaño finding massive audiences, and I've always sensed that about my own readership. They're not intimidated by strange things: they just don't like boring, pretentious self-indulgence. There's a readership out there hungry for new adventures.

Never Let Me Go is a completely weird novel, but I tried to make it not pretentious. I tried to make every aspect of it something people would understand. And the end result is something that doesn't look so weird. Okay, some people say it's sci-fi, but I don't feel odd giving that novel to anybody. I would like to think I can continue the *Unconsoled* experiment, if you like, in a manner that's not going to alienate people who usually read me. In many ways the climate now is more conducive to the kind of writing I was doing in *The Unconsoled* more than twenty years ago.

SG: This assumption that your audience has changed reminds me of Virginia Woolf, who wrote in 'Mr Bennett and Mrs Brown' (1924) that 'on or about December 1910' human character changed. Now, a century later, I was wondering what your thoughts about that statement are, and whether you think that we have experienced another important 'turn' in human consciousness since Woolf's claim.

KI: People usually put this moment of change after the First World War. They point to *Ulysses*, *The Waste Land*, Picasso, Stravinsky and French composers such as Ravel and Debussy. That is a conventional way of thinking. I don't know to what extent there is a causal connection between the socio-historical context and artistic representation. What disturbs me about that approach is that often less good work is remembered and survives because it is seen as a representation of particular historical events. An 'angry young men' novel from the fifties, such as John Braine's *Room at the Top*, is preserved because the history books tell us that it exemplifies something about that era. In other words, literary history isn't autonomous; it's always made to piggyback on history. It's that tendency I don't like. It leads to the preservation of mediocre books whilst some brilliant books are forgotten because they don't fit the clear historical model.

I'm more attracted to the idea of 1910, where we go before the First World War. It was the first time when the masses were educated and becoming literate, and when culture for the masses was introduced in a serious way. There was a reaction on the part of the educational and social elite, who wanted to produce an art form that would baffle and exclude the new members who'd come rushing through the door with their yellow jacket paperbacks. You could argue that Eliot's poetry is the celebration of a certain elitist background and education. But it's just as plausible to say that because aeroplanes had recently appeared and industrialization had come to many parts of the world, people started to adopt stream of consciousness or the strange Imagist techniques of Eliot and Pound.

There was, at least to a certain extent, a retrenching of elitism in the face of mass culture and mass education. That doesn't mean to say that the work of Eliot and Pound was automatically important and good. It's possible that wonderful art can be born out of not entirely admirable motives, or unconscious motives. Artists have a certain relationship to what they believe to be mass culture. In order to function for all of us, we do have to sometimes create this uncouth beast, which these days is made up of people watching reality television and those who make crackling noises behind you in the cinema. You have to believe you're a high priest of an elite part of society that is more civilized and that's why what you do is important.

Now, writers are going in the opposite direction. Writers want to claim the middle ground, and to some extent have their cake and eat it too. They want to be part of the mainstream, and this reflects the way society has changed. You don't any longer have to belong to some kind of minority culture to be part of the cultural elite. The Sunday supplements appeal to a large chunk of the society, as does television. Artists want to be part of that. They want to be culturally important in a massive sense. It's possible to be a serious artist but use popular art, street art and, in the case of Quentin Tarantino, pulp fiction. Tarantino achieves a synthesis of the high brow and the popular. David Mitchell is another good example. In a book like *Cloud Atlas* [2004] he breezes through all these popular genres and he turns them into a dazzling, postmodern performance – but the whole thing is unmistakably liter-ary. Mitchell's nodding towards very pulpy fiction, second-rate thrillers, genre sci-fi, but it's all mixed up in a recipe that produces something very interesting and apocalyptic. Things have changed enormously. It's much easier for the younger generation of writer to think that there's nothing contradictory about appealing to a mass audience, thinking about how commercial one's work is, and at the same time saying this is dead serious. This is high art. It's not a compromise, but you embrace it. We're moving away from elitism, to something which isn't afraid of modern culture, pop culture. We're moving towards a new seriousness.

SG: Your use of the word 'synthesis' is interesting because it suggests we've moved on from the overtly self-conscious playfulness of high postmodernist work but also, for instance, from postcolonial literature as a category after the collapse of imperial structures. Zadie Smith is always categorized as a postcolonial author whilst I'm not sure this is the case. She seems to move beyond such oppositional categories. Your work too poses similar challenges to such categorization.

KI: I've never understood the categorization of postcolonial writing. I've been sent papers where I'm talked about as a postcolonial novelist, but I'm never sure about the definition. Does 'postcolonial' mean writing that came out in the postcolonial era? Or does it have to come from a country that used to be part of an empire, and which, after the colonies started to devolve, changed into an independent state? Or does it mean writing by people who don't have white skins? I often suspect the latter is the accurate definition. It seems to me defined by the writer, not the work. Whether somebody is postcolonial seems to be defined by the writer's biography rather than by their writing, and that's what makes me very suspicious of postcolonial writing as a category.

I'm also wondering whether, not so much because of postmodernism, but because of things like gender studies and colonial studies, that academics and university departments are not allowed to say which books are better than others, or to say what is important. It's become harder to argue for a particular reading list purely for literary merit and to champion works equivalent to *Ulysses* today. That confidence has disappeared in the relativist period, and as an academic you're much more vulnerable to having to justify the teaching of books in terms of other disciplines, such as history, for example.

In the fifties you had people like F. R. Leavis, who were very confident about what a good book was, to the point where it was dodgy. You don't get academic figures like that any more, people who lead the way, who shape taste. It's that very activity that people are dubious about. The right to say if there's any philosophical soundness to making a judgement at all has gone and we just have a kind of review-pages consensus in which new writers should rise to prominence and older writers are preserved. It's a relatively arbitrary process by which we are selecting a future canon. I wonder what the universities are doing about this; if they think it is their business to be worrying about the canon of the future – whether, say, William Golding needs to be preserved for the future generation or whether he can drop off the map; whether we care or not.

This conversation took place at Kazuo Ishiguro's London home on 11 September 2009.

bibliography

primary sources

novels

(1982) *A Pale View of Hills*. London: Faber and Faber.
(1986) *An Artist of the Floating World*. London: Faber and Faber.
(1989) *The Remains of the Day*. London: Faber and Faber.
(1995) *The Unconsoled*. London: Faber and Faber.
(2000) *When We Were Orphans*. London: Faber and Faber.
(2005) *Never Let Me Go*. London: Faber and Faber.

short stories

(1981a) 'A Strange and Sometimes Sadness', in *Introduction 7: Stories by New Writers*. London: Faber and Faber, pp. 13–27.
(1981b) 'Getting Poisoned', in *Introduction 7*, pp. 38–51.
(1981c) 'Waiting for J', in *Introduction 7*, pp. 28–37.
(1983a) 'A Family Supper', in T. J. Binding (ed.), *Firebird 2*. Harmondsworth: Penguin, 121–31; also in M. Bradbury (ed.) (1987), *The Penguin Collection of Modern Short Stories*. Harmondsworth: Penguin, pp. 434–42; and *Esquire*, March 1990, 207–11.
(1983b) 'The Summer after the War', *Granta* 7, 121–37.
(2001) 'A Village after Dark', *The New Yorker*, 21 May, 86–91.
(2009) *Nocturnes: Five Stories of Music and Nightfall*. London: Faber and Faber.

screenplays

(1984) *A Profile of Arthur J. Mason*. Dir. M. Whyte, prod. A. Skinner for Skreba/Spectre. Unpublished. Broadcast in the UK, Channel 4, 18 October 1984.
(1993) *The Gourmet*, in *Granta*, 43, 89–127. Dir. M. Whyte, prod. A. Skinner for Skreba/Spectre. Broadcast in the UK, Channel 4, 8 May 1986.
(2003) *The Saddest Music in the World*. Dir. Guy Maddin, prod. N. Finchman for IFC. Unpublished. Released in UK, 25 October; released in USA, 14 February 2004.
(2005) *The White Countess*. Dir. James Ivory, prod. Ismail Merchant for Merchant/Ivory. Unpublished. Released 21 December 2005.

film adaptations of ishiguro's work

(1993) *The Remains of the Day*. Dir. James Ivory, adapted by Ruth Prawer Jhabvala. Merchant Ivory Productions. Released 12 November.
(2010) *Never Let Me Go*. Dir. Mark Romanek, adapted by Alex Garland. DNA Films.

musical adaptations of ishiguro's work

(2010) *The Remains of the Day*. Dir. Chris Loveless; music, book and lyrics Alex Loveless. Premiere 1 September at Union Theatre, London.

other

(1983) 'I Became Profoundly Thankful for Having Been Born in Nagasaki', *Guardian*, 8 September, 9.
(1986) 'Introduction' to Yasunari Kawabata's *Snow Country and Thousand Cranes*, trans. E. G. Seidensticker. Harmondsworth: Penguin, pp. 1–3.
(1993) 'Letter to Salman Rushdie', in S. McDonogh (ed.), *The Rushdie Letters: Freedom to Speak, Freedom to Write*. London: Brandon, pp. 79–80.

secondary sources
books

Beedham, M. (2010), *The Novels of Kazuo Ishiguro: A Reader's Guide to Essential Criticism*. London: Palgrave Macmillan.
Cheng, C. (2010) *The Margin Without Centre: Kazuo Ishiguro*. Oxford: Peter Lang.
Lewis, B. (2000), *Kazuo Ishiguro*. Manchester: Manchester University Press.
Parkes, A. (2001), *The Remains of The Day: A Reader's Guide*. New York: Continuum Contemporaries.
Petry, M. (1999), *Narratives of Memory and Identity: The Novels of Kazuo Ishiguro*. Frankfurt: Peter Lang.
Porée, M. (1999), *Kazuo Ishiguro: The Remains of the Day*. Paris: Didier Érudition-CNED.
Shaffer, B. W. (1998), *Understanding Kazuo Ishiguro*. Columbia: University of South Carolina Press.
Veyret, P. (2002), *Kazuo Ishiguro: L'encre de la mémoire*. Bordeaux: Presses Universitaires de Bordeaux.
Wong, C. (2000), *Kazuo Ishiguro*. Tavistock: Northcote House.

edited collections

Fluet, L. (2007), 'Ishiguro's Unknown Communities', *Novel: A Forum on Fiction*, 40 (3), 2007.
Gallix, F., V. Guignery and P. Veyret (eds.) (2004), *Kazuo Ishiguro, Études Britanniques Contemporaines, Revue de la Société d'Études Anglaises Contemporaines*, 27.
Matthews, S. and S. Groes (eds.) (2009), *Kazuo Ishiguro: Contemporary Critical Perspectives*. London and New York: Continuum.

book chapters

Bradbury, M. (1987), 'The Floating World', in Bradbury, M., *No, Not Bloomsbury*. London: André Deutsch, pp. 363–66.

——— (1993), *The Modern British Novel*. London: Secker and Warburg, pp. 423–25.

Childs, P. (2005), *Contemporary British Novelists: British Fiction since 1970*. New York: Palgrave Macmillan, pp. 123–140.

Connor, S. (1996), 'Outside In', in *The English Novel in History: 1950–1995*. London: Routledge, pp. 83–127.

Döring, T. (2006), 'Sherlock Holmes – He Dead: Disenchanting the English Detective in Kazuo Ishiguro's *When We Were Orphans*,' in C. Matzke and S. Mühleisen (eds.), *Postcolonial Postmortems: Crime Fictions from a Transcultural Perspective*. Amsterdam: Rodopi, pp. 59–86.

Doyle, W. (1993), 'Being an Other to Oneself: First Person Narration in Kazuo Ishiguro's *The Remains of the Day*', in E. Labbé (ed.), *L'Altérité dans la littérature et la culture du monde Anglophone*. Le Mans: University of Maine Press, pp. 70–6.

Foster, J.W. (2006), '"All the Long Traditions": Loyalty and Service in Barry and Ishiguro', in C. H. Mahony (ed.), *Out of History: Essays on the Writings of Sebastian Barry*. Dublin: Catholic University of America Press, pp. 99–119.

Glaubitz, N. (2009), 'Transcribing Images–Reassembling Cultures: Kazuo Ishiguro's Japan', in S. Säckel, W. Göbel and N. Hamdy (eds.), *Semiotic Encounters: Text, Image and Trans-Nation*. Amsterdam: Rodopi, pp. 175–90.

Goody, I. (2005), 'Fin de siècle, fin du globe: Intercultural Chronotopes of Memory and Apocalypse in the Fictions of Murakami Haruki and Kazuo Ishiguro', in E. Eoyang (ed.), *Intercultural Explorations*. Amsterdam: Rodopi, pp. 95–203.

Gordon, G. (1998), *Philosophy of the Arts: An Introduction to Aesthetics*. London and New York: Routledge, pp. 121–27.

Hall, L. (1995), 'New Nations, New Selves: The Novels of Timothy Mo and Kazuo Ishiguro', in A. R. Lee (ed.), *Other Britain, Other British: Contemporary Multicultural Fiction*. London: Pluto Press, pp. 90–110.

Hitchens, C. (1993), 'Kazuo Ishiguro', in *For the Sake of Argument: Essays and Minority Reports*. London: Verso, pp. 320–22.

Holmes, F. M. (2005), 'Realism, Dreams and the Unconscious in the Novels of Kazuo Ishiguro', in J. Acheson and S. C. E. Ross (eds.), *The Contemporary British Novel since 1980*. New York: Palgrave Macmillan, pp. 11–22.

King, B. (1991), 'The New Internationalism: Shiva Naipaul, Salman Rushdie, Buchi Emecheta, Timothy Mo and Kazuo Ishiguro', in J. Acheson (ed.), *The British and Irish Novel since 1960*. New York: St Martin's Press, pp. 192–211.

Lewis, B. (2009), 'Kazuo Ishiguro', in J. Parini (ed.), *British Writers: Retrospective Supplement 3*. New York: Charles Scribner's Sons, pp. 149–64.

Lodge, D. (1992), 'The Unreliable Narrator', in *The Art of Fiction*. New York: Viking, pp. 154–57.

Luyat, A. (1994), 'Myth and Metafiction: Is Peaceful Co-Existence Possible? Destruction of the Myth of the English Butler in Kazuo Ishiguro's *The Remains of the Day*', in M. Duperray (ed.), *Historicité et metafiction dans le roman contemporain des Iles Britanniques*. Aix-en-Provence: University of Provence, pp. 183–196.

Massie, A. (1990), *The Novel Today: A Critical Guide to the British Novel 1970–1989*. London and New York: Longman, p. 64.

Newton, A. Z. (1997), 'Telling Others: Secrecy and Recognition in Dickens, Barnes and Ishiguro', in *Narrative Ethics*. Cambridge: Harvard University Press, pp. 241–85.

Page, N. (1991), 'Speech, Culture and History in the Novels of Kazuo Ishiguro', in M. Chan and R. Harris (eds.), *Asian Voices in English*. Hong Kong: Hong Kong University Press, pp. 161–68.

Phelan, J. and M. P. Martin (1999), 'The Lessons of "Weymouth": Homodiegesis, Unreliability, Ethics, and *The Remains of the Day*', in D. Herman (ed.), *Narratologies: New Perspectives on Narrative Analysis*. Columbus: Ohio State University Press, pp. 88–109.

Rennison, N. (2005), *Contemporary British Novelists*. London: Routledge, 91–94.

Salecl, R. (1996), 'I Can't Love You Unless I Give You Up', in R. Salecl and S. Zizek (eds.), *Gaze and Voice as Love Objects*. Durham: Duke University Press, pp. 179–207.

Spark, G. (2008), 'The Mysterious Case of the Disappearing Empire: History and the Golden-Age Detective Genre in Kazuo Ishiguro's *When We Were Orphans*', in P. MacPherson, C. Murray, G. Spark, and K. Corstorphine (eds.), *Sub/Versions: Cultural Status, Genre and Critique*. Newcastle upon Tyne: Cambridge Scholars Press, pp. 124–34.

Stanton, K. (2006), 'Foreign Feeling: Kazuo Ishiguro's *The Unconsoled* and the New Europe', in *Cosmopolitan Fictions: Ethics, Politics, and Global Change in the Works of Kazuo Ishiguro, Michael Ondaatje, Jamaica Kincaid, and J. M. Coetzee*. Abingdon: Routledge.

Stevenson, R. (1993), *A Reader's Guide to the Twentieth Century Novel in Britain*. Lexington: University Press of Kentucky, pp. 130–36.

Sutherland, J. (1998), 'Why Hasn't Mr. Stevens Heard of the Suez Crisis?', in *Where Was Rebecca Shot?: Puzzles, Curiosities and Conundrums in Modern Fiction*. London: Weidenfeld and Nicolson, pp. 185–89.

Weiss, T. (2003), 'Where is Place? Locale in Ishiguro's *When We Were Orphans*', in R. Ahrens, D. Parker, K. Stierstorfer, and K.-K. Tam (eds.), *Anglophone Cultures in Southeast Asia: Appropriations, Continuities, Context*. Heidelberg: Universitätsverlag, pp. 271–94.

Wood, M. (1995), 'The Discourse of Others', in *Children of Silence: Studies in Contemporary Fiction*. London: Pimlico, pp. 171–81.

journal articles

Adams, A. M. (2008), 'Tradition and the Individual Servant: Kazuo Ishiguro and the Aesthetic Ends of Modernism', *The Kentucky Philological Review*, 23, 31–8.

Adelman, G. (2001), 'Doubles on the Rocks: Ishiguro's *The Unconsoled*, *Critique: Studies in Contemporary Fiction*, 42 (2), 166–79.

Appiah, K. A. (2001), 'Liberalism, Individuality, and Identity', *Critical Inquiry*, 27 (2), 305–32.

Arai, M. (1990), 'Ishiguro's Floating Worlds: Observations on his Visions of Japan', *General Education Review*, 22, 29–34.

Ash, J. (1994), 'Stick it up Howard's End', *Gentleman's Quarterly*, 8, 43.

Atkinson, R. (1995), 'How the Butler Was Made To Do It. The Perverted Professionalism of *The Remains of the Day*', *Yale Law Journal*, 10, 177–220.

Bain, A. M. (2007), 'International Settlements: Ishiguro, Shanghai, Humanitarianism', *Novel: A Forum on Fiction*, 40 (3), 240–64.

Bao, X. (2009) 'Symbols in Kazuo Ishiguro's *The Remains of the Day*', *Foreign Literature Studies*, 31 (3), 75–81.

Bhabha, H. K. (1995), 'Unpacking My Library Again', *Journal of Midwest Modern Language Association*, 28 (1), 5–18.

Bigliazzi, S. (2007), 'Inside (Counter-)Factuality: Reassessing the Narrator's Discourse in Kazuo Ishiguro's *The Remains of the Day*', *Rivista di Letterature Moderne e Comparate*, 60 (2), 219–44.

Birch, D. (2008), 'A Brief History of the Future', *Times Literary Supplement*, 30 January.

Black, S. (2009), 'Ishiguro's Inhuman Aesthetics', *Modern Fiction Studies*, 55 (4), 785–807.

Britzman, D. P. (2006), 'On Being a Slow Reader: Psychoanalytic Reading Problems in Ishiguro's *Never Let Me Go*', *Changing English: Studies in Culture and Educations*, 13 (3), 307–18.

Capri, D. (1997), 'The Crisis of the Social Subject in the Contemporary English Novel', *European Journal of English Studies*, 1 (2), 165–83.

Cardullo, B. (1995), 'The Servant', *Hudson Review*, 47 (4), 616–22.

Cheng, C. (2005), 'Making and Marketing Kazuo Ishiguro's Alterity', *Post-Identity*, 4 (2).

Chertoff, D. and L. Toker (2008), 'Reader Response and the Recycling of Topoi in Kazuo Ishiguro's *Never Let Me Go*', *Partial Answers: Journal of Literature and the History of Ideas*, 6 (1), 163–80.

Cunningham, H. C. (2004), 'The Dickens Connection in Kazuo Ishiguro's *When We Were Orphans*', *Notes on Contemporary Literature*, 34 (5), 4–6.

Davis, R. G. (1994), 'Imaginary Homelands Revisited in the Novels of Kazuo Ishiguro', *Miscelánea*, 15, 139–54.

——— (1995), '*The Remains of the Day*: Kazuo Ishiguro's Sonnet on his Blindness', *Cuadernos de Investigación Filológica*, 21–2, 57–67.

Ekelund, B. G. (2005), 'Misrecognizing History: Complicitous Genres in Kazuo Ishiguro's *The Remains of the Day*', *International Fiction Review*, 32 (1–2), 70–90.

Finney, B. (2002), 'Figuring the Real: Ishiguro's *When We Were Orphans*', *Jouvert: A Journal of Postcolonial Studies*, 7 (1).

Fluet, L. (2003), 'The Self-Loathing Class: Williams, Ishiguro and Barbara Ehrenreich on Service', *Key Words: A Journal of Cultural Materialism*, 4, 100–30.

——— (2007a), 'Ishiguro: Unknown Communities', *Novel: A Forum on Fiction*, 40 (3), 205–304.

———— (2007b), 'Immaterial Labours: Ishiguro, Class and Affect', *Novel: A Forum on Fiction*, 40 (3), 265–88.

Forsythe, R. (2005), 'Cultural Displacement and the Mother–Daughter relationship in Kazuo Ishiguro's *A Pale View of Hills*', *West Virginia University Philological Papers*, 52, 99–108.

François, P. (2004), 'The Spectral Return of Depths in Kazuo Ishiguro's *The Unconsoled*', *Commonwealth Essays and Studies*, 26 (2), 77–90.

Furst, L. (2007), 'Memory's Fragile Power in Ishiguro's *The Remains of the Day* and W. G. Sebald's "Max Ferber"', *Contemporary Literature*, 48 (4), 530–53.

Garland, A. (1998), 'On the Shelf: *An Artist of the Floating World*', *Sunday Times: Books*, 10 May, 9.

Griffin, G. (2009), 'Science and the Cultural Imaginary: The Case of Kazuo Ishiguro's *Never Let Me Go*', in *Textual Practice*, 24 (4), 645–63.

Griffiths, M. (1993), 'Great English Houses/New Homes in England?: Memory and Identity in Kazuo Ishiguro's *The Remains of the Day* and V. S. Naipaul's *The Enigma of Arrival*', *Span*, 36, 488–503.

Guth, D. (1999), 'Submerged Narratives in Kazuo Ishiguro's *The Remains of the Day*', *Forum for Modern Language Studies*, 35 (2), 126–7.

Hama, M. (1991) 'A Pale View', *Switch*, 8 (6), 76–102.

Hassan, I. (1990), 'An Extravagant Reticence', *The World and I*, 5 (2), 369–74.

Henke, C. (2003), 'Remembering Selves, Constructing Selves: Memory and Identity in Contemporary British Fiction', *Journal for the Study of British Culture*, 10 (1), 77–100.

Ingersoll, E. G. (2001), 'Desire, the Gaze, and Suture in the Novel and the Film: *The Remains of the Day*', *Studies in the Humanities*, 28 (1–2), 31–47.

———— (2007), 'Taking Off the Realm of Metaphor: Kazuo Ishiguro's *Never Let Me Go*', *Studies in the Humanities*, 34 (1), 40–59.

Janik, D. I. (1995), 'No End of History: Evidence from the Contemporary English Novel', *Twentieth Century Literature*, 41 (2), 160–89.

Jerng, M. (2008), 'Giving Form to Life: Cloning and Narrative Expectations of the Human', *Partial Answers: Journal of Literature and the History of Ideas*, 6 (2), 369–93.

Jirgens, K. E. (1999), 'Narrator Resartus: Palimpsestic revelations in Kazuo Ishiguro's *The Remains of the Day*', *Q/W/E/R/T/Y: Arts, Littératures & Civilisations du Monde Anglophone*, 9, 219–30.

Lang, J. (2000), 'Public Memory, Private History: Kazuo Ishiguro's *The Remains of the Day*', *CLIO: A Journal of Literature, History and the Philosophy of History*, 29 (2), 143–65.

Lee, H. (1990), 'Quiet Desolation', *New Republic*, 22 January, 36–39.

Luo, S.-P. (2003), '"Living the Wrong Life": Kazuo Ishiguro's Unconsoled Orphans', *Dalhousie Review*, 83 (1), 51–80.

Ma, S.-M. (1999), 'Kazuo Ishiguro's Persistent Dream for Postethnicity: Performance in Whiteface', *Post Identity*, 2 (1), 71–88.

Mallett, P. J. (1996), 'The Revelation of Character in Kazuo Ishiguro's *The Remains of the Day* and *An Artist of the Floating World*', *Shoin Literary Review*, 29, 1–20.

Marcus, A. (2006), Kazuo Ishiguro's *The Remains of the Day*: The Discourse of Self-Deception', *Partial Answers: Journal of Literature and the History of Ideas*, 4 (1), 129–50.

Mason, G. (1989), 'Inspiring Images: The Influence of the Japanese Cinema on the Writings of Kazuo Ishiguro', *East-West Film Journal*, 3 (2), 39–52.

McCombe, J. P. (2002), 'The End of (Anthony) Eden: Ishiguro's *The Remains of the Day* and Midcentury Anglo-American Tensions', *Twentieth Century Literature: A Scholarly and Critical Journal*, 48 (1), 77–99.

McDonald, K. (2007), 'Days of Past Futures: Kazuo Ishiguro's *Never Let Me Go* as "Speculative Memoir"', *Biography*, 30 (1), 74–83.

Medalie, D. (2004), 'What Dignity is There in That?: The Crisis of Dignity in Selected Late Twentieth-Century Novels', *Journal of Literary Studies*, 20, 48–61.

Nunokawa, J. (2007), 'Afterword: Now They are Orphans', *Novel: A Forum on Fiction*, 40 (3), 303–4.

O'Brien, S. (1996), 'Serving a New Order: Postcolonial Politics in Kazuo Ishiguro's *The Remains of the Day*', *Modern Fiction Studies*, 42 (2), 787–806.

Park, S. (2008), '"Spontaneous Mirth" out of "a Misplaced Respectfulness": A Bakhtinian Reading of Kazuo Ishiguro's *The Remains of the Day*', *Review of International English Literature*, 39 (3), 45–71.

Patey, C. (1991), 'When Ishiguro Visits the West Country: An Essay on *The Remains of the Day*', *Acme*, 44 (2), 135–55.

Pégon, C. (2004), 'How to Have Done With Words: Virtuoso Performance in Kazuo Ishiguro's *The Unconsoled*', in *Études Britanniques Contemporaines, Revue de la Société d'Études Anglaises Contemporaines*, 27, 83–95.

Popa, C. (2006), 'Functions of Modality in Kazuo Ishiguro's *The Remains of the Day*', *Studia Universitatis Babes-Bolyai*, 51 (1), 47–56.

Puchner, M. (2008), 'When We Were Clones', *Raritan: A Quarterly Review*, 27 (4), 34–49.

Quill, L. (2009), 'Ethical Conduct and Public Service Loyalty Intelligently Bestowed', *American Review of Public Administration*, 39 (3), 215–24.

Reitano, N. (2007), 'The Good Wound: Memory and Community in *The Unconsoled*', *Texas Studies in Literature and Language*, 49 (4), 361–86.

Robbins, B. (2001), 'Very Busy Just Now: Globalisation and Harriedness in Ishiguro's *The Unconsoled*', in *Comparative Literature*, 53 (4), Autumn, 426–42.

——— (2007), 'Cruelty is Bad: Banality and Proximity in *Never Let Me Go*', in *Novel: A Forum on Fiction*, 40 (3), 289–302.

Robinson, R. (2006), 'Nowhere, in Particular: Kazuo Ishiguro's *The Unconsoled* and Central Europe', *Critical Quarterly*, 48 (4), 107–30.

Roos, H. (2008), '"Not Properly Human": Literary and Cinematic Narratives about Human Harvesting', *Journal of Literary Studies*, 24 (3), 40–53.

Rothfork, J. (1996), 'Zen Comedy in Postcolonial Literature: Kazuo Ishiguro's *The Remains of the Day*', *Mosaic*, 29 (1), 79–102.

Rushton, R. (2007), 'Three Modes of Terror: Transcendence, Submission, Incorporation', *Nottingham French Studies*, 46 (3), 109–20.

Sarvan, C. (1997), 'Floating Signifiers and *An Artist of the Floating World*', *Journal of Commonwealth Literature*, 32 (1), 93–101.

Sauerberg, L. O. (2006), 'Coming to Terms – Literary Configurations of the Past in Kazuo Ishiguro's *An Artist of the Floating World* and Timothy Mo's *An Insular Possession*', *EurAmerica: A Journal of European and American Studies*, 36 (2), 175–202.

Scanlan, M. (1993), 'Mistaken Identities: First-Person Narration in Kazuo Ishiguro', *Journal of Narrative and Life History*, 3 (2/3), 139–54.

Seaman, M. J. (2007), 'Becoming More (than) Human: Affective Posthumanisms, Past and Future', *Journal of Narrative Theory*, 37 (2), 246–75.

Seltzer, M. (2009), 'Parlor Games: The Apriorization of the Media', *Critical Inquiry*, 36 (1), 100–133.

Sim, W. (2005), 'Kazuo Ishiguro', *Review of Contemporary Literature*, 25 (1), 80–115.

Slay, J. (1997), 'Ishiguro's *The Remains of the Day*', *Explicator*, 55 (3), 180–2.

Su, J. J. (2002), 'Refiguring National Character: The Remains of the British Estate Novel', *MFS: Modern Fiction Studies*, 48 (3), 552–80.

Sumners-Bremner, E. (2006), '"Poor creatures": Ishiguro's and Coetzee's Imaginary Animals', *Mosaic: A Journal of the Interdisciplinary Study of Literature*, 39 (4), 145–60.

Suter, R. (1999), '"We're Like Butlers": Interculturality, Memory and Responsibility in Kazuo Ishiguro's *The Remains of the Day*', *Q/W/E/R/T/Y: Arts, Littératures & Civilisations du Monde Anglophone*, 9, 241–50.

Tamaya, M. (1992), 'Ishiguro's *The Remains of the Day*: The Empire Strikes Back', *Modern Language Studies*, 22 (2), 45–56.

Terestchenko, M. (2007), 'Servility and Destructiveness in Kazuo Ishiguro's *Remains of the Day*', *Partial Answers: Journal of Literature and the History of Ideas*, 5 (10), 77–89.

Teverson, A. (1999), 'Acts of Reading in Kazuo Ishiguro's *The Remains of the Day*', in *Q/W/E/R/T/Y: Arts, Littératures & Civilisations du Monde Anglophone*, 9, 251–58.

Toker, L. and D. Chertoff (2008), 'Reader Response and the Recycling of Topoi in Kazuo Ishiguro's *Never Let Me Go*', *Partial Answers: Journal of Literature and The History of Ideas*, 6 (1), 163–80.

Trimm, R. S. (2005), 'Inside Job: Professionalism and Postimperial Communities in *The Remains of the Day*', *Lit: Literature Interpretation Theory*, 16 (2), 135–61.

—— (2009), 'Telling Positions: Country, Countryside, and Narration in *The Remains of the Day*', *Papers on Language and Literature*, 45 (2), 180–211.

Veyret, P. (2005), 'The Strange Case of the Disappearing Chinaman: Memory and Desire in Kazuo Ishiguro's *The Remains of the Day* and *When We Were Orphans*', *Études Britanniques Contemporaines, Revue de la Société d'Études Anglaises Contemporaines*, 29, 159–72.

Vinet, D. (1999), 'The Butler's Woman, a Strategy of Avoidance in Kazuo Ishiguro's *The Remains of the Day*', *Études Britanniques Contemporaines, Revue de la Société d'Études Anglaises Contemporaines*, 16, 63–80.

—— (2000), 'The Avatars of the Father in *The Remains of the Day*', *Études Britaniques Contemporaines, Revue de la Société d'Études Anglaises Contemporaines*, 19, 53–67.

—— (2004), 'Fugal Tempo in *The Unconsoled*', in *Études Britaniques Contemporaines, Revue de la Société d'Études Anglaises Contemporaines*, 27, 127–41.

———— (2005), 'Revisiting the Memory of Guilt in Ishiguro's *When We Were Orphans*', *Études Britanniques Contemporaines, Revue de la Société d'Études Anglaises Contemporaines*, 29, 133–44.

Wain, P. (1992), 'The Historical-Political Aspect of the Novels of Kazuo Ishiguro', *Language and Culture*, 23, 177–205.

Walkowitz, R. L. (2001), 'Ishiguro's Floating Worlds', *ELH*, 68 (4), 1049–76.

———— (2007), 'Unimaginable Largeness: Kazuo Ishiguro, Translation, and the New World Literature', *Novel: A Forum on Fiction*, 40 (3), 216–39.

Wall, K. (1994), '*The Remains of the Day* and its Challenges to Theories of Unreliable Narration', *Journal of Narrative Technique*, 24 (1), 18–42.

Watson, G. (1995). 'The Silence of the Servants', *Sewanee Review*, 103 (3), 480–86.

Westermann, M. (2004), '"Is the Butler Home?" Narrative and the Split Subject in *The Remains of the Day*', *Mosaic: A Journal for the Interdisciplinary Study of Literature*, 37 (3), 157–70.

Whyte, P. (2007), 'The Treatment of Background in Kazuo Ishiguro's *The Remains of the Day*', *Commonwealth Essays and Studies*, 30 (1), 73–82.

Winsworth, B. (1999), 'Communicating and not Communicating: The True and the False Self in *The Remains of the Day*', *Q/W/E/R/T/Y: Arts, Littératures & Civilisations du Monde Anglophone*, 9, 259–66.

Wong, C. (1995), 'The Shame of Memory: Blanchot's Self-Dispossession in Ishiguro's *A Pale View of Hills*', *Clio*, 24 (2), 127–45.

Wroe, N. (2005), 'Living Memories', *Guardian: Review*, 19 February, 20–1.

Yoshioka, F. (1988), 'Beyond the Division of East and West: Kazuo Ishiguro's *A Pale View of Hills*', *Studies in English Literature*, 71–86.

Zinck, P. (2005), 'The Palimpsest of Memory in Kazuo Ishiguro's *When We Were Orphans*', *Études Britanniques Contemporaines, Revue de la Société d'Études Anglaises Contemporaines*, 29, 145–58.

reviews

A Pale View of the Hills

Bailey, P. (1982), 'Private Desolations', *Times Literary Supplement*, 19 February, 179.

Campbell, J. (1982), 'Kitchen Window', *New Statesman*, 19 February, 25.

King, F. (1982), 'Shimmering', *Spectator*, 27 February, 25.

Lively, P. (1982), 'Backwards and Forwards', *Encounter*, 58/59, (6/1), 86–91.

Milton, E. (1982), 'In a Japan Like Limbo', *New York Times Book Review*, 9 May, 12–13.

Spence, J. (1982), 'Two Worlds Japan Has Lost Since the Meiji', *New Society*, 9 May, 266–67.

Thwaite, A. (1982), 'Ghosts in The Mirror', *Observer*, 14 February, 33.

An Artist of the Floating World

Chisholm, A. (1986), 'Lost Worlds of Pleasure', *Times Literary Supplement*, 14 February, 162.

Dyer, G. (1986), 'On Their Mettle', *New Statesman*, 4 April, 26.

Hunt, N. (1987), 'Two Close Looks at Faraway', *Brick*, 31, 36–8.

Morton, K. (1986), 'After the War was Lost', *New York Times Book Review*, 8 June, 19.
Parrinder, P. (1986), 'Manly Scowls', *London Review of Books*, 6 February, 16.
Stuewe, P. (1986), 'Genuine Japanese . . . Slush-Pile Saviour . . . for God and Greed', *Quill and Quire*, 52 (12), 31.
Wasi, J. (1987), 'Book Reviews', *Indian Horizons*, 36 (1/2), 52–4.

The Remains of the Day
Annan, G. (1989), 'On the High Wire', *New York Review of Books*, 7 December, 3–4.
Coates, J. (1989), 'Deceptive Calm', *Chicago Tribune Books*, 1 October, 5.
Dyer, G. (1989), 'What the Butler Did', *New Statesman and Society*, 26 May, 34.
Gray, P. (1989), 'Upstairs, Downstairs', *Time*, 30 October, 55.
Gurewich, D. (1989), 'Upstairs, Downstairs', *New Criterion*, 8 (4), 77–80.
Hutchings, W. (1990), 'English: Fiction', *World Literature Today*, 64 (3), 463–4.
Iyer, P. (1991), 'Waiting upon History', *Partisan Review*, 58 (3), 585–9.
Kamine, M. (1989), 'A Servant of Self-Deceit', *New Leader*, 13 November, 21–2.
King, F. (1989), 'A Stately Procession of One', *Spectator*, 27 May, 31–2.
Rafferty, T. (1990), 'The Lesson of The Master', *New Yorker*, 15 January, 102–4.
Rubin, M. (1989), 'A Review of *Remains of the Day*', *Christian Science Monitor*, 13 November, 13.
Rushdie, S. (1991 [1989]) 'What the Butler Didn't See', *Observer*, 21 May, 53; repr. as 'Kazuo Ishiguro', in *Imaginary Homelands: Essays and Criticism 1981–1991*. London: Granta, 244–6.
Strawson, G. (1989), 'Tragically Disciplined and Dignified', *Times Literary Supplement*, 19 May, 4494, 535.
Thwaite, A. (1989), 'In Service', *London Review of Books*, 18 May, 17–18.

The Unconsoled
Brooke, A. (1995a), 'Leaving Behind Daydreams for Nightmares', *Wall Street Journal*, 11 November, A12.
—— (1995b), 'A Superb Achievement', *Spectator*, 24 June, 40–41.
Chaudhuri, A. (1995), 'Unlike Kafka', *London Review of Books*, 8 June, 30–31.
Cunningham, V. (1995), 'A Pale View of Ills without Remedy', *Guardian*, 7 May, 15.
Cusk, R. (1995), 'Journey to the End of the Day', *Times*, 11 May, 38.
Eder, R. (1995), 'Meandering in a Dreamscape', *Los Angeles Times Book Review*, 8 October, 3, 7.
Gray, P. (1995) 'Bad Dreams: After *The Remains of the Day*, a Weird Non-Sequitur', *Time*, 2 October, 81–82.
Hughes-Hallet, L. (1995), 'Feeling No Pain', *Sunday Times: Books*, 14 May, 7, 9.
Innes, C. (1995a), 'Fiction without Frontiers', *Los Angeles Times*, 5 November, 11.
—— (1995b), 'Dr. Faustus Faces the Music', *Nation*, 6 November, 546–8.
Iyer, P. (1995), 'The Butler Didn't Do It, Again', *Times Literary Supplement*, 28 April, 22.
Janah, M. (1995), 'A Dreamscape of Music and Memory', *San Francisco Chronicle*, 8 October, R-V 4.
Kakutani, M. (1995), 'A New Annoying Hero', *New York Times*, 17 October, C17.
Kauffmann, S. (1995), 'The Floating World', *New Republic*, 6 November, 42–5.

Kaveney, R. (1995), 'Tossed and Turned', *New Statesman and Society*, 12 May, 39.

Kiely, R. (1995), 'In an Unknown City to an Unknown Destination', *Boston Book Review*, 1 October, 32.

Menand, L. (1995), 'Anxious in Dreamland', *New York Times Review*, 15 October, 7.

Passaro, V. (1995), 'New Flash from an Old Isle', *Harper Magazine*, 10 October, 71–5.

Rorem, N. (1996), 'Fiction in Review', *Yale Review*, 84 (2), 154–9.

Rorty, R. (1995), 'Consolation Prize', *Village Voice Literary Supplement*, 10 October, 13.

Rubin, M. (1995), 'Probing the Plight of Lives "Trapped" in Others' Expectations', *Christian Science Monitor*, 4 October, 14.

Shone, T. (1995), 'Chaos Theory', *Harper's Bazaar*, 1 October, 132.

Simon, L. (1996), 'Remains of the Novelist', *Commonwealth*, 22 March, 25–26.

Smith, J. (1995), 'Lost Worlds, Memories form the Basis of His Brilliant Writing', *San Francisco Chronicle*, 12 November, B.

Steinberg, S. (1995), 'A Book about Our World', *Publisher's Weekly*, 18 September, 105–6.

Sweet, N. (1995), 'Kafka Set to Music', *Contemporary Review*, 10 October, 223–24.

Todd, T. (1995), 'Down and Out in Central Europe', *Austin Chronicle*, 7 June, 32.

Wilhelmus, T. (1996), 'Between Cultures', *Hudson Review*, 49 (2), 316–22.

Wood, J. (1995), 'Ishiguro in the Underworld', *Guardian*, 5 May, 5.

Wood, M. (1995), 'Sleepless Nights', *New York Review of Books*, 21 December, 17–18.

When We Were Orphans

Anastas, B. (2000), 'Keeping It Real', *Village Voice*, 3 October.

Barrow, A. (2000), 'Clueless in Shanghai', *Spectator*, 25 March, 44–45.

Bouldrey, B. (2000), 'A Life in Pieces', *San Francisco Chronicle*, 24 September, www.sfgate.com/cgi-bin/article.cgi?file=/chronicle/archive/2000/09/24/RV63071.DTL.

Carey, J. (2000) 'Few Novels Extend the Possibilities of Fiction. This One Does', *Sunday Times: Culture*, 2 April, 45.

Francken, J. (2000), 'Something Fishy', *London Review of Books*, 13 April, 45.

Gorra, M. (2000), 'The Case of Missing Childhood', *New York Times*, 24 September.

Gray, P. (2000), 'The Remains of Shanghai', *Time*, 18 September, www.time.com/time/magazine/article/0,9171,997979,00.html.

Hensher, P. (2000), 'It's The Way He Tells It . . .', *Observer*, 19 March, www.guardian.co.uk/books/2000/mar/19/fiction.bookerprize2000.

Jaggi, M. (2000), 'In Search of Lost Crimes', *Guardian*, 1 April, 8.

Jones, R. C. (2000), 'Shanghai Search', *Times: 2*, 6 April, 15.

Kakutani, M. (2000), 'The Case He Can't Solve: A Detective's Delusions', *New York Times*, 19 September, E-7.

Leith, S. (2000), 'Shanghai Sherlock', *Daily Telegraph: Arts and Books*, 25 March, 4.

McWilliam, C. (2000), 'Painful, Lovely, Limpid in Freezing Fog', *Financial Times: Weekend*, 8 April, 4.

Oates, J. C. (2000), 'The Serpent's Heart', *Times Literary Supplement*, 31 March, 21–22.

Sutcliffe, W. (2000), 'History Happens Elsewhere', *Independent on Sunday: Review*, 2 April, 56–58.

Never Let Me Go

Atwood, M. (2005), 'Brave New World', *Slate*, 1 April, slate.msn.com/d/2116040.

Browning, J. (2005), 'Hello Dolly', *Village Voice*, 22 March, www.villagevoice. com/2005-03-22/books/hello-dolly/.

Deb, S. (2005), 'Lost Corner', *New Statesman*, 7 March, 55.

Desai, A. (2005), 'A Shadow World', *New York Review of Books*, 52 (14), 22 September, www.nybooks.com/articles/article-preview?article_id=18261.

Dyer, G. (2005), '*Never Let Me Go*, by Kazuo Ishiguro', *Independent*, 27 February, www.independent.co.uk/arts-entertainment/books/reviews/neverlet-me-go-by-kazuo-ishiguro-746712.html.

Freeman, J. (2006), 'Never Let Me Go: A Profile of Kazuo Ishiguro', *Poets and Writers*, 5 June, 41.

Giles, G. (2005), 'Like Lambs to Slaughter', *Newsweek*, 4 April, 52.

Grossman, L. (2005), 'Living on Borrowed Time', *Time*, 11 April, www.time.com/ time/magazine/article/0,9171,1044735,00.html.

Harrison, M. J. (2005), 'Clone Alone', *Guardian: Features and Reviews*, 26 February, 26.

Hensher, P. (2005), 'School for Scandal', *Spectator*, 26 February, 32, www.spectator. co.uk/books/21309/part_4/school-for-scandal.thtml.

Hill, T. (2005), 'England's Dreaming', '*Never Let Me Go*', *Times*, 31 August, entertainment.timesonline.co.uk/tol/arts_and_entertainment/books/fiction/ article561005.ece.

Inverne, J. (2005), 'Strange New World', *Time International*, 28 March, 68.

Jennings, J. (2005), 'Clone Home', *Artforum International*, 4 March, 1.

Kakutani, M. (2005), 'Sealed in a World That's Not as It Seems', *New York Times*, 4 April, E-8.

Kermode, F. (2005), 'Outrageous Game', *London Review of Books*, 21 April, 21.

Kerr, S. (2005), 'When They Were Orphans', *New York Times*, 17 April, 16.

Kipen, D. (2005), 'Love Among Clones', *San Francisco Chronicle*, 14 February, E-1.

Menand, L. (2005), 'Something about Kathy: Ishiguro's Quasi-Science-Fiction Novel', *New Yorker*, 28 March, 78–9.

Messud, C. (2005), 'Love's Body', *The Nation*, 16 May, 28–31.

Moore, C. (2005), 'Meanings Behind Masks', *Daily Telegraph*, 6 March, www.telegraph.co.uk/arts/main.jhtml?xml=/arts/2005/03/06/boish06. xml&sSheet=/arts/2005/03/06/bomain.html.

O'Neill, J. (2005), 'New Fiction', *Atlantic Monthly*, May, www.theatlantic.com/ doc/200505/oneill.

Sandhu, S. (2005), 'Raw Emotional Intensity', *Daily Telegraph*, 26 February, 1.

Schiefer, N. (2005), *London Free Press*, 16 April, D8.

Siddhartha, D. (2005), 'Lost Corner', *New Statesman*, 7 March, 55.

Wood, J. (2005), 'The Human Difference', *New Republic*, 12 May, 36.

Yardley, J. (2005), 'Never Let Me Go', *Washington Post*, 17 April, 2.

Nocturnes

Coe, J. (2009), 'Nocturnes', *Financial Times*, 16 May, www.ft.com/cms/ s/2/65193848-40db-11de-8f18-00144feabdc0.html.

Fleming, T. (2009), 'Heartbreak in Five Movements', *Observer*, 10 May, www. guardian.co.uk/books/2009/may/09/kazuo-ishiguro-nocturnes.

Kermode, F. (2009), 'Exercises and Excesses', *London Review of Books*, 31 (9), 14 May, 33.

Mukherjee, N. (2009), 'Unhappy Endings', *Time*, 15 May, www.time.com/time/magazine/article/0,9171,1902710,00.html.

Robson, L. (2009), 'Laughter in the Dark', *New Statesman*, 14 May, (5), www. newstatesman.com/books/2009/05/ishiguro-laugh-novel-world.

Tayler, C. (2009), 'Scenes from an Italian Café', *Guardian*, 16 May, www.guardian. co.uk/books/2009/may/16/nocturnes-music-nightfall-kazuo-ishiguro.

interviews and profiles

Adams, T. (2005), 'For Me, England is a Mythical Place: Interview with Kazuo Ishiguro', *Observer: Features*, 20 February, 17.

Anonymous and Ishiguro, K. (1989), 'The Butler in Us All', *Bookseller*, 14 April, 1327–28.

—— (2008), 'The Art of Fiction', *Paris Review*, Spring, 23–54.

Bates, K. G. (2005), 'Interview with Kazuo Ishiguro', broadcast on NPR Radio on 4 May, transcript published in B. W. Shaffer and C. Wong (2008), pp. 199–203.

Bigsby, C. (1987), 'In Conversation with Kazuo Ishiguro', 'An Interview with Kazuo Ishiguro', *European English Messenger*, Zero Issue, 26–29; repr. in B. W. Shaffer and C. F. Wong (2008), pp. 15–26.

Bradbury, D. (2000), 'Making up a Country of His Own', *Times*, 2, 6 April, 12–13.

Bradbury, M. (1995), 'Breaking Loose', *W Magazine*, 1, 34–37.

Chira, S. (1989), 'A Case of Cultural Misperception', *New York Times*, 28 October, 13.

Crummet, G. and C. F. Wong (2006), 'A Conversation about Life and Art with Kazuo Ishiguro', in B. W. Shaffer and C. F. Wong (2008), pp. 204–20.

De Jongh, N. (1982), 'Life after the Bomb', *Guardian*, 22 February, 11.

Field, M. (1988), 'This Britisher is Japanese', *Sydney Morning Herald*, 12 March, 74.

Freeman, J. (2005), 'Never Let Me Go: A Profile of Kazuo Ishiguro', *Poets and Writers Magazine*, May–June; repr. in B. W. Shaffer and C. F. Wong (2008), pp. 194–98.

Frumkes, L. B. (2001), 'Kazuo Ishiguro', *The Writer*, 114 (5); repr. in B. W. Shaffer and C. F. Wong (2008), pp. 189–193.

Gallix, F. (2000), 'Kazuo Ishiguro: The Sorbonne Lecture', *Études Britanniques Contemporaines, Revue de la Société d'Études Anglaises Contemporaines*, 18 June; repr. in B. W. Shaffer and C. F. Wong (2008), pp. 135–55.

Hawley, J. (1988), 'Grousebeating with Royals', *Sydney Morning Herald*, 5 March, 72.

Hensher, P. (1995), 'Books', *Harper's and Queen*, June, 21.

Hogan, R. (2000), 'Kazuo Ishiguro', *Beatrice.com*; repr. in B. W. Shaffer and C. F. Wong (2008), pp. 156–60.

Howard, P. (1989), 'A Butler's Tale Wins Booker for Ishiguro', *Times*, 27 October, 24.

—— (1993), 'A Comedy of Authors', *Times: Supplement*, 21 September, vi.

Iyer, P. (1996), 'A New Kind of Travel Writer', *Harper's Magazine*, 30 February, 32j.

Jaggi, M. (1995a), 'Dreams of Freedom', *Guardian*, 29 April, 28.

——— (1995b), 'Kazuo Ishiguro Talks to Maya Jaggi', *Wasafiri*, 22, 20–24.

——— (2004), 'Kazuo Ishiguro with Maya Jaggi' [1995], in S. Nasta (ed.), *Writing Across Worlds: Contemporary Writers Talk*. London: Routledge, 159–170; repr. in B. W. Shaffer and C. F. Wong (2008), pp. 110–19.

Kellaway, K. (1995), 'The Butler on A Bender', *Observer Review*, 16 April, 6–7.

Kelman, S. (1991), 'Ishiguro in Toronto', Spalding, L. and M. Ondaatje (eds.), *The Brick Reader* (Toronto: Coach House press, 1991); repr. in B. W. Shaffer and C. F. Wong (2008), pp. 42–51.

Krider, D. (1998), 'Rooted in a Small Space: An Interview with Kazuo Ishiguro', *Kenyon Review*, 20 (2), 146–154; repr. in B. W. Shaffer and C. F. Wong (2008), pp. 125–34.

Mackenzie, S. (1996), 'Into the Real World', *Guardian*, 15 February, 12.

——— (2000), 'Between Two Worlds', *Guardian: Weekend*, 25 March, 10–11; 13–14; 17.

Mason, G. (1989), 'An Interview with Kazuo Ishiguro', *Contemporary Literature*, 30 (3), 335–47.

Morrison, B. (1989), 'It's a Long Way from Nagasaki', *Observer*, 29 October, 35.

Mullan, J. (2006), 'Kazuo Ishiguro Talks to John Mullan', *Guardian*, 23 March, blogs.guardian.co.uk/culturevulture/ishiguro.mp3 [audio interview, 39 minutes].

Newsweek (2005), 'Like Lambs to The Slaughter: An Interview with Kazuo Ishiguro', 4 April.

Ōe, K. and K. Ishiguro (1991), 'The Novelist in Today's World: A Conversation', *Boundary 2*, 18, 109–122; repr. as 'Wave Patterns: A Dialogue', in *Grand Street*, 10, 75–91; repr. in B. W. Shaffer and C. F. Wong (2008), pp. 52–65; originally published in (1989) *Kokusai Koryu*, 53, 100–8.

Ohno, B. (1996), 'Who is The Unconsoled?: A Profile of Novelist Kazuo Ishiguro', *Mars Hill Review*, 5, 137–42.

Oliva, P. (1996), 'Chaos as Metaphor: An Interview with Kazuo Ishiguro', *Filling Station Magazine*, Winter, 9; repr. in B. W. Shaffer and C. F. Wong (2008), pp. 120–124.

Patterson, C. (2005), 'The Samurai of Suburbia', *Independent: Books*, 4 March, www.independent.co.uk/arts-entertainment/books/features/kazuoishiguro-the-samurai-of-suburbia-527080.html.

Richards, Linda. (2000), 'January Interview: Kazuo Ishiguro', *January Magazine*, October, januarymagazine.com/profiles/ishiguro.html.

Sandhu, S. (2005), 'The Hiding Place', *Telegraph*, 6 March, www.telegraph.co.uk/arts/main.jhtml?xml=/arts/2005/03/06/boishiguro.xml.

Sexton, D. (1987), 'Interview: David Sexton Meets Kazuo Ishiguro', *Literary Review*, January, 16–19.

Shaffer, B. W. (2001), 'An Interview with Kazuo Ishiguro', *Contemporary Literature*, Spring, 1; repr. in B. W. Shaffer and C. F. Wong (2008), pp. 161–74.

Shaffer, B. W. and C. Wong (eds.) (2008), *Conversations with Kazuo Ishiguro*. Jackson, MS: University of Mississippi Press.

Sinclair, C. (1987a), 'The Land of the Rising Son', *Sunday Times: Magazine*, 11 January, 36–7.

——— (1987b), 'Kazuo Ishiguro in Conversation', *The Roland Collection* [video, 34 minutes].

Smith, J. L. (1995), 'A Novel Taste of Criticism: Kazuo Ishiguro', *Times*, 3 May, 17.

Swaim, D. (1990), 'Don Swaim Interviews Kazuo Ishiguro', in B. W. Shaffer and C. F. Wong (2008), pp. 89–109.

Swift, G. (1989), 'Kazuo Ishiguro', *Bomb*, Autumn, 22–23; repr. in B. W. Shaffer and C. F. Wong (2008), pp. 35–41.

Tonkin, B. (2000), 'Artist of His Floating World', *Independent: Weekend Review*, 1 April, 9.

Tookey, C. (1986), 'Sydenham, mon amour', *Books and Bookmen*, March, 33–34.

Vorda, A. and K. Herzinger (1991), 'An Interview with Kazuo Ishiguro', *Mississippi Review*, 20, 131–54; repr. as 'Stuck on The Margins: An Interview with Kazuo Ishiguro', in A. Vorda (ed.), *Face to Face: Interviews with Contemporary Novelists*. Houston, TX: Rice University Press, 1993, 1–36; repr. in B. W. Shaffer and C. F. Wong (2008), pp. 66–88.

Wachtel, E. (ed.) (1996), 'Kazuo Ishiguro', in *More Writers & Company*. Toronto: Alfred A. Knopf, 17–35.

Wilson, J. (1995), 'The Literary Life: A Very English Story', *New Yorker*, 6 March, 96–106.

Wong, C. (2001), 'Like Idealism is to the Intellect: An Interview with Kazuo Ishiguro', *Clio*, 30, 309–25; repr. in B. W. Shaffer and C. F. Wong (2008), pp. 174–188.

on the web

www.litencyc.com/php/speople.php?rec=true&UID=2318
www.contemporarywriters.com/authors/?p=auth52
www.en.wikipedia.org/wiki/Kazuo_Ishiguro
www.faber.co.uk/author/kazuo-ishiguro/

index

280

landscapes and 9, 211–24;
 unreliable 97
Mendelsohn, F. 238, 244
mental evasion 91
mental landscapes 213–15
Merchant–Ivory films 126
migration 14–15, 254, 255–6
militarism 74–80
Milton, J., *Paradise Lost* 215
minor literature 9, 157–68
 characteristics of 160–2
Mitchell, D. 262–3
Mitford, D. 120
Mitford, N. 120
 Wigs on the Green 120–1
Mitford, U. 120
Miura, M. 74, 77, 80
Miyamoto, S. 10, 77, 78
Miyata, S. 78
Mo, T. 14
modernism 5, 8, 13–30, 222–3
 continental/European 8, 16
 high 8, 14–16, 20, 222
moral agents 106–8
moral choices
 anagnorisis and 113–17
 in autonomy-denying systems
  106–17
mortality 209
Mosley, O. 119–20, 123, 129
Mukai, J. 78
Mulisch, H. 6
Munich Agreement (1938) 122
Murakami, H. 3, 8, 46, 49, 51, 261
music 9, 44, 144–56
 and contemporary British
  fiction 144–6
 Nocturnes 150–5
 The Unconsoled 60–1, 146–50,
  154–5, 158
myth 127–8

Nachkriegskind, D. 5–6
Nagasaki 6, 47–8
Nakamura, K. 78
nakedness, fear of 26–7
names, translation of 70–1
narrative
 agency 95–8
 compression 199–210

gaps in 4
Japanese translations: *An Artist
 of the Floating World* and linear
 narrative 74; regular form and
 polite form 51–2
 modes in *The Remains of the
 Day* 98–104
National Museum of Modern Art,
 Tokyo 75, 78
Nazism 120, 122
Never Let Me Go 1, 2, 3, 6, 17, 26, 55,
 56, 82, 259–60, 261
 art, emotion and social justice 22–5
 autonomy-denying systems 7,
  106–17
 concertina effect 9, 199–210
 in context 239–42
 female narrator 55–6, 61–5
 genesis of 236–9
 Japanese translation 51–2
 landscapes and memory 9,
  211–24
 and 'outsider science fiction' 7,
  236–46
 rites of passage 41–4
 scientific discourse 7, 225–35
 title taken from a song 115, 144–5
New Party 119
Nicholas of Myra, Saint 166
Nietzsche, F. 28
Nocturnes 1, 9, 150–5, 215, 248
nomadism 14–15
Norfolk 216, 217–18
nostalgia 16, 48, 88, 138–9
 émigrés 255–6
novum 237, 239, 245
nuclear technology 227

objective correlative 20, 21, 24, 29
Öe, K. 15
Olympia Rally 119, 120
Onodera, K. 70
opium trade 177, 186, 187
Opium Wars 186
oratorical autobiography 100–1
organ donation 42, 199, 227, 239
organic resonance 150–4
Other, the 61–2, 64–5
'outsider science fiction' 7, 236–46
Ozu, Y. 48–9

7449014141R00173